Staycation Station
Funded by a
Library Services & Technology Act (LSTA) grant

WITHDRAWN

CITY OF
RIVERSIDE

Riverside Public Library

Enlivening the individual spirit no matter what the journey

"BRAVE AND NOBLE ELEPHANT! WE ENTREAT YOU TO BANISH
EVERY WISH TO STAY IN THE FOREST!"

SIAMESE BRAHMINIC CHANT

Photograph: Elephant hunt at Ayutthaya, c. 1890

"BANGKOK! I THRILLED. I HAD BEEN SIX YEARS AT SEA, BUT HAD
ONLY SEEN MELBOURNE AND SYDNEY, VERY GOOD PLACES,
CHARMING PLACES IN THEIR WAY – BUT BANGKOK!"
                                                    JOSEPH CONRAD

Photographs: Chao Phraya River, c. 1890. Wat Arun gate, c. 1890.

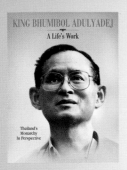

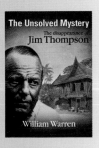

"BANGKOK HAS BEEN APTLY STYLED THE
'VENICE OF THE EAST,' FOR ITS
THOROUGHFARES AND HIGHWAYS OF
TRAFFIC ARE SIMPLY INTERSECTING
CANALS AND BRANCHES OF THE RIVER;
AND THE MAJORITY OF THE HOUSES ARE
EITHER FLOATING, BUILT UPON RAFTS,
OR UPON PILES ON THE SIDES OF THESE
WATERWAYS."

FRANK VINCENT

Photographs: Floating houses, Bangkok, c. 1890.

Thailand

CONTENTS

NATURE, *8*

Wild habitats, *9*
Tropical forests, *10*
Orchids, *11*
Mangroves, *12*
Ricefields, *13*
Butterflies, *14*
Birds' nests, *15*
Coral reefs, *16*

HISTORY, *16*

People of Siam, *17*
Prehistory, *18*
The first millennium, *18*
The Siamese kingdom, *19*
The Lanna kingdom, *20*
Contemporary history, *21*

ARTS AND TRADITIONS, *23*

Buddhism, *24*
Buddhism in Thai life, *25*
Flower arrangements, *26*
Offerings, *27*
Spiritual abodes, *27*
Elephants, *28*
Royal barges, *29*
Costume, *30*
Regal costume, *31*
Special attire, *32*
Thai classical music, *33*
Theater, *34*
Popular theater, *35*
Thai puppets, *36*
Thai pleasures, *37*
Festivals, *38*
Baskets in traditional life, *39*
Thai food, *40*
Kaeng Phed Ped Yang, *41*
Thai fruits and sweets, *42*
Thai language, *43*

ARCHITECTURE, *43*

Thai village, *44*
Traditional Thai houses, *45*
Thai temple, *46*
Siamese architecture, *47*
Rattanakosin architecture, *48*
Lanna religious architecture, *49*
Thai religious monuments, *50*
Lanna chedis, *51*

THAILAND AS SEEN BY PAINTERS, *51*

THAILAND AS SEEN BY WRITERS, *58*

BANGKOK, *70*

The Grand Palace, *74*
Wat Po, *78*
Old Town Sights, *80*
The Chao Phraya, *87*
The klongs of Thonburi, *90*
Chinatown, *91*
Dusit district, *92*
Modern Bangkok, *93*
Private museums, *94*
Shopping, *95*
Bangkok side trips, *96*
Kanchanaburi and River Kwai, *97*
Pattaya and vicinity, *98*

THE SOUTH, *99*

Phetchaburi, *100*
Hua Hin to Surat Thani, *102*
Koh Samui, *104*
Nakhon Si Thammarat, *106*
Songkhla, Haadyai and Pattani, *107*
Phuket, *108*
Phangnga Bay, *112*
Phi Phi Islands, *114*
Krabi and offshore islands, *115*
Islands of the Andaman Sea, *116*

THE NORTHEAST, *116*

Khmer temples, *118*
Along the Mekong, *121*
National parks, *122*

THE CENTRAL PLAINS, *123*

Ayutthaya, *124*
Lopburi, *127*
Kamphaeng Phet, *128*
Sukhothai, *129*
Si Satchanalai, *131*
Phitsanulok, *132*

THE NORTH, *132*

Chiang Mai, *133*
Lamphun, *141*
Lampang, *142*
Nan Valley, *146*
Mae Hong Son, *148*
Mae Rim and Fang, *150*
Chiang Rai, *151*
Hill tribes, *152*
Chiang Saen/The Golden Triangle, *156*

APPENDICES, *158*

Directory, *160*
List of illustrations, *171*
Index, *174*

The Spirit of Thailand

With its course running through most of the Southeast Asian region, Mekhong river is intrinsically a lifeline of Thailand's rich culture and civilization. Throughout the history, not only has its sublime natural beauty resonated with its inhabitants on the riverbanks, but also with visitors from far and wide, making it one of the world's most legendary waterways. Like its namesake river, Mekhong captures the kingdom's myriad charms and embodies the age-old Thai wisdom that has been synonymous with the brand for over 70 years since its establishment in 1941. Trusted for many generations, Mekhong is the true spirit of Thailand.

A scene of Mekhong River at Kaeng Khut Khu, Chiang Khan, Loei Province, Thailand

AN INSPIRATIONAL RESORT

How to Use this Guide

The symbols at the top of each page refer to the different parts of the guide.

- ■ NATURAL ENVIRONMENT
- ● UNDERSTANDING VENICE
- ▲ ITINERARIES
- ◆ PRACTICAL INFORMATION

The itinerary map shows the main points of interest along the way and is intended to help you find your bearings.

The mini-map locates the particular itinerary within the wider area covered by the guide.

● ▲ ■ ◆
The symbols alongside a title or within the text itself provide cross-references to a theme or place dealt with elsewhere in the guide.

★ The star symbol signifies that a particular site has been singled out by the publishers for its special beauty, atmosphere or cultural interest.

At the beginning of each itinerary, the suggested means of transport to be used and the time it will take to cover the area are indicated:

- 🚤 By boat
- 🚶 On foot
- 🚲 By bicycle
- 🕐 Duration

THE GATEWAY TO VENICE ★

PONTE DELLA LIBERTA. Built by the Austrians 50 years after the Treaty of Campo Formio in 1797 ● *34,* to link Venice with Milan. The bridge ended the thousand-year separation from the mainland and shook the city's economy to its roots as Venice, already in the throes of the industrial revolution, saw

BRIDGES TO VENICE

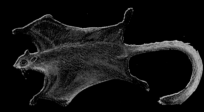

NATURE

WILD HABITATS, *9*
TROPICAL FORESTS, *10*
ORCHIDS, *11*
MANGROVES, *12*
RICEFIELDS, *13*
BUTTERFLIES AND MOTHS, *14*
BIRDS' NESTS OF
SOUTHERN THAILAND, *15*
CORAL REEFS, *16*

RED RHODODENDRON

HORNBILL
The strong and often ornate beak of the hornbill is perfectly molded for picking and cracking large fruit and seed pods from a wide range of forest plants.

Much of Thailand's natural heritage is due to the shape of the country, a stretched ribbon of land over 900 miles long, spanning both seasonally dry zones and habitats where rain falls throughout the year. The present-day Thai landscape has been molded by the actions of various colonists in the past, with farming being the most important influence. About 20,000 square miles of the country are set aside as conservation areas (for example, northeast Thailand national parks ▲ *122-3)*, many of which are open to the public, offering visitors an opportunity to encounter a wide range of plants and animals within a natural environment.

Tropical rain forest
Savanna
Monsoon forest

LEAF MONKEY (1) AND GIBBON (2)
These primates dwell in the forest canopy and feed on fruit and leaves. The leaf monkey has a large, especially adapted stomach similar to that of a cow.

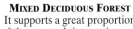

1
2

ASIAN BLACK BEAR
The Asian black bear is a forest dweller that feeds mainly on nuts and fruit, as well as ants, insect larvae and carrion.

MONTANE EVERGREEN FOREST
This is typified by an open canopy with trees festooned in lichens and epiphytes. Trees are also much shorter and less straight when compared with those of lowland forest.

HILL EVERGREEN RAIN FOREST
Climbing from montane evergreen forests, an unclear transition zone of slightly smaller trees that are widely spaced apart lies at an altitude of 2,300–2,600 feet above sea level.

EVERGREEN RAIN FOREST
True evergreen rain forest exists only in the extreme southern region of peninsular Thailand, near the Malaysian border.

WILD GINGER
One of a large number of economically valuable plants that grow wild in the forests of Thailand, the wild ginger plant is believed to have a number of medicinal healing properties that are now being investigated.

KOUPREY
Once a widely distributed species, the kouprey is today one of the most seriously threatened large mammals in the world.

BARKING DEER
Also called *muntjac,* these solitary animals are found in woodlands, rain forests and monsoon forests with dense vegetation.

MIXED DECIDUOUS FOREST
It supports a great proportion of the country's interesting and varied wildlife.

BANTENG
The banteng is a species of wild ox native to Southeast Asia.

UNDERWATER WORLD

TROPICAL RAIN FOREST
It is one of the richest ecosystems on the planet today.

FUNGI
As part of the nutrient recycling scheme of the natural forest, fungi play an essential role in all forests and woodlands.

MANGROVES
Coastal mangrove formations help protect shorelines from erosion and also provide a safe haven and nursery ground for a huge variety of fish species.

RIVERINE GRASSLANDS
Open patches of riverine grassland and savanna are important feeding and browsing areas for many forest herbivores. Many areas of grassland were formerly forested but regular outbreaks of fire prevent woody regeneration of these areas.

DRY DECIDUOUS WOODLANDS
Extensive dry deciduous woodlands with some dipterocarp species still occur in the north and east of the country.

BAMBOO FOREST
Bamboo stands are present in monsoon forests and generally thrive in areas previously cleared by man, blocking out most growth beneath their lofty foliage.

GREEN PEAFOWL
The only viable population of green peafowls remaining in Thailand is found in the Huai Kha Khaeng Wildlife Sanctuary where about 300 birds gain refuge.

GLORIOSA SUPERBA

MONITOR LIZARD
The monitor lizard is a diurnal species that feeds on insects, eggs, fish, other lizards, snakes, nestling birds and small mammals.

N   Ph   K   Ca   Mg   C

Tropical forests are like a kaleidoscope of different worlds. They cover a fifth of the earth's land surface and are home to about half of the known species of animal and plant life. The forests ▲ *122-3* are confined to a belt around the equator, where the stable climate, temperature and humidity permit a great diversity of vegetation and wildlife.

PIG-TAILED MACAQUES
These are diurnal primates, living in groups of 15–30 animals, feeding on fruit, small vertebrates and insects. They are mostly found in hill forests.

Constant temperature and high humidity levels favor the growth of lianas, trailing vines, lichens and epiphytes.

The buttress or stilt-like roots of the trees help support them in the shallow soil.

The dark forest floor is alive with communities of omnivorous insects such as ants and termites.

162 FEET

EMERGENT LAYER
The few emergent trees above the canopy are home to insectivorous bats and birds such as eagles and hornbills.

122 FEET

CANOPY LAYER
The canopy is a continuous layer of foliage about 22 feet deep that supports a broad variety of animals. Mammals like flying squirrels, gibbons and macaques feed on the rich supply of fruit, leaves, bark and nuts.

FOLIAGE
The leaves of the canopy can change their positions in order to catch the maximum amount of sunlight. Their drip-tips allow the rain to drain away and the waxy coating is a protection against algae and moss.

FLYING SQUIRREL

79 FEET

UNDERSTORY
Mammals like the peculiar binturong, pangolin and civet move freely in the understory between the ground and the upper tree layer in search of morsels and a safe place to rest.

41 FEET

FOREST FLOOR
At the top of the food chain are predators such as tigers or leopards that stalk their wary prey in the shade of the lower canopy and the forest floor.

GROUND

The plants, insects and fungi that dwell at ground level are fed upon by mammals and birds.

TAPIR
A shy forest-dweller, this herbivore is often found near quiet rivers and wallows, feeding on leaves and small trees.

SILVER-EARED MESIA

BLACK-THROATED SUNBIRD

BINTURONG
Resembling a small bear, the binturong has a bushy, prehensile tail that enables it to feed in the trees as well as on the ground.

PALM CIVET
The agile small-toothed palm civet is a nocturnal species that searches for insects, fruit and small mammals in the branches of tall secondary forests.

SLOW LORIS
This is a solitary nocturnal primate with large eyes and a thickly furred body.

TIGER
This is the largest member of the cat family; fewer than 250 now survive in Thailand.

NUTRIENT STORAGE
While in temperate forests a high proportion of nutrients is held in the soil (left-hand bar, above); in the poorer tropical soil, they are held in the biomass (right-hand bar, above). As the scarce soil nutrients are found near the surface, the roots of the trees seldom grow deeper than 26 feet.

ELEPHANT
The largest land mammal in Thailand, the Asian elephant is now a rare sight, with fewer than 3,000 animals remaining. Most of them are found in the national parks of the northeast.

CLOUDED LEOPARD
Living in tall secondary forests, the clouded leopard is a nocturnal predator that feeds on pigs, deer, monkeys and smaller animals.

PANGOLIN
The scaly armor plating of the pangolin allows it to roll into a tight ball when threatened. It feeds exclusively on ants and termites.

NUTRIENTS RECYCLING
Different forms of plants and animals have evolved in harmony on the forest floor to recycle decaying materials such as leaves and tree trunks, returning valuable nutrients back to the soil. In time these are taken up by other plants, sustaining the incredible diversity that exists in the forest and thereby continuing the natural cycle that began millions of years ago. The harmony and natural balance of this network is threatened by deforestation, shifting agriculture and human intrusions.

ZEN is the iconic department store that offers 7 levels of exciting merchandise and theatrically inspirational store ambience for the Young and Young-@-Hearts. Being at the forefront of fashion, the unique ZEN is highly popular among Trendy Thais and Foreign Visitors.

This one-of-a-kind sensational megastore also boasts Thailand's most entertaining and creative eating establishments:

Ying Yang Asian Gastro Bar, Level 1
FoodLoft Gourmet Food Court with Tasteful Ambience, Level 7

Plus 4 scintillating rooftop dining choices:
ZENSE Gourmet Deck & Lounge Panorama with 5 Acclaimed Restaurants
Shintori Japanese Art Cuisine
HORIZONS Tapas Cuisine Bar
Heaven on ZEN, the Private Escapade

There are still more reasons to make ZEN your One-Stop Location. The ZEN World building features True Fitness, the best gym in town, as well as an Urban Spa, Aesthetic Services, and a variety of Education Services. CentralWorld Live and ZEN Event Gallery are perfect for large gatherings, seminars and banquets.

ZEN is The Lifestyle Destination.

最前卫的购物氛围带来最时尚的购物体验

ZEN Lifestyle Megastore @CentralWorld
Shopping Complex, 4/ 4,5 Rajadamri/ Rama I Rd., Bangkok
(A short walk from BTS Skytrain Stations Siam and Chidlom)
Open daily 10 a.m. till 10 p.m.

Ample parking / Valet parking services
VIP Customer Lounge & Concierge Services
VAT refunds
Attractive in-store discounts

Tel. 0-2100-9999
/ZENMegastore   www.zen.co.th

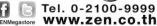

ORCHIDS

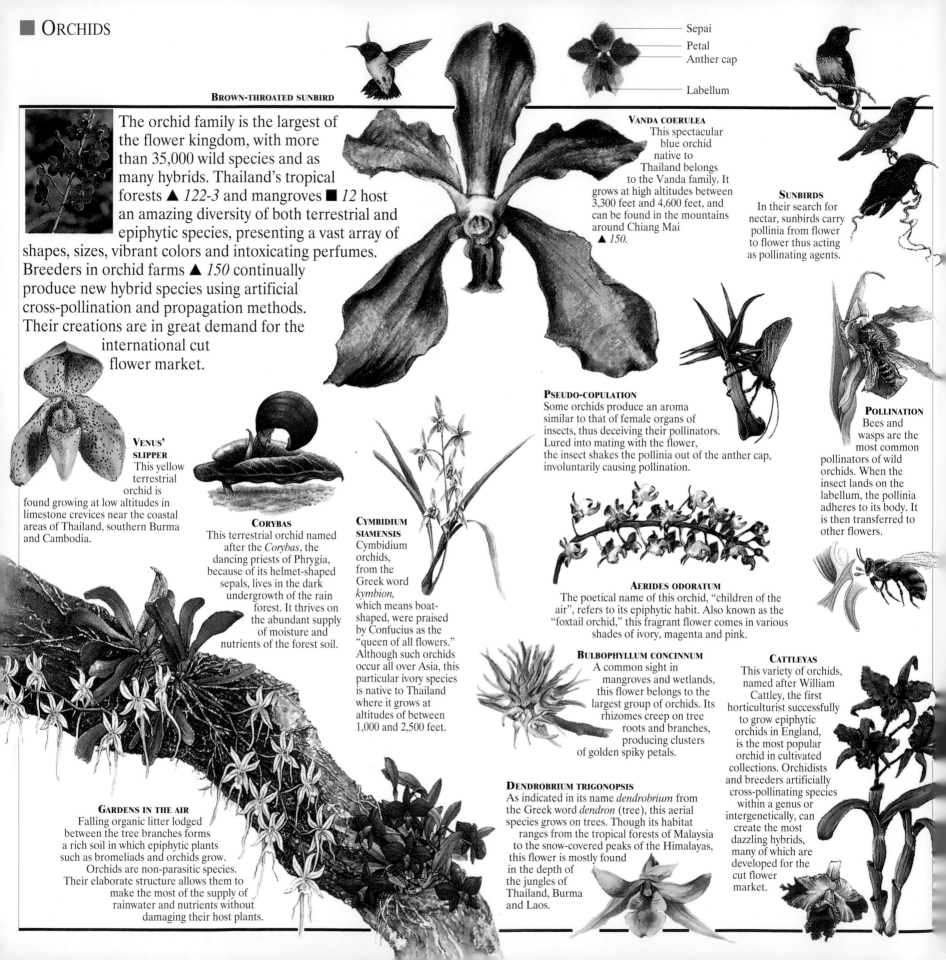

BROWN-THROATED SUNBIRD

Sepal
Petal
Anther cap
Labellum

The orchid family is the largest of the flower kingdom, with more than 35,000 wild species and as many hybrids. Thailand's tropical forests ▲ *122-3* and mangroves ■ *12* host an amazing diversity of both terrestrial and epiphytic species, presenting a vast array of shapes, sizes, vibrant colors and intoxicating perfumes. Breeders in orchid farms ▲ *150* continually produce new hybrid species using artificial cross-pollination and propagation methods. Their creations are in great demand for the international cut flower market.

VANDA COERULEA
This spectacular blue orchid native to Thailand belongs to the Vanda family. It grows at high altitudes between 3,300 feet and 4,600 feet, and can be found in the mountains around Chiang Mai ▲ *150*.

SUNBIRDS
In their search for nectar, sunbirds carry pollinia from flower to flower thus acting as pollinating agents.

VENUS' SLIPPER
This yellow terrestrial orchid is found growing at low altitudes in limestone crevices near the coastal areas of Thailand, southern Burma and Cambodia.

CORYBAS
This terrestrial orchid named after the *Corybas*, the dancing priests of Phrygia, because of its helmet-shaped sepals, lives in the dark undergrowth of the rain forest. It thrives on the abundant supply of moisture and nutrients of the forest soil.

CYMBIDIUM SIAMENSIS
Cymbidium orchids, from the Greek word *kymbion,* which means boat-shaped, were praised by Confucius as the "queen of all flowers." Although such orchids occur all over Asia, this particular ivory species is native to Thailand where it grows at altitudes of between 1,000 and 2,500 feet.

PSEUDO-COPULATION
Some orchids produce an aroma similar to that of female organs of insects, thus deceiving their pollinators. Lured into mating with the flower, the insect shakes the pollinia out of the anther cap, involuntarily causing pollination.

POLLINATION
Bees and wasps are the most common pollinators of wild orchids. When the insect lands on the labellum, the pollinia adheres to its body. It is then transferred to other flowers.

AERIDES ODORATUM
The poetical name of this orchid, "children of the air", refers to its epiphytic habit. Also known as the "foxtail orchid," this fragrant flower comes in various shades of ivory, magenta and pink.

BULBOPHYLLUM CONCINNUM
A common sight in mangroves and wetlands, this flower belongs to the largest group of orchids. Its rhizomes creep on tree roots and branches, producing clusters of golden spiky petals.

CATTLEYAS
This variety of orchids, named after William Cattley, the first horticulturist successfully to grow epiphytic orchids in England, is the most popular orchid in cultivated collections. Orchidists and breeders artificially cross-pollinating species within a genus or intergenetically, can create the most dazzling hybrids, many of which are developed for the cut flower market.

DENDROBRIUM TRIGONOPSIS
As indicated in its name *dendrobrium* from the Greek word *dendron* (tree), this aerial species grows on trees. Though its habitat ranges from the tropical forests of Malaysia to the snow-covered peaks of the Himalayas, this flower is mostly found in the depth of the jungles of Thailand, Burma and Laos.

GARDENS IN THE AIR
Falling organic litter lodged between the tree branches forms a rich soil in which epiphytic plants such as bromeliads and orchids grow. Orchids are non-parasitic species. Their elaborate structure allows them to make the most of the supply of rainwater and nutrients without damaging their host plants.

A BOLD AND REVOLUTIONARY NEW ERA IN LIFESTYLE DINING & ENTERTAINMENT IS HERE

A Spectacular Dining and Entertainment Paradise on the rooftop of the iconic ZEN Lifestyle Megastore in Bangkok. Visiting this 6,800 square metre concept is a definite must! Spread over 4 levels with indoor and outdoor spaces, each with its own unique presence and amazing concept, visitors will be captivated by a truly sensational experience.

The Place to see and be seen.

Expected to be one of the most Trendsetting Food Entertainment Greats of the World.

**Five Top-Rated Restaurants with Hip Indoor & Outdoor Bars
and Seats that command a great view of Metropolitan Bangkok**
ZENSE Gourmet Deck & Lounge Panorama: Larger than Life.
Dine and Chill Out with great Lounge Rhythms and have fun. Italian, Thai, Indian, Contemporary European, Japanese Fusion & ZENSE Patisserie.
www.zensebangkok.com info@zensebangkok.com Tel: 662 100 9898   Level 17

Shintori, The Japanese Art of Cuisine
The highly acclaimed and inspirational Japanese cuisine is now in Bangkok! Diners will enjoy a spectacular presentation of food that even highly experienced Food Stylists and Critics will rave about. Whether in the Grand Dining Hall or our 4 unique private Urban Villas, Shintori is synonymous with elegant simplicity combined with classy chic.
www.shintoribangkok.com info@shintoribangkok.com Tel: 662 100 9000   Level 18

**Gastronomy + Mixology + Musicology
+ 360° Panorama Bangkok**
Horizons Bangkok is the Tapas Cuisine Bar with the most stunning 360 degree panoramic view. Our Chefs will present you with Food Designs, our Mixologists will give you our Special Cocktails and Concoctions, our Spin Doctors will entertain you with music that makes you want to dance and our Service Managers will give you that smile that brings you home safe and sound.
www.horizonsbangkok.com info@horizonsbangkok.com Tel: 662 101 0900 Level 19

Heaven on Zen is the Ultimate Private Escapade.
This Heavenly space with our special daily menu selection of Food and Drinks from the Horizons team will escalate your sensation to the Top of this World!
www.Heaven-on-ZEN.com info@Heaven-on-ZEN.com Tel: 662 101 0900 Level 20

A Dining Zensationo Limited Establishment.
**Levels 17-20 ZEN World. The Heart of Downtown Bangkok.
Open from 5pm till late. Dress Code applies.
Ample Parking, Valet Parking & Conceirge Services.**
Head Office: Level 16 ZEN World

ZEN Lifestyle Megastore
Asia's Most Dynamic and Trendy Shopping Destination
CentralWorld
4, 4/5 Rajadamri Road, CentralWorld, Pathumwan, Bangkok 10330 Thailand
Telephone: +66 2100 9988 Fax: +66 2100 9966 www.zen.co.th

■ MANGROVES

A mangrove coast in southern Thailand, covering sinking limestone ranges millions of years old. As the sea level changes, the mangrove forest cover advances or retreats.

Mangroves and intertidal mudflats are of great conservation value in Thailand, helping sustain valuable inshore fisheries and protecting the coast from erosion. With a constant supply of water, sunlight and nutrients the rate of growth of mangrove trees is very fast. The most extensive and species-rich mangrove ecosystems are found along the west coast of the peninsula ▲ *112-5*. There are also several important mangroves and mudflats on the east coast, as well as in the inner gulf, although large areas have been converted to prawn ponds. The total area of mangrove forest is about 2,300 square miles most of which are along the west coast.

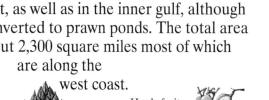

The Brahmini kite circles above the mangrove.

This large estuarine crocodile is rarely seen. Forest clearance and aquaculture projects are responsible for its dwindling numbers ▲ *98*.

The mangrove snake is particularly adapted to this unusual habitat and is found just above the water level.

Crab-eating macaques are one of the numerous mammal species living in this environment.

The fruit of the Nipa palm is edible. The Nipa borders waterways in the mangrove deltas off the open sea and usually covers much of the swamp area.

Hardy fruits of *Amoora calcullata* and *Xylocarpus gremata*. There are few flowers or fruits in the mangrove forest.

1

2

3

The collared kingfisher (1), gray heron (2) and little cormorant (3) are bird species common in the coastal swamps and mud flats.

Charcoal making is one of the many threats facing the coastal mangrove forest. Shrimp farming is another.

Rhizophora mucronata produces pointed spikes (right) that form effective instant seedlings. Equipped with tiny leaves at the top end, they drop off the parent into the mud below and take root at once. Apart from this unusual mode of propagation, *Rhizophora mucronata* produces conventional seeds as well.

Free form furniture, made from the roots of the mangrove.

Cross-section of the mangrove coastline. The swamps are criss-crossed by tidal channels, which are often bordered by the Nipa palm. The mangrove's enormous root systems are the dominant feature of the habitat. It extends to the low tide mark, below which the roots cannot obtain enough oxygen for growth. Where the ground rises above high tide mark level away from the open sea, the surroundings gradually assume the character of lowland rain forest.

Below the water level, the mud and the roots give shelter to a plethora of marine life, including fish, crabs and molluscs.

RICEFIELDS

CRIMSON HERON

An extraordinary amount of human energy is invested in producing the rice crop throughout the year. Rice plays an important role in the daily lives of the people, providing the staple diet for the Thai population as well as being a major export crop. Many cultural rituals are closely tied to the cultivation of rice and complex calculations are made to predict forthcoming rainfall patterns and the bounty of future crops. Little has changed in the ricefields of Thailand ▲ 126 over the centuries and, in addition to providing an important wildlife refuge for a large number of species, they also remain a source of great spiritual and intellectual inspiration.

PAPAYA TREES
All available land is cultivated. Papaya and banana trees are frequently planted on the verges of the ricefields.

BIRDS OF THE RICEFIELDS
The ricefields provide a rich feeding haven for a variety of birds. Some of the most common of these are the munias, a group of small, seed-eating birds that feed on ripening rice. These, in turn, attract aerial predators such as the black-shouldered kite and marsh harrier, which may also feed on amphibians such as frogs.

The bright green seedlings clustered in ricefields prior to transplanting and the sun-drenched fields of rice that await harvesting are familiar sights in Thailand.

EGRETS AND HERONS
The rich aquatic and terrestrial life of the ricefields attracts large numbers of herons and egrets in all seasons. Although egrets and herons usually feed alone, they often roost together, which probably assists in detecting predators ▲ 107.

3. RIPENING
Through careful management of the water level, the plants flourish, grain heads develop and swell as the sun ripens the swaying stalks. This stage of growth is the least demanding in terms of labor input, but there are always water levels to be controlled, dykes to be repaired and nursery beds to be tended elsewhere in the ricefields.

BEAST OF BURDEN
Although mechanical means of plowing ricefields are now available, most farmers still prefer traditional means of cultivation involving the use of the water buffalo as a general beast of burden. Known locally as the "Asian tractor", the water buffalo is also an important source of milk and meat for many people. Its hide is used in clothing and its dung is collected as a fertilizer or as a source of fuel for burning.

1. PREPARING THE LAND
The farmer and the water buffalo drag a heavy plow to loosen up the water-logged soil, and their trampling actions also help to redistribute the valuable nutrients stored in the soil. Prior to planting, a heavy log is pulled across the muddy base to prepare a firm bed for the young seedlings.

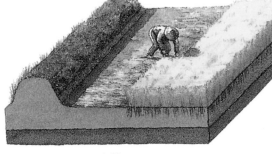

COMB DUCK
The comb duck is a frequent visitor to ricefields and it nests on the edges of wooded marshland. It flies with broad wing beats.

HARVESTING THE RICE AND THRESHING
The long stalks of ripe corn are harvested and then beaten over a drum to dislodge the grains from the chaff. Winnowing sifts off any remaining waste while the plump rice grains are dried in the sun before being stored.

LIFE AT THE WATER'S EDGE
The ricefield provides an ideal habitat for reptiles, fish and amphibians. Many of the fields are deliberately stocked with carp and catfish, which feed on decaying plants, algae and insect larvae. Frogs also help control the level of harmful insects, thereby eliminating the use of costly and often destructive pesticides.

2. TRANSPLANTING THE SEEDLINGS
Once the ricefield has been flooded and suitably prepared, bunches of bright green seedlings are transplanted from the tiny nursery beds where they were raised. This work is done entirely by hand, people laboring all day to set out row upon row of tender young plants. The softened mud base facilitates the planting process and seedlings quickly take root in this habitat.

4. HARVESTING
The harvesting of a paddy crop marks the end of a long period of hard labor and no time is lost in cutting the ripened golden stalks lest wild animals or inclement weather threaten to destroy the season's efforts. Rice stalks are harvested using a sharp sickle; the cutter lays the stalks tenderly on the ground in his wake. Later these will be collected and stacked, prior to threshing.

PESTS IN THE RICEFIELDS
The ricefield mouse and rat are common inhabitants of all ricefields and open grasslands, feeding on fallen grain, seeds and insects. The rat may also feed on rice plants and may be a pest in granaries where the dry grain is stored.

TRADITIONAL SILK LOOM

Several spectacular species of butterfly are found in the mountain ranges of north and northwest Thailand, near Chiang Rai, Pai, Mae Hong Son, and in the national park northwest of Chiang Mai ▲ *140*. In the cultivated zones, ricefields and rubber plantations, few species have survived the process of deforestation. The entire zone from Lampang to Chiang Mai is undergoing reforestation but the plant species being used do not produce a habitat favorable to the reestablishment of butterfly species. Certain "cosmopolitan" species of butterfly can travel for miles across oceans. The first explorers to arrive in Siam found several well-known European, African and North American species.

LIFE CYCLE OF THE MULBERRY BOMBYX

4–6 days Silk spinning

15–18 days Ecdysis

4–12 days Pupation

10–12 days Hatching

1–2 days Ovigenesis

1. Doi Inthanon, highest point in Thailand (8,547 feet), poor soil and cold climate where small mountain butterflies are found.
2. Chedi (6,600–8,250 feet), few cultivated areas and little highland forests. Habitat of small butterflies.
3. Chiang Mai plains, *pierides* and swallow-tail butterflies.
4. Mae Chaem, cultivated valley (1,580 feet) with a wide range of butterflies within the low vegetation.
5. Mae Surin rain forest (330–4,950 feet), privileged home to the most beautiful specimens in Thailand.
6. Khun Yuan (1,650–3,300 feet), a zone where rain forest butterflies live side by side with the small valley species.

THE SILK INDUSTRY
The silk industry in Thailand is now located mainly in the northeast of the country. The larvae of the *Mulberry bombyx*, probably the best-known Thai moth, produce silk. This moth does not exist in the wild. Having long been domesticated, it has even lost the ability to fly.

ATROPHANEURA POLYEUCTES
A jungle butterfly that sometimes ventures into towns and villages.

STICOPHTALMA CAMADEVA
This is the biggest diurnal butterfly in Thailand and South East Asia with a wing span of 5.6 inches.

TROIDES AEACUS
The *Troides aeacus* reigns in the north. Its caterpillar deters birds and insectivorous reptiles by living on a poisonous liana, the *aristoloche,* which protects it against predators. This butterfly has recently been designated an endangered species.

ACHERONTIA LACHESIS
The *Acherontia lachesis,* which lives in the northern mountains, is the Thai cousin of the European "death's head hawk moth" (*A. atropos*). It is a nocturnal butterfly and will risk its life to penetrate beehives to gorge itself on the honey.

TERINOS CLARISSA
The *Terinos clarissa* belongs to the *nymphalides* family. This small butterfly is mauve, varying in shade with the angle of vision. It flies discreetly close to the ground in the deep forest and at rest it is camouflaged against the vegetation.

PAPILIO ARCTURUS
The black part of the wings of the *Papilio arcturus* looks as though it is sprinkled with emerald dust. This spectacular butterfly can often be seen along mountain tracks.

BHUTANITIS LIDDERDALI
This butterfly is from the northern mountain valleys. At rest, its hind wings are covered by the fore wings, hiding their magnificent colors and allowing the insect to blend with its surroundings.

After ecdysis the silkworms are placed on bamboo trays, known as *jo*, where they secrete a fibrous slime that protects them until metamorphosis.

A mural painting from Wat Phumin in Nan Province, showing a Lanna lady selecting spools of yarn while working at a Thai frame loom.

The filaments are spun and eventually skeins are produced. Each cocoon yields about 2,000 feet of usable thread (*mai luad*), although in total a mature cocoon can contain over 1 mile of thread in about 30 layers. Silk made from thread still coated with sericin is called raw silk. Natural silk or *tussah* is the silk produced by undomesticated caterpillars living in trees.

Cocoons are taken from the *jo* and boiled to remove the sticky sericin coating the silk filaments.

The raw thread is bright yellow. Before weaving it is washed first in a herbal mixture made from the bark and leaves of the banana tree, and then in a *ke* solution made from a thorny vine that is commonly found on hillsides, then dyed. Traditional dyes used include lac, indigo, krajai berries and thalang roots. To the east of Chiang Mai, on the way to Charoen Muang, it is possible to visit a *magnanerie* (silkworm rearing house) and to taste chrysalides which have been grilled after the removal of their silk filaments.

Thailand is one of the major producers of edible birds' nests, a delicacy in Chinese cuisine dating as far back as the Ming and Qing dynasties of the 17th century. The swiftlets (*nok kin lom*) nest in caves along the southwestern coast and on the offshore islands ▲ *110, 114*. They find their way by echolocation. A series of up to 20 audible clicks per second is emitted and the echoes reflecting off the walls enable the birds to maneuver in the darkness. Already an expensive delicacy, these birds' nests could become more expensive as overcollection threatens the normal cycle of nest building.

CAVES
Besides the swiftlets, an interacting community of animals known as troglodytes may be found in the caves. Bats are abundant. Both bats and swiftlets produce guano, which is fed upon by insects such as moths and cockroaches. These insects in turn provide food for other predators such as bugs, centipedes and geckos. The most common predators of the swiftlets and their nestlings are the snakes, hawks and eagles that hunt in the surrounding areas, and the egg-eating crickets.

BAT HAWK

CRICKET

TYPES OF NESTS
The black nest swiftlet (*Aerodramus maximus*) uses its black feathers to build nests, hence the name "black nests." In contrast, the white nest swiftlet (*Aerodramus fuciphagus*) builds its nest wholly with saliva.

GRADES OF BIRDS' NESTS
The price of edible birds' nests varies according to their quality. White nests, wholly made of saliva, are more expensive. The best birds' nests are the first ones built during the breeding season. Thicker and translucent white, they expand to almost 20 times their volume upon soaking. Second and third nests are of lower grade, appearing dirtier and thinner.

BUILDING THE NEST
The bird makes chewing and retching movements of the bill and throat, as the saliva is regurgitated and worked around the mouth. Saliva is smeared on the edge of the nest with the sides of the bill. The nest takes shape as a pad of hardened saliva adhering to the wall. Subsequently a rim is added and material is laid down in layers until a small cup-shaped nest is finally formed.

DRY LONGAN

DRY BABY ABALONE

GINGER

COLOR AND QUALITY
Some supposedly high-quality nests are reddish. However, the coloration bears no relation to blood and may have leached into the nest from the substrate.

NEST COLLECTING TOOLS

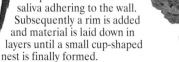

HONEY ROCK SUGAR

RED DATES

ROCK SUGAR

SHARKS' FINS

COLLECTING BIRDS' NESTS
In Thailand this is carried out between February and July. Three collections are made each breeding season. Birds' nests are usually found in the lofty and dark interiors of caves. The nest collector, armed with a small torchlight and rope, stealthily climbs up the bamboo stilt that leads him to the nest ▲ *110*.

A SOUP TONIC
Bird's nest soup made with traditional ingredients has long been used as a tonic in Chinese medicine, and to protect the body against various ailments. Recent research on the nutritional value of birds' nests has shown the presence of a soluble glycoprotein that may promote growth, tissue repair and cell division within the immune system.

DRY SNOW FROG

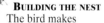

CORAL REEFS

GREEN TURTLE
Green turtles are exploited for their shell, flesh and eggs, and their numbers have been decimated wherever they occur.

The coral reef ecosystem is one of the richest habitats on earth. Coral colonies are composed of countless individuals – polyps – that feed on plankton. Although coral reefs can cover a large area, they grow very slowly: it may take 1,000 years for a reef to grow just 3 feet. When corals die, their skeletons remain and a new generation of polyps can grow on top of them. Each type of coral has its own distinctive shape, adding further to the splendor of the reef ecosystem.

COACHMAN FISH
The name of this fish derives from the long, whip-like appendages that often hang from its dorsal fin.

SURGEON FISH
Originating in the Indo-Pacific region, this species is quite aggressive.

EMPEROR FISH
This fish has one of the largest territories of all coral-reef dwellers.

TRIGGERFISH
Its common name refers to an erect spine in its dorsal fin, which cannot be released until a second spine (the trigger) is withdrawn.

PARROT FISH
Parrot fish have large scales and a typically bird-like beak formed of fused teeth.

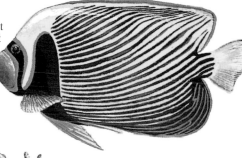

CORAL REEFS AND POLYPS
Coral reefs provide an important source of food and income to local Thais. A coral polyp is a soft, almost transparent animal that builds its skeleton outside its body. Polyps feed at night by extending their tentacles, each of which is armed with a series of stinging cells that paralyse any passing prey. The moray eel is a key predator in the reef ecosystem; it hides in crevices, lunging out to seize unsuspecting fish.

TRIPLE BANDIT CLOWN FISH
This fish lives in close association with sea anemones.

PEOPLE OF SIAM, *17*
PREHISTORY, *18*
THE FIRST MILLENNIUM, *18*
THE SIAMESE KINGDOM, *19*
THE LANNA KINGDOM, *20*
CONTEMPORARY HISTORY, *2*

PEOPLE OF SIAM

DEMOGRAPHY
Thailand has a total population of 69 million; about one third is below the age of 20.

Thailand is a mosaic of peoples and cultures, and has had remarkably little racial conflict. This may be due to the fact that the central Thai have ruled more by consensus than by force. The widespread practice of Theravada Buddhism has also promoted racial harmony.

THE THAIS. At the beginning of the first millennium, a people known as the Tai migrated from what is now southern China into the Chao Phraya River valley. When the Tai first arrived, the region was inhabited by Austro-Asiatic groups speaking Mon and Khmer; the present-day Thais are the product of the assimilation and fusion of these three groups. Many Thais still live in southern China (particularly in Yunnan, Guangdong, and Guangxi). Today four subdivisions of Thais are recognized in the country: the central Thais (from the region between Sukhothai and Phetchaburi), who speak the standard Thai taught in schools; the Pak Isan Thais (a mixture of Thai and Khmer in the northeast), who also speak standard Thai; the Pak Tai Thais (south of Phetchaburi), who have a darker complexion and speak a dialect largely incomprehensible to central Thais; the northern Thais, who speak a different dialect and who are a fusion of Thai immigrants with Karens and Lawas (Austro-Asiatic). Each of these groups had largely independent histories until recent centuries.

LIFE EXPECTANCY
The average life span for Thai men is 71.3 years, while for women, it is 76.3 years.

BUDDHISTS
95 percent of its population are Buddhists, making Thailand the largest Theravada Buddhist country in the world.

THE CHINESE. As traders, the Chinese arrived long before the Thais. They settled more permanently, at first in coastal cities in the south and then in other areas. The peak period of Chinese migration was in the 19th and early 20th centuries, and they now form a substantial part of most urban populations. Thanks to extensive assimilation, it is difficult to distinguish them as a separate ethnic group.

THE LAOS. Much of the northeast is inhabited by groups of Lao-speaking people – Lao Wieng, Yuai, Yo, Lao Kao and Phutai – who migrated (some were forcibly moved) mostly during the last century and are today among the poorest in the country. Like the Thais, they belong to the Sino-Tibetan group. They are renowned for their weaving skills, and some groups were once distinguished by their dress, rather like today's hill tribes; these elaborate costumes can still be seen during village festivals. Though Buddhist, many still practice older animistic rituals.

THE NORTHEAST
Much of the population decends from Laos.

THE KHMERS. Khmer-speaking people are also numerous in some parts of the northeast, particularly in Surin province near the Cambodian border. Most of them migrated during the 19th century when Siam occupied a large part of Cambodia. In the 1970s, the war in Cambodia drove millions of Khmer refugees into Thailand. The refugees' repatriation or resettlement took over a decade to complete.

THE SHANS. The Thai Yai (right), called the Ngiaw by the Thais, belong to the Tai linguistic family and migrated from the Shan states of Burma in the 19th century. Today the Shans are scattered throughout the north, especially in Mae Hong Son and Mae Sariang.

THE MUSLIMS. Thailand's largest religious minority, Muslims live mainly in the southernmost provinces. In Narathiwat, Pattani and Yala, separatist violence has erupted where an ethnic Malay majority speaks Yawi (ancient Malay), though not among the Thai-speaking Muslims of Satun. Ninety-nine percent of Thai Muslim are Sunni. Those Muslims who are not ethnic Malays are mainly descendants of Persian, Middle Eastern and Indian traders (left) who had settled in Siam during the Ayutthaya and early Bangkok periods.

MUSLIMS
More than 2 million Muslims, most of whom are Sunni, live in Thailand. There are about 3,200 mosques in the country.

THE MONS. These people, who live mostly in Nakhon Pathom, Samut Songkram and Samut Prakan, are not ancestors of the ancient Mon culture that once ruled over portions of central Thailand, but relatively recent Buddhist immigrants from Burma.

HILL TRIBES. The majority of the hill tribes ▲ *146, 152-5* in northern Thailand are relatively recent immigrants to the region. Only the Karens and the Lawas (right) were settled in the country before the arrival of the Thais. The hill tribes form a minority. In 1999, their total population was about 873,700. Apart from the Karens and the Lawas, this group also includes the Miens (Yaos), Lisus, Lahu Shis and the Blue and White Hmongs. While aspects of religions such as Christianity, Buddhism and Islam have been adopted by some hill tribes, animism is still in evidence.

A Karen with traditional pendants.

PREHISTORY

ROCK PAINTINGS
Several caves or rock faces are decorated with paintings from simple handprints to complete tableaux showing scenes of hunting, fishing and dancing. These could date back to the 4th century BC. Some are easily accessible, like those at Khao Chiang Ngam, 124 miles from Bangkok on the road to Khorat.

PLEISTOCENE. Evidence of Pleistocene cultures, dating from 600,000–130,000 BC, have been found in various parts of Thailand, from Lampang in the north to Krabi in the south. The earliest implements found were pebble tools, followed by early flake tools (300,000–290,000 BC), then by Proto-Hoabinhian pebble tools (140,000–13,000 BC)

TRIPOD
(c. 2000 BC)
This pottery tripod was found at Ban Kao, in the Kanchanaburi province. It was probably copied from a tin prototype, and is reminiscent of the Chinese bronzes of the Han dynasty.

HOABINHIAN. This term was coined by a French archeologist in Vietnam in the 1920's and covers a period from around 120,000 –2000 BC. The earliest Hoabinhian tools in Thailand were found in caves in Mae Hong Son and Kanchanaburi. In the former, the American archeologist Chester Gorman found tools and seeds of various cultivated plants including betel nut, black pepper, bottle gourd and cucumber. These have been dated by carbon-14 tests to as far back as 9700–6000 BC, far earlier than previously suspected. More sophisticated tools like the polished adze and the edge-ground knife appeared in the cave around 6800 BC. Pottery has also been found at the same level.

BAN CHIANG ▲ 117. The discoveries of a prehistoric culture at Ban Chiang, in the northeastern province of Udon Thani, have aroused considerable archeological controversy, with some historians questioning the early dates originally ascribed to the appearance of copper and bronze. Most now accept that the initial dating of 4000 BC is too early but still maintain that the two metals could possibly be dated to between 2500 BC and 2000 BC – later than their first appearance in the Middle East but approximately contemporaneous with copper in China – and that Thailand had a true Bronze Age. Painted pottery found in the burial sites at Ban Chiang and elsewhere in the northeast was produced relatively late in the culture's history, between 1000 BC and 500 BC. The most recent level of the Ban Chiang excavation is dated at around 250 BC.

3000 BC
First civilizations in Mesopotamia.

2700–2300 BC
Egyptian pyramids of Kheops, Khephren and Mykerinos built.

1765–1122 BC
Shang Dynasty.

566–486 BC
Buddha.

219 BC
Hannibal crosses the Alps.

THE FIRST MILLENNIUM

THE INDIAN INFLUENCE. In the 1st century AD, Indian merchants began arriving in peninsular Thailand in search of new products to trade. They brought with them Indian ideas of art, architecture, religion and government that dominated the south over the next five centuries and later spread to other parts of the country. At first Hindu images were produced, but, from the 5th century onward, Buddhist images appeared in greater numbers, reflecting this new religion, which also came from India.

SRIVIJAYA ▲ 103. Beginning in the 8th century AD a new, more warlike empire called Srivijaya was established in the southern peninsula, originating from Sumatra. It remained the principal force in the region until the 13th century. Many historians disagree about the exact center of the empire, but one of its important centers was Ligor, or Nakhon Si Thammarat. Wholly Hindu at first, Srivijaya later also practiced Mahayana Buddhism and beautiful images were created for both religions.

DVARAVATI ▲ 81-2. What is traditionally called the Dvaravati Period extends from the 7th to 11th centuries AD; a more accurate name might be Mon, for during this period, several Mon kingdoms rose in central Thailand, first at U Thong near the subsequent Thai capital of Ayutthaya, and later at Lopburi and Nakhon Pathom. All three were centers of Theravada Buddhism, the sect eventually adopted throughout the country. The Mons eventually succumbed to the more powerful Khmers.

KHMER EMPIRE. In the 7th century AD the rising Khmer Empire began to extend its power over the northeastern region. By the 11th century it had reached the Chao Phraya River valley. The great period of Khmer monument building commenced with the reign of Suriyavarman I (AD 1002-50) ▲ 118. The principal religion in the early centuries was Hinduism, which was replaced with Mahayana Buddhism by the late 12th century. Khmer power began to wane in the 13th century.

MIGRATION OF THE THAIS. It is thought that in the 11th century AD Thais migrated in large numbers from Yunnan in southern China, driven by a desire for greater independence and better farmland. They formed two groups of kingdoms, in the north near the Mekong River and further south at the edge of the Chao Phraya River valley.

27 BC–AD 14
Foundation of the Roman Empire.

AD 330
Foundation of Constantinople.

Votive tablet of the Srivijaya era.

AD 348
Buddhist settlements at Dunhuang.

AD 395
Fall of the Roman Empire.

AD 518–907
Tang Dynasty.

AD 571–632
Mohammed

WHEEL OF THE LAW
This wheel dates from the 7th century and is a symbol of the law taught by Buddha.

AD 762
Foundation of Baghdad.

AD 800–14
Reign of Charlemagne, Holy Roman Emperor.

AD 960–1274
Sung Dynasty.

AD 1066
The Norman Conquest in England.

AD 1096–9
The First Crusade.

Soldiers and elephants, in celadon, from the Sukhothai era.

THE SIAMESE KINGDOM

1245
Jean de Plancarpin travels to Karakorum.

1253
Guillaume de Rubrouck travels to Karakorum.

1274
Death of Thomas Aquinas.

1276
Arrival of Marco Polo in China.

1279–1368
Yuan Dynasty.

1338
Beginning of the Hundred Years War between England and France.

1348
Black Death reaches Europe.

1368–1644
Ming Dynasty.

1492
Christopher Columbus discovers the Americas.

1602
Foundation of Dutch East India Company.

1644–1911
Qing Dynasty.

POWER STRUGGLE IN SUKHOTHAI. In the first half of the 13th century, probably in the 1240's, a Thai chieftain later known as King Intradit joined forces with several other groups, overthrew the Khmer overlord at Sukhothai ▲ *128, 130,* and established an independent Thai kingdom of the same name. Sukhothai remained small under its first two rulers; it expanded dramatically, however, during the reign of King Ramkhamhaeng (left), exerting either direct or indirect power over much of present-day Thailand through force and strategic alliances. Ramkhamhaeng is also credited with devising the Thai alphabet as well as a paternalistic system of monarchy that is regarded as ideal even to this day. Aside from its political achievements, Sukhothai is also remembered for its superb Buddhist art and architecture, which were distinctively Thai, and which are still considered the finest ever created in the country. Also notable were the beautiful ceramics produced first at Sukhothai and later at the satellite city of Si Satchanalai. Sukhothai's empire began to fall apart rapidly after Ramkhamhaeng's death and by 1320 it had once more become a small kingdom of little regional significance. By 1378 it had become a vassal state of Ayutthaya.

THE RISE OF AYUTTHAYA.
Ayutthaya was founded on the Chao Phraya River by King Ramathibodi in 1350. Over the next four centuries, it grew from a small, fortified city into one of the great capitals of the region, its power reaching far beyond the fertile river valley. The capital fell to the Burmese in 1569, but less than two decades later regained independence under the able leadership of the future King Naresuan, who proceeded to extend its rule over most of the southern peninsula, the north, and both Cambodia and Laos. Relations with Europe began with a treaty between Siam and Portugal in 1516. The Dutch received permission to build a trading station in 1604, followed by the British in 1612. By King Narai's reign in 1656, Ayutthaya already had a cosmopolitan population of nearly a million. The first French Catholic missionary arrived in Ayutthaya in 1662, joined by others two years later. Given land on which to build churches and schools by King Narai, they became an important force in relations between the two countries. The first Thai embassy sent to France was lost at sea in 1681, but a second arrived safely in 1684 and formally requested a French mission to Ayutthaya. The first of these missions arrived in 1685, headed

by the Chevalier de Chaumont; a second arrived two years later. A Thai embassy accompanied the first on its return to France, and was received at the court of Louis XIV. Following the death of King Narai in 1688, conservative elements assumed control and expelled many Europeans during the latter part of Ayutthaya's rule ▲ *124.*

1762–96
Reign of Catherine II of Russia.

1787
American Constitution drafted.

THE FALL OF AYUTTHAYA. Shortly after King Ekatat assumed the throne in 1758, Ayutthaya was attacked once more by the Burmese under King Alaungpaya. A second invasion led by Alaungpaya's son, Hsinbyushin, succeeded in capturing Ayutthaya, after a siege lasting more than a year. The city was burned and looted by the victors and more than 30,000 of its inhabitants were taken to Burma. Son of a Chinese father and a Thai mother, the future King Taksin was a military officer at the time of Ayutthaya's fall. Within seven months he managed to rally Thai forces, expel the Burmese from the ruins of the city, and establish a new capital at Thonburi, further down the Chao Phraya River.

1789
The French Revolution.

1804–14
Napoleon Bonaparte, Emperor.

THE CHAKRI DYNASTY. In March 1782 a revolt broke out against King Taksin ● *20* ▲ *134,* who was thought to have become insane. He was replaced by a prominent military commander who, as King Rama I, founded the Chakri Dynasty and, for strategic reasons, moved the seat of government across the river to a small trading port known as Bangkok. King Rama IV, or King Mongkut (r. 1851–68, left), is best known as the hero of *The King and I.* To the Thais, however, he is remembered as one of the most far-sighted Chakri rulers, who negotiated important treaties with European powers, introduced modern sciences, and set his kingdom on the path to reforms that undoubtedly helped save it from the colonial fate that befell all its immediate neighbors. During his reign from 1868 to 1910, King Rama V (below), or King Chulalongkorn as he is better known, carried his father's reforms further. He abolished slavery, reorganized the governmental system, and built the first railways. The first Thai king to visit European capitals, Rama V also sent most of his sons abroad for further education. Though forced to concede a considerably large sector of Thai territory to France and England, Rama V was able to preserve his country's independence.

1868–1912
Meiji Period in Japan.

1869
Suez Canal opened.

RAMA V SURROUNDED BY HIS FAMILY
This portrait was painted by the Italian artist Gelli.

THE LANNA KINGDOM

6TH CENTURY AD
Arab invasions.

571–632
Mohammed.

982
Erik the Red discovers Greenland.

A Bodhi tree at Wat Pong Yang Kok in Lampang Luang.

1099
The First Crusade – Jerusalem taken.

1325
Foundation of Tenochtitlan by the Aztecs.

1453
Constantinople taken by the Turks.

1497
Vasco da Gama discovers sea route to India.

Wat Ched Yod at Chiang Mai, built in 1455.

Northern Thailand, which has a history largely independent from the rest of the country, appears to have been populated by different groups of Thais, who assimilated with local inhabitants and settled in the fertile valleys of the north around the first millennium. Present-day Chiang Saen was the seat of the Ngong Yang kingdom, and was one of the main centers. Chiang Saen ▲ *156* and Payao, another center, were both in contact with India, through Burma, and traded with the Srivijaya empire. The decline of the latter led to the emergence of a trade route to China and ultimately to the birth of a powerful kingdom in the north.

HARIPUNCHAI (LAMPHUN) ▲ *141.* Mon immigrants from the Dvaravati kingdom of Lopburi founded the city of Haripunchai in the 7th century, as well as a string of fortified towns around it. Devout Buddhists, the Mons were a key force in the conversion of the Thais in the north and Haripunchai remained an important cultural center for centuries.

KING MENGRAI. Unification of the small northern principalities was achieved by King Mengrai, a Ngong Yang chief of mixed Thai and Lawa blood. Embarking on a grand scheme for conquering the whole region, he founded Chiang Rai ▲ *151,* seized Haripunchai in 1292, annexed Payao and, in 1296, founded his new capital of Chiang Mai. He thus established the powerful Lanna kingdom, which was to last for 600 years before being annexed by Siam. For a considerable period, toward the end of the kingdom, it was in effect under Burmese or Central Thai control ▲ *134, 136.*

THE GOLDEN AGE OF LANNA. The 15th century saw the flowering of the Lanna kingdom, which was powerful enough to host an international Buddhist gathering in 1455. Trade, art and education flourished, despite the occasional feudal battles between vassals and princes. The west bank of the Mekong (today parts of Laos, Burma and Thailand) was also ruled by the King of Lanna.

THE BURMESE INVASION. Quarrels over the possession of a powerful talisman, an image of the Buddha, led to a Burmese invasion in 1558 and Lanna became a vassal state of the King of Pegu, governed by Burmese-appointed rulers. King Naresuan of Ayutthaya, fighting the Burmese who had invaded Siam, expelled these rulers from Lanna in 1598 and for the next 17 years Ayutthaya remained the dominant power in the north.

THE BURMESE ERA. In 1615, the Burmese King of Ava reestablished control over Lanna, which lasted for more than a century. Actual Burmese presence in the north, however, remained minimal and had very little effect on most of the population. The darkest period in the history of the north began with the rebellion of General Thip, who defeated a Burmese army and proclaimed himself King of Lampang in 1727. His successors eventually ruled in the 19th century, but before that, the King of Ava sent army after army into Lanna and Siam. After the fall of Ayutthaya, Kawila of Lampang and King Taksin of Thonburi joined forces against the Burmese. Having reconquered Chiang Mai in 1776, however, the Thais were forced to abandon the impoverished city. Lanna and Laos were decimated by the endless war; towns such as Chiang Saen, Luang Prabang and Vientiane, previously spared by the Burmese, were destroyed by the Thais to prevent their recapture. The strain, accumulated over many hard-fought battles, took its toll on Taksin and affected his mental health. He became eccentric and cruel toward his subordinates. In 1782, an élite group of officials led by Phya San rebelled, forcing Taksin to abdicate.

THE 19TH CENTURY. Independent but impoverished, 19th-century Lanna was governed by the family of Kawila ▲ *143,* nominally a vassal of Thailand, but in fact autonomous. Not until 1874 was a Thai High Commissioner sent to administer the north and during the reign of King Rama V the region was slowly incorporated into the Thai kingdom. Laos, east of the Mekong, annexed by King Rama I during the Burmese War, was ceded to France in 1893, following a show of force by gunboats.

1588
Spanish Armada defeated.

The old walls of Chiang Mai.

1733
John Kay invents flying shuttle.

1769
Richard Arkwright erects spinning mill.

A BURMESE PRINCE
Mural painting at Lampang (left).

1837–1901
Reign of Queen Victoria.

1894
Japan declares war against China.

Chao Kaew Nawarat, last king of Chiang Mai (1911–39).

CONTEMPORARY HISTORY

1910
Annexation of Korea by Japan.

In 1910, at the time of King Rama V's death, Thailand had become a modern nation recognized by the Western world, its boundaries apparently more or less secure. The following 80 years, however, were to be turbulent and marked by momentous events both inside the country and beyond.

1914
Outbreak of World War One.

FROM RAMA VI TO MODERN LEADERS. The first Thai ruler to be educated abroad, King Rama VI continued many of the reforms initiated by his father. In 1913, a law was passed requiring Thai citizens to have surnames for the first

1917
Russian Revolution.

1918
End of World War One.

time; the first university, Chulalongkorn, was established in 1917; the country entered World War One on the side of the Allies; and unequal treaties with Western powers were renegotiated in Thailand's favor.

1922
Mussolini's Fascists march on Rome.

END OF THE ABSOLUTE MONARCHY. King Rama VI's successor, Rama VII (above and below), inherited numerous economic and social problems. On June 24, 1932, a small group of foreign-educated military officers and civil servants staged a coup d'état calling for a constitutional monarchy. The king, who had already been thinking along such lines himself, granted their request. Later, he became disillusioned and abdicated in 1935, spending the rest of his life in England. Prince Ananda Mahidol, then a boy of 10, was named his successor and a regency council was appointed until he completed his studies in Switzerland.

1927
Lindbergh makes first solo flight across the Atlantic.

1933
Hitler appointed chancellor.

POWER STRUGGLES. The two dominant figures in Thai politics during the 1930's were Luang Pibulsonggram, later known as Field Marshal Pibul, and Dr Pridi Panomyong. Both men were educated in France. These two leaders held

1936–9
Spanish Civil War.

different views on many issues and were in frequent conflict. By the end of the decade, Pibul had become the country's Prime Minister and Dr Pridi had held several senior posts, including that of Minister of Foreign Affairs.

1939
Outbreak of World War Two.

THE PACIFIC WAR. In 1940, following the fall of France, skirmishes broke out along the borders of Thailand and Indo-China which resulted in the return of areas in Laos and Cambodia to Thailand the following year. Upon the outbreak of the Pacific War on December 8, 1941, Japan demanded free passage through southern Thailand for its attack against British territories. Unable to resist, Pibul granted permission and, further, issued a declaration of war against Great Britain and the United States in January 1942. A Free Thai underground movement was organized by Pridi during the war, not only bringing him back to power but also enabling Thailand to avoid being treated as an enemy nation following Japan's defeat.

1941
Japanese attack on Pearl Harbor.

1945
Atomic bomb dropped on Hiroshima. End of World War Two.

THE NEW KING. On June 9, 1946, the young King Ananda (right) was found shot dead in his room at the Grand Palace during a visit from Switzerland. His younger brother thus came to the throne as King Bhumibol Adulyadej, Rama IX, in circumstances that were both tragic and politically explosive.

1947
Indian Independence.

1948
Assassination of Mahatma Gandhi.

TUMULTUOUS TIMES. The next three decades saw a number of coups and counter-coups. Accused of complicity in the death of the king, Pridi was forced into exile by Pibul. Though Pridi attempted two comebacks, in 1949 and 1951, both ended in failure and he retired first to China and finally to France. Pibul remained in power until he, too, was overthrown by Field Marshal Sarit Thanarat in 1957. In October 1973 Thai students staged a series of massive demonstrations that overthrew the military government and sent its leaders into exile. Three years of chaotic democracy ensued, but in 1976, alarmed by the unrest and by the fall of Indo-China to communists, rightist elements returned to power in a violent coup in which several hundred students were killed.

1950–3
Korean War.

1953
Edmund Hillary and Sherpa Tenzing reach summit of Everest.

A UNIQUE MONARCHY. One of the outstanding forces in contemporary Thailand is the monarchy that has evolved under King Bhumibol Adulyadej (below) following his official coronation in 1950. The world's longest-serving head of state and one of its most inspiring leaders, he has reshaped the monarchy in his own image, initiating development, health, and education projects across the country and bringing the institution closer to the people than ever before. In recent years, the elderly king has spent much time in hospital due to a variety of illnesses. However, his public projects are ongoing. The great respect earned through these endeavors has enabled the king to act as a decisive mediator in times of severe civil unrest, particularly during the student revolution of 1973 and, even more dramatically, during the political upheaval of 1992 when he made an unprecedented television appearance to effect a compromise between the opposing groups.

1958
Treaties establishing EEC come into force.

1963
Assassination of John F. Kennedy.

1969
First men land on the moon.

MODERN THAILAND.

Thailand's recent history has been marked by further military coups, successful and otherwise, but it has also enjoyed steady economic and social progress. During the eight-year premiership of General Prem Tinsulanonda (1979–88), a local communist insurgency ended, relations with neighboring countries improved, and the incremental reintroduction of democratic institutions gained increasing public support among the general population. Meanwhile, Thailand achieved the status of a "Newly Industrialized Country", with manufactured exports overtaking agricultural produce in national revenue. In a temporary setback, bloody suppression of anti-

1975
End of Vietnam War.

1979
Phnom Penh, capital of Cambodia, falls to the Vietnamese. First European space shuttle launched.

1986
People Power movement unseats Philippines President Ferdinand Marcos.

1989
Berlin Wall is demolished. Tiananmen Square massacre takes place.

dictatorship protests forced the resignation of the non-elected Prime Minister General Suchinda Kraprayoon in May 1992. While this unrest damaged the country's image of stability, many knowledgeable observers saw this as an encouraging sign that predominantly middle-class demonstrators succeeded in resisting the traditional military dominance in politics. For the next fourteen years a series of democratically elected, if fractious governments avoided military interference. Peaceful elections continued in spite of an unprecedented economic upheaval that began with a devaluation of the Thai baht in 1997 and spread throughout Asia. Thailand suffered the closure of many financial companies, banks, and manufacturing plants, resulting in social problems and scores of unfinished building projects that had started during the boom. A bail-out effort by the International Monetary Fund, together with positive steps by the Chuan Leekpai government, put the country on the road to recovery. Fortunately, Thailand was able to avoid the serious social disruption that afflicted some of its neighbors, with villages reabsorbing migrants and the middle class calmly reverting to simpler lifestyles discarded during the pre-1997 consumer boom.

1990
Iraq invades Kuwait.

1991
Operation Desert Storm liberates Kuwait. Collapse of the Soviet Union.

CONTEMPORARY CULTURE.

The economic crash had positive effects too. It brought a reassessment of things lost during the boom, when the emphasis was on development and consumption of imported brands. A renewed pride in Thai products and traditions emerged, combined with new cosmopolitanism. Initially, this focused on small-scale fairs. Soon designers incorporated indigenous materials and forms into Thai brands with a contemporary style. Now exported worldwide, this fusion style predominates in furniture, fashion clothing, lifestyle objects and the interiors of increasingly upscale shops, bars, restaurants, hotels and spas. Thailand was an early focus of the world spa boom, which has helped revive traditional massage and herbal therapies. Thai cuisine has also received imaginative attention as high-quality culinary practices have swept cities and resorts. This refinement has been mirrored in the arts. With international film festivals becoming frequent, Thai films have improved in quality and number, winning awards at Cannes and earning more abroad than at home. Thai contemporary art has experienced huge innovation, diversity and international acclaim. Even in music, Thai singers are starting to record in English for foreign sales. Greater sophistication has also brought new thinking. Many young urbanites identify as "indie", or independent. This less deferential outlook will likely bring further changes to a society already transformed.

HIGH-TECH FUTURE.

Thailand aspires to be regarded as a fully developed country and a regional hub in myriad activities. This involves vast construction and huge budgets. The SkyTrain and subway, launched in 1999 and 2004 respectively, have already changed life in Bangkok and more lines will follow. Bangkok's new Suvarnabhumi Airport is among the world's biggest, though many problems plagued its opening in 2006. By virtue of its location, the country is becoming a transit hub. Highways and possibly railroads will soon traverse Thailand from Vietnam to Burma, and China to Malaysia. China has blasted rapids and built ports on the Mekong to turn the river into a trading channel while damming it for hydro-electric power. Various construction plans will open up remote or protected areas to development. As well as new dams and roads, a long-mooted shipping canal and oil "land bridge" across the narrow Kra Isthmus would create a shortcut between the Indian and Pacific Oceans. Although the tourist industry aims to shift from quantity to quality, arrivals will doubtless grow, especially from Korea and China. It is becoming clear that after periods under the influence of Japan and America in the 20th century, Thailand in the 21st century will once again turn its attention northwards.

1992
Bill Clinton (Democrat) elected President of the United States.

1993
UN-sponsored elections take place in Cambodia.

1994
End of US embargo on Vietnam.

1997
Asian economic crisis. Handover of Hong Kong to China. ASEAN accepts Burma, Laos as members.

1998
India & Pakistan test nuclear weapons. Fall of President Suharto in Indonesia.

1999
Cambodia joins ASEAN.

2000
George W Bush becomes US President.

2001
Sept 11 attacks on the World Trade Center in the US.

2002
Bali bombing. Taliban ousted in Afghanistan.

2003
The US sends troops to Iraq.

2004
Indian Ocean Tsunami

2005
Hurricane Katrina

2006
North Korean nuclear test

THAKSIN'S RISE AND FALL. The liberal constitution of 1997 ushered in an era of strong governance, with consolidated parties ultimately not restrained by new watchdog institutions. Thaksin Shinawatra, a telecommunications tycoon and Thailand's richest man, won the January 2001 election with his populist party Thai Rak Thai (Thais Love Thais, TRT). After narrowly winning a corruption trial, Thaksin brought about unprecedented reforms, including farm debt moratoriums, cheap universal healthcare, and cash handouts to each village. Encouraging entrepreneurship and expecting officials to act like CEOs, Thaksin's cabinet stoked booms in stock, property and consumer credit. Fuelling nationalism, it repaid the IMF loan early. The economy withstood a series of calamities: the Severe Acute Respiratory Syndrome (SARS) and Avian Flu epidemics, the Bali bombings and the Indian Ocean Tsunami. Inundating resorts along Thailand's Andaman Sea coast on 26 December 2004, the tsunami led to some safety and planning improvements, though land grabs and hasty re-building repeated the ad hoc development of Thai tourist infrastructure. In political and social policy, TRT appeared to be emulating Singapore. A "social order campaign" included violent drug suppression, random raids on bars, earlier closing times, youth curfews, the taming of Patpong's adult shows and proclamations against revealing clothing. Increased bloodshed in the Muslim deep south raised concern about human rights that led to a reconciliation commission, though separatist violence continued. Allegations against Thaksin of corruption, rights abuses and offending the monarchy snowballed into mass demonstrations in late 2005. Protests intensified when Thaksin's family sold its telecoms firm to Singapore, avoiding tax. After the opposition boycotted Thaksin's snap re-election in April 2006, politics entered hiatus during celebrations for the King's Diamond Jubilee in June 2006. The Army Chief, General Sothi Boonyaratglin, broke the impasse through a bloodless coup on 19 September 2006, stranding Thaksin in exile. The period that followed has been one of the most tumultuous in Thai history. Thai society has split into pro-Thaksin and anti-Thaksin sides, and protests and counter-protests ultimately boiled into violence in 2010 when the anti-Thaksin government of the time cracked down. In 2011, Thaksin's sister was elected prime minister. Her main challenge was handling the 2011 floods, which were the most devastating in decades. In 2012, Thailand was more stable but the divisions have yet to heal.

ARTS AND TRADITIONS

BUDDHISM, *24*

BUDDHISM IN THAI LIFE, *25*

FLOWER ARRANGEMENTS, *26*

OFFERINGS, *27*

SPIRITUAL ABODES, *27*

ELEPHANTS, *28*

ROYAL BARGES, *29*

COSTUME, *30*

REGAL COSTUME, *31*

SPECIAL ATTIRE, *32*

THAI CLASSICAL MUSIC, *33*

THEATER, *34*

POPULAR THEATER, *35*

THAI PUPPETS, *36*

THAI PLEASURES, *37*

FESTIVALS, *38*

BASKETS IN TRADITIONAL LIFE, *39*

THAI FOOD, *40*

KAENG PHED PED YANG (A THAI DISH), *41*

THAI FRUITS AND SWEETS, *42*

THAI LANGUAGE, *43*

BUDDHISM

The primary aim of Buddhists is to overcome the suffering of this world by salvation through enlightenment. Mahayana (Greater Vehicle), or northern Buddhism, is found in China, Korea, Tibet and Japan. Theravada, or southern Buddhism, the only surviving school of the Hinayana (Lesser Vehicle) system, originated in Sri Lanka and incorporates elements of Hinduism and local beliefs. It predominates in Thailand, Burma, Laos and Cambodia.

BODHI TREE
The tree under which the future Buddha obtained full enlightenment was a fig (*Ficus religiosa*). There he sat, vowing not to move until he had gained enlightenment, successfully resisting Mara's assaults. Many temples in Thailand were built around sacred Bodhi trees brought back as cuttings from India by pilgrims.

MERCIFUL BODHISATTVA
Avalokitesvara is one of the most popular Bodhisattvas, who sees all the misery of the world and treats it with compassion, and is often depicted with 11 hands and 1,000 arms, each symbolizing one aspect of the help he can provide.

BODHISATTVAS
In Theravada Buddhism, only a chosen few can ever reach full enlightenment and terminate the chain of rebirths. However, in Mahayana Buddhism, Bodhisattva intercessors and enlightened individuals voluntarily postpone their own nirvana indefinitely in order to devote themselves to the salvation of mankind.

WHEEL OF THE LAW
Known as *dharmacakra*, the wheel symbolizes the living nature of Buddhist teachings, the perpetual changing of all objects and beings, and the constant quest for salvation. The deer refers to a deer park near Benares, where Buddha preached his first sermon, "setting in motion the Wheel of the Law."

DIVINE KING
This bejeweled image of Buddha shows the identification of Buddhahood with kingship in Cambodia, where under Jayavarman II, Mahayana Buddhism was declared the state religion. This *devaraja* (divine king) cult was introduced by Jayavarman II in the early 9th century and influenced Buddhist iconography in the 11th century when the Central Plains of Siam were under Khmer rule.

VICTORY OVER MARA
Mara, the god of death, tried to prevent Sakyamuni's salvation, fearing that his own kingdom of deaths and rebirths would be in peril. He vainly attempted to dislodge Sakyamuni from his meditations by sending an army of demons and by tempting him with his beautiful daughters and their voluptuous dancing. But when Sakyamuni performed the earth-touching *mudra*, and the earth trembled, Mara fled.

A SYMBOLIC ACT
Siddhartha Gautama (563–483 BC), the founder of Buddhism and better known as Sakyamuni or Buddha, was educated as an Indian prince. One day he rode from his palace accompanied by his groom, Chana, while the gods muffled the sound of the hooves with their hands. In the countryside, he cut off his long hair and beard, and donned plain clothes to symbolize his renunciation of the world and decision to become an ascetic.

"MUDRA"
Mudra are the hand gestures found in Buddhist iconography. This 14th-century image of Buddha shows the *bhumisparsa mudra* (touching the earth), made when Sakyamuni called the earth to witness his attainment of Buddhahood.

MEDITATION
It is one of the many ways of reaching enlightenment, a state that can be described in Buddha's own words: "There is a sphere which is neither earth, nor water, nor fire, nor air, which is not the sphere of the infinity of space, nor the sphere of the infinity of consciousness, the sphere of nothingness, the sphere of neither perception nor non-perception, which is neither this world nor the other world, neither sun nor moon. I deny that it is coming or going, enduring, death or birth. It is only the end of suffering."

Thailand is one of the most strongly Buddhist countries in the world; 95 percent of the population practice Theravada Buddhism (a branch of Hinayana Buddhism). As Buddhism is the state religion, the King has the right to appoint the supreme patriarch of the *sangha* (Buddhist clergy). General awareness of the way of life of the *sangha* is strong, half the male population has gone through a period of monkhood in their lifetime. Monks are highly revered. In towns and villages the wat (temple) is the heart of social and religious life.

MEDITATION
The purpose of meditation is to cleanse the mind of irrelevant thoughts and enhance concentration on the central aim of achieving nirvana. There are a variety of schools, with different teachers and methods, all with the same ultimate purpose.

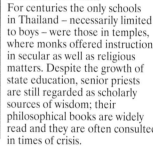

BUDDHIST ART
Buddhism has been the greatest source of inspiration in Thai art, producing not only countless images but also temples and their elaborate decorations. The purpose is not to create objects of beauty but to express the piety of the artist and thus gain merit.

ROLE OF A MONK
Some monks pass their time studying Buddhist scriptures and practicing meditation. Many others, however, perhaps the majority, play an active role in daily life, sometimes as teachers, sometimes as advisors in village disputes. Monks are called on, too, to preside over a wide variety of ceremonial occasions, from funerals to the opening of a new business.

RENUNCIATION OF WORLDLY GOODS
This 19th-century photograph reflects the typical life of monks, who in following the footsteps of Prince Siddhartha, renounce material possessions, pain and passion in pursuit of enlightenment.

MONKS AS TEACHERS
For centuries the only schools in Thailand – necessarily limited to boys – were those in temples, where monks offered instruction in secular as well as religious matters. Despite the growth of state education, senior priests are still regarded as scholarly sources of wisdom; their philosophical books are widely read and they are often consulted in times of crisis.

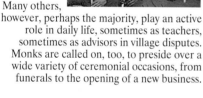

ACQUIRING MERIT
Thai Buddhists acquire merit through a number of traditional acts. The most common is offering food to monks in the early morning, while others include presenting robes and other necessities to monasteries, releasing caged birds, and building new temples.

ORDINATION
At some point in his life, generally just before he marries and starts a family of his own, a young Thai may undergo training as a monk, often for three months during the rainy season. In villages, the entire population takes part in the ordination ceremony, which involves both religious solemnity and enthusiastic celebration ▲*149*. The *nak*, or future novice, has his head shaved and is dressed in white

robes symbolizing purity; carrying an incense stick, a candle and a flower, he is then carried in a gala procession to the temple, where the ordination ceremony is conducted by resident monks.

Short-lived though they may be, traditional Thai flower arrangements qualify as genuine works of art. The object is not to reflect nature but to fashion something that, at first appearance, could hardly be less natural; Thai flower arrangements are often reminiscent of the complex patterns on painted porcelain or intricately set pieces of jewelry. Women of the royal court were celebrated for their skill at producing such creations and the art still continues today in numerous offerings for both religious and secular occasions ▲ *135*.

"MALAI"

Exquisitely fashioned *malai*, or garlands, play an important part in Thai social and religious life. In the most common kind, fragrant white jasmine buds are threaded thickly together, with accents of color provided by other flowers such as roses, marigolds and orchids. There are also highly complex versions requiring many hours of work. Nearly everyone who visits a shrine brings a *malai* as an offering to the resident spirit. Taxi drivers hang a garland from the dashboard to avoid accidents, and Buddhist altars in Thai homes receive a fresh one daily. You are also likely to be given a *malai* if you move into a new house, get engaged, or depart from or arrive at a party.

"BAI-SRI"

Bai-sri are special creations used in a number of Thai ceremonies. These are based on a structure of deftly folded banana leaves, which are then further adorned with such flowers as jasmine and sometimes food. *Bai-sri cham*, for instance, has a central banana-leaf cone filled with cooked rice topped by a hard-boiled egg; surrounding it are other cones decorated with various flowers. This is often given as a token of respect by a student to a teacher or presented as a good-luck offering to infants.

GIFT PRESENTATION

Flowers and garlands are used to embellish gifts. This beautiful flower arrangement covers robes and items presented to monks on special occasions.

BASIC "KRATHONG"

Krathong, the elegant little boats set adrift on waterways during the Loy Krathong festival ● *38*, belong to the *bai-sri* category, the base being composed of banana leaves folded to resemble an open lotus blossom. This is then decorated with flowers, incense sticks and lighted candles and sent out as an offering to the water spirits on the night of the full-moon in the 11th lunar month, usually in late October or early November. In recent years, *krathong* have been made of colorful papers arranged around a base of styrofoam.

"JAD PAAN"

Jad paan, or bowl arrangements, are also called *poom*, because of the traditional rounded pyramidal shape, which resembles a budding lotus. The core, 4 to 8 inches high, is made of moistened earth, sawdust, or styrofoam. The entire core is tightly embedded with flowers which resemble multi-colored pieces of porcelain. Bowl arrangements are often used in wedding ceremonies, when they are placed beneath the hands of the bride and groom, to receive holy water poured by the guests.

ORNATE "KRATHONG"

According to legend, Loy Krathong originated in Sukhothai ▲ *128, 135*, as a palace pastime in which royal ladies competed to see who could produce the most spectacular *krathong*. The same sense of competition remains today, with some creations towering more than 3 feet high in a variety of fantastic shapes. Prizes are awarded to the most imaginative.

A wide variety of traditional Thai occasions call for an offering of one kind or another. Some are secular: an auspicious birthday celebration, greeting an honored guest or the opening of a business. By far the greatest number, however, are religious in nature, presented during special merit-acquiring rituals and almost any visit to a Buddhist temple or shrine. The composition of such an offering varies considerably and may range from flowers and symbolic items to food and paper money – all, of course, arranged attractively.

Far older than Buddhism in Thailand is belief in spirits, as well as various gods and demigods. There are spirits who guard individual pieces of land, for instance, and others who watch over villages and capital cities or make their home in trees and caves. The general term for such invisible beings is *phi* ▲ *150*, but special names are given to many who enjoy demigod status. To avoid difficulties and ensure harmony and prosperity, all must be placated, sometimes with a special abode of their own, always with carefully prepared offerings. Such animistic beliefs do not clash with Buddhism; rather they coexist comfortably and often overlap in ways mystifying to outsiders.

DAILY PLACATIONS
To promote harmony and goodwill, the guardian spirit is placated with daily offerings by household members, the most basic being fragrant incense sticks, candles and flowers. Employees and shopkeepers regularly present offerings at the spirit house of their workplace while actors and dancers do so before a performance. Chinese shop-keepers usually have a spirit house for the local spirits and a small shrine painted in red, dedicated to the Taoist gods.

BASIC OFFERINGS
The basic offering made to images of Buddha and on ceremonial occasions consists of incense sticks, candles and flowers, usually lotus buds. The first symbolizes life's fragrance, the second suggests its transitory nature, and the third is a reminder of the impermanence of beauty – all significant concepts in the Buddhist faith.

MONEY TREES
Thod kathin, held at the end of the annual Rains Retreat, are ceremonies in which groups visit temples to present various necessities to the resident monks. Besides new robes and Buddhist literature, offerings may include financial donations, in which case the money is elegantly arranged in the form of a tree that is proudly carried in a gala procession to the monastery. Such trees are often displayed for several days in front of the house of the donor, and anybody can join the merit-acquiring ceremony by adding their own contribution to the tree.

MEALS FOR MONKS
On Buddhist holy days the laity often offers the midday meal to monks at a temple as a means of acquiring. Much care goes into the presentation of the various dishes, which are traditionally displayed on shaped banana leaves and decorated with fresh flowers and delicately carved fruits.

SPIRIT HOUSES
The guardian spirit of a particular compound, whether residential or commercial, is generally provided with a small house on the property; the exact site must be determined by an expert and has nothing to do with esthetic considerations. Elevated on a post, the houses come in a wide variety of forms, some simple wooden replicas of a traditional Thai dwelling, others ornate cement creations that resemble miniature Buddhist temple buildings down to the smallest decorative detail.

ELABORATE OFFERINGS
Spiritual abodes in wealthier compounds are lavishly supplied with a variety of elaborate offerings. In addition to small dolls to symbolize attendants, these may include floral displays, fresh fruits, and culinary delicacies ranging from sweets to full meals, carefully arranged on plates.

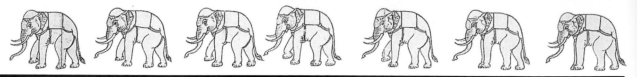

The elephant, which once roamed wild in large numbers in Thai forests, has played an important cultural and economic role for centuries ▲ *117*. "White elephants" were revered as symbols of royalty; the Thai national flag used to show a white elephant on a red background, until the adoption of the present striped flag in 1917. The royalty of Ayutthaya rode into battle on war elephants, and King Rama IV offered a supply of the animals to US President Buchanan. Valued for their skill and might, elephants once provided the main work force in the teak forests of the North. Now, most of the remaining domesticated elephants entertain tourists ▲ *140*.

ELEPHANTS IN WAR

Their value in war may well have been a major catalyst in the taming of elephants. About 22,000 supposedly took part in ancient Indian battles, leading the charge, and a 16th-century Burmese invasion force against Ayutthaya consisted of 300,000 men, 3,000 horses and 700 elephants. One of the most celebrated encounters in Thai history was an elephant-back duel between the Ayutthayan King Naresuan and a Burmese Crown Prince in 1592, resulting in victory for Naresuan.

ELEPHANT TUSKS

While their collection is deplored by environmentalists today, elephant tusks were treasured possessions in the past; some, like the ones shown above, were carved with Buddhist motifs, while others were mounted for display in palaces.

MYTHICAL ELEPHANTS

Elephants figure not only in Buddhism but also in Hindu mythology. The three-headed Erawan, for example, is the mount of the god Indra, while the *gajasingha* was a lion with the head of an elephant and Ganesha was the elephant-headed son of Shiva and Parvati, regarded as the god of arts or knowledge.

ELEPHANTS IN HUNTING

Kings and royal princes often rode on elephants while hunting, as seen in this illustration from an ancient manuscript.

HOWDAHS

Howdahs, or elephant chairs, came in a wide variety of forms. Some were relatively simple wooden seats secured to the animal's back with leather straps, while those for royalty could be ornate, comfortably appointed palanquins. Palaces had special platforms for mounting and descending.

TRAINING MANUALS

As far back as 2,000 years ago, Sanskrit manuals outlined precise procedures for capturing and, most importantly, training wild elephants. The manuscript book shown above, written during the reign of King Rama II, undoubtedly drew on these ancient sources, as well as on the practical experience of Thai trainers. While force was sometimes required, the most important part was winning the animal's confidence and affection ▲ *144, 150, 157*.

SOUTHERN ROUNDUP

In southern Thailand, as elsewhere, wild elephants were captured by driving them with drums, trumpets and gunfire into stockades, where they were tamed and trained.

THE WHITE ELEPHANT

White elephants – actually a silvery gray – were revered as auspicious symbols by rulers in the past. Even today, when one of these rare animals is discovered in Thailand, it is presented to the king and kept in a special enclosure at Chitralada Palace, the royal residence. Ten have been found so far during the reign of King Rama IX.

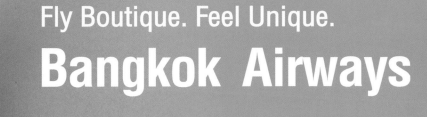

An aspect of Ayutthaya noted by almost every early European visitor was the spectacle of the ornately carved and gilded royal barges, sometimes hundreds of them rowed by chanting oarsmen in elaborate costume. The custom was continued in Bangkok, where new barges were built by King Rama I and used to deliver offerings to monasteries along the river. Long in disuse following the end of the absolute monarchy in 1932, the barges have since been restored or rebuilt, and processions have been held during the Bangkok bicentennial celebrations (1982), King Rama IX's Golden Jubilee (1996) and 6th Cycle Birthday (1999), as well as the Apec Summit (2003).

CLASSIC FORMATIONS

The royal barge procession held in 1982 was based on the formation shown in a 19th-century manuscript, probably a copy of a much earlier one. The procession extended for 3,220 feet and involved a total of 51 principal barges, all richly decorated, and 2,192 men. In addition, there were numerous smaller craft, known as *rua dang* and *rua saeng*, which acted as outer escorts and attendants; most of these were plain, with slightly raised stem and stern pieces, though a few performed special duties and were decorated with gold leaf. The crews consisted of officers and men of the Royal Thai Navy, who were carefully trained in traditional ways of propelling the long boats.

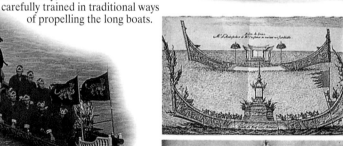

EKACHAI BARGE
There are two Ekachai barges in the procession, used to carry religious items. The prows are stylized horns of *hera*, or horned dragons, the bodies of which are painted in gold-and-black lacquer.

SUPHANAHONGSA
The most important of the barges is the Suphana-hongsa or Golden Hansa – the mythical, swan-like mount of Brahma – in which the king rides ▲ *90*. The present one, built by King Rama VI in 1911, is made from a single teakwood trunk, 150 feet long and over 10 feet wide at the beam; a full crew consists of fifty oarsmen, two steersmen, two officers fore and aft, one standard-bearer, one signalman, one chanter and seven royal insignia bearers.

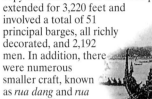

GUNBOATS
In early times, the barges were used in fighting. They were manned by crews of 60 to 70 oarsmen, or *rua chai*. Later they were armed with cannons protruding through the prow, which subsequently began to be decorated with figureheads from mythology, partly, perhaps, for identification but also to bring good fortune in battle.

EARLY IMPRESSIONS
The first visual impressions of the royal barges, in the 17th century, came in the form of sometimes fanciful engravings that accompanied books written by members of the two French embassies that came to the court of King Narai.

BOAT SONGS
"It was a breathtaking sight," wrote Father Guy Tachard, a Jesuit priest who witnessed a royal barge procession in late 17th-century Ayutthaya. "The sound of traditional chanting reverberated along both banks of the river which were crowded with people waiting to see the spectacular event." The rhythmic barge songs still survive, varying in pace to match the different speeds and strokes of the oarsmen.

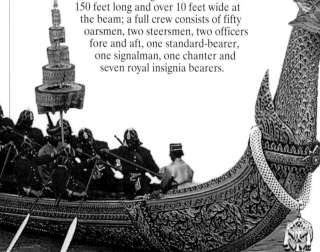

ADORNMENT
Intricately woven floral wreaths, resembling thick bejeweled necklaces, adorn the prows of the barges during a procession.

"They wear few clothes," wrote Simon de la Loubère of the ordinary Thais he saw in 17th-century Ayutthaya, "not so much by reason of the heat as by the simplicity of their manners." In everyday traditional life, the only apparel for both men and women was a length of homespun cotton that could be worn as skirt or trousers. Silk was reserved for royalty ▲ *117*. Despite the growing popularity of Western fashions, many people in the countryside still regard the old-style dress as being more suited to their ways of life.

"JONGKRABANE"
The *jongkrabane* ● *54*, a length of cloth was wrapped around the waist then pulled through the legs and secured at the back, was popular with women in the past. A similar fashion worn by men was called a *pannung*.

ADORNMENT
Elegant jewelry – gem-studded brooches, buckles, pendants, tiaras, heavy gold belts and body chains – has been worn in Thailand since the Dvaravati period. An innovation of the Ayutthaya period was the wearing of particular colors

on different days of the week: red for Sunday, yellow for Monday, pink for Tuesday, green for Wednesday, orange for Thursday, blue for Friday, and purple for Saturday.

MENSWEAR
Traditionally, Thai men wore only a sarong, sometimes pulled between the legs to form pantaloons. This fashion survives today in the all-purpose length of cotton called a *phakama* ▲ *138*, which can also be used as a head-covering, a wash cloth, or an impromptu tent for a siesta in the ricefields.

PRINTED FABRICS
In the late Ayutthaya and early Bangkok periods, some pieces of cloth used by the aristocracy, both silk and cotton, were printed in India, using Thai motifs (above) that denoted various degrees of rank. The most popular of these was called *pha lai-yang*, or "designed cloth," and had to meet stringent esthetic requirements; less prized varieties were called *pha lai-nok-yang*, "cloth not according to design," and *pha liang-yang*, "copied design."

"MOR HOM"
A basic item of attire for most Thai farmers is the loose cotton shirt called *mor hom*, traditionally fastened with string at the front. These are dyed dark blue with indigo and worn by both men and women, often with a broad-brimmed hat of woven palm leaf to ward off the sun.

HAIRSTYLES
In former times, Thai men and women cut off almost all their hair except for a growth on the crown, as shown in the above detail from an early 19th-century mural; the remaining hair was compared to a lotus flower. Sometimes after childbirth or on the death of a close relative, women shaved their heads as completely as men did when entering the monkhood. Even today, older countrywomen often wear their hair closely cropped like a man's.

NORTHEASTERN ELEGANCE
In northeastern Thailand, where a sizeable part of the population is ethnically Lao, numerous striking costumes can be seen, particularly during festivals, when the best clothing is brought out. Lao embroidery is a notable skill of the region and is used to adorn sarongs as well as *sabai*; the latter are long pieces of cloth about a foot wide that are draped diagonally over the shoulder and fall to the waist.

NORTHERN "PASIN"
In northern Thailand *pasin*, as women's sarongs are called, have horizontal stripes and richly decorated areas at the bottom; on silk *pasin* the decorations are often in gold brocade, a craft for which the region is noted. Certain bright color combinations are deemed appropriate only for young, unmarried girls, while older women wear more subdued hues like dark blue and purple. Extending almost to the ankles, *pasin* are worn tightly tucked around the waist and often further secured with a belt.

TATTOOS
Tattoos are worn by Thai men less for esthetic purposes than to ward off a variety of dangers and bring good fortune; on some men of the far north elaborate designs

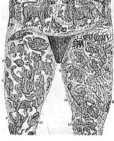

of auspicious animals once covered large areas of the body, almost like a suit of clothing. The practice has declined in modern times, but still it has its adherents and master tattooists command great respect from believers.

Thai royal attire was designed to impress, particularly on ceremonial occasions when the king, sitting high on his throne, wore so many ornaments and jewel-encrusted robes that he resembled a statue more than a living man. Royal children wore similarly elaborate clothing on important occasions, such as the top-knot cutting ceremony when they came of age. The costumes of court officials – including the patterns of the silk they wore and the accessories they carried – usually varied according to their rank. Each costume was strictly prescribed by royal order.

A KING IN STATE

Despite a few Western innovations, full ceremonial dress for royalty has changed remarkably little from the ancient past, as demonstrated in this photograph (left) of King Rama VI (1910–25). Prominent among its features are the tiered Great Crown of Victory with wing-like appendages on either side, a tight-fitting, high-necked tunic and trousers of gold-brocaded silk, special slippers and a richly embroidered and bejeweled robe. Some of the same features can be seen on images of the Buddha in royal attire made in the late Ayutthaya and early Rattanakosin periods.

DRESSED FOR THE OCCASION

At important ceremonies, princes would wear clothing and jewelry similar to that of their elders.

TONSURE CEREMONY

In the past, both boys and girls had shaven heads except for a tuft of hair on the crown. The cutting of this top-knot marked their official coming of age and, especially in the palace, was accompanied by elaborate ceremonies that extended over several days.

A ROYAL PRINCE

Royal princes of the mid-19th century wore rich gowns and sarongs of silk, the patterns of which were forbidden to those of lesser rank. Imported cloth from China and Japan was highly esteemed because of its comparative rarity, but Cambodian and Laotian silks were also prized. The gilded, broad-brimmed hat came into fashion during the Ayutthaya period, probably as a result of foreign influence.

A KING AND QUEEN

It was during the reign of King Rama IV, shown here with one of his queens, that Western fashions first appeared in royal circles. When British photographer John Thompson was invited to take some royal photographs in 1865, the King posed for one in "a sort of French Field Marshal's uniform" as well as others in more traditional dress.

WESTERN INFLUENCE

Western dress became widespread under King Rama V, shown on the right, the first Thai ruler to travel abroad and experience European culture at first hand. Men of the court adopted European suits and uniforms so enthusiastically that within a short time the old Thai costumes had virtually disappeared in palace circles.

ROYAL REGALIA

The royal regalia, received by each king on his coronation, include a number of swords, jeweled slippers, a fan and a staff, among other items, most dating back to the first Chakri ruler.

ROYAL WOMEN

The women of King Rama V's court were inspired by the fashions of England's Queen Alexandra, particularly her blouses with puffed sleeves. Sometimes these were worn with cumbersome Victorian skirts, sometimes with more graceful Thai *pasin*, or sarongs.

As well as the clothing already described as being worn by royalty and ordinary people, both past and present, there is another category in Thailand: that of special attire, real and imagined. The real includes the saffron robes prescribed for monks, a familiar sight in and out of Thailand's numerous temples, as well as certain military uniforms and costumes for special ceremonies. The imaginary takes in most of the early Western views of Thailand and its people, some recorded on the scene but many executed later by artists more influenced by fantasy than by a desire to portray reality.

THE AMBASSADOR'S HAT
In 17th-century French engravings of Ayutthaya, Thais are often shown wearing what some called the "ambassador's hat," known thus because it was worn by the three ambassadors who were received at Versailles.
In reality, such a costume was never worn by commoners.

A MONK'S ROBES
After ordination, a monk discards the clothing of the outside world and adopts priestly robes made of saffron-colored cotton cloth. These consist of three pieces of cloth, one worn sarong-like around the waist, another as a shoulder sash, and a third long enough to envelop the entire body. Only the first two are worn inside the monastery. New priests are instructed in the prescribed way of tying the robes. Vegetable dyes were traditionally used, but today most cloth is dyed with chemicals.

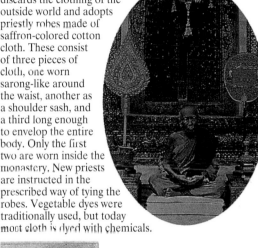

A MONK IN FULL ROBES
This old engraving shows a monk wearing the full set of three robes and standing near one of the gilded, tiered parasols seen in Buddhist temples.

A MANDARIN
The figure, from Simon de la Loubère's account of his visit to 17th-century Ayutthaya, is labeled "A Siamese Mandarin" and shows a silk *pannung* tucked between the legs, a blouse and an ambassador's hat.

THE ORIGINAL HAT
An original specimen of the ambassador's hat is preserved at Lopburi National Museum.

AMBASSADOR'S ATTIRE
One of the ambassadors who were received by Louis XIV in Paris is shown above.

CEREMONIAL COSTUME
The figure on the right is dressed in one of the ornate costumes worn during the plowing ceremony, an ancient Brahminic ritual that originated in Ayutthaya to mark the beginning of the rice-planting season. It is similar to a court costume, consisting of a tall hat, richly brocaded tunic and pantaloons, and a semi-transparent gown trimmed with gold brocade. The ceremony was revived by the present king and is held annually in Bangkok during May at Sanam Luang, across from the Grand Palace.

SOLDIERS
Military uniforms have changed considerably over the years, becoming more Westernized. The soldier shown above is wearing one favored in late Ayutthaya and early Bangkok.

THAI AMBASSADORS AT VERSAILLES
The three Thai ambassadors who were received by Louis XIV in 1686 at Versailles caused a sensation, because of the lavish gifts they brought and also because of their exotic dress. Thai motifs appeared on French textiles and tapestries and their fancy costumes became the subject of endless engravings and calendars.

The earliest Thai musical instruments were given names that reflected the sounds they made, such as *krong, chap, ching, so* and *khong*. Later more complex instruments were created, many adapted from foreign cultures like Indian and Khmer. During the Ayutthaya period, an instrumental ensemble was composed of four to eight musicians; this was expanded to twelve in the early Bangkok reign of King Rama II. There are now about fifty different types of Thai musical instruments, including many regional variations. Music accompanies most traditional Thai occasions, from the classical dance festivals to folk theater and boxing matches.

XYLOPHONE

Closely akin to the Western xylophone is the instrument called *ranad*, one of the six basic components of most musical groups that accompany classical dancing and many ceremonies. The *ranad* comes in a number of types, some slightly curved and others flat, producing different tones. Its musical purpose is usually to produce variations on the principal melody and the rhythm. The keys are made of bamboo or seasoned wood mounted on a wooden frame.

AN EVOLVING ART

Music dates back to the earliest days of the kingdom, as suggested by the stucco frieze below showing a group of musicians in the Dvaravati period (7th–11th century). Dvaravati instruments, the result of Indian influence, were adopted by the Thais, who went on to produce a number of new instruments. These are mentioned in the *Tribhumikatha*, one of the first books written in Thai, as well as on a stone inscription attributed to King Ramkhamhaeng of Sukhothai.

THE LONG DRUMS

The beat of a drum is essential to Thai music, providing a rhythmic excitement that rises and falls. In small ensembles, the most common type is the relatively small, double-ended *klong tad thapon*, but in the north huge drums called *klawng yao*, often several yards long and requiring several men to carry them, are frequently heard at festivals.

"KHONG WONG"

Known as *khong wong lek* (small) or *khong wong yai* (large) depending on their size, these consist of a circular series of small gongs suspended on a rattan frame and provide the melody in a Thai musical performance. There is no doubling in parts, so if two are involved only one plays the melody while the other plays variations.

GONG

Large gongs ▲ *141* are often elaborately mounted, like the one above, which is suspended between a pair of elephant tusks. Smaller versions are used in most ensembles, along with xylophones, drums, the oboe-like *pinai*, the circular *khong wong yai*, and a set of small cymbals called *ching lek*. In addition to the role they play in music, gongs were traditionally struck to announce important events.

ENSEMBLE

A typical small musical ensemble is called a *phipat* band. The majority of the instruments are percussive but there is always at least one reed, the *pinai*, which sounds somewhat like a bagpipe. In the illustration above, the man on the right is using a flute-like instrument composed of varying lengths of hollow bamboo; this is most often heard in the northeast and is of Lao origin.

STRINGED INSTRUMENTS

The *chakhay* is a thick-necked guitar-like instrument requiring great skill, it is heard only in larger orchestras and played on a low table, almost always by a woman. Another popular traditional Thai stringed instrument is the *saw sam sai*, a fiddle composed of a triangular coconut shell, an ivory neck, and three silk strings; King Rama II was a noted *saw sam sai* performer, so enthusiastic that he exempted from taxation all plantations that grew the triangular coconuts needed for its manufacture.

The classic Thai theater is the *khon*, a masked drama performed in dance and gesture at the royal court; it probably originated in Indian temple rituals and came to Thailand by way of Indonesia. The story lines are drawn from the *Ramakien*, the Thai version of the Indian *Ramayana*. During the Ayutthaya period, men played both male and female roles because the movements were thought too strenuous for women to perform, though by the early 19th-century Bangkok period both men and women were appearing on the stage together. All records of the story were lost with the destruction of Ayutthaya in 1767; King Rama I of Bangkok, together with literary members of his court, wrote a new version in 1798 and later additions were made by King Rama II.

MASKS
Khon masks are creations made of lacquered papier mâché, decorated with gold and jewels, reflecting the personalities of the characters being portrayed.

THEATERS
Traditional *khon* performances were presented by torchlight in palace halls and courtyards with no complicated scenery to distract from the characterizations. Gradually, however, they moved outside the palaces in the early Bangkok period and could be seen in public theaters especially erected for the purpose during festivals and ceremonies. The shorter version of the *Ramakien* written by King Rama II is the most popular, and only selected episodes are offered to contemporary audiences. Even these are comparatively rare, however; the average visitor sees only brief excerpts performed between courses at Thai restaurants catering for tourists.

"KHON" TROUPES
Khon performers are trained from early childhood in the dance steps and gestures which require considerable physical strength and agility. A royal troupe was part of the palace retinue in both Ayutthaya and early Bangkok; later, a number of high-ranking princes had troupes of their own.

GESTURES
The familiar story is told through stylized postures and gestures, which express action, thought and feeling. Anger is shown by stamping a foot. Raising the upper lip with a pinch of the fingers conveys a smile and, thus, pleasure. Stiffening of the body with a certain arm motion suggests ambition, while supporting the brow bending and with one hand expresses sorrow. Discriminating audiences decipher the most subtle gestures and evaluate a performance on the basis of them.

NARRATION
Narrative verses accompany *khon* performances. The verses are recited or sung either by a chorus or by a

single narrator sitting with a musical ensemble consisting of woodwinds, gongs, drums and other traditional instruments.

THE "RAMAKIEN"
The *Ramakien* ▲ 77, on which the *khon* is based, is an epic account in lyrical verse of the triumph of good over evil. The hero is Phra Ram, a king of Ayutthaya and also a reincarnation of the god Vishnu. His consort, Nang Sida, is abducted by the wicked King Thotsakan of Longka (Sri Lanka) and the lengthy drama recounts the ultimately successful efforts of the King and his brother Phra Lak, assisted by the clever monkey-god Hanuman, to rescue her. Performances were often staged on two consecutive nights for a total of more than 20 hours; a *khon* staging of the entire *Ramakien* would require 311 characters and take more than a month of continuous performance.

COSTUMES
Khon costumes are made of heavy brocades decorated with costume jewelry and closely resemble the dress of royalty and celestial beings in classical Thai mural paintings. The major characters are identifiable by the color of their dress; Phra Ram, the hero, wears deep green, while his brother Phra Lak wears gold and the monkey-god Hanuman wears white. Phra Ram, Phra Lak and Nang Sida usually do not wear masks; Thotsakan, the villain, has a green mask on which small faces are painted to indicate that he is a 10-headed demon and Hanuman, a white simian one with a mischievous expression. Green masks denote high rank and purple and blue masks are for minor characters.

«THE GREATER PART OF THE PERFORMANCE CONSISTED OF MERELY TWISTING THE FINGERS AND HANDS AND ARMS IN SUCH POSITIONS AS TO MAKE THEM APPEAR OUT OF JOINT.»

CARL BOCK

When the *khon* moved outside the limited confines of the royal palace and became part of the popular culture, it did so in a form known as *lakhon*. This is less formal and the movements are less angular, more graceful and sensual. The stories are drawn not only from the *Ramakien* but also from a collection of morality tales called the *Jataka* and from a Javanese historical romance known in Thai as *Inao*. *Lakhon* is subdivided into several variations, the three major ones being *lakhon chatri*, *lakhon nok* and *lakhon nai*; another form of popular theater, relying more on social satire and pantomime than on pure dance, is the *likay*.

ACTORS

Unlike *khon*, skilled *lakhon* and *likay* performers are able to earn a living from their talents outside places mainly limited to tourists. There are resident troupes of female *lakhon* dancers at nearly every major shrine, for example, and their services are often called upon by people wishing to thank the resident deity for answered prayers; *lakhon* dancing is also often a feature of festivals and private entertainments. Similarly, *likay* troupes tour the country presenting their shows at fairs held in towns and villages, some of the performers becoming major stars among rural audiences.

"MANORA"

One of the principal sources of *lakhon chatri* is a Javanese romance called *Manora*, in which the heroine is half-human and half-bird. Long, curving metal extensions (below) amplify her graceful fingers. Simpler performances of *lakhon chatri* can be seen regularly at popular shrines in Bangkok such as the *lak muang* (the city's foundation stone) and the one near the Erawan Grand Hyatt Hotel, where supplicants whose wishes have been granted pay resident troupes of dancers to perform.

GRACEFUL FINGERS

In *lakhon* performances, especially those by women, the hands are particularly expressive, assuming gestures that

are only possible after years of training. The use of long metal nails, which originated in southern Thailand with the *Inao*, can now be seen in other parts of the country; one of the best-known variations is the romantic fawn *lep*, or "nail dance," a mainstay of northern celebrations.

THEATER TRAINING

Training for the Thai dance begins at an early age, with boys and girls at first learning to move their heads, bodies, limbs and fingers to music. Only later do they begin to practice the sixty-eight separate movements that comprise the more intricate alphabet of the dance, each movement having a picturesque name such as "the bee caressing the flower" or "the stag walking in the forest."

"LIKAY"

Likay performances can be seen at most Thai temple fairs. This combines a burlesque of *lakhon* with low comedy; the plots vaguely follow classical lines, with traditional characters, but much of the humor is spontaneous, involving double meanings and puns as well as allusions to local scandals and prominent figures.

Puppets were once an important part of traditional Thai theater. Predating both the *khon* and the *lakhon* was the shadow play, subdivided into *nang yai* and *nang talung*. Introduced from the Sumatran empire of Srivijaya, this was a form of entertainment in 17th-century Ayutthaya. Also seen were *hun* marionettes, little carved figures that enacted classical stories in the royal court. A popular version was *hun krabok* ("rod puppets").

"NANG YAI"
In *nang yai*, or "big *nang*," the cowhide shadow-play figures are huge, up to 6 feet tall and intricately designed, depicting characters from the *Ramakien* and other classical romances. Each is mounted on two sticks and held behind a brilliantly backlit white screen by bearers who dance their parts to the accompaniment of music and choral singing. Some scholars believe the movements of the bearers later evolved into a stylized dance and eventually led to the *khon* masked drama.

"HUN KRABOK"
A variety of *hun* marionette, *hun krabok* have detailed wooden heads and costumes that conceal a central rod; there are no arms or legs, only hands operated by two sticks hidden within the robe. Chakraphand Posayakrit, a contemporary artist, has fashioned a beautiful new set, which can be seen in occasional performances.

PUPPET DRAMA
Puppets were often dressed in the same costumes and masks found in *khon* dances, though some were used to perform Chinese dramas and were appropriately attired; considerable skill was required to paint the miniature faces and create the accessories.

Puppet theater was a palace diversion and because of its slow pace never became widely popular outside until recent revivals by Joe Louis Theater, pictured above with *hun lakorn lek* puppets.

A DECLINING ART
A common form of night-time entertainment in the royal court of Ayutthaya, *nang yai*'s appeal gradually declined, because of the popularity of the *khon*.

"NANG TALUNG"
Nang talung is a more popular version of the shadow-play found at festivals in southern Thailand. The figures are smaller and have one or more moveable parts such as a chin or an arm. Concealed behind the screen along with the manipulators are singers and comedians whose witty contributions to the performance probably account for the continuing popularity of the form.

SHADOW-PLAY FIGURES
Shadow-play figures are carved from the hides of water buffaloes or cows that have been soaked, dried and scraped, then darkened with charcoal or tinted with herbs and berries.

"HUN LEK"
Hun lek, small *hun* marionettes, date from the reign of King Rama V; they were modeled either on characters from the *khon* or from Chinese dramas and manipulated by concealed threads pulled from below rather than from above. These puppets have almost vanished from Thailand's art scene, though one superb set can be viewed at Bangkok's National Museum.

● THAI PLEASURES

Sanuk, a Thai term usually translated as "fun," is a much-valued pursuit and covers a wide range of activities. Prominent among them are various traditional sports that, despite such innovations as Western football and bowling, have never lost their appeal to the vast majority of Thais, especially in rural areas. During leisure time, almost any open field or festival offers a display of some kind, from the balletic ferocity of Thai-style boxing to more esoteric amusements such as a struggle between two giant horned beetles or multicolored Siamese fighting fish.

"CHULA" KITES
The detail above, from an old mural painting, shows a *chula*, or "male", kite caught on a temple roof. On breezy afternoons during the hot season, kites of all kinds can be seen in the sky above Sanam Luang, the great oval field across from the gold spires of the Grand Palace.

"TAKRAW"
In its traditional form, the game of *takraw*, which is also popular in neighboring countries such as Malaysia, involves keeping a hollow rattan ball aloft as long as possible. The circle of players can use their feet, knees, elbows and head but not their hands. Groups of young men start a casual *takraw* game almost anywhere during a break from work or school, demonstrating remarkable grace and footwork.

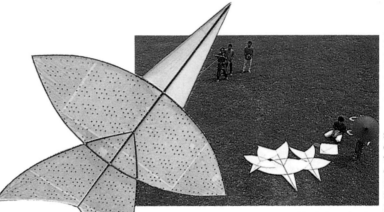

KITE-FIGHTING
Kite-fights in Thailand are actually a symbolic battle of the sexes. The "female" is a small diamond-shaped kite called a *pukpao*, while the "male", called a *chula*, is a huge star-shaped creation that requires teams of up to seventy men to send it aloft and maneuver it. The object is for one of the *chula* to snare a *pukpao* with a bamboo hook and bring it down in "male" territory; alternatively, the more agile *pukpao* often succeed in looping their lines around a *chula* and bring it crashing to earth on their side of the field.

PROFESSIONAL "TAKRAW"
Over the years, more professional forms of *takraw* have evolved, using nets to separate opposing teams or high baskets through which the ball must be sent, along with strict rules of play. *Takraw* competitions of this kind are often held in Bangkok at Sanam Luang and also at the Asian Games.

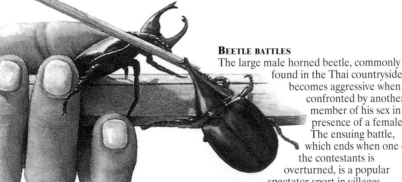

BEETLE BATTLES
The large male horned beetle, commonly found in the Thai countryside, becomes aggressive when confronted by another member of his sex in the presence of a female. The ensuing battle, which ends when one of the contestants is overturned, is a popular spectator sport in villages, with wagers on the outcome.

THE MARTIAL ARTS
As this old illustrated manuscript shows, boxing was an important part of self-defense. In the old days, no gloves were used and both hands and feet were bound in cloth that often contained bits of ground glass for added effect. Several Ayutthaya kings were famed for their skill in this graceful yet lethal art.

THAI BOXING
In modern Thai-style boxing, gloves are used but in most other ways it is similar to the sport of the past. Any part of the body, except the head, can be used as an offensive weapon and any part, including the head, is a fair target. The foot is the most effective of all, usually swung in a wide arc at lightning speed.

Festivals are liberally sprinkled throughout the Thai year: religious and secular, national and local, high-spirited and gravely reverent. This has been true since the earliest days of the kingdom; a Sukhothai stone inscription, describing an annual merit-acquiring event, says, "They join together in striking up the sound of musical instruments, chanting and singing. Whoever wants to make merry, does so; whoever wants to laugh, does so." Today Thais seize almost any occasion for a chance to don their best clothes and celebrate, whether it be one of the several milestones in the Buddhist calendar or merely some notable village event.

CANDLE FESTIVAL
The beginning of Buddhist Lent, or Phansa, during July, is observed in the northeastern city of Ubon Ratchathani with the Candle Festival, when hundreds of beautifully carved candles, some several feet tall, are carried in gala parades before being presented to local temples.

PLOWING CEREMONY
The royal plowing ceremony, an ancient Brahminic ritual marking the start of the rice-planting season, had been allowed to lapse for many years when it was revived by the present king in 1960. Held every May at Sanam Luang, across from the Grand Palace, it is a colorful event that climaxes with a prediction of the coming harvest for Thailand's farmers.

ROYAL HOLIDAYS
Many of Thailand's annual events celebrate the monarchy and involve lavish public decorations as well as festivities. These include the birthdays of the King (December 5) and the Queen (August 12), the date of the founding of the present Chakri Dynasty (April 6), Coronation Day (May 5), and Chulalongkorn Day (October 23), which honors the dynasty's beloved fifth ruler.

SONGKRAN
Officially, Thailand begins the new year on January 1; at the same time, however, the old solar New Year, called Songkran, continues to be a major two-day celebration in mid-April. This is a typically Thai blend of solemn ritual and riotous festival. Offerings are brought to various temples, where both the abbot and the principal Buddha images are anointed with lustral water, while homes are given a thorough cleaning and homage paid to senior family members. Outside, pleasure reigns in the form of lavishly decorated parades, beauty contests, and buckets of water cheerfully thrown at anyone passing in the streets ▲ *137, 139.*

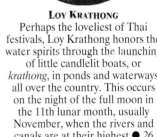

LOY KRATHONG
Perhaps the loveliest of Thai festivals, Loy Krathong honors the water spirits through the launching of little candlelit boats, or *krathong*, in ponds and waterways all over the country. This occurs on the night of the full moon in the 11th lunar month, usually November, when the rivers and canals are at their highest ● *26* ▲ *128, 139, 149.*

ROCKET FESTIVAL
Known as *bun bang fai*, northeastern rocket festivals combine Brahminic, Buddhist and animist elements and are basically concerned with bringing rain through the firing of homemade skyrockets and high-spirited village merrymaking that go on for two days.

BUDDHIST OBSERVANCES
This detail from a mural painting shows the making of miniature sand chedis ● *51*, or chedi *sai*, in temple compounds during the celebration of Songkran, the traditional New Year; the act reflects the origins of the oldest form of Buddhist monument. The importance of Buddhism can be discerned in many festivals.

● BASKETS IN
TRADITIONAL LIFE

Of all traditional Thai crafts,
none plays a more significant
and continuing role than baskets
▲ *140*. Made from a variety of easily
obtainable materials – bamboo is the most common but certain
reeds, grasses, palms and even ferns are also used – they were
born of rural necessity and serve a wide range of needs: catching
and keeping fish, carrying rice, storing household goods and
steaming food, to mention only a few. Such baskets are basically
utilitarian; at the same time, however, many of them display an
undeniable elegance of form and delicacy of workmanship that
raises them to the level of
genuine folk art.

"SAI" (FISH TRAP)
This bomb-shaped trap, called a *sai*, is found in all regions and is used for trapping prawns or small fish, which swim into the opening and are prevented from escaping by bamboo slivers around the inside of the mouth. The average length is around 3 feet. Such traps are placed in ponds or rivers, and are usually fastened to stilts for locating purposes.

GLUTINOUS RICE BASKETS
Baskets like these are common in northern and northeastern Thailand, where they are used by farmers as a kind of lunch pail to carry glutinous rice with them when they go to work in the fields. The wooden foot keeps the basket raised from the ground, while the cord makes it easy to transport; the contrasting weaves add an esthetic touch.

WATER BASKET
This ingenious device (called *mah* or *timah)*, made with palm leaves and fitted with a wooden handle, is found in the south. Water can be scooped from a pond or, with the aid of a rope, drawn from a well.

SEED CONTAINER
Made of lacquered basketry to make it waterproof and also deter insect pests, this seed container is also decorated with stylized motifs and an outside frame of bamboo slivers. It is used in the north for storing seeds that will be sown during the next planting season.

DUCK-SHAPED CONTAINER
All over Thailand, one can spot narrow-necked baskets like the one below, cleverly designed to keep a trapped fish alive while preventing it from escaping. The loose string attached at the neck makes it easy to carry.

RICE BASKET
Known as a *krabung*, this sort of basket is found in all regions of the country. It is neatly woven with bamboo supports up to its widest part and is used for measuring and carrying rice; four loops on the sides enable it to be strung on a carrying pole. *Krabung* may vary in shape from area to area.

"SARB" (FISH TRAP)
This kind of fish trap is normally found in the northeast and is about 3 feet long. It is placed in streams and irrigation systems supplying the ricefields ▲ *13*, where it is left to trap any fish that might pass when the ricefields are flooded.

Thai food, like Thai culture, is the product of various influences, blended to form one distinctive cuisine. Ordinary fare in Sukhothai and early Ayutthaya was simple: mainly fish, fresh or dried, mixed with rice, vegetables, a few spices, and a salty sauce made from fermented fish or shrimp. Other ingredients and flavors came through increased contact with foreign cultures, China and India in particular, and also Europe. Today it covers a wide range of dishes, many of them regional specialties; those of the northeast, for instance, are generally regarded as the spiciest; in the south seafood is plentiful and Muslim specialties appear on the menu.

STICKY RICE
A glutinous variety of rice, or *khao niaow*, is the staple in north and northeastern Thailand, largely due to the influence of neighboring Laos. Traditionally, this is rolled into small balls with the right hand and then dipped into the various liquid dishes. Special woven bamboo baskets are used to serve the rice at tables and to carry it into the fields by working farmers.

FISH SAUCE
Nam pla is a pungent sauce made from fermented fish, served as a salt substitute in early Thai cooking and still an essential condiment on any table. A number of brands are available on the market, each with its devoted adherents, and several coastal towns on the Gulf of Thailand are famous for the production of the sauce.

CHILLIES
Chillies, known in Thai collectively as *prik*, were introduced to Asia by the Portuguese from South America in the 16th century and quickly spread so widely that their searing flavor is now basic to numerous cuisines. Thai cooking employs over forty varieties of chilli, ranging from large and mild to tiny bombshells called *prik-kee-nu*, which translates as "mouse-dropping pepper," on account of their shape.

A THAI MEAL
A Thai meal, even in rather grand households, is an informal affair. Steamed rice forms the centerpiece – loose-grained in most parts of the country, glutinous in the north and northeast – and the other dishes are placed around it, to be eaten in any order a diner prefers. There may be many or few of these, depending on economic status, but there is usually some kind of curry, a soup and a spiced salad, along with fish sauce, chopped chillies and other condiments, and fresh fruit as a dessert.

NOODLES
Originally introduced from China, noodles often take the place of rice in quick meals supplied by vendors and sidewalk food shops. They come in numerous sizes, the most common being made from rice, flour or mung beans.

ROYAL CUISINE
Thai food that is prepared and served with enhanced elegance is often referred to as "royal cuisine" since it is supposed to have been inspired by palace chefs. Fruit and vegetables are carved into exquisite shapes, with colors and textures carefully matched, turning each dish into edible art.

FRESH SEASONINGS
Besides chillies, a number of fresh herbs and roots are regularly used in Thai cooking. Coriander leaves and lemon grass are two of the most popular, while others include root ginger, basil, galangal, garlic and the kaffir lime (both leaves and fruit).

DRY SPICES
Black pepper, used as a hot spice before the introduction of chillies, is still a popular dry ingredient. Among the others are crushed coriander seeds, turmeric, cinnamon, cloves and sesame seeds.

This spicy dish from central Thailand is typical of Thai cuisine with its use of *nam pla*, chillies and other spices and herbs such as coriander. *Kaeng* is a common type of dish meaning "with spicy gravy" and there are many variations on its basic theme. This particular dish can be made with chicken, pork or beef, and is always served with rice and sometimes with salted hard-boiled eggs.

INGREDIENTS
for KAENG PHED PED YANG
1 roast duck, boned and cut into small pieces
3 cups of coconut milk
½ cup water
2-3 tablespoons red chilli paste (see "Ingredients for Chilli Paste," opposite)
2 stalks lemon grass
5 small tomatoes
3 tablespoons *nam pla* (fish sauce)
½ cup peas
4 green or red chillies
10 leaves of Asian basil

RECIPE FOR CHILLI PASTE
Fry the cumin and coriander seeds for 1–2 minutes until golden brown. Chop the dried peppers, shallots, garlic and galangal finely. Pound all the paste ingredients, including the fried cumin and coriander, until a smooth paste is obtained. Set the chilli paste aside.

INGREDIENTS FOR CHILLI PASTE
2 teaspoons cumin seeds
1 teaspoon coriander seeds
8 dried peppers
1 teaspoon salt
1 teaspoon dried lemon grass
2 tablespoons chopped shallots
1 teaspoon chopped garlic
1 teaspoon galangal
1 teaspoon shrimp paste
2 teaspoons water

Mortar and pestle are indispensable utensils in Asian kitchens.

RECIPE FOR KAENG PHED PED YANG

1. Cut the chillies and soak them in water for 10 minutes. Cut the tomatoes into halves. Leave the chillies and tomatoes to one side.

2. In a pan, add two thirds of the coconut milk to the water and bring it to the boil. Leave to simmer.

3. Add the chilli paste and stir well. Cook for a few minutes.

4. Add the pieces of duck to the warmed coconut milk and paste mixture. Turn up the heat and cook for 10 minutes.

5. Add the *nam pla*, peas, tomatoes and chillies. When the peas are cooked, add the remaining coconut milk and bring to the boil. Scatter the basil onto the dish and turn off the heat.

6. Serve *kaeng phed ped yang* with white rice.

An old engraving showing Thai women seated round a mat, eating a meal with their fingers.

Thailand is blessed not only with a wide selection of delectable fruits but also with some of the best varieties to be found in Southeast Asia. There are more than two dozen kinds of bananas, including a small, finger-sized species noted for its sweetness, as well as mango, durian, pineapple, jackfruit, rambutan, mangosteen, melons, lychee, papaya, guava, fresh coconuts and countless others. Fruit frequently serves as the dessert course, but there are also other choices, including a variety of confections that are eaten as snacks between meals.

ORNAMENTAL FRUITS
On special occasions, miniature fruits called *look choop* are made from a mixture of mung-bean paste and sugar, then flavored with fragrant essences and realistically colored with food dyes. The creation of these requires considerable skill, and, like fruit and vegetable carving, was once associated with the women of royal and aristocratic households. Decorative baskets of the little fruits are often presented as gifts on birthdays and other celebrations.

COCONUT MILK
A number of Thai desserts consist of various ingredients in sweetened coconut milk. Thin glass noodles may be served in this way, as well as tapioca, rice-flour dumplings that resemble lotus seeds, and sweet blackened jelly cubes. These are often colored with shocking pink and green food dyes and served with ice.

STREET SWEETS
Khanom is the general Thai word for "sweet," and many street vendors specialize in one kind or another to tempt passers-by. The woman shown above is preparing a popular delicacy known as *khanom krok*, in which a mixture of thick coconut milk, rice flour, eggs, and sugar is cooked on the spot in a special clay mold.

FRUIT AND VEGETABLE CARVINGS
The art of fruit and vegetable carving was a renowned skill among women of the royal palace and even today many otherwise ordinary dishes in restaurants are enhanced by a radish or spring onion transformed into an unexpected flower. In the hands of a true expert almost any firm-fleshed fruit becomes an object of extraordinary beauty.

PORTUGUESE INFLUENCES
The Portuguese were the first Europeans to open trade relations with Ayutthaya, in the 16th century. Among their cultural influences that still survive are a number of delicate sweets

based on egg yolks and sugar, sometimes spun into a mass of thin threads through a special device made for the purpose.

SWEET SELECTION
Presentation is an important part of the appeal of Thai sweets. Coconut custards and jellies are often wrapped individually in banana leaves, which imparts a subtle flavor as well as serving as a useful container, while egg-yolk confections are rolled into golden balls and cakes are cut into varied shapes. Other popular ingredients include glutinous rice, sweet potatoes, pumpkin, palm sugar, slivers of fresh young coconut and mung-bean paste.

DURIAN
A controversial fruit among Westerners because of its distinct smell ("like rotten onions and stale cheese," one writer described it), the durian is highly prized by Thais, fetching high prices during its short fruiting season. The creamy flesh is usually eaten together with sweet sticky rice. Numerous hybrids have been produced by Thai growers, bearing such imaginative names as "Golden Pillow," "Frog" and "Transvestite," the last so called because its seeds will not germinate.

FRUIT AND FRUIT VENDORS
Few Thai street scenes would be complete without a fresh-fruit vendor; his moveable shop dispenses a selection of succulent pineapple, green mango, crisp guava (often dipped into a mixture of dried chillies and salt), banana fritters, prickly rambutans, ruby-red mangosteens, and juicy slices of chilled watermelon.

Thai is a pentatonal language belonging to the so-called group of Tai-Kadai languages that includes Shan and Khun in Burma, Thô in Vietnam, Buyi and Zhuang in Yunnan and Guizhou provinces of China, and long-extinct languages such as Ahom in Assam. Most of the words are monosyllabic. There are five main dialects in Thailand. Literature is mostly written in the central dialect spoken in and around Bangkok. Due to the early importance of Buddhism, a strong Sanskrit and Pali influence can be felt in the vocabulary as well as in the syntax. One of the main difficulties in learning Thai lies in the various conversational styles. There are several speech levels in spoken Thai, which depend on age, sex and social factors. The first-person pronoun, for instance, can be rendered in numerous ways ranging from the very humble, when speaking to the king, to the most dismissive.

THAI ALPHABET

According to tradition, the first Thai alphabet was created in 1283 by King Ramkhamhaeng, Rama the Powerful of Sukhothai, who based it on Mon and Khmer versions of an old South Indian script. All these scripts are organized around a horizontal line that runs throughout the words. The script of modern Thai follows very strict phonological rules. It consists of 44 consonants and 32 basic vowels that cannot be used alone and are written in close relationship to the consonants in order to create syllables.

MANUSCRIPTS

Old Thai manuscripts were written on two kinds of material: *khoi* paper, made from the bark of a local tree, and palm leaf. To make the latter, the leaves of palm fronds were dried and trimmed to form flat sheets; the calligraphy was etched with a sharp needle and the surface rubbed with ink to fill in the engraved areas. Palm leaf books were used only for religious texts and were rarely illustrated. *Khoi* books consisted of sheets folded concertina-fashion into a series of panels. These were often illustrated and dealt not only with religious subjects but also, especially in early Bangkok, with such secular matters as anatomy, warfare, the martial arts and auspicious elephants.

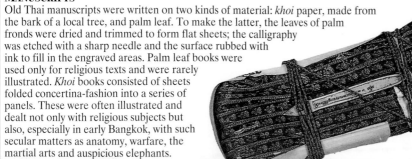

ARCHITECTURE

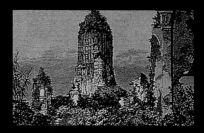

THAI VILLAGE, *44*

TRADITIONAL THAI HOUSES, *45*

THAI TEMPLE, *46*

SIAMESE ARCHITECTURE, *47*

RATTANAKOSIN ARCHITECTURE, *48*

LANNA RELIGIOUS ARCHITECTURE, *49*

THAI RELIGIOUS MONUMENTS, *50*

LANNA CHEDIS, *51*

1. TEMPLE
2. SCHOOL
3. MARKET AND SHOPHOUSES
4. HOUSES ON STILTS
5. VEGETABLE FARM

The typical Thai village is built along a waterway; these form the principal artery of communication in the countryside. Each village is self-contained, comprising a Buddhist temple, a school and a market. Usually, a cluster of Chinese shophouses make up the village market. To stay above floodwaters, many of the houses in the village are built on stilts.

● TRADITIONAL THAI HOUSES

The basic Thai house of the past, rarely seen today, was a simple structure of bamboo and thatch, raised off the ground for protection against floods and wild animals. Most family life took place on a veranda-like platform outside the one or two rooms that served as sleeping quarters. In time, this model evolved into more complex structures of wood, varying in both form and decoration to suit conditions in different regions but always retaining their essential simplicity.

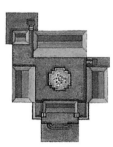

FLOATING HOUSES
Early Bangkok had many floating shophouses, where the family lived and traded. The floorboards in such structures are loosely fitted to allow for movement as the water rises and falls. ▲ 72.

ROYAL HOUSES
Royal houses were similar in design to those of commoners except that they were generally closer to the ground and had more decorative features.

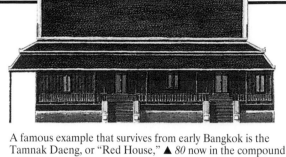

A famous example that survives from early Bangkok is the Tamnak Daeng, or "Red House," ▲ 80 now in the compound of the National Museum. Built by King Rama I as a residence for one of his queens, it was originally in Ayutthaya style but acquired more Rattanakosin elements during several moves. King Rama V presented the house to the museum as a reminder of an architectural style then becoming rare.

CENTRAL PLAINS HOUSES
The best-known traditional house style is found in the Central Plains. Elevated on stout round posts, it has steep roofs with curved bargeboards and paneled walls leaning slightly inward; the various components are prefabricated to enable easy dismantling and reassembly. The simplest house consists of a single unit with an outside veranda, while those accommodating larger families might have several separate units arranged around a central platform ▲ 94, 126.

"SALA"
Sala, or pavilions, are open structures with characteristic Thai roofs where people relax and watch the world go by. They can still be seen in many parts of the country: near the entrance to temples, along roadsides and canals, and in several private compounds.

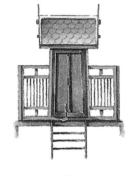

THE NORTHERN HOUSE
The northern Thai house differs significantly from its counterpart in the Central Plains. The walls lean outward, giving it a sturdier look, and windows are often smaller. A notable decorative feature, especially in the Chiang Mai area, are the V-shaped designs at the ends of the roof, called *kalae*. Some authorities believe they represent a pair of buffalo horns.

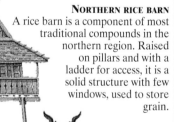

NORTHERN RICE BARN
A rice barn is a component of most traditional compounds in the northern region. Raised on pillars and with a ladder for access, it is a solid structure with few windows, used to store grain.

ROOF GABLE ("NGAO")
A distinctive feature of the Central Plains house is the elegant curved decoration at the ends of the peaked bargeboards surrounding the gables. Known as *ngao*, it evolved from Khmer architecture and appears in elaborate forms on religious buildings and palaces. A stylized version can also be seen in domestic houses.

PANELING
Paneled walls are a relatively recent addition to the Thai house.

GATE
Houses belonging to more prosperous families usually have a gate, often sheltered by a Thai-style roof that opens on to the central platform. A jar of water is placed at the bottom of the steps so that visitors and residents can wash their feet before ascending.

1. "BOT"

The bot, or ubosot, where new monks are ordained, is the most important building in the wat compound, though it may not be the largest or most impressive. It is always surrounded by eight boundary stones (*bai sema*) demarcating the consecrated area, which is outside the authority of any governing body.

The Thai temple, or wat, is actually a complex of buildings and religious monuments within a single compound, often varying in both age and artistic value, designed to serve a number of practical purposes in the surrounding community. One section houses the resident monks, for instance, while elsewhere there are structures for worship, for meetings, for education, for cremations, for enshrining relics and ashes of the deceased.

The focal point of village life, a wat is erected as an act of merit by the community as a whole or by a private patron and is best appreciated through an understanding of its different functions.

"VIHARN" (NOT FEATURED)

The viharn is an assembly hall used by monks and the laity who come to hear sermons. The compound shown here is without a viharn; other compounds may have several. Viharns and bots are similar architecturally, only distinguishable by the presence of the *bai sema*.

2. "CHEDI"

A chedi, or stupa, is a reliquary monument where relics of the Buddha or the ashes of important people are enshrined. The chedi is often the main reason behind the construction of the wat compound.

3. BELL TOWER

Most wat compounds contain a bell tower. The bell is rung to summon resident monks to prayers in the late afternoon.

4. MONKS' QUARTERS

The monks' quarters in a wat consist of individual houses where the resident monks live, the largest unit being reserved for the abbot.

5. & 6. "HO TRAI"

Ho trai, or libraries, are usually built in the middle of a pond (5) or on a raised platform (6) to keep the manuscripts away from termites and other domestic pests.

7. "SALA KANPRIEN"

The *sala kanprien* usually serves as a meeting hall.

8. "SALA"

Other *sala* in the compound are used by visitors and pilgrims.

9. CREMATORIUM

Cremations are held in a tall, tower-like structure with steps leading to the area where the body is consigned to flames.

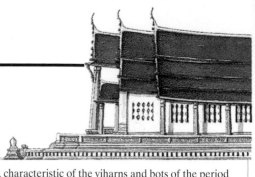

Thai architecture evolved from various cultural influences, adapted and subtly transformed into something distinctly different. The process began at Sukhothai, where the first models were stone-roofed Khmer temples and Mon structures. The Thais introduced wooden roofs and more ornamental features, such as colored tiles and ceramic adornments. Other architectural forms came from India, China and Sri Lanka. During the Ayutthaya period, Thai architecture achieved its own unique style.

Ayutthaya temple buildings
Ayutthaya-style religious structures ▲ *125* were designed to impress with their size and splendor.

A characteristic of the viharns and bots of the period was a concave curve of the base called *thong sampao*. Interiors tended to be dark, to emphasize the mystery and royalty of the Buddha, while elaborate decorations were used on the outside. The example shown above is Wat Na Phra Meru, built in the 15th century and restored by King Rama III of Bangkok.

Sukhothai viharn
No Sukhothai-period viharns exist today in their original form, but as shown by this model displayed at the Sukhothai Archeological Park, they were rectangular, open-sided structures with sloping wood roofs in two sections, the lower part supported by pillars with lotus capitals. Ceramic decorations were liberally used ▲ *129, 130*.

Ayutthaya-period library window
This window of gilded wood, adorned with inlaid mosaic, is in an Ayutthaya-period *ho trai*, or library; the late 17th-century structure was moved from the old capital to Bangkok.

Ayutthaya-period doors
Shown here are doors at Wat Yai Suwannaram in Phetchaburi, which date from the Ayutthaya period. Beautifully carved and gilded, they are particularly fine examples of the graceful curves that characterize Ayutthaya style.

Ayutthaya-period slit windows
Windows with narrow openings, like the one shown here from Wat Na Phra Meru in Ayutthaya, were of Khmer origin and contributed to the darkness of the interior.

Sukhothai mondop
Mondop, like this one at Wat Si Chum in Sukhothai, were cube-like structures, adapted from Sri Lanka through the Mons. The buildings, which had thick brick walls, were used to house an object of worship, such as a Buddha image or a sacred footprint. The name comes from the Sanskrit word *mandapa*, though in India the structure is designed either as an open hall or as a pavilion ▲ *129*.

Throne hall
Though the original has vanished, Ayutthaya's splendid Sampet Prasat Throne Hall at the ancient city has been reconstructed from its remains and from the evidence of records. It clearly shows the ship-hull shape – a prominent feature then – that may have symbolized a ship carrying Buddhist pilgrims to salvation.

Lotus capital
Columns surmounted by water-lily or lotus-bud decorations were common on structures dating from the Sukhothai to Ayutthaya periods; in Bangkok, the lotus capital was replaced entirely by the water-lily motif. This example is from the Viharn Daeng in Ayutthaya Province.

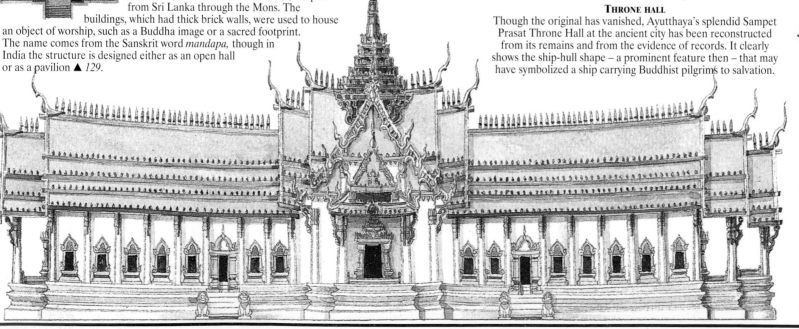

● RATTANAKOSIN ARCHITECTURE

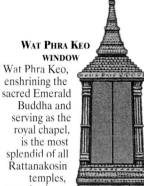

At the beginning of the Rattanakosin, or Bangkok, period, a conscious attempt was made to recreate the splendor of Ayutthaya. Some of the first buildings were replicas of former ones, with careful attention paid to every detail. Later Rattanakosin decorations became even more elaborate than those of Ayutthaya, influenced by Chinese motifs and love of color. Western influences became predominant under King Rama V, when foreign architects were brought in to design palace buildings and even temples reflected the new styles.

GATE OF WAT TEPIDARAM
Both Chinese and Western influences are revealed in the external walls of Wat Tepidaram, which are made of whitewashed brick and decorated with Chinese tiles and statues.

WAT SUTHAT DOOR
Leading to the bot enclosure, this door in Wat Suthat is framed with marble and displays the graceful curving lines typical of Rattanakosin.

WAT PO BELL TOWER
Covered with glazed tiles and adorned with pointed finials and ornate decorations, the bell tower at Bangkok's Wat Po ▲ 79 exemplifies all the best qualities of Rattanakosin art. The temple was a favorite with early Chakri rulers, particularly King Rama III.

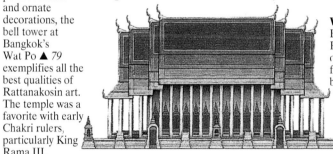

WAT SUTHAT BOT
Built by King Rama I, founder of Bangkok, the finely proportioned bot of Wat Suthat is 264 feet long and stands on two terraces, adding to its imposing appearance. A colonnade surrounds the structure and bears the weight of the massive four-tier roofs. The interior is decorated with well-preserved mural paintings.

WAT PHRA KEO WINDOW
Wat Phra Keo, enshrining the sacred Emerald Buddha and serving as the royal chapel, is the most splendid of all Rattanakosin temples, constituting a virtual textbook of classical architecture and decoration. The window shown above reflects the richness and intricate detail of its adornment.

WAT RAJABOPIT WINDOW
Wat Rajabopit, built by King Rama V, displays both traditional and Western styles. Windows like the one above are decorated with mosaics and carvings, and walls and pillars in the temple are covered with colored porcelain tiles.

WAT SUTHAT VIHARN
Wat Suthat viharn, one of the finest surviving structures of early Bangkok, has a double-layered roof and eight doors preceded by porticoes. The gables have magnificently carved decorations of various religious symbols, while the interior is divided into three sections by two rows of columns.

WAT PHRA KEO MONDOP
The *mondop* at Wat Phra Keo, dating from the reign of King Rama I, is regarded as the most beautiful example of Rattanakosin architecture. Square-shaped and surmounted by a slender spire, it is supported outside by tall elegant columns and is covered with an incredible profusion of lavish decorations.

CHINESE INFLUENCE
Chinese architectural styles and decorations were popular during the reign of King Rama III, as can be seen in the viharn of Wat Tepidaram.

WAT BENCHAMABOPIT (MARBLE TEMPLE)
Popularly known as the Marble Temple, Wat Benchamabopit ▲ *92, 132* was built toward the end of King Rama V's reign and displays an eclectic blend of cultural influences. The walls are covered with marble brought from Carrara, Italy, while the yellow roof tiles are Chinese. The bot has stained-glass windows as well as massive marble Khmer-style *singha* (guardian lions), flanking the doors.

Religious architecture in the northern Lanna kingdom developed independently from that of Ayutthaya in the Central Plains and is linked more with the Thai people of Yunnan, the Shan states and Laos. Thanks to the surrounding teak forests, wood was used extensively in construction and also in decorative carvings to adorn temples. Old Lanna viharns were open, like those of Sukhothai, and the columns supporting the roof were often low.

VIHARN OF WAT CHIENG KHONG

Originally located in Chiang Rai, this example of early Lanna style ▲ 51 was dismantled and brought to the ancient city outside Bangkok to be reassembled. Except for a brick base, the viharn is built entirely of wood, including wooden tiles, and is open on all four sides; low columns support the huge tiered roof.

VIHARN LAIKAM OF WAT PHRA SINGH

This early 19th-century viharn at Wat Phra Singh is possibly the finest example of late Lanna style surviving in Chiang Mai. It is a closed structure with brick walls and a wooden façade; guardian serpents stand on the entrance stairs ▲ 136.

LIBRARY OF WAT PHRA SINGH

Wat Phra Singh's library is a small wooden building, raised on a high brick base, decorated with stucco deities. The library itself is adorned with intricate inlaid decorations and reflects pure Lanna style at its best ▲ 136.

KU OF WAT PHRA THAT LAMPANG LUANG

A unique feature of Lanna architecture is the *ku*, a brick structure used to house the Buddha image. Similar to a chedi, it is gilded and placed inside a temple. The *ku* above is in Lampang province ▲ 142, 145.

WAT PHUMIN

Wat Phumin in Nan province ▲ 146 was established in 1596 by a local ruler and restored in 1865 and 1873. Its main building, serving as both bot and viharn, is a unique structure built on a perfect cruciform plan, with four axial porches leading to four Buddha images placed in the center. On the interior walls are lively murals depicting the Jataka stories and painted about a hundred years ago. The stairways of two opposite entrances are flanked by *naga* with the tail at one doorway and the head at the other. The chapel has a five-tier roof, decorated with *naga* symbolizing the water flowing down from Mount Meru.

MONDOP OF WAT PONGSANUK TAI

This graceful *mondop* at Wat Pongsanuk Tai in Lampang ▲ 143 is a typical example of old Lanna style. Completely open on all sides, it has a tiered roof with false upper stories and a cage enclosing four Buddha images flanking a Bodhi tree. The decorations display a wit and ingenuity lacking in many modern temples of the region, which have been influenced by Bangkok tastes.

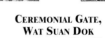

CEREMONIAL GATE, WAT SUAN DOK

Monumental gates, like this one at Wat Suan Dok in Chiang Mai, are typical of the north and were also a feature of now-vanished palaces. Wat Suan Dok was once a *wiang*, or fortified monastery, built on the site of a royal garden ▲ 137, 143.

RELIQUARY CHEDI
A reminder of the original significance of the chedi is this example, made of limestone and standing 19 inches high; dating from the 7th and 8th centuries, it was found in Saraburi Province and is now in the National Museum.

It is traditionally claimed that, as the Buddha was dying, one of his disciples asked how they could remember him and his doctrines. He replied that they could make a mound of earth in which a relic of his body could be placed after his cremation. Thus began what has become known as a chedi, a monument that over the years became taller, narrower, and often of considerable size, used to enshrine relics of the Buddha or the ashes of important people, religious and royal. Chedis are found in every wat, often along with prangs, an older type of monument adapted from Hindu architecture, and introduced to Thailand by the Khmers.

AYUTTHAYA PRANG
The prang as a form came to Thailand with the Khmers, who had acquired it from India. In Hindu mythology, it represents the 33 levels of heaven, which in Buddhism became the 33 stages of perfection. It was revived in Ayutthaya to emphasize the concept of divine kingship, as seen here in the prang of Wat Raja Burana ▲ *124*, built of stuccoed brick and laterite in 1424. A rare collection of gold objects was found in 1957 in a large crypt beneath the prang.

BELL-SHAPED CHEDI
The bell-shaped chedi originated in Sri Lanka and first appeared in Thai religious architecture during the Sukhothai period; it has been used since throughout Thai history up to the present. The one shown above, at Wat Yai Chai Mongkol in Ayutthaya, is 238 feet high, composed of brick and stucco, and was built by King Rama-thibodi in 1358 ▲ *125*.

SRIVIJAYA CHEDI
Chedis of the Srivijaya period, which lasted in the southern peninsula from the 7th to the 13th centuries, were built of brick and stucco and had strongly Javanese characteristics. The only surviving example in good condition is the one shown on the right, which stands on a square foundation and has four square tiers ascending in decreasing size; located at Wat Phra Boromathat in Chaiya ▲ *103*, it dates from the 8th century but has been restored several times, most recently in 1901 and 1930.

PHRA PATHOM CHEDI
The orange-tiled, bell-shaped Phra Pathom Chedi at Nakhon Pathom is reputed to be the tallest in the world, 352 feet high and 315 feet in diameter. It was built in the 19th century during the reigns of King Rama IV and Rama V, and encases a much earlier 132-foot monument dating from the Dvaravati period. Several monuments are similarly built around one or more older structures ▲ *96*.

WAT ARUN
Wat Arun, or the Temple of Dawn, is one of Bangkok's major riverside landmarks ▲ *88*. The central prang, 221 feet high, stands on a 122-foot base; originally only 50 feet high, it was raised to its present height during the reigns of King Rama II and Rama III. Stairways lead up at the four cardinal points, and there are smaller prangs at each of the four corners. All are decorated with multicolored ceramic.

SUKHOTHAI LOTUS-BUD CHEDI
The monument after which Wat Chedi Chet Thaew is named was built during Sukhothai's classic period, in the mid-14th century, at the satellite city of Si Satchanalai. An almost identical copy of one at Wat Mahathat in Sukhothai, it has a lotus-bud finial, a feature unique to Sukhothai religious architecture and found on other Sukhothai monuments throughout the kingdom ▲ *131*.

Early Lanna chedis display a number of Sinhalese features and are similar to those of Sukhothai. The region had extensive religious contacts with the outside world; in 1455, during the reign of King Tilokaraja, Chiang Mai was the site of an international Buddhist gathering. Later, in the 19th century, Burmese influences ▲ *137, 144,* altered both temple buildings and monuments.

Generally, Lanna chedis are smaller than those in the Central Plains, with the notable exception of Wat Chedi Luang in Chiang Mai, which was raised to 300 feet before its destruction by an earthquake in 1545.

CHEDI AT WAT PHRA SINGH
This chedi at Chiang Mai's Wat Phra Singh consists of a square block topped with a tiered spire, an ancient Lanna form that is related to some in Sukhothai ▲ *136.*

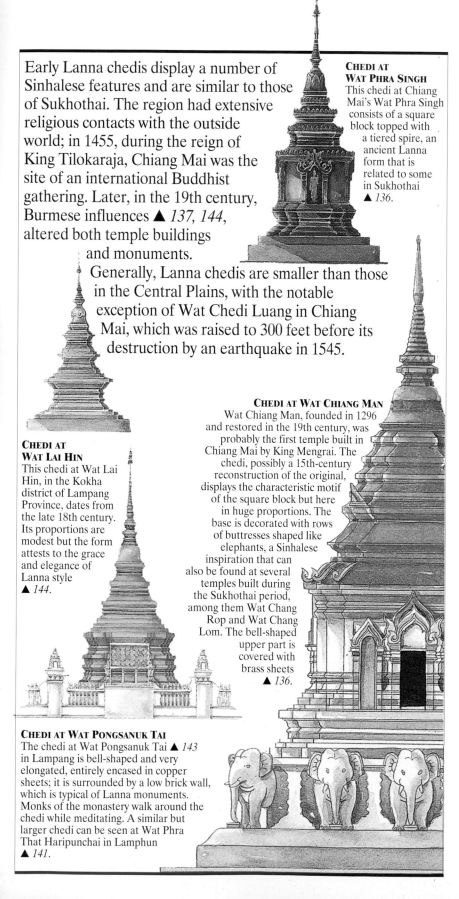

CHEDI AT WAT LAI HIN
This chedi at Wat Lai Hin, in the Kokha district of Lampang Province, dates from the late 18th century. Its proportions are modest but the form attests to the grace and elegance of Lanna style ▲ *144.*

CHEDI AT WAT CHIANG MAN
Wat Chiang Man, founded in 1296 and restored in the 19th century, was probably the first temple built in Chiang Mai by King Mengrai. The chedi, possibly a 15th-century reconstruction of the original, displays the characteristic motif of the square block but here in huge proportions. The base is decorated with rows of buttresses shaped like elephants, a Sinhalese inspiration that can also be found at several temples built during the Sukhothai period, among them Wat Chang Rop and Wat Chang Lom. The bell-shaped upper part is covered with brass sheets ▲ *136.*

CHEDI AT WAT PONGSANUK TAI
The chedi at Wat Pongsanuk Tai ▲ *143* in Lampang is bell-shaped and very elongated, entirely encased in copper sheets; it is surrounded by a low brick wall, which is typical of Lanna monuments. Monks of the monastery walk around the chedi while meditating. A similar but larger chedi can be seen at Wat Phra That Haripunchai in Lamphun ▲ *141.*

THAILAND AS SEEN BY PAINTERS

AYUTTHAYA AS SEEN BY FRENCH ENVOYS, *52*
ARUNOTHAI: LIFE IN THE HAREM, *53*
JEK SENG: COSTUMES OF THE NORTHERNERS, *54*
KHRUA IN KHONG: THE GREEN COUNTRYSIDE, *55*
HILDEBRANDT: THE CHAO PHRAYA, *56*
CHINI: GLIMPSES OF BANGKOK, *57*

> «WE WENT FOR A WALK OUTSIDE THE TOWN. I PAUSED
> FREQUENTLY TO ADMIRE THE STRONG GREAT CITY, SEATED UPON
> AN ISLAND ROUND WHICH FLOWED A RIVER THREE TIMES THE
> WIDTH OF THE SEINE.» ABBÉ DE CHOISY

The first Western impressions of Siam are found in early atlases and accounts of voyages and explorations. There are many interesting engravings that accompany the publications of the travels of French Jesuits and the two French embassies to Ayutthaya in 1685 and 1687. The flurry of diplomatic activities and the arrival in Paris of Siamese ambassadors increased the interest in this newly discovered exotic land. One of the most popular subjects was the grand parade of royal barges carrying the Chevalier de Chaumont and his retinue to the king's palace. While the original theme was engraved in the book by Father Guy Tachard, the subject was elaborated and developed in countless prints such as that shown left (1).

Royal elephants and their rich caparisons were another favorite subject (2). This image comes from La Loubère's works. Prints were rarely drawn first-hand and were produced from descriptions and sketches by missionaries. The Cabinet des Estampes in Paris preserves a collection of 33 watercolors that cover most of the themes depicted in the engravings. Reproduced here are a map of Ayutthaya (3) and two views (4 and 5) of the observatory that was constructed by King Narai and given to the Jesuits to pursue their astrological studies.

1		3
		4
2		5

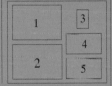

«VIVID PICTURES OF ANATOMY AND JEWELRY, GARDENS AND
POOLS, KIOSKS AND MATTED DORMITORIES MAKE THIS WING OF
THE PALACE A STUNNING BLEND OF REALITY AND POETRY.»

THE MARQUIS DE BEAUVOIR

The languid tempera ladies who appear on these pages are the work of Arunothai Somsakul, a contemporary Thai artist. He is inspired by his affection for the elegance of turn-of-the-century court life in Bangkok, which he portrays in a decadent, almost Symbolist manner. A large portion of Arunothai's output is manifestly erotic, and even his more decorous works are suffused with an air of almost palpable sensuality.

The oblique looks and whispered conversations of the palace ladies suggest either intrigues or assignations, the imminence of scandal. Even the figures carved in relief on the walls seem privy to many an exciting secret. The concupiscent atmosphere is sometimes reinforced by the presence of small erotic embellishments hidden within the composition that go unnoticed at first – or even second – glance.

The figures conspire in detailed settings that accurately portray the objects of court life at the time. Specific situations are often recognizable: the Vimarn Mek Palace seen through the window behind the gossiping ladies, for example. The paintings are, as is usual with Arunothai, set during the fifth reign, when Western fashions, often somewhat modified, were already being adopted by Bangkok society.

«THE NORTHERN SCHOOL IS CLEARLY DISTINGUISHED BY ITS VIVID
PORTRAYAL OF FAMILIAR SCENES CONVEYING A STRONG FEELING
OF INTIMACY.»

JEAN BOISSELIER

JEK SENG: ●
COSTUMES OF THE NORTHERNERS

A record of the colorful mosaic of races and cultures of northern Thailand is preserved in the murals at Wat Phra Singh, Chiang Mai. The surviving Lanna murals are engaging portraits of life in the north, before the irresistible influence of the culture of Bangkok overwhelmed the more delicate Lanna traditions. The murals were probably painted by a local artist named Jek Seng, who completed them during the late 19th century. The changing fashions and growing cosmopolitanism of the period are depicted in a detail from a mural (1), where the man watching the buffaloes wears a Bangkok-style *pannung* ● *30,* evidence that the culture of the capital was already spreading northward at this time. On the same mural, the lofty personages asking for directions are Shan, as is evident from the turbans and striped shawls they wear (2). Their Lue guide is heavily tattooed about the legs and loins and is armed with a red umbrella. The ladies of the market are more conservatively attired; their classic striped sarongs, bare bosoms and thin shoulder-cloths are typically Lanna (3). Life in a typical northern Thai house is also clearly shown (4).

«KHRUA IN KHONG, WITH ALL HIS INNOVATIONS, STRANGE LIFESTYLE AND ODD AND FORCEFUL PERSONALITY, MAY BE CONSIDERED THE FIRST ARTIST IN THE WESTERN MEANING OF THE WORD IN THAILAND.» PIA PIERRE

The lush green countryside of Thailand did not appear in Thai paintings until relatively late. The religious nature of the works and the flat two-dimensional style confined naturalistic elements to the role of embellishments, with which Thai artists filled up small empty corners of their compositions. The influence of Chinese landscape painting was first felt in the 19th century, gradually filtering into the work of Thai muralists and causing larger areas of their paintings to be treated as landscape. Even so, it was not until the advent of the artist-monk from Phetchaburi, Khrua In Khong ▲ 101, that the landscape per se became a subject in Thai art. An intimate of King Rama IV, Khrua In Khong found inspiration in the traditions of Western painting, which he discovered in the form of reproductions brought to Thailand by ambassadors and missionaries. Khrua In Khong introduced the concept of perspective to Thai painting; he also showed affection for the American neo-classical style of architecture, which made its earliest appearance in Thailand during the 19th century. Khrua In Khong added new colors to the Thai painter's palette, showing a clear preference for darker tones. The two images here of a river scene (1) and town life (2) were finished at Wat Bowornivet, Bangkok, around 1860, and are intended as figurative depictions of religious teachings. The metaphorical landscapes depicted are recognizably Thai; the abundance of water and rolling limestone hills in the background are almost certainly a remembrance of his native Phetchaburi. Khrua In Khong's stormy skies, however, are not particularly Thai; the treatment of clouds and sunlight effects owe a visible debt to the *Tempesta* of Giorgione, a work that was fresh in Khrua In Khong's mind at the time. The geometric perspective of some of the buildings is inspired by the *Flagellazione* of Piero della Francesca.

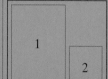

«THERE IT WAS…THE ORIENTAL CAPITAL WHICH HAD AS YET
SUFFERED NO WHITE CONQUEROR; AN EXPANSE OF BROWN HOUSES
OF BAMBOO…SPRUNG OUT OF THE BROWN SOILS ON THE
BANKS OF THE MUDDY RIVER.»   JOSEPH CONRAD

Following the expulsion of the French from Ayutthaya in 1688, a century of isolationism followed. During this time few foreigners visited Siam. As a result most of the atlases and books printed contained illustrations adapted from those of La Loubère and Father Guy Tachard. Normal relations with Western countries were resumed during King Rama IV's reign (1851–68) and Siam once again received the attention of writers and publishers, though still very few artists traveled in the country. One of the few artists to visit Siam was Eduard Hildebrandt (1818–69), who produced a series of watercolors of Bangkok and had them published as chromolithographs in his book, *Drei Reise um die Erde* (London, 1867). The two reproduced here show the banks of the Chao Phraya, which at that time was the main thoroughfare of the city. In the first painting, beyond the floating houses, Wat Arun, a famous landmark, can clearly be seen (1). The second provides a glimpse into one of the many floating shophouses that lined both banks (2). The Chinese temple behind would have been one of the few edifices at the time to be built of brick.

1
2

«I WILL LEAVE! STEAMSHIP WITH SWAYING MASTS, WEIGH ANCHOR
TOWARD EXOTIC NATURE.»

STEPHANE MALLARMÉ

CHINI: ●
GLIMPSES OF BANGKOK

By the turn of the century, in that period of revolutionary ideas that was to transform the art scene in the West, many artists felt a special fascination for the Orient and its exotic themes. However, only a few were able to experience at first hand the colors and atmosphere of the East. One artist who did was Galileo Chini (1873–1956). He was summoned to Bangkok in 1911 to decorate the ceiling of the new throne hall there, which had recently been completed by Annibale Rigotti. Chini spent two and a half years in Siam, painting the vaulted ceiling of the throne room with friezes in the Secessionist style and large frescoes depicting the glory of the Chakri Dynasty. The artist's long, prolific career subsumed many crucial phases in the development of modern art: the Pre-Raphaelite movement, Secessionism, Symbolism and Divisionism. Underlying these explorations was a solid Florentine mastery of his craft. The friezes in Bangkok are among the most charming of Chini's paintings. However, the work he completed during the Siam years ranks among his finest in that period. The mood suggested in *Mesu the Performer* (1), a study of a Thai dancer against a stark black background, is almost erotic, with a touch of the Symbolist manner. Another of Chini's masterpieces is undoubtedly the *Chinese New Year Festival in Bangkok* (2), its phantasmagoric quality achieved through strength of color and diffused light from an apparent multiplicity of sources. A vague hint of the Futurist work of Boccioni is visible here. *Nostalgia by the River* (3), painted in 1913 in the Divisionist style, creates a suggestive mood around what has long been one of the most popular Thai themes among artists: the river with its decadent, sensual atmosphere.

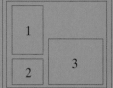

THAILAND AS SEEN
BY WRITERS

THE KINGDOM OF SIAM, 59
SUKHOTHAI/PATTANI, 60
AYUTTHAYA, 61
CHIANG MAI, 62
BANGKOK, 63
NAKHON PATHOM, 66

Chini was fascinated by the elaborate costumes of the Siamese court and pursued his studies with a series of large temperas of figures which are almost scenographic cartoons rather than paintings. The Brahmins shown in the picture above are an exemplary study on white with the translucent and transparent nuances of their immaculate clothes rendered with luminous precision.

It is sad to contemplate a great city, which once contained seventy-five temples, deserted by all, and even its ruins lost in the jungle; but old Chieng Sen has little hopes of recovery now, for it lies off the main road and the cost of clearing the plantations and undergrowths of brushwood which now choke the city would be too great to repay the undertaking. How are the mighty fallen and the weapons of war perished! So the old city sleeps, a prey to the wild beast of the jungle and those craftier two-legged animals, who come to seek what they can find among the ruins which lie to hand. **"**

REGINALD LE MAY, *AN ASIAN ARCADY*, CAMBRIDGE 1926,
REPRINTED BANGKOK 1986

BANGKOK

AN AUDIENCE WITH THE KING OF SIAM

After the assassination of Phaulkon and the expulsion of the French from Ayutthaya, Siam remained in almost complete isolation for nearly 150 years. Among the many unsuccessful delegations from the West was that of John Crawfurd, an Englishman. He came to the court of King Rama II in 1822. The following is an extract from Crawfurd's account of his first audience with the king.

"The curtain placed before the throne was drawn aside as we entered. The whole multitude present lay prostrate on the earth, their mouths almost touching the ground: not a body or limb was observed to move; not an eye was directed towards us; not a whisper agitated the solemn and still air....Raised about twelve feet above the floor, and about two yards behind the curtain alluded to, there was an arched niche, on which an obscure light was cast, of sufficient size to display the human body to effect, in the sitting posture. In this niche was placed the throne, projecting from the wall a few feet. Here, on our entrance, the King sat immovable as a statue, his eyes directed forwards. He resembled, in every respect, an image of Buddha placed upon his throne; while the solemnity of the scene, and the attitude of devotion observed by the multitude, left little room to doubt that the temple had been the source from which the monarch of Siam had borrowed the display of regal pomp. **"**

JOHN CRAWFURD, *JOURNAL OF AN EMBASSY FROM THE GOVERNOR GENERAL OF INDIA TO THE COURTS OF SIAM AND COCHIN-CHINA*, LONDON 1828,
REPRINTED SINGAPORE 1971

THE FLOATING CITY

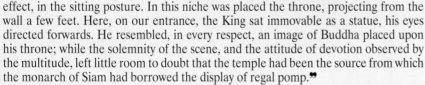

Mrs Anna Leonowens, an English widow, arrived in Bangkok in 1862, engaged to teach English to some of King Rama IV's wives and children. She wrote two books about her experiences, "The English Governess at the Siamese Court" and "The Romance of the Harem", which later formed the basis of the popular musical "The King and I". Although her books, written in the style of the serial melodrama, are largely inaccurate, her description of Bangkok is quite realistic.

"The situation of the city is unique and picturesque. When Ayutthaya was 'extinguished,' and the capital established at Bangkok, the houses were at first built on the banks of the river. But so frequent were the invasions of cholera, that one of the kings happily commanded the people to build on the river itself, that they might have greater cleanliness and better ventilation. The result quickly proved the wisdom of the measure. The privilege of building on the banks is now confined to members of the royal family, the nobility and residents of acknowledged influence, political or commercial...At night the city is hung with thousands of covered lights, that illuminate the wide river from shore to shore. Lamps and lanterns of all imaginable shapes, colours, and sizes combine to form a fairy spectacle of enchanting brilliancy and beauty. The floating tenements and shops, the masts of vessels, the tall, fantastic pagodas and minarets, and, crowning all, the walls and towers of the Grand Palace, flash with countless charming tricks of light, and compose a scene of more than magic novelty and beauty. So oriental fancy and profusion deal with things of use, and make a wonder of a commonplace...

A double, and in some parts a triple, row of floating houses extends for miles along the banks of the river. These are wooden structures, tastefully designed and painted, raised on substantial rafts of bamboo linked together with chains, which, in turn, are made fast to great piles planted in the bed of the stream. The Meinam itself forms the main avenue, and the floating shops on either side constitute the great bazaar of the city, where all imaginable and unimaginable articles from India, China, Malacca, Burma, Paris, Liverpool and New York are displayed in stalls...

Naturally, boats and canoes are indispensable appendages to such houses; the nobility possess a fleet of them, and to every little water-cottage a canoe is tethered, for errands and visits. At all hours of the day and night processions of boats pass to and from the palace, and everywhere bustling traders and agents ply their dingy little craft, and proclaim their several callings in a Babel of cries. **"**

ANNA LEONOWENS, *THE ENGLISH GOVERNESS AT THE SIAMESE COURT*,
LONDON 1870

THE WOMEN'S BURDEN

George Windsor Earl (1805–65) was a British officer in the Far East and Australia. Linguist, antiquarian and author, he wrote several books. His first work, and probably his best, "The Eastern Seas", recounts his travels in the Far East. The book stands out among contemporary literature for its acute judgment and sense of observation.

"The Siamese empire is apparently on the decline, a circumstance which may be attributed to the ruinous wars in which it is continually engaged, and to the enormous church establishment. Every man is obliged to serve as a soldier when called for, and to bring with him provisions for his own subsistence sufficient for his supply for several months. Wars, therefore, entail little expense on the government which may account for the readiness with which they are undertaken. The men who are engaged in their usually inglorious campaigns, acquire habits of idleness which are never afterwards corrected, and consequently the support of these drones, and of the enormous mass of priesthood, falls entirely on the women. The body of Talapoins or priests is enormously disproportioned to the rest of the inhabitants. In Bangkok alone, their numbers exceed thirty thousand. Like lilies of the valley 'they toil not, neither do they spin,' but are idle consumers of the produce of the soil. They do not even cook their own provisions, not being permitted to do so by their creed, but the younger members of the community go from house to house to collect the viands which are bountifully supplied by the people. The Talapoins received a great accession to their ranks during a late period of scarcity,

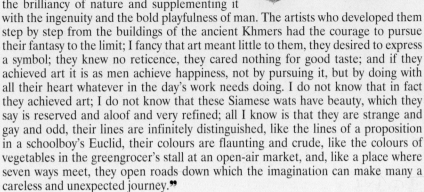

indeed it must be a matter of surprise that all the males do not become members of the priesthood, since among the privileges of their order may be reckoned exemption from labour, taxation, and military service, while they are at liberty to retire from the office whenever they please; the mode of life, however, led by these lazy vagabonds is found to be so agreeable, that they rarely take advantage of the latter privilege. The males affect to consider the women in the light of an inferior order of beings, but these lordly personages seldom enter upon any undertaking of moment without first consulting their wives. The women indeed, may be said to compose the most important portion of the community. They transact the greater part of the mercantile business, and are the principal cultivators of the soil, cheerfully undertaking the most laborious employments in the support of their families."

GEORGE WINDSOR EARL, *THE EASTERN SEAS*, LONDON, 1837, REPRINTED SINGAPORE, 1971

CONRAD ARRIVES IN BANGKOK

The future author Joseph Conrad (1857–1924) came to Bangkok in 1888 as a seaman named Josef Teodor Konrad Korzeniowski, to take his first command as captain of a ship called the "Otago". In "The Shadow-Line", he describes his arrival in the city.

"One morning, early, we crossed the bar, and while the sun was rising splendidly over the flat spaces of land we steamed up the innumerable bends, passed under the shadow of the great gilt pagoda, and reached the outskirts of the town…There it was, spread largely on both banks, the Oriental capital which had yet suffered no white conqueror; an expanse of brown houses of bamboo, of mats, of leaves, of a vegetable-matter style of architecture, sprung out of the brown soil on the banks of the muddy river. It was amazing to think that in those miles of human habitations there was not probably half a dozen pounds of nails…
Some of those houses of sticks and grass, like the nests of an aquatic race, clung to the shores, others seemed to grow out of the water; others again floated in long anchored rows in the very middle of the stream. Here and there in the distance, above the crowded mob of low, brown roof ridges, towered great piles of masonry, king's palace, temples, gorgeous and dilapidated, crumbling under the vertical sunlight, tremendous, overpowering, almost palpable, which seemed

to enter one's breast with the breath of one's nostrils and soak into one's limbs through every pore of the skin."

JOSEPH CONRAD, *THE SHADOW-LINE*, LONDON 1986

MAUGHAM ON THAI TEMPLES

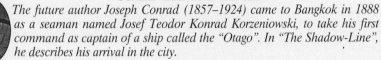

Somerset Maugham (1874–1965) was a doctor before he gained fame as a novelist and short-story writer. He served as a British agent in the two world wars. Maugham came to Thailand overland through Burma in 1923. The following extract from one of his travel books, "The Gentlemen in the Parlour", records his vivid impressions of Bangkok's famous Buddhist temples.

"They are unlike anything in the world, so that you are taken aback, and you cannot fit them into the scheme of the things you know. It makes you laugh with delight to think that anything so fantastic could exist on this sombre earth. They are gorgeous; they glitter with gold and whitewash, yet are not garish; against that vivid sky, in that

dazzling sunlight, they hold their own, defying the brilliancy of nature and supplementing it with the ingenuity and the bold playfulness of man. The artists who developed them step by step from the buildings of the ancient Khmers had the courage to pursue their fantasy to the limit; I fancy that art meant little to them, they desired to express a symbol; they knew no reticence, they cared nothing for good taste; and if they achieved art it is as men achieve happiness, not by pursuing it, but by doing with all their heart whatever in the day's work needs doing. I do not know that in fact they achieved art; I do not know that these Siamese wats have beauty, which they say is reserved and aloof and very refined; all I know is that they are strange and gay and odd, their lines are infinitely distinguished, like the lines of a proposition in a schoolboy's Euclid, their colours are flaunting and crude, like the colours of vegetables in the greengrocer's stall at an open-air market, and, like a place where seven ways meet, they open roads down which the imagination can make many a careless and unexpected journey."

A WELCOME FROM MISS PRETTY GIRL

A calling card was given to Somerset Maugham by a street tout during his visit to Thailand in 1923. Reproduced here is its message, which was recorded in the same book. The gentleman, incidentally, refused the invitation.

"Oh, gentleman, sir, Miss Pretty Girl welcome you Sultan Turkish Bath, gentle polite massage, put you in dreamland with perfume soap. Latest gramophone music. Oh, such service. You come now! Miss Pretty Girl want you, massage you from tippy-toe to head-top, nice, clean, to enter Gates of Heaven."

SOMERSET MAUGHAM, *THE GENTLEMEN IN THE PARLOUR*, LONDON 1930

THE TEMPLE OF DAWN

"The Temple of Dawn" was one of a cycle of four novels by the Japanese author Yukio Mishima (1925–70), the last of which was completed just before his ritual suicide in 1970. Much of the novel takes place in Bangkok, shortly before and during World War Two; in this passage the young hero visits Wat Arun, the Temple of Dawn, in the early morning:

"It was still darkish, and only the very tip of the pagoda caught the first rays of the rising sun. The Thonburi jungle beyond was filled with the piercing cries of birds…The repetitiveness and the sumptuousness of the pagoda were almost suffocating. The tower with its color and brilliance, adorned in many layers and graduated toward the peak, gave one the impression of so many strata of dream sequences hovering overhead. The plinths of the extremely steep stairs were also heavily festooned and each tier was supported by a bas-relief of birds with human faces. They formed a multicolored pagoda whose every level was crushed with layers of dreams, expectations, prayers, each being further weighted down with still other stories, pyramid-like, progressing skyward… With the first rays of dawn over the Menam River,… thousands of porcelain fragments turned into so many tiny mirrors that captured the light. A great structure of mother-of-pearl sparkling riotously…The pagoda had long served as a morning bell tolled by its rich hues, resonant colors responding to the dawn. They were created…to evoke a beauty, a power, an explosiveness like the dawn itself."

YUKIO MISHIMA, *THE TEMPLE OF DAWN*, NEW YORK 1973

A HUMORIST IN BANGKOK

S.J. Perelman, a leading American humorist, was a regular contributor to the "New Yorker" magazine as well as a playwright and the author of early film scripts for the Marx brothers. Shortly after World War Two he made a trip through Asia, which under the title of "Westward Ha!" became a bestseller; the following extract gives his impressions of Bangkok at a time when it was relatively untouched by mass tourism.

❝From the very beginning I was charmed by Bangkok, and I propose to be aggressively syrupy about it in the most buckeye travelogue manner. I liked its polite, gentle, handsome people, its temples, flowers, and canals, the relaxed and peaceful rhythm of life there. Apart from its shrill and tumultuous central thoroughfare swarming with Chinese and Indian bazaars, it struck me as the most soothing metropolis I had thus far seen in the East. Its character is complex and inconsistent; it seems at once to combine the Hannibal, Missouri of Mark Twain's boyhood with Beverly Hills, the Low Countries, and Chinatown. You pass from populous, glaring streets laden with traffic into quiet country lanes paralleled by canals out of a Dutch painting; a tree-shaded avenue of pretentious mansions set in wide lawns becomes a bustling row of shops and stalls, then melts into a sunny village of thatched huts among which water-buffalo graze. The effect is indescribably pleasing; your eye constantly discovers new vistas, isolated little communities around every corner tempting you to explore them.**❞**

S.J. PERELMAN, *THE MOST OF S.J. PERELMAN*,
NEW YORK, 1978

THE COUNTRYSIDE AND THE CITY

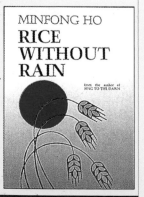

Minfong Ho is a Singaporean, but she spent most of her childhood in Thailand, and was for many years a teacher at the University of Chiang Mai. Her first novel, "Rice without Rain", was based on her experiences in northern Thailand during the 1976 student uprising, and it describes the politicization of an impoverished northern Thai village by a group of idealistic young students. The novel opens with a scene from the ricefields.

❝Heat the colour of fire, sky as heavy as mud, and under both the soil – hard, dry, unyielding. It was a silent harvest. Across the valley, yellow ricefields stretched, stopped and dry. The sun glazed the afternoon with a heat so fierce that the distant mountains shimmered in it. The dust in the sky, the cracked earth, the shrivelled leaves fluttering on brittle branches – everything was scorched. Fanning out in a jagged line across the fields were the harvesters, their sickles flashing in the sun. Nobody spoke. Nobody laughed. Nobody sang. The only noise was wave after wave of sullen hisses as the rice stalks were slashed and flung to the ground. A single lark flew by, casting a swift shadow on the stubbled fields. From under the brim of her hat, Jinda saw it wing its way west. It flew to a tamarind tree at the foot of the mountain, circled it three times, and flew away. A good sign…**❞**

The 1976 student movement was put down by the army, with considerable violence. Many of the student leaders fled to the jungle to take up arms with the Communist Party of Thailand (CPT). But most soon found themselves at odds with the CPT's hierarchy. Through a skillful policy of coercion and reconciliation, the Thai government was able to diffuse the Communist threat, and bring the guerillas out of the hills. Today, members of the 1976 movement are among the professional middle classes of Bangkok, and it was this group's willingness to take risks that led to the eventual victory of the pro-democracy forces, after a bloody confrontation in Bangkok's Sanam Luang square in 1992.

MINFONG HO

RICE WITHOUT RAIN

from the author of
SING TO THE DAWN

❝I am Jinda, daughter of Inthorn Sriboonrueng,' she began. To her surprise she found that her voice was steady. It reverberated from all corners of the square, and even from the wall of the temple. She felt awed that her voice could reach so far. She had practised the speech so many times that it had become automatic, and it flowed effortless from her now, separate and yet a part of herself. Like a kite with a lovely long tail, tugging its way upwards as she held the string, her words flew up. It was an exhilarating feeling, and Jinda's voice grew stronger with it. 'My father has farmed all his life,' she said, 'and yet he has never had enough to eat. Why?' She paused, and in that brief silence she felt that maybe, just maybe, she could help change a bit of Thailand after all. 'Because he has had to pay half of his harvest to the landlord, year after year. Flood or drought.'

'Commie bitch!' A shrill voice pierced the air.

Startled, Jinda stopped. Who had shouted that? Why?

Suddenly, a heavy object sailed towards her, landing where the shoe-shine boy had been. There was a loud explosion, and bits of dirt and glass shattered out. In the rolls of smoke which poured forth, people screamed, and started to run.

Ned grabbed the microphone from Jinda, and urged the crowd to be calm. 'Nothing serious has happened,' he announced. 'A small homemade bomb has just been tossed at us. This has happened in previous rallies. It hasn't hurt anyone. Do not panic, I repeat, do not panic. The speech will continue.'

But something was happening on the far side of the square. The soldiers in their olive green fatigues had fanned out in front of the ambulances, and were advancing towards the centre, pushing the crowd forward.

There was another explosion. It landed further away, but the bomb was deafening and devastating. As the smoke cleared, Jinda stared, stunned. At least five students sprawled motionless on the grass…that was when the distant gunfire started. At first Jinda did not know what it was, this sharp staccato rattle. Then she saw students dropping to their knees, in crumpled heaps, and she understood.**❞**

MINFONG HO, *RICE WITHOUT RAIN*,
SINGAPORE 1986

BANGKOK NIGHTLIFE

Born in England, Pico Iyer wrote for "TIME" magazine. He has also written for the "Partisan Review", "The Village Voice" and the "Times Literary Supplement". He came to Thailand in the 1980's while gathering material for a travel book later published as "Video Night in Kathmandu", from which the following excerpt is taken.

❝In seedy and improvident Manila, the bars were the fast-buck stuff of a puritan's nightmare; while in high-tech and prosperous Bangkok, they were quicksilver riddles, less alarming for their sleaze than for their cunning refinement, embellished by the country's exquisite sense of design, softened by the ease of Buddhism, invigorated by the culture of *sanuk* (a good time). In Manila girls tried to sell themselves out of sheer desperation; in Bangkok, the crystal palaces of sex were only extra adornments in a bejeweled city that already glittered with ambiguities…In Bangkok, moreover, the ambivalence of the girls only intensified the ambiguity of the bars…no gaze was direct, and no smile clear-cut in the city of mirrors. And the mirrors were everywhere: one-way mirrors walling the massage parlors, mirrors lining the ceilings of the 'curtain hotels,' mirrors shimmering in the bars, pocket mirrors in which each girl converted herself into a reflection of her admirer's wishes. Look into a bar girl's eyes, and you'd see nothing but the image of your own needs; ask her what she wanted, and she'd flash back a transparent 'up to you.' Everything here was in the eye of the beholder; everything was just a trick of the light.**❞**

PICO IYER, *VIDEO NIGHT IN KATHMANDU*,
NEW YORK 1988

NAKHON PATHOM

THE WORLD'S BIGGEST PAGODA

Sunthorn Phu (1786–1856) is generally regarded as Thailand's greatest poet, the first to bring realism into Thai verse. Born shortly after the establishment of Bangkok as the capital, he was a particular favorite of King Rama II, during whose reign he wrote perhaps the most famous of his works, "Khun Chang and Khun Phan". Sunthorn Phu is also noted for his works in a Thai genre called the "nirat", a sort of travel poem that blends descriptions of actual places with meditations on life and love by the poet. The following is from his "Nirat Phra Pathom", about a journey to the famous chedi in what is today called Nakhon Pathom.

"At last, we arrive at the Pagoda of the Sleeping Buddha's Temple.
It stands alone and high on a hill;
Colossally solid like a parapet,
Mounted on a manmade promontory.
It was constructed with sharp corners, showing the front gable,
Covered with a thin sheet of tin up to the top,
Stretching staunch and seamless in brick-and-stucco walls,
Wrought with time-honored and meticulous workmanship.
We walk around the Pagoda at the base,
Seeing deer's traces and hearing wild cocks crowing.
The spot is overgrown with wild creepers,
Winding and sticking in a thick green cluster.
We see secluded cubicles built for monks
Who may take shelter in their pilgrimages.
We are moved by their ardent faith.
At the stairs, we gaze up the slope:
It's so steep that our faces remain upturned.
That must be the way to heaven when we die.
We make an effort to help one another upward.
Once reaching the upper level, we are high spirited.
Pity my sons who also come up.
They are not so tired as us adults, though.
We hold candles in reverential attitude
And walk clockwise around the Pagoda
Three times, according to ceremonious practice.
Then we sit down and pay respects.
We offer incense sticks, candles, and flowers,
Also the candles entrusted to us by many others.
The owners had already made their wishes.
May they keep their beauty to the end.
May they be happy, every one of them,
Until they become enlightened by faith.
I've brought these candles with a desire
To be related to them in every life to come.
May our mutual love materialize now
And, in the future, may it be complete.
I salute the Pagoda of the Holy Relics:
May the true religious live forever.
I make merit, so the Buddha helps me
Increase my power to attain enlightenment.
And I'd like my words, my book,
To preserve, till the end of time and heaven,
Sunthorn the scribe who belongs
To the King of the White Elephant."

SUNTHORN PHU, *NIRAT PHRA PATHOM*,
TRANSLATED BY MONTRI UMAVIJANI,
BANGKOK 1986

ITINERARIES

BANGKOK, *70*
THE SOUTH, *99*
THE NORTHEAST, *116*
THE CENTRAL PLAINS, *123*
THE NORTH, *132*

▲ An image of His Majesty King Bhumibol Adulyadej adorns the side of a Bangkok skyscraper.

▲ The banks of the Chao Phraya River.

▲ Traffic on the Chao Phraya River, Bangkok's main river.   ▼ Lumpini Park and modern Bangkok.

▲ Two teenage girls shopping in Bangkok.   ▼ Wat Thong Thammachat, Thonburi, in Bangkok.

▲ Phangnga Bay.　　　　▼ West Coast, Phuket.　　　　▲ Koh Phi Phi Le.　　　　▼ Kata Yai Beach, Phuket.

▲ Wat Phra Si Sanphet, Ayutthaya.

▲ Wat Mahathat, Sukhothai.　　　　▼ Life on the river, Ayutthaya.

▲ Monks collecting alms in Chiang Mai.　　▼ Duck farm, Singhburi.

▼ Floating market, Damnern Saduak.

BANGKOK

BANGKOK, 71

HISTORY OF THE CITY, 72

THE GRAND PALACE, 74

WAT PO, 78

RATTANAKOSIN ISLAND, 80

THE CHAO PHRAYA RIVER, 87

KLONGS OF THONBURI, 90

CHINATOWN, 91

DUSIT DISTRICT, 92

MODERN BANGKOK, 93

PRIVATE MUSEUMS, 94

SHOPPING, 95

BANGKOK EXCURSIONS, 96

KANCHANABURI AND RIVER KWA

PATTAYA AND ENVIRONS, 98

BEYOND PATTAYA, 99

▲ BANGKOK

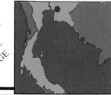

KLONG BANGLAMPHU
NATIONAL GALLERY
KHAO SAN ROAD
WAT BOWORNIVET
RAJADAMNOEN AVENUE
OCTOBER 14 MONUMENT
DEMOCRACY MONUMENT
QUEEN'S GALLERY
RAMA VII MUSEUM
MAHAKAN FORT
WAT RAJANADDA
WAT SAKET (GOLDEN MOUNT)
GIANT SWING
WAT SUTHAT
WAT RAJABOPIT
SARAROM PARK
RAILWAY STATION
PAK KLONG TALAAD FLOWER MARKET
MEMORIAL BRIDGE

WAT ARUN

NATIONAL THEATER
NATIONAL MUSEUM
PATRAVADI THEATER
THAMMASAT UNIVERSITY
WAT MAHATHAT
WAT RAKHANG
SANAM LUANG
LAK MUANG
MINISTRY OF DEFENSE
WAT PHRA KEO
WAT RAJAPRADIT
ROYAL PALACE
WAT PO

« THE GENERAL APPEARANCE OF BANGKOK IS THAT OF A LARGE,
PRIMITIVE VILLAGE, SITUATED IN AND MOSTLY CONCEALED BY A
VIRGIN FOREST OF ALMOST IMPENETRABLE DENSITY.»

FRANK VINCENT, 1871

An early view of Bangkok from the murals of Wat Rajapradit, painted in 1864. Behind the roofs of the Royal Palace runs the Chao Phraya, lined with floating houses on its banks. Chinese shophouses and Western-style homes stand among Thai temples and orchards.

Both literally and metaphorically, all roads in Thailand lead to Bangkok (derived from *bang makok*, which means "Village of the Wild Plum"), the center of almost everything: of power both temporal and spiritual, of the ancient monarchy, of commerce and communications, of higher education and the arts, of that indispensable part of life the Thais call *sanuk*, or "fun." It has a dynamic modern façade, sprawling and often confusing to the newcomer, best comprehended perhaps by looking back to the city's early days.

THE FOUNDING OF BANGKOK

Following the 1767 destruction of Ayutthaya, after 400 years of rule from there, the Thai capital was moved first to Thonburi on the west bank of the lower Chao Phraya River and then, in 1782, to a small trading port called Bangkok on the opposite bank. King Rama I, who decreed the move, felt the position of the new capital was more defensible and that it offered the space for a capital worthy of the Chakri Dynasty, which he had founded. He gave it a

lengthy official title, which the Thais have shortened to Krung Thep, "City of Angels," while foreigners continue to use the old name; the period of Thai history thus inaugurated is called Rattanakosin. As a matter of interest, Krung Thep is adapted from its actual name (listed in the *Guinness Book of Records* as the world's longest place name): *Krungthep Mahanakhon Bovorn Rattanakosin Mahintharayutthaya Mahadilokpop Noparatratchathani Burirom Udomratchaniveymahasathan Amornpiman Avatansathit Sakkathattiya-avisnukarmprasit.*

RATTANAKOSIN ISALAND

The Grand Palace and its adjacent royal chapel, the Temple of the Emerald Buddha – both replicas of Ayutthayan structures – were built first on an artificial island created by digging a canal where the river curved sharply, a strategy that had been used at Ayutthaya. Walled and fortified, the island was the political and cultural heart of the capital for more than a century. A group of Chinese traders who had occupied the site were moved outside the walls, where they formed the nucleus of a flourishing community of narrow streets, wharfs and warehouses that still exists. Spurred by increasing trade with the outside world, relative political stability and immigration (mainly Chinese), the city of Bangkok expanded rapidly. Two new canals were excavated and rows of floating houses ● *45* appeared on both banks of the Chao Phraya, and ships began arriving from Europe as well as neighboring countries. The floating houses served as both shops and residences for most of the population. Not until the 1820's did non-royal homes begin to appear on land, the majority on the Thonburi side of the river. By the mid-19th century, Bangkok had a population of 300,000 and was well on its way to becoming a major metropolis.

THE FOUNDER OF BANGKOK
King Rama I was a former military commander who succeeded King Taksin of Thonburi as ruler in 1782; he also began the Chakri Dynasty, of which the present king is the ninth monarch. The original buildings of the Grand Palace, as well as numerous temples, date from his seventeen-year reign.

FLOATING HOUSES
Thousands of floating houses, anchored to stout posts, lined the river and canals of early Bangkok.

EARLY TIMES

Early Bangkok was a water-oriented city, with the river and an intricate system of canals, or klongs, serving as the means of communication. The first proper street appeared in 1862, during the reign of King Rama IV, and ran parallel to the river for a considerable distance. Along it were most of the embassies, trading companies and shophouses selling the latest imported goods. Soon roads began to radiate from the Chao Phraya, through former orchards and across ricefields, accommodating ever-growing numbers of rickshaws, carriages, trams and, in 1902, automobiles. King Rama V, inspired by his visits abroad, attempted to create an orderly, European-style city in the Dusit district, with broad, tree-lined avenues and parks. But Bangkok resisted any such systematic planning; by World War Two it was sprawling in all directions from the original walled island. A building boom that started in the 1950's and continues to this day has transformed the capital almost beyond recognition to older Thais.

BANGKOK'S FIRST RICKSHAW
A wealthy Chinaman presented the first rickshaw to King Rama V in 1871; within a generation there were so many on the streets of Bangkok that, in 1901, a law was passed limiting their number. Automobiles arrived the following year. By 1908, there were over 300 cars; the invasion of this modern form of transportation spelled doom for the city's once numerous canals.

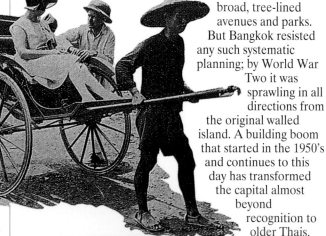

MODERN-DAY-BANGKOK

Present-day Bangkok covers an area of some 600 square miles, on both sides of the river – forty-five times larger than its nearest provincial rival – and is home to an estimated ten million people, half of them below thirty years of age. (The exact population would be impossible to calculate; many are part-time laborers who come to work between farming chores, while others are still registered as residents of their hometowns despite years in the capital.) They live and work in a variety of centers, often commuting for several hours each day by bus, for long the city's only form of public transport, but now joined by an elevated "Sky Train" and a subway system. Government offices are concentrated mainly in the area around the Grand Palace and Ratchadamnoen Road, while Yaowarat Road and its environs are largely devoted to Chinese business firms and the powerful military has its headquarters behind high walls in the Dusit district. Silom and Sathorn Roads have emerged as the financial district, with Patpong as a major attraction after nightfall; a number of leading hotels are also in this area. Though the streets off Sukhumwit Road comprise the prime residential and entertainment district, new suburban housing estates can be found all around the city with new shopping and recreational facilities constantly arising.

RECENT DEVELOPMENTS

The past decade or so has seen extensive construction along the Chao Phraya, especially on the Thonburi side, not only hotels but also residential condominiums for affluent Thais seeking a location more convenient to their offices. Nearly all of the country's major domestic and foreign businesses are located in Bangkok, along with the official residence of the royal family, government ministries, the most prestigious universities and preparatory schools, and the leading sports and cultural facilities. Thanks to this concentration of wealth and power, 90 percent of all the motor vehicles in the country are registered in the city, creating traffic congestion that an extensive network of overpasses and expressways has yet fully to solve. Though government policy encourages decentralization of industry into provincial areas, most of the modern factories are located in or near Bangkok, which is still the focus of the aviation, railway and communications systems, not to mention the extremely busy port of Klong Toey on the river, through which most of the country's imports and exports pass.

THAI TRAMS
Horse-drawn trams appeared on the streets of Bangkok in 1888; by the end of the century, the trams ran on electricity and continued to operate in decreasing numbers along New Road until the 1960's. The above painting, by contemporary artist Arunothai ● 53, shows fashionably dressed tram passengers in the past.

CHINATOWN IN THE 1950'S
Yaowarat Road ▲ 91 is pictured in Chinatown during the 1950's, when trams were no longer the only public transport as buses were growing in popularity.

The mythical half-bird, half-human *garuda* (above right) – legendary steed of the Hindu god Vishnu – is part of the royal insignia and appears among the decorations on many buildings within the palace compound.

As residence of the Lord of Life, as Thai kings are known, the royal palace has been the center of every capital in the country's history. The Grand Palace, surrounded by a high wall, covers nearly a square mile and, in its original form, was a conscious evocation of the one in Ayutthaya, divided into an outer part for government offices, a central portion containing the king's living quarters and audience halls, and an inner area for female members of the royal family and their attendants. Buildings were added to the palace compound by each of the first five Chakri rulers, particularly King Rama V, during whose reign Westernization was rapid.

EARLY BUILDINGS

The Dusit Maha Prasat depicted in a mid-19th-century engraving.

DUSIT MAHA PRASAT. Among the original palace buildings that still remain, though modified by later kings, is the Dusit Maha Prasat throne hall. Covered with four-tier tiled roofs and surmounted by a seven-tier gilded spire, it contains a blackwood throne inlaid with mother-of-pearl dating from the reign of King Rama I. The remains of kings, queens and royal family members are placed in the Dusit Maha Prasat prior to cremation. The building is open to the public.

THE PHRA THINANG APHONPHIMOK PRASAT. King Rama IV introduced Western architecture to the palace and was also responsible for one of its most beautiful traditional structures:

King Rama V alighting at the Phra Thinang Aphonphimok Prasat pavilion at the turn of the century. The pavilion is a major attraction today.

the Phra Thinang Aphonphimok Prasat (right). This pavilion on the east wall surrounding the Dusit Maha Prasat was where the king changed his robes before descending a flight of steps to mount a palanquin.

The structure displays graceful elegance and a distinctive blend of simple with sumptuous decoration epitomizes classic Thai architecture. It was reproduced at the Brussels Exposition in 1958.

THE GRAND RESIDENCE GROUP. Also from the earliest period of the palace is a group of connecting buildings known as Phra Maha Monthien, "the Grand Residence." The first three kings of the dynasty lived in one of these, the Phra Thinang Chakraphat Phiman – Phra Thinang is a title bestowed on any structure (building, pavilion, throne and so on) used by a king. It contains the royal bedchamber and it is still traditional for new monarchs to spend a night here upon assuming the throne, symbolizing their assumption of residence in the palace of their ancestors. In front and connected by a flight of stairs is the Phra Thinang Phaisan Taksin, where coronation ceremonies are held. It also houses two historic thrones, the Royal Regalia, and a small, much venerated image called Phra Siam Thewathirat, regarded as the tutelary deity of the Thai nation. The first Chakri king is supposed to have made regular use of this hall and, when old, to have held private audiences from one of its windows with people in the courtyard below. From the Octagonal Throne on the east side, new kings formally receive the invitation to rule over the kingdom, while from the Phattrabit Throne on the west, they receive the Royal Regalia, consisting of the crown, a sword, a royal staff, a fan, a whisk made of yak's tail, bejeweled slippers, and the Great White Umbrella of State. In the northern wall of the Phaisan Taksin is a gate known as Thewarat Mahesuan, through which only the king, the queen, and the royal children may walk. This leads to the Phra Thinang Amarin Winitchai, originally the principal audience hall of the Middle Palace where officials of state and foreign ambassadors were received. Dominating this hall – the only one in the group now open to the public – is the Phra Thinang Busbok Mala, an open-pillar construction of ornately carved wood with a tiered roof, made during the reign of King Rama I; to the left and right of the base are lateral extensions that make the structure appear to be floating in the air. The whole rests on a gilded masonry dais that dates from the reign of King Rama III. Curtains were drawn to conceal the king when he entered from the Phaisan Taksin; when it was time for the audience a fanfare sounded, the curtains dramatically parted, and the ruler was revealed in all the magnificence of his Royal Regalia. The Phra Thinang Busbok Mala throne (above right) is reserved for kings and objects of veneration. It holds the urns containing the ashes of previous Chakri kings. From his place on the throne, the reigning Chakri king receives offerings and pre-sides over the prayers of the royal family. Another throne in the building from the first reign, known as the Phra Thaen Sawetachat, is still used by the King for some of the investiture ceremonies as well as for the annual birthday audience.

View of the palace walls and roofs of Wat Phra Keo (above).

The Phra Thinang Busbok Mala throne, which contains funerary urns of the Chakri kings (below).

A large collection of ancient topiary – shrubbery trimmed into fancy shapes – adorns the front courtyard of the palace, a decorative technique that was probably inspired by plants in Chinese gardens.

«HOW CAN I DESCRIBE THE BARBARIC GRANDEUR, THE PARADE, THE SHOW, THE GLITTER, THE REAL MAGNIFICENCE, THE PROFUSE DECORATIONS OF TODAY'S ROYAL AUDIENCE!»

SIR JOHN BOWRING

"Ah! well, travelers who spoke of Siam as a dream of the Arabian Nights only told the truth; the colours of the East are so brilliant, the outlines so eccentric, the architecture so dazzling and covered with ornament, and these twenty palaces joined together hold so much that is wonderful, that it is worth taking the voyage for this one view…"

The Marquis of Beauvoir, 1867

LATER PALACE BUILDINGS

THE REGENT QUEEN
Queen Sowabha Phongsri, the principal queen of King Rama V, was the first of the royal wives to take up residence with the king outside the Inner Palace. She also served as regent during his trips abroad, and founded the first Thai girls' school and the Thai Red Cross, and, in general, was an important force in the liberation of Thai women from male domination.

THE TONSURE CEREMONY
One of the grandest rituals held in the Grand Palace was the Tonsure Ceremony, which marked the coming-of-age of children in the Inner Palace. After the tuft of hair was cut by Brahmin priests, the climax of a celebration that lasted several days, male children had to move out of the women's quarter to an outside residence.

AUDIENCE HALL
Thai kings since Rama V have traditionally received foreign ambassadors in the Central Audience Hall of the Chakri Maha Prasat, standing before a splendid wooden throne plated with silver and gold niello. On the walls are several large, European-style paintings of celebrated meetings between Thai ambassadors and King Louis XIV at Versailles.

The first Western-style buildings appeared in the palace enclosure during the reign of King Rama IV. These included a suite of rooms in the Siwalai Gardens, behind the Phra Maha Monthien, where the king lived and kept his collection of scientific instruments, and a tall structure with clocks on four sides. None of these remain today; they were torn down during the next reign, which saw the most extensive additions since the palace was built. King Rama V, the first Thai ruler to travel to Europe, ordered the construction of a new throne hall and royal residence. They were completed in time for the celebration of Bangkok's centenary in 1882.

CHAKRI MAHA PRASAT. Designed in neoclassical style by an English architect, the Chakri Maha Prasat was originally planned as a domed building, wholly Western in appearance; before completion, however, the dome was replaced with the older structures around it. The king and his principal queen moved to quarters on the upper floors of this structure and used the lower levels for state entertainment; a grand stairway reserved only for the king led down to the women's quarters behind the throne hall.

SIWALAI GARDENS. Also added most of the present buildings which now contains the the Boromphiman Mansion designed by a German for the Crown Prince, and a few Western-style residences for queens and consorts in the Inner Palace. The gardens were used for receptions as well as a recreation area for the royal women and their children. Toward the end of his reign, King Rama V moved out of the Grand Palace to new during the fifth reign were in the outer area, one of Royal Household Bureau, in the Siwalai Gardens, architect as a residence

quarters in the Dusit district but continued to use the older buildings for royal ceremonies, a tradition that was continued by subsequent rulers of the dynasty.

THE INNER PALACE. This was a secret world that much intrigued European visitors to Thailand in the 19th and early 20th centuries. According to Dr Malcolm Smith, an English physician who attended to King Rama V's principal queen and other royal patients, it "was a town complete in itself, a congested network of houses and narrow streets with gardens, lawns, artificial lakes and shops. It had its own government, its own institutions, its own laws and law courts. It was a town of women, one controlled by women. Men on special construc-tion or repair work were admitted, and the doctors when they came to visit the sick. The king's sons could live there until they reached the age of puberty; after that they were sent to live with relations, or with the governors in the provinces. But the only man who lived within its walls was the king." At its peak, in King Rama V's reign toward the end of the 19th century, about 3,000 women lived in this part of the palace, most of them servants or daughters of noble families who were sent here to learn various refined skills such as cooking, embroidery, and making floral wreaths. With the advent of royal monogamy in the next reign, the number steadily decreased as wives and princesses were allowed to move outside. A few stayed on, however, and the last resident died in the 1970's.

MUSEUMS IN THE PALACE COMPOUND

Just beyond the entrance is the Coins and Royal Decorations Museum. Early Thai coins and other items used as money are displayed here, in addition to medals and other decorations presented by Chakri kings for outstanding service, many of them set with precious stones. On the ground level of the Chakri Maha Prasat is a display of ancient weapons while near the Dusit Maha Prasat another museum contains stone inscriptions and palace decorations replaced during various renovations.

WAT PHRA KEO

Wat Phra Keo, the Temple of the Emerald Buddha, serves as the royal chapel and as such is located in one corner of the Grand Palace compound; unlike other Buddhist temples, it has no resident monks.

THE EMERALD BUDDHA ▲ *88.* The fabled statue – the Phra Keo – was discovered when lightning struck an ancient stupa in northern Thailand in the early 15th century. Over the next five centuries, legends accumulated around the small seated image – 26 inches high and 19 inches wide at the lap span, actually carved from a semiprecious form of jade. It was enshrined in a number of northern cities and also, for more than 250 years, in Laos; the future King Rama I brought it back to Thailand after having destroyed Vientiane to take possession of it, and later made it the principal Buddha image of his new capital at Bangkok. The image is the most venerated of all the thousands in the country.

Today the Emerald Buddha sits high atop an ornate throne of gilded wood in the bot of Wat Phra Keo,

constructed by King Rama I but extensively refurbished and added to by later kings. The carved gable boards of the building show the god Vishnu astride a *garuda* ▲ *74*, while the outer walls are richly decorated with gilded stucco and glass mosaics. Three times a year, at the beginning of each season – cool, hot and rainy – the robes of the image are changed in an elaborate ceremony presided over by the king; countless ordinary Thais also come regularly to make offerings at the temple and pray for various wishes to be granted.

OTHER BUILDINGS. On the side of the bot, also aligned on an east-west axis, are three elaborate buildings set very close to each other: the Prasat Phra Thep Bidom, reconstructed by Rama V, and converted by Rama VI into the royal pantheon; a library in the shape of a square *mondop* ● *47*, a replica of the Temple of the Buddha's Footprint in Saraburi; and a gilded chedi built with a design similar to those of Wat Si Samphet in Ayutthaya, with the explicit intention of recreating the splendor of the ancient capital and the magical powers of its landmark buildings. Khmer-style prang are positioned at every corner of the cloister, a clear political statement by the early Chakri kings repeating the imperialist attitude of the Khmer rulers.

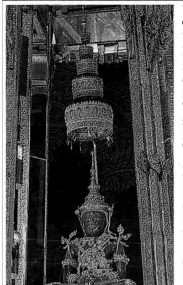

PALLADIA
The Emerald Buddha is the most eminent example of the Palladia, images reputed to be endowed with supernatural powers and considered protectors of a town, a king, or a dynasty.

THE ROYAL PANTHEON
The reconstructed Prasat Phra Thep Bidom contains statues of previous Chakri kings. Usually closed, it is open to the public only on special occasions. According to temple caretakers, the reason for its closure is that the bare-chested images of the first three sovereigns are now deemed an embarrassing sight not quite befitting royalty.

1. BOT
2. PRASAT PHRA THEP BIDOM (ROYAL PANTHEON)
3. LIBRARY
4. CHEDI
5. MONDOP

«THIS SACERDOTAL DISNEYLAND IS ENTERED
THROUGH A GATE SET IN CLOISTERS WHOSE INNER WALLS
CARRY MURALS DEPICTING THE "RAMAKIEN"».

ALISTAIR SHEARER

MYTHOLOGICAL CREATURES
Many of the divinities whose statues adorn the compound of Wat Phra Keo are of Hindu origin, further evidence of the blending of Buddhism with other religions. Some are fabulous animals that inhabited an imagi-nary forest in the Himalayas called the Himavat (the Himaphan in Thai). These include the *tantima* bird, a strange creature with a cock's comb and a parrot-like beak; the more graceful, swan-like *hong,* often at the top of a pole with a bell in its beak; and the elegant bird-humans, the *kinnon* (male) and *kinnari* (female). Also present is the *garuda,* traditional mount of the god Vishnu; Siva's steed, the sacred bull called *nandi;* and *ganesha,* the elephant-headed son of Siva and his consort Parvati.

ARCHITECTURAL DECORATIONS. The various structures at Wat Phra Keo display a virtual textbook of classic Thai decorative techniques and mythological statuary. Entire walls are transformed into shimmering, jewel-like expanses through the use of glass mosaics or carefully fitted pieces of multicolored porcelain; wooden gables and roof supports are richly carved and gilded, and doors and windows are adorned either with intricate mother-of-pearl inlay designs or gold-and-black lacquer paintings. All of them were restored for the 1982 Bangkok bicentennial celebrations, having fallen into a state of disrepair. The multitiered roofs are covered with colored tiles, chedis and stupas with layers of glittering gold leaf, while the interiors of most buildings are decorated with complex mural paintings. The gates leading into the courtyard are flanked by huge statues of *yaksa,* or demons, supposed to ward off evil spirits. They are brightly painted and covered with glass mosaic decorations. Several bronze statues scattered around the buildings represent mythical animals of the Hindu and Buddhist pantheon. Around the basement where the chedi, the *mondop* and the pantheon are built, there are a number of small Chinese gardens embellished by Qing statues of animals and heavenly guards.

MURAL PAINTINGS OF THE "RAMAKIEN". On the walls of the galleries surrounding Wat Phra Keo are a series of panoramic mural paintings that depict the story of the *Ramakien,* the Thai version of the *Ramayana,* an Indian epic dealing with the triumph of good over evil. The tale is told in 178 panels, each occupying the area between two pillars of the many that support the gallery; poems about the action, composed in the reign of King Rama V, are inscribed on marble slabs set into the relevant pillar. Though originally painted by order of King Rama I when the temple was built, the murals have been restored many times, most recently for the 1982 Bangkok bicentennial celebrations. These works are almost identical to the original 1930 compositions executed under the direction of Phra Thewapinimmit, and reflect the style of that era with Western perspective, the use of shadows, and naturalistic rendering of the landscape, and with characters drawn in a conventional Thai manner.

THE "RAMAKIEN"
The *Ramakien,* the Thai version of the *Ramayana,* appears in mural paintings, as in the galleries of Wat Phra Keo, in bas-relief carvings, like those at Wat Po, and also in illustrated manuscript books. It provides the stories for the *khon* (classical masked dance) ● *34.* Though all the manuscripts recounting the legend from the Ayutthaya period were destroyed when the capital fell to the Burmese in 1767, the story was already an established part of Thai cultural tradition. King Rama I himself rewrote it after the founding of Bangkok, and the second king of the Chakri dynasty also produced a version for the dance.

REPLICA OF ANGKOR WAT
A model of Angkor Wat, the famous center of Khmer culture, was placed in the temple compound by King Rama IV, as a reminder of the time when Cambodia was a vassal state of Thailand. The territory was lost in the late 19th century when the French exerted pressure on King Rama V and redefined the borders of Indo-China.

The oldest and largest temple in Bangkok, Wat Phra Chetuphon, popularly known as Wat Po – derived from its original name of Wat Bodharam – was founded in the 16th century during the Ayutthaya period. It was a particular favorite with the early Chakri kings, most of

whom restored or added buildings to its huge compound. Chetuphon Road, along which King Rama I supposedly rode on his way to Thonburi when he was crowned in 1782, separates the monastic buildings housing some 300 priests from the enclosure containing the structures used for religious ceremonies. In its heyday, this was the home of more than 500 monks and 750 novices, and the monks' quarters are still a veritable city within the city. Most of the buildings were reconstructed during the fifth reign, replacing older wooden houses, and the mansions of the most reverend monks are often embellished with precious gilded stucco.

Wat Po's greatest benefactor was King Rama III (1824–51), who was responsible not only for most of the buildings the visitor sees today but also for turning the temple into a kind of open university, filled with displays of educational material. Twenty small hills scattered around the compound, for example, contain geological specimens from all parts of Thailand; a collection of stone Rishi, or hermits,

STONE BALLASTS
Literally hundreds of Chinese stone figures – animals both realistic and whimsical, humans both small and fearsomely huge – are scattered throughout Wat Po; similar ones can be seen in other major Bangkok palaces and temples. Most came to Thailand in the early 19th century as ballast on ships returning empty from the lucrative rice trade and were placed in the temple during King Rama III's reign, a period that also saw an increase in Chinese influence on architecture and decorative motifs. Prominent among the statues are the towering door guardians, or protective demons, that stand beside each of the sixteen monumental gates leading into the temple and beside those that divide the various compounds. The latter represent Europeans, as shown by their tall, brimmed hats that the sculptors had perhaps observed in Chinese port cities and assumed all foreigners wore.

demonstrates various yoga positions; and inscriptions and mural paintings deal with such diverse subjects as warfare, medicine, astrology, botany and history. Anyone who was interested in either religious or secular knowledge could study the wealth of information compiled from ancient textbooks and presented to the public in this most democratic way. It was an unprecedented move in a society where knowledge had always been the privilege of the few. King Rama I, who was the founder of Bangkok and the first restorer of Wat Po, is credited with salvaging 1,200 statues from the ruins of Ayutthaya. The collection contains 689 of the rescued statues. Many others were added to it by later kings. The temple is a veritable gallery of Thai art, practically covering every historical period. Most of the images are displayed along the cloisters and serve to top the chedis containing ashes of the illustrious deceased. In an attempt to preserve these rows of statues, renovation work has since been carried out, and they are now encased in glass.

SCHOOL FOR TRADITIONAL MEDICINE. One aspect of Wat Po's old educational function that remains very much alive today is the School for Traditional Medicine, in the eastern part of the temple compound. Besides offering courses of instruction in herbal medicines and Thai-style massage, authorized members of the profession offer treatment to the public in the late afternoons; marble engravings on the walls, placed there in the reign of King Rama III, give various rules regarding the subject. Foreigners can take a fifteen-day course in traditional massage, with classes held for two hours daily, while skilled masseurs are usually available from 200 baht per hour.

Within the monks' quarters on the other side of Chetuphon Road, expert masseurs attend to local patients using ancient techniques under the watchful eyes of monks who sanction the operation by spitting holy water on the ailing part, while assistants beat furiously on the drums.

TEMPLE ASTROLOGERS. This temple, very popular with local and foreign visitors, also attracts a large number of street vendors, snake charmers, astrologers, palmists and other entertainers to its premises. It is well known for its colony of resident astrologers.

RISHI FIGURES
The stone Rishi, or hermits, in the outer courtyard of Wat Po, were formerly located in a series of sixteen pavilions and moved to their present site during the reign of King Rama V. They demonstrate yoga positions to relieve physical and mental complaints and promote meditative contemplation, a reminder of the time when the temple was a leading center of public education.

TREATISE ON MASSAGE
Small buildings around the cloister that encircles the chedis of the Four Kings display a series of murals, showing the techniques of Thai massage. The subject is further illustrated by statues of hermits in various yoga stances and self-massage techniques.

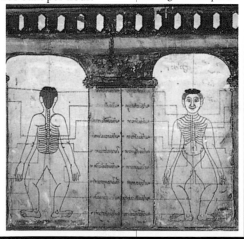

«OH! WAT PO IS THE MONASTERY BUILT BY A KING; IT IS NEVER NEGLECTED AND IT IS RESPLENDENT LIKE HEAVEN...»

SUNTHORN PHU

THE BOT. Founded in 1835 on the ruins of an older edifice, the huge bot is encircled by a cloister and is possibly the finest in the city, with four viharns (one at each of the cardinal points). The presiding image was moved here from Ayutthaya and placed on a high pedestal in a most dramatic fashion. The murals depicting the life of forty-one disciples of the Buddha and scenes inspired by Buddhist cosmologists are still relatively well preserved, while those of the viharns have completely vanished. Of particular interest are the main doors of the bot, which boast mother-of-pearl decorations depicting scenes from the *Ramakien.*

THE RECLINING BUDDHA. The huge Reclining Buddha of Wat Po (above), measuring 150 feet long and 50 feet high, and covered with layers of gold leaf, represents the dying Buddha at the moment he entered Nirvana. Its most impressive artistic feature is the inlaid mother-of-pearl designs that adorn the soles of its feet, depicting the legendary signs by which the true Buddha can be recognized. Only the upper parts remain of the once superb mural paintings that adorned the interior walls of the building housing the image, constructed during the reign of King Rama III.

CHEDIS OF THE FOUR KINGS. Not far from the bot, in a low-walled enclosure, stand four tall chedis, or stupas, decorated with porcelain and dedicated to the first four Chakri kings: the green one, containing a standing Buddha from Ayutthaya, to Rama I; the white one to Rama II; the yellow one to Rama III; and the blue one to Rama IV.

THE LIBRARY. Founded by Rama I but restored in the third reign, the library is one of the most graceful edifices in Bangkok. The central chamber is topped by an elaborate crown-like cupola and spire; four extended porticoes create a Greek-cross plan. The building is decorated with glazed tiles and polychrome ceramic pieces. John Crawfurd, who led a British embassy to the court of King Rama II in 1822, noted the gardens surrounding the building, one of which had a pond with crocodiles. Today, the library is set in an elegant Chinese-style garden.

THE BODHI TREE. Next to the library stands an ancient Bodhi tree, whose imposing presence is enhanced by two Chinese pavilions, where a statue of Guan Yin (also known as the Goddess of Mercy), is the object of devotion. The area is called the "Garden of the Transplanted Tree," referring to the tree that grew from a cutting of the Bodhi tree in Anuradhapura, Sri Lanka.

"RAMAKIEN" PANELS Around the base of the bot are a series of 152 marble panels engraved with scenes from the *Ramakien,* the Thai version of the *Ramayana.* The panels show one of the main episodes, the abduction of Sida and her eventual recovery after several battles. The incompleteness of the episode and its abrupt ending suggest that they may have been salvaged from other temples – perhaps in Ayutthaya – and subsequently moved to Bangkok. There is, however, no record of their origin. The marble panels were once used to make stone rubbings for sale to tourists; similar rubbings are now made from copies of the carvings ▲ 151.

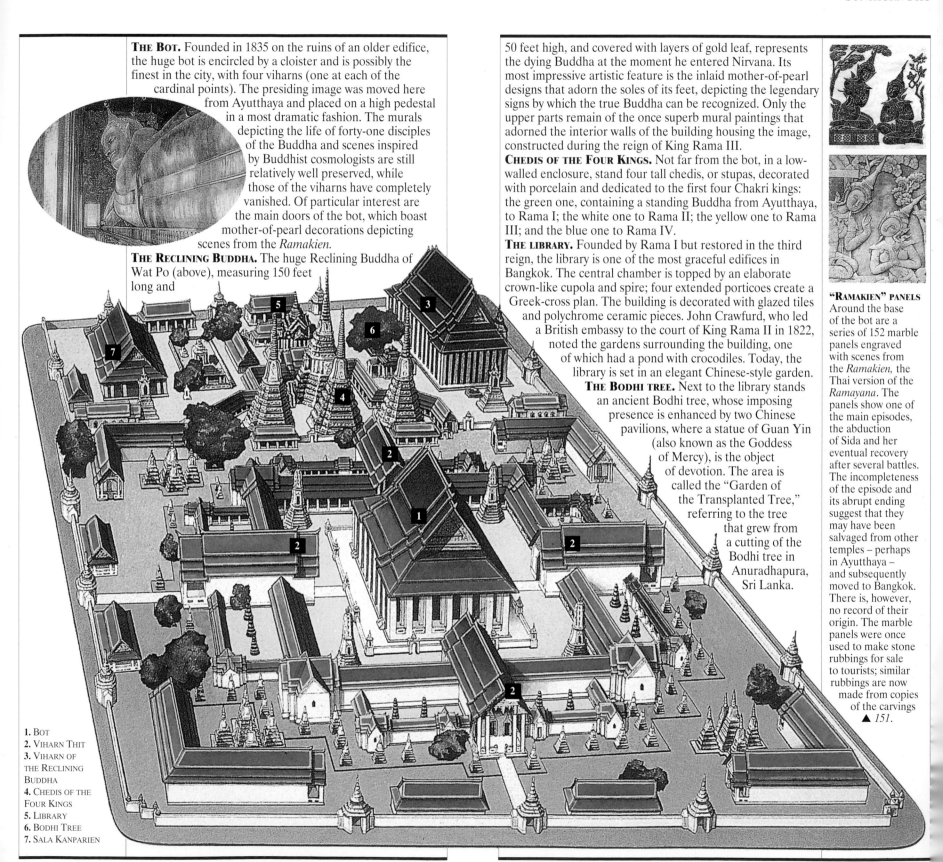

1. BOT
2. VIHARN THIT
3. VIHARN OF THE RECLINING BUDDHA
4. CHEDIS OF THE FOUR KINGS
5. LIBRARY
6. BODHI TREE
7. SALA KANPARIEN

A watercolor sketch of Sanam Luang at the turn of the century, when rickshaws were still in existence. A few pedal pedal rickshaws were recently reintroduced for tourists.

SANAM LUANG

"...The Siamese attach great importance to seals, which take the place of signatures in Western civilization. These seals are mostly made of ivory, in the shape of a *phrachedee*, the devices representing a *Hoalaman* or a *Ruchasee*, an angel or a lotus-flower… no sealing wax is used with these seals, but always a vermillion-red dye."

Carl Bock

The large oval field across from the Grand Palace is popularly known as Sanam Luang, "the Royal Field." More formally, it is called the Pramane Ground, the place where royal cremations are held, the last having been that of the mother of King Rama IX, in 1996. The Plowing

Ceremony to forecast the coming agricultural crop is held here in May, while on the King's Birthday and at New Year Sanam Luang becomes a giant festival, with staged entertainments. On the eastern side are ministries and the city pillar Lak Muang, while on the west are Silpakorn University, Wat Mahathat, Thammasat University and the National Museum. Facing Sanam Luang across a road from the northern side stands the National Gallery ▲ 84.

THE SECOND KING
The office of the Second King, who served as vice-ruler, was a peculiarly Thai institution that began in the Ayutthaya period. The position was abolished in the reign of King Rama V, when the heir apparent became known as the Crown Prince.

NATIONAL MUSEUM

Bangkok's National Museum – which has over thirty branches throughout the country – is housed partly in the palace of the Second King, a sort of vice-ruler, built during the reign of King Rama I. The collection was moved there from the Grand Palace by King Rama V in 1887, and under King Rama VII (1925–34) it was expanded and placed under the Royal Institute of Literature, Archeology and Fine Arts,

later the Fine Arts Department. Two modern buildings were constructed on either side of the old palace in 1967, while a new gallery on Thai history was opened during Bangkok's bicentennial celebrations (1982).

BUDDHAISAWAN CHAPEL. The Buddhaisawan Chapel was built in 1787 to enshrine an important northern Buddha image called the Phra Buddha Si Hing, and is now within the grounds of the museum. The interior walls are painted with exceptionally fine murals showing scenes from the life of the Buddha, while the building itself is an outstanding example of early Bangkok religious architecture.

TAMNAK DAENG. Tamnak Daeng, or "Red House," was the residence of an elder sister of King Rama I. It was moved from Thonburi by King Rama II to the Grand Palace compound and later, in the fourth reign, to its present location in the museum grounds. Furniture and other items of the early Bangkok period are displayed inside ● 45.

THE MUSEUM COLLECTION. The National Museum's collection covers the whole range of art found in the country, religious and secular, fine and decorative, Thai and otherwise. The Prehistoric Gallery, for instance,

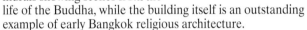

includes Neolithic tools and pottery dating as far back as 10,000 BC, in addition to painted pots and bronze objects unearthed at excavations in the northeast. Numerous creations of the pre-Thai Srivijaya, Dvaravati and Khmer kingdoms are also displayed, as well as those of the early Thai settlements of the far north. Thai Buddhist art encompasses images in stone, bronze and terracotta from the Sukhothai, Ayutthaya and Rattanakosin (Bangkok) periods, together with such religious items as illustrated scripture books, manuscript cabinets and votive plaques. Open daily except Mondays and Tuesdays, the museum also contains a large selection of miscellaneous arts, among them Thai and Chinese ceramics, theatrical costumes, textiles, furniture, funeral chariots, palanquins, elephant howdahs, weapons, puppets and assorted objects used in royal households. Guided tours in English are offered on certain days of the week by the National Museum Volunteer Group.

PRIZED AMULETS
Amulets, usually in the form of a clay votive plaque bearing the image of the Buddha or of a particularly revered monk, are highly prized by most Thais. Mounted in gold or silver, they are worn on chains around the neck to avert misfortune. Many are sold on the sidewalks near Sanam Luang, particularly around Wat Mahathat.

The earliest reminder of Buddha's teachings was a mound of earth, which eventually evolved into the stupa. Later, feeling the need for a more concrete symbol, adherents to the faith began to make images. Various schools of thought arose concerning the exact features and *mudra*, or gestures, of such images, eventually resulting in a wide range of choices as revealed in the different periods of Thai art. This evolution of the image of Buddha can be seen in those displayed in the National Museum.

CASTING BUDDHA IMAGES

Bronze Buddha images are cast by the "lost wax" process, which involves a clay core in the rough form desired, a covering of wax carved into the shape of the image, and an outer mold of clay. The wax is then melted and drained off and molten bronze poured in to replace it. Casting often takes place in a temple compound, accompanied by a variety of ceremonies. The mural shown on the right, in Wat Bowornivet ▲ *85*, Bangkok, depicts the castings of three famous images, namely the Phra Buddha Chinaraj, Phitsanulok, and two large images now in Wat Bowornivet. The event took place in the late Sukhothai period.

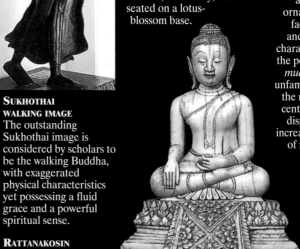

DVARAVATI

Dvaravati images (7th–11th century), mostly in stone, stucco, or terracotta, are heavy-featured and realistic in appearance, with prominent curls.

LOPBURI

Strongly influenced by Khmer images, those of Lopburi (7th–14th century) have stylized faces with broad mouths that seem to be faintly smiling; later ones are often in royal attire.

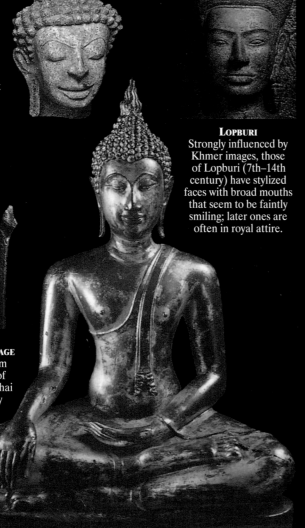

SUKHOTHAI SEATED IMAGE

Bronze was the medium preferred by sculptors of 13th–15th-century Sukhothai and the one in which they produced their greatest work. Most images are seated with the hand in the gesture called *bhumisparsa mudra*, or "touching the earth."

SUKHOTHAI WALKING IMAGE

The outstanding Sukhothai image is considered by scholars to be the walking Buddha, with exaggerated physical characteristics yet possessing a fluid grace and a powerful spiritual sense.

RATTANAKOSIN

A beautiful ivory image of Buddha, late 19th century.

AYUTTHAYA

Ayutthaya images (14th–18th century) display a variety of styles; the most characteristic is richly attired and adorned, reflecting the Ayutthaya association of kingship and religion.

LANNA

The typical northern 13th–20th-century Lanna image has a round face, large curls, a prominent chin, and a thick, solid body; it is often seated on a lotus-blossom base.

RATTANAKOSIN

Rattanakosin or 18th–20th-century Bangkok images are frequently standing and heavily ornamented, the faces narrow and somewhat characterless, and the postures and *mudra* often unfamiliar; after the mid-19th century they display an increased sense of realism.

Thepanom Sukhothai glazed stone figure, 14th–15th century.

The stone Bodhisattva Avalokitesvara (left) stands just over 3 feet tall and exhibits Indian influence, which was very important throughout the early to middle centuries of the first millennium. This statue, originally from Chaiya ● *50* ▲ *98*, dates from the 6th–7th century.

A fine example of Sukhothai ceramics, this glazed stoneware figure of a horseman dates from the 14th–15th century.

A pair Sukhothai-period praying deities in terracotta.

The stone Vishnu from Takua Pa (left), 7 feet tall, dates from the 8th–9th century and is among the large display of early Hindu statues that make up one of the most interesting sections of the museum's collection.

There are many bronzes of Hindu gods dating from the Sukhothai period. These were once worshiped at the Brahmin temple of Bangkok, having been moved there from the ruins of Sukhothai by King Rama I. Depicted here (left) is a 10-foot-tall image of Shiva.

The Buddhaisawan Chapel, within the grounds of the National Museum, contains some of the best mural paintings of the Bangkok School, executed during the reign of Rama I. On the right is a detail from a mural showing the descent of Buddha from heaven on a ladder made of *naga* and jewels. On his left is a golden ladder for Indra and on his right a silver ladder for Brahma. These two gods accompanied him back to earth after he preached to his mother and the gods for three months. A gold-lacquered screen from the early 19th century displays a scene from the *Ramakien* (left) ▲ *77*.

The Lanna bronze elephant (right) dates from AD 1575 and was originally used as a support for presenting offerings. The duck-shaped water vessel (below) dates from the 14th–15th century.

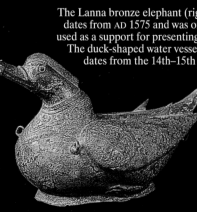

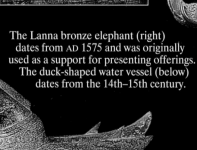

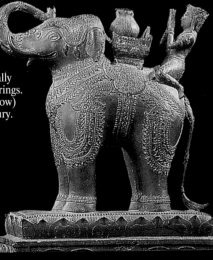

The art of the early Mon kingdom of Dvaravati can be seen in the large collection of terracottas and stuccos ▲ *96*. Above is a stucco *yaksa* dating from the 9th century and found in Nakhon Pathom. The head (right), dating from slightly earlier, was found at Ku Bua.

«ENTERTAIN NOT THY THOUGHTS WITH WORLDLY THINGS.
DO NO WORK BUT THE WORK OF CHARITY AND TRUTH.»

BUDDHIST PRECEPTS

RATTANAKOSIN ISLAND PLAN
A long-term blueprint intends to "restore" Rattanakosin Island to a state that never existed, with modern buildings since the reign of Rama V to be demolished and broad open vistas opened up, especially along the river. Though offering more grandeur, the plan faces strong opposition since it would destroy the charming communities of Phra Chan, Phra Arthit, Pak Klong Talaad and Tha Tien, which are as old as Bangkok and provide a living link to the past. The old shops, markets, apothecaries and other local trades are themselves a popular tourist sight. The plan would also bulldoze the National Theater so a lesser known temple could be seen from Sanam Luang.

A VENERATED PIG
Overlooking Klong Lord near Saranrom Palace is a large statue of a pig, covered with layers of gold leaf offered by supplicants. This was erected in honor of Queen Sowabha Phongsri, the principal Queen of King Rama V, who was born in the year of that animal. It has become an important shrine for people of the area, who believe it has the power to grant various wishes.

OTHER SIGHTS IN SANAM LUANG

WAT MAHATHAT. This temple dates from before the founding of Bangkok, but was extensively restored during the reign of King Rama I and became one of the city's most important monasteries. The future King Rama IV served as one of its abbots. Today, Wat Mahathat (above) houses a college for Buddhist priests and offers meditation classes for foreigners. On weekends, the temple is usually filled with peddlers who display and sell amulets to visitors.

"LAK MUANG." Standing outside the walls of Wat Phra Keo, the *lak muang* (the city's foundation stone pillar) is in the form of a *lingam* that serves as the abode of Bangkok's guardian spirit and as the spot from which distances in the city are measured. First erected by King Rama I in 1782, it is now sheltered by an ornate pavilion (below right) and was joined with the *lak muang* of Thonburi after the cities merged. Large numbers of supplicants come here to ask for almost anything, from matrimonial harmony to a winning ticket in the national lottery. In addition to making offerings of flowers and incense, many also pay for dancers to perform a propitiatory kind of *likay* ▲ 35.

SILPAKORN UNIVERSITY. Silpakorn

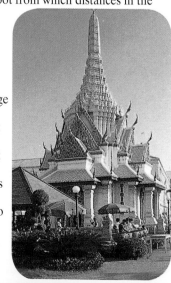

(Fine Arts) University is housed partly in an old palace of the first reign. It owes its existence largely to Corrado Feroci, an Italian sculptor. Feroci began working for the Thai government in 1924, founded the School of Fine Arts in 1933, and lived in the country under the Thai name of Silpa Bhirasri until his death in 1962. The building fronting Sanam Luang is decorated with a frieze in Art Nouveau style painted by Italian artists.

NATIONAL THEATER. Erected in the early 1970's, this huge edifice became the hub of cultural and musical activities: dance troupes and foreign orchestras once performed here. Today only a few classical drama performances and official foreign shows get staged here, and the building may be demolished to allow a view of a temple that was formerly part of the palace of the Second King. The Thai classical dance school that was once located here has recently moved out.

WAT RAJAPRADIT ★

A small, serene temple built during King Rama IV's reign, Wat Rajapradit (above right) is located in a compound adjacent to the garden of the former Saranrom Palace, where King Rama IV often said he wished to retire. The main building is sheathed in gray marble from China and raised on a high stone platform, while on both sides of the building are Khmer-style prangs; on the terrace behind the temple is a stupa also covered with gray marble. The doors are adorned with gold-and-black lacquer paintings and the gables and eaves are decorated with fine carvings. Wat Rajapradit has a restful atmosphere not very often found in larger temple compounds, but as the doors are often locked, tourists may only visit the temple on the 1st and the 15th of each lunar month, when the local folk come to pray and present alms to the monks.

Wat Rajapradit.

MURALS OF 1864
The bot of Wat Rajapradit is decorated with an unusual set of murals painted in 1864, during the reign of King Rama IV. These depict various royal ceremonies held during the twelve months of the year and constitute a rare historical record of early Bangkok since many of those ceremonies are no longer performed ▲ 72.

BANGLAMPHU

This triangular neighbourhood north of Sanam Luang – bordered by Rajadamnoen Klang Avenue, Klong Banglamphu and the river – was historically associated with artists who performed in the royal palaces. Today, it remains a hub of cultural activity, with a vibrant streetlife thanks to Banglamphu Market and Khao San Road, Bangkok's district for foreign backpackers. The road and adjacent alleys are lined with travel agencies, bookshops, silver shops, souvenir stalls, bars, restaurants and guesthouses made famous by the book and film "The Beach". Now a destination in its own right for curious Thais, who come here for the nightlife, Khao San Road is going upmarket. The first permanently pedestrianized road in Thailand, it now includes boutique hotels and stages official events at festivals like Songkran.

NATIONAL GALLERY. This Italianate classical building facing Sanam Luang which once housed the Royal Mint now acts as a repository of Thai art. The small permanent collection includes works by major modern Thai artists, though it has not kept pace with the boom in contemporary Thai art that has drawn international acclaim since the 1990's. Museums proposed at the Thailand Cultural Center on Rajadaphisek Road, and possibly at a downtown site beside Siam Discovery Center, would showcase today's artistic trends. The National Gallery does, however, host major exhibitions of Thai and international art.

National Gallery.

RIVERSIDE WALKWAY AND TOURIST BUREAU. On the riverbank under Phra Pinklao Bridge stands the Bangkok Tourist Bureau Headquarters, from which one can catch several guided walking or bicycle tours. A river promenade built on pilings in the Chao Phraya river heads north past several fine mansions now put to diplomatic or cultural use and ends at Santichaiprakarn Park.

PHRA ARTHIT ROAD AND SANTICHAIPRAKARN PARK. This picturesque riverside road is a major hub of contemporary Thai arts. Several of its small restaurant-bars and bookshops hold exhibitions, performances and other events, often in conjunction with the arts festivals held frequently in Santichaiprakarn Park, such as the Bangkok Theater Festival in November. This green space on the river bank contains a Thai-style pavilion, a performance area and Phra Sumen Fort.

Riverside walkway at Santichaiprakarn Park.

WAT BOWORNIVET. Built by King Rama III for his brother, who spent the better part of his life as a monk before ascending the throne as King Rama IV, this monastery is renowned for the murals of the *ubosot*, painted for the first time in Thai history in Western perspective by the monk artist Khrua In Khong ● 55. The temple houses three important large Sukhothai images ▲ 82 and a Buddha from Borobodur donated by the Dutch government to King Rama V. It is the residence of the Supreme Patriarch of Thai Buddhism.

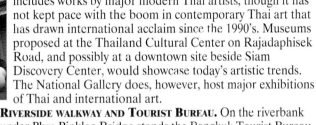

RAJADAMNOEN ROAD

Rajadamnoen (Royal Progress) Road was created by King Rama V to be a processional avenue from the Grand Palace to his new palace complex in Dusit. Its central stretch, Rajadamnoen Klang Road, is lined with buildings in the grand, streamlined style of the 1940's and served as Saigon in the film "Good Morning Vietnam". Decorated with lights and ornamental displays during royal birthdays and important national celebrations, it holds several monuments related to Thai democracy and offers fine vistas of both Wat Rajanadda and the Golden Mount of Wat Saket. New plans intend to turn Rajadamnoen Klang road into a Thai "Champs Elysées", lined with upmarket shops and offices.

October 14th Monument.

DEMOCRACY MONUMENT. Commemorating Thailand's transition in 1932 from an absolute to a constitutional monarchy, the Democracy Monument is a vast sculpture by the Italian artist Corrado Feroci. It depicts an ornamental tray holding the Constitution, surrounded by four wings stretching upward, all set dramatically on a traffic island in the avenue. This was the focus of huge anti-dictatorship demonstrations in 1973, 1976 and 1992. These all ended in bloodshed and a memorial to the victims of the October 14th, 1973, incident now stands nearby at the junction with Tanao Road on the south side of Rajadamnoen Klang Road. Images from the democratic struggles, and occasionally staged performances, ring its central spire.

KING PRAJADIPHOK MUSEUM. This turreted building at Phan Fah Bridge, where Rajadamnoen Road turns north towards Dusit, now houses a newly opened museum dedicated to King Rama VII, also known as King Prajadiphok. As well as focusing on his life and reign it explains the circumstances surrounding the King's efforts to cultivate democracy, his transformation into Thailand's first constitutional monarch, and his later abdication.

THE QUEEN'S GALLERY. Facing King Prajadiphok Museum across Phan Fah Bridge at the bend in Rajadamnoen Road, this building owned by Bangkok Bank was converted into Bangkok's first gallery of modern art. Opened in honor of Queen Sirikit's sixth cycle birthday anniversary, it hosts major exhibitions from home and abroad, including work by royal family members. Changing displays also draw from a permanent collection of pieces by distinguished National Artists and from the Bangkok Bank's annual art competition, which has launched the careers of many prominent contemporary painters.

Phra Sumen Fort.

A RESTING PLACE
Wat Saket appears in most 19th-century accounts of Bangkok not only because of its Golden Mount but also because it was a resting place for the dead during cholera epidemics. Too numerous for conventional cremation, the bodies were laid out at the temple for vultures to devour. Anna Leonowens, the Englishwoman who was hired by King Rama IV to teach some of his wives and children, wrote: "None but the initiated will approach these grounds after sunset, so universal and profound is the horror the place inspires – a place the most frightful and offensive known to mortal eyes." Paupers and unidentified dead bodies were also brought to Wat Saket for more conventional cremation.

WAT SAKET AND THE GOLDEN MOUNT

"Just outside the city wall is the Golden Mount, a bell-shaped mound faced with brick, but so overgrown by trees that it has the appearance of a natural hillock…From here we look down upon a forest of palms and plane-trees, through which break the red roofs of the houses. Everywhere rising above the trees are graceful spires and the manifold roofs of temples, with their tiles of rich orange or deep purple, great splashes of color against the clear blue sky…" That was a description by P.A. Thomson in 1910 of the view from the Golden Mount. Today a visitor to the mount enjoys a different view. Phu Khao Thong, the Golden Mount, is an artificial hill topped by a large gilded stupa that has long been the highest

elevation in Bangkok and one of the city's most celebrated landmarks. The stupa is 260 feet from its base to the tip of its spire. A replica of a similar hill in Ayutthaya, this was a feat of 19th-century engineering, begun by King Rama V but not completed until the following reign. The stupa, reached by a flight of 300 steps, contains relics of the Buddha presented to King Rama V by Lord Curzon, Viceroy of India, in 1897. The Golden Mount lies within the compound of Wat Saket. Built by King Rama I, Wat Saket is one of the oldest temples in Bangkok, though it has often been restored and few of the original murals and other decorations remain. One of its sanctuaries has a large standing Buddha image brought from Sukhothai by the first Chakri king. The temple contains a pavilion that was once a temple library and that was moved to its present location from Ayutthaya. It dates from the late 17th century and features gilded panels with Chinese-style motifs and classic lacquered windows. Some of the windows were exhibited in Paris on the occasion of the third centenary of Thai-French diplomatic relations.

The window panels of the library of Wat Saket portray a series of foreigners – merchants, traders and ambassadors – who used to frequent cosmopolitan Ayutthaya in its heyday.

CITY WALLS

Like Ayutthaya, Rattanakosin island was once surrounded by a high wall. Most of the wall has been pulled down, though stretches remain near the two remaining forts and facing Wat Boworniwet. Phra Sumen Fort has been restored as part of Santichaiprakarn Park. A park is planned for Mahakan Fort.

The city walls fronting Wat Saket at the turn of the century.

MONK'S BOWL VILLAGE

Just south of the Golden Mount is Bangkok's last remaining 'village' of metalworkers devoted to making black lacquered bowls of steel and copper with which monks beg for alms. It may be possible to see this handicraft on Soi Baan Baat, off Boriphat Road south of Bamrung Meuang Road. These rare, expensive items are now mostly bought as ornaments.

The Lohaprasad in the compound of Wat Rajanadda.

WAT RAJANADDA

With the removal of a movie theater that long concealed it, the architectural beauties of Wat Rajanadda are now visible to passers-by. Its most interesting feature is the Lohaprasad, started by King Rama III but only completed a decade ago by the Fine Arts Department. It has six levels, each housing small ornamental pavilions, is 110 feet high and overlooks Rajadamnoen Klang Avenue. A new pavilion outside the temple serves as a reception area for important foreign visitors to Bangkok. The temple also holds a major amulet market.

This road, which leads to the square with the Giant Swing, is almost entirely devoted to shops selling various Buddhist items – images of all sizes, mostly bronze, as well as robes, fans and alms bowls for monks, carved altar tables, little gilded Bodhi trees, ceremonial umbrellas, candles and incense sticks and countless other items used in temple adornment. These are presented by laymen to the temples on a variety of religious occasions.

WAT SUTHAT

Wat Suthat is one of the most important temples in Bangkok. Work on the temple started during the reign of King Rama I, was continued by his successor, and finally completed under King Rama III. The temple's principal attractions are two unusually large buildings, the bot and the viharn, both of which exhibit outstanding classic Thai religious art and architecture.

THE VIHARN ● 46. Noted for its graceful proportions, the viharn is raised on two platforms and surrounded by a cloister; at the corners of the platform are pavilions enshrining Buddha images in various positions. The gables are richly adorned with mythological animals and religious symbols, and the huge doors, carved in three layers, are attributed to King Rama II, who was noted for his artistry. The interior walls and the two rows of supporting columns are covered with fine mural paintings of the early Bangkok period. The principal Buddha image, Phra Buddha Chakyamuni, was moved to Bangkok from Wat Mahathat in Sukhothai and dates from the 14th century. It was cast together with another much revered image called the Prabu Chinaraj, which is now housed in Phitsanulok.

THE BOT ● 46. Constructed between 1839 and 1843 by King Rama III, the bot contains an image known as Phra Trai Lok Chet, in front of which is a group of disciple figures. Well-preserved murals also cover the interior walls of this structure. The door of the low brick wall that surrounds the bot are guarded by statues imported from China, all representing Western sailors and soldiers and reflecting the low opinion both the Thai and the Chinese had of Westerners in those days. The statues of the Westerners, they were fully convinced, were monstrous enough to ward off the evil spirits lurking outside their houses.

BRAHMIN TEMPLE. Overlooking the square containing the Giant Swing is the Brahmin temple called Devastan. While of little interest architecturally, it is a reminder of the powerful influence white-robed Brahmin priests once exerted in Thailand, particularly in the royal court. Even today Brahminic rituals play a vital part in many ceremonies.

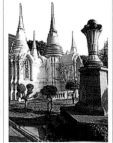

Sao Chin Cha, the Giant Swing.

THE GIANT SWING. Across Wat Suthat is the Giant Swing, or Sao Chin Cha, once the focus of a colorful Brahmin ceremony honoring the god Siva, when teams of young men swung to great heights in an effort to snatch sacks of money with their teeth, the highest sack being on a 76-foot pole. The ceremonial practice was abolished during the reign of King Rama VII for being too dangerous.

WAT RAJABOPIT

Located on a road of the same name, Wat Rajabopit was built in 1870, shortly after King Rama V ascended to the throne, and displays the eclectic approach to architecture that was characteristic of the fifth reign. Its central feature is a graceful gilded stupa, modeled after the famous one in Nakhon Pathom, with a courtyard surrounded by a circular cloister with marble columns and two-tiered roofs, interrupted by the bot and three viharns; the exterior walls of the bot, the lower part of the stupa, and the cloister are covered with glazed Chinese tiles in a subtle blending of colors, while the doors and windows of the bot are decorated with mother-of-pearl inlays depicting the five royal orders. The interior of the bot has a vaulted roof that suggests a Gothic cathedral, and its color scheme of pale blue and gold also has a European flavor that contrasts with the classic Thai surroundings.

MINI CEMETERY
To the west of Wat Rajabopit is an atmospheric little cemetery crowded with tombs in assorted styles of architecture, including Gothic and Khmer. These mostly enshrine members of King Rama V's extensive family, evidence of the high regard in which he held the temple.

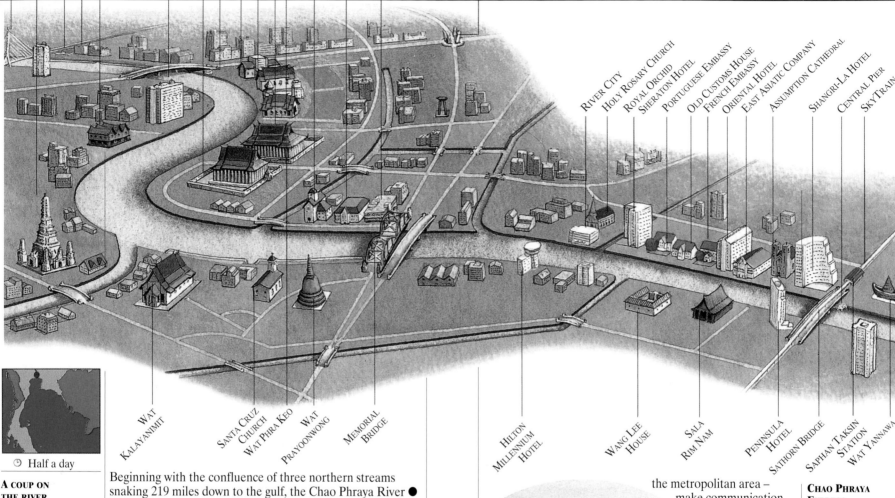

Labels (top, left to right):
RAMA VIII BRIDGE · WAT ARUN · SANTICHAIPRAKARN PARK · PHRA SUMEN FORT · WAT RAKHANG · KOSITHARAM · SIRIRAT HOSPITAL · WAT PO · BANGKOK TOURIST BUREAU · NATIONAL THEATER · NATIONAL MUSEUM · GRAND PALACE · WAT MAHATHAT · CHAKRABONGSE HOUSE · RACHINI SCHOOL · PAK KLONG TALAAD · DEMOCRACY MONUMENT · RIVER CITY · HOLY ROSARY CHURCH · ROYAL ORCHID · SHERATON HOTEL · PORTUGUESE EMBASSY · OLD CUSTOMS HOUSE · FRENCH EMBASSY · ORIENTAL HOTEL · EAST ASIATIC COMPANY · ASSUMPTION CATHEDRAL · SHANGRI-LA HOTEL · CENTRAL PIER · SKYTRAIN

Labels (bottom, left to right):
WAT KALAYANIMIT · SANTA CRUZ CHURCH · WAT PHRA KEO · WAT PRAYOONWONG · MEMORIAL BRIDGE · HILTON MILLENNIUM HOTEL · WANG LEE HOUSE · SALA RIM NAM · PENINSULA HOTEL · SATHORN BRIDGE · SAPHAN TAKSIN STATION · WAT YANNAWA

⏱ Half a day

A COUP ON THE RIVER

In May 1950, elements of the navy staged a coup on a landing near the Grand Palace. The prime minister of the time was taken at gunpoint to a battle-ship anchored in the middle of the river and held hostage overnight. In the morning, planes from the air force bombed and sank the ship. However, the premier was not aboard: his captors had gallantly told him to swim for it when the bombs began to fall. He reached the shore, rallied his forces and within 36 hours was back in full command of the situation.

Beginning with the confluence of three northern streams snaking 219 miles down to the gulf, the Chao Phraya River ● 56 has played a decisive role throughout much of Thailand's history. It waters the broad Central Plains, creating one of the world's most fertile rice-growing areas; at the same time, it provides access to the outside world, making possible the trade that has nurtured three capital cities on its banks – first Ayutthaya, then Thonburi, and last Bangkok – over more than six centuries. The river was the focal point of Bangkok, not only in its early years but also well into the present century. The double and triple rows of floating houses that once lined its banks have vanished, and bridges – seven in the metropolitan area – make communication with Thonburi easier than the old network of canals. Nevertheless, even today, a relatively short cruise along the Chao Phraya reveals a succession of major landmarks, both cultural and commercial: the Grand Palace enclosure and countless important Buddhist temples, the oldest foreign embassies, Catholic churches, the wharfs and godowns of trading companies, wholesale markets for agricultural produce brought to the capital by boat, spacious palaces and houses of old, where the city's élite once resided (and, in some cases, still do). The same trip will also suggest a residential revival along the Chao Phraya in the form of new hotels and towering condominiums rising on both sides amid those nostalgic sights; thanks to the increasingly congested traffic and the difficulty of commuting to distant suburbs, residents are now returning to Bangkok's timeless traditional heart.

CHAO PHRAYA EXPRESS

These ferries operate from 6am to 7pm. It connects to the Sky Train station at Sathorn Bridge.

CROSS-RIVER FERRIES

Operated by the Chao Phraya Express Boat Company, these run between the two riverbanks during the day and until midnight.

This 1920's guidebook to Wat Arun shows that the temple has been a popular tourist attraction for many years.

WAT ARUN

With the possible exception of the Grand Palace, no Chao Phraya attraction is as celebrated as the soaring 343-foot central prang of Wat Arun ● 50, the Temple of Dawn, on the Thonburi bank. Dating from the Ayutthaya period and considerably restored, the temple served as the royal chapel during the Thonburi reign of King Taksin. The Emerald Buddha ▲ 76 was enshrined here before being brought to its present home at Wat Phra Keo. King Rama II of Bangkok first conceived the idea of raising the great

SOMDET YA PARK

A small riverside park dedicated to the late Princess Mother, whose sons became Kings Rama VIII and IX. Named after her formal title, Somdet Phra Srinagarindra Boranarajajonani Memorial Park contains a museum in a house resembling the home where she grew up as commoner goldsmith's daughter. A ceramic frieze celebrates her years in nursing and community projects. The park is just downstream of the Memorial Bridge on the Thonburi bank.

Khmer-style prang, but due to engineering problems, it was not completed until the following reign. This, as well as the four smaller ones that flank it, are adorned with ceramic tiles and fragments of multicolored porcelain, creating a jewel-like effect in the sunlight. A platform halfway up the tower offers a panoramic view of the river and Bangkok. Traditionally, at the end of the rainy season, the king visits Wat Arun and presents robes to the resident monks in a ceremony, a trip that in the past was made from the Grand Palace using a fleet of carved and gilded royal barges ● 29.

OTHER TEMPLES ALONG THE RIVERSIDE

WAT KALAYANIMIT ★. This imposing edifice, standing where Klong Bangkok Yai enters the Chao Phraya, was built during the reign of Rama III. The *ubosot* shelters a huge bronze Buddha image especially popular with Thai Chinese, who honor the image as Sam Poh Kong in memory of the famous Ming eunuch admiral. The temple grounds contain impressive Chinese statues brought as ballast by the rice-trade junks. A stone polygonal chedi was also made in China and assembled behind the *ubosot*. The murals are very well preserved and give a glimpse of life during that period. A small alleyway and new riverside walkway lead to a charming little Chinese temple and Santa Cruz Church ▲ 89.

WAT PRAYOONWONG. Built during King Rama III's reign, Wat Prayoonwong boasts fine lacquered doors decorated with mother-of-pearl. The temple is also known for its artificial hill surrounded by a pond of turtles that are fed by Buddhist visitors to acquire merit.

THE MEMORIAL BRIDGE

Just before the towering spire of Wat Prayoonwong, the Memorial Bridge was the first to link Bangkok with Thonburi. It was opened by King Rama VII at precisely 8.16 in the morning – the auspicious time chosen by royal astrologers – on April 6, 1932, which was also the 150th anniversary of the capital's founding.

WAT RAKHANG KOSITHARAM. Across the river from the Grand Palace, a ferry from Tha Chang Pier leads to this wat built in the reign of King Rama I. "Rakhang" means "bell," and the name is partly derived from the numerous bells rung here in the morning and evening. The main building is a particularly beautiful example of early Rattanakosin architecture ● 48, with fine Ayutthaya-style stucco decorations around the doors and windows, while the *ho trai* ● 46, a library on a raised platform, contains some well-preserved murals depicting the *Ramakien* epic and the Buddhist cosmology. Of special interest are three traditional Thai houses that were occupied by King Rama I before he became the ruler and moved to the temple. The houses, as well as their gold-and-black lacquered windows and ornate entrance-way, were restored for Bangkok's bicentennial in 1982. North of the wat stands Patravadi Theater, the leading space for contemporary dance and drama, and where five traditional works are staged.

HO PHRA TRAI PIDOK

When King Rama I donated his former residence to Wat Rakhang to be converted into a library, the buildings were re-arranged, and murals were added. In the early 1980's, these were restored with the help of a well-known Thai painter, Fua Haripitak.

PAK KLONG TALAAD

Formerly Bangkok's main wholesale market, this sprawling collection of buildings had for over a century served as a central exchange for vegetables, fruit, cut flowers, and other produce brought by boat (right) from the gardens and orchards of Thonburi, as well as others further upriver. Located next to Memorial Bridge and not far from Chinatown, the market features an awe-inspiring variety of flowers, and is a wonderful place to stroll around at night or in the wee hours, when vendors come to buy their flowers for the coming day's sales.

THE WANG LEE HOUSE

In between rows of godowns on the Thonburi bank, this is one of the best preserved of the Chinese-style residences once common in 19th-century Bangkok. Like the others, it was built by a Chinese immigrant who came to profit from the city's growing rice trade and who founded several other still-thriving businesses. Most of these houses have fallen into disrepair, but the Wang Lee family has maintained its ancestral home in good condition.

THE PICKLED MURDERER

An unusual feature of Sirirat Hospital, on the bank of the river next to the Phra Pink Lao Bridge, is the ten museums that it contains. The most famous is the Museum of the Department of Forensic Medicine, where the focus is on crime. The most celebrated exhibit here is the preserved body of Si-Oui, a Chinese immigrant who murdered seven children before he was captured and executed in the 1950's. Si-Oui suffocated his victims, then ate their internal organs in the belief that it would promote longevity – a theory best disproved by his own fate.

«EVERY CURVE OF THE RIVER IS BEAUTIFUL WITH AN UNEXPECTEDNESS OF ITS OWN.»

ANNA LEONOWENS

View of the Chao Phraya at the end of the 19th century

COLONIAL INFLUENCE Overlooking the river, both the French Embassy and the Oriental Hotel date from the second half of the 19th century and originally had the louvered shutters and spacious verandas typical of European buildings of the time. The French Embassy has been slightly remodeled recently.

THE OLD COLONIAL QUARTER

FOREIGN EMBASSIES. All the early foreign embassies – or legations, as they were then called – were located by the river. The earliest was built by the Portuguese, who had also been the first to establish relations with Ayutthaya, and who were granted permission to erect a trading post and consulate in 1820, during the reign of King Rama II; part of the trading office still remains at the back of the property, while the embassy residence, facing the river, was built later. The British came later, on the site now occupied by the General Post Office, followed by the Americans nearby, the French (next to the Oriental Hotel) and others, all with landings from which the diplomats traveled upriver to the Grand Palace on official business. Today, only the Portuguese and French remain at their respective original sites.

ORIENTAL HOTEL. This building started as a small guest house in 1865, calling itself the Oriental and overlooking the river. The guest house burned down that year, and was replaced with a more substantial establishment, which in turn was acquired by H.N. Andersen, founder of the nearby East Asiatic Company, in 1884. Feeling that Bangkok was ready for a really luxurious hotel, he built a new one, designed by an Italian architect, which opened its "forty commodious and well furnished" rooms in 1887. The Oriental quickly established itself as the place to stay in the Thai capital and accommodated countless distinguished visitors, among them royalty, movie stars and traveling writers such as Somerset Maugham and Noël Coward. Today, the only part of the original structure that remains is the Author's Wing, graced by a pediment that displays a golden rising sun facing the river by which most of its early guests arrived.

EAST ASIATIC COMPANY. Now one of the world's largest trading conglomerates, the East Asiatic Company evolved from a firm founded by H.N. Andersen in 1884, in a group of wooden buildings next to the Oriental Hotel. The present building dates from 1901. Andersen later returned to his native Denmark, where he served as the Thai Consul-General until his death in 1938.

OLD CUSTOMS HOUSE. Built in the 1880's, during the reign of King Rama V, this finely proportioned structure served as the main customs house for Bangkok until the development of the port facilities at Klong Toey, down river. The building was taken over by the fire brigade, but will soon be retrofitted and converted to a luxury hotel. Just behind the building, a narrow lane leads to a small Muslim settlement and cemetery.

CATHOLIC CHURCHES Catholic missionaries began work in Thailand during the Ayutthaya period and one of the buildings of the Church of the Immaculate Conception, near the Krung Thon Bridge, dates from this time, when visitors stopped at Bangkok on their way to the capital. Bishop Jean-Baptiste Pallegoix, who taught the future King Rama IV Latin and French, later resided here. Another river landmark is Santa Cruz Church, near the Memorial Bridge, originally built by Portuguese residents after the fall of Ayutthaya and reconstructed by Bishop Pallegoix in 1834; the present cathedral dates from 1913 ▲ 88. Also erected by Portuguese Catholics around the same time was the first Holy Rosary Church (pictured), beside the Royal Orchid Sheraton Hotel. The present building, though, is of later vintage. The imposing Assumption Cathedral, standing by the Oriental Hotel, is one of Bangkok's largest, and was built in 1910 to replace an older church on the site.

WAT YANNAWA

Built in the early 19th century, Wat Yannawa was particularly popular with Chinese residents who began to settle in that part of Bangkok as the city expanded. Though of no great artistic interest, it contains a notable feature – a building designed in the shape of a Chinese junk, complete with huge eyes to ward off evil spirits and surmounted by two chedis. This was added to the compound by order of King Rama III, who had observed the increasing number of steam-powered ships calling at the capital and wanted his subjects to remember the older kind of vessel to which they owed so much of their prosperity.

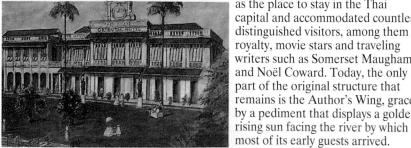

"HUNG HUNTRAA" Robert Hunter, an English businessman, was granted royal permission to build the first Western-style house on the river in the reign of King Rama II. Known as "Hung Huntraa," it continued to be used as a guest house for notable visitors even after Hunter's departure.

SIAMESE TWINS Crossing the Chao Praya in 1824, Hunter noticed a strange creature swimming near his boat. It proved to be the famous Siamese twins, Chang and Eng, who, partly with Hunter's support, went on to become celebrated attractions abroad. They eventually settled in America, where they died in 1874.

THE LONG TAIL

The *hong yao*, or "long-tail," boat (below) is perhaps the most often seen (and heard) conveyance along the Thonburi klongs. Reportedly developed in Thailand, it has a propeller on a long pole that can be raised to navigate shallow waterways.

Another, 149 feet long, is adorned with a many-headed *naga*, or sacred serpent, while other figureheads include horned dragons, *garuda*, and characters from the *Ramakien*. Royal barge processions today are rare, being held on occasions like Bangkok's Bicentennial in 1982, the King's 60th and 72nd birthdays and the King's Golden Jubilee in 1996.

KLONG VENDOR

Selling by water is still as much a part of klong life as it was in the distant past. Vendors in small boats offer almost everything needed by waterside residents. Ernest Young in his book *The Kingdom of the Yellow Robe* observed, "There is a water market, but unlike the land market which remains open all day, this one opens and closes before the sun has risen very high. Scores of boats are massed together in one compact crowd. Each boat is sunk to the gunwale with piles of fruit or fish. The occupants barter and bargain with the same incessant deafening noise of shouting, laughing, and swearing that is characteristic of all markets the world over. The women wear flat-topped hats made of leaves, which slope outwards from the crown, and are stuck on their heads by a circular framework of cane placed inside."

Most of the once numerous klongs, or canals, of Bangkok have vanished, filled in to widen narrow roads or to create new ones. In Thonburi, however, development has come more slowly, due largely to the lack of bridges across the Chao Phraya until fairly recently, and the klongs retain much of their old atmosphere.

ROYAL BARGE MUSEUM

The Royal Barge Museum, on Klong Bangkok Noi near the point where it enters the river, displays but a few of the spectacular craft that were once used for royal processions along the Chao Phraya. Such processions began in Ayutthaya when, according to one foreign observer, as many as 200 barges were involved, propelled by chanting, uniformed oarsmen "all rowing in synchronized movement and rhythm." The most impressive of the contemporary barges is the gilded Suphanahongsa ● 29 in which the king rides, over 150 feet long and requiring a crew of sixty-four, with a prow in the shape of a mythical, swan-like bird.

LIFE ALONG THE KLONG ★

"To unaccustomed eyes it is surprising to see a decent old woman with a mop of grey hair deftly maneuvering her canoe amid the traffic as she goes methodically about her day's shopping…On houseboats, people lounge about idly; men mostly half-naked wash themselves or their children, and here and there half-a-dozen urchins scramble about in the water." This description, written by Somerset Maugham in 1923, is still remarkably close to what one sees today on a cruise through the Thonburi klongs. Weathered old wooden houses, some in the steep-roofed traditional style, still crowd the banks; families still bathe from their doorsteps in the late afternoon, the women preserving their modesty with a sarong; and vendors in straw hats still paddle small craft laden with various goods. Thonburi has long been famous for its mangoes and durians, and, while some of the orchards have been turned into building sites, many remain along the waterways. Among the most popular klongs are Bangkok Yai and Bangkok Noi, though smaller ones lead off in all directions and offer glimpses of a fast-disappearing way of life.

WAT SUWANNARAM ★

On the southern bank of Klong Bangkok Noi not far from where it joins the river, this well-proportioned temple was built on the foundations of an Ayutthaya-period temple by King Rama I and renovated by King Rama III. In addition to being a good example of transitional architecture of the Ayutthaya and Rattanakosin periods, it is noted for the beautiful mural paintings in its sanctuary; these works of art are attributed to Luang Vichit Chetsada and Krua Khonpae, two prominent painters of the third reign, and have been restored using modern techniques. On the south wall, behind the principal Buddha image, are scenes from the three worlds of Buddhist cosmology. The entrance wall is covered with a huge mural depicting the victory of Buddha over Mara while the side walls are decorated with rows of praying figures facing the altar and scenes of the last ten Jataka tales of the Buddha's previous lives.

❝The procession of the royal barges, borne along the bosom of the great mother Menam, with all the accessories of splendour that Bangkok could produce, afforded a sight the beauty of which is hardly to be equalled in any part of the gorgeous East.❞
Carl Bock

«HALF OF THE POPULATION OF THE MENAM DELTA IS CHINESE AND VERY FEW PEOPLE ARE WITHOUT SOME TRACE OF THE CHINESE BLOOD IN THEM.»

HOLT S. HALLETT, 1890

"The Chinese here are a model of peaceful intrusion. The several thousands who immigrated into Siam have monopolised trade. Whatever is related to labour in the kingdom is stimulated, organised and soon thriving in their hands. While the Siamese represents sheer idleness, his bustling sycophant counterpart from the Celestial empire is a paragon of greediness and painstaking toil."
The Marquis de Beauvoir

LION CARICATURE
The painting above reflects the traditional lion dance, regarded as an essential part of the ceremonies that accompany the official opening of many buildings and also suggesting the importance of Chinese customs in Thai life.

Occupying the site selected by King Rama I for his royal palace in 1782 was a community of Chinese traders. They moved to a new location, just outside the city walls, where they created a teeming district that became Bangkok's Chinatown, long the center of commercial life in the capital.

SAMPHENG LANE

Beginning at Wat Pathum Khongka – an old temple also known as Wat Sampheng, built a century before Bangkok became the capital – and running for seven blocks parallel to Yaowarat Road, Sampheng Lane is a noisy covered alleyway lined with shops selling goods of all kinds: wedding mementoes, buttons, imported textiles, kitchenware, gold chains, beads, toys and clothing, to mention only a few. The road eventually emerges at Pahurat, just across from Klong Ong Ang, a market famous for its numerous shops and stalls selling textiles at prices substantially lower than anywhere else in the city.

YAOWARAT ROAD

Yaowarat ▲ 73 is the main street of Chinatown. The thoroughfare is congested and the air heavily polluted but it is nevertheless full of life and fascinating discoveries, especially down the narrow lanes leading off each side. It once boasted a large number of opium dens, gambling houses, burlesque shows, and brothels (proclaimed by green lanterns hanging outside); these have mostly disappeared, at least on the surface, but the area still retains a raffish, faintly mysterious ambience at night.

Paul Morand, writing at the turn of the century, captured the atmosphere of the area in *Rien que la Terre*: "With the noise of the street, the fanfare of gramophones, the clattering of mahjong, like hail on a tin roof, one is reminded of China, but it is the pawnshops which give the impression reality. Gamblers come to pawn their jewels, their silken robes, their pipes. The more the pipes have been smoked and filled with opium, the more they gain for them. Lotteries, cockfights, fish fights, betting on Shanghai races, ten days' journey from here; all are played. Bets are even placed on the number of pips in a melon! It is reported that naval officers, under arrest and confined to their boats, continue to play at sea, by signal!" Near the end of Yaowarat Road is an area called Nakorn Kasem, once known as the "Thieves' Market" because of its many shops selling antiques and secondhand goods.

CHINATOWN TEMPLES

Chinatown contains temples both large and small, some for Mahayana Buddhists, some for Taoists, and others for Theravada Buddhists. The leading Mahayana Buddhist temple is Wat Mangkon Kamalawat, on Charoen Krung Road, where enormous candles decorated with Chinese figures are among the altar offerings. Off Plabplachai Road is Wat Kanikaphon, founded by a former brothel owner, where elaborate paper models of luxury items such as automobiles, planes, computers and houses are burned in honor of deceased relatives. This temple is better known as Wat Mae Lao Fang after the brothel owner. Li Thi Miew, a Taoist temple on Plabplachai, has interesting Chinese paintings on the interior walls. Wat Traimit is located close to where Yaowarat Road meets Charoen Krung Road. It contains the Golden Buddha that was found during construction work at a temple near the river in the 1950's. Originally covered in stucco, the solid gold Buddha was revealed when it was accidentally dropped during moving, shattering the stucco. The statue weighs over 5 tons. At Odeon Circle nearby, a huge ornamented Chinese gate honors the King's 72nd birthday in 1999.

FORTUNE SEEKER
A client eagerly awaits the verdict as a Chinatown fortune-teller consults his almanac. They are consulted on everything from health to the most auspicious dates for marriage or opening a new business.

Vegetarian food offerings at Wat Mangkon Kamalawat.

ITALIAN ARTISTS
While in Europe, King Rama V made contact with many artists and posed in their studios. He later commissioned several Italian artists to work in Bangkok; Cesare Ferro was the first to become a Siamese court painter in 1904. Besides various portraits of the king, Ferro's works also included the wall decorations of the Amphornsathan Throne Hall in the palace. Prince Naris, who was in charge of the public works department, was also keen to promote innovative ideas such as Siamese subjects and Western techniques. He worked closely with a team of craftsmen and painters, notably Carlo Rigoli, on various projects such as Wat Rajathiwat and the Borom-phiman Mansion. All the Italian artists gave art lessons to Thai painters and influenced the local art scene. However, the one who left a lasting impression was Corrado Ferroci, who came to Thailand in 1923 and lived there until his death. Ferroci produced a number of royal statues and eventually became a teacher. He founded the institute now known as Silpakorn University, which trains hundreds of young artists ▲ 72.

King Rama V was the first Thai ruler to travel to Europe. The result of such trips was a determination to transform Bangkok into a Western-style capital. The main focus of his effort was the Dusit district, which he linked with the traditional center by Ratchadamnoen (Royal Progress) Avenue and where he proceeded to build a new throne hall and palace, residences for members of the royal family (among them Chitralada Palace, where the present king and queen live), and numerous tree-lined avenues suitable for carriage rides. His successor Rama VI followed up his plans on an even larger scale. Since most of Bangkok's expansion has taken place elsewhere, largely to the east, this district still retains much of its early 19th-century flavor, with many of the old buildings occupied by the military and government offices.

ANANDA SAMAKHOM THRONE HALL. The center of Rama V's Dusit district was the elaborate, Western-style throne hall. Construction began in 1907, directed by a group of Italian architects and engineers, notably Annibale Rigotti, Carlo Allegri, E.G. Gollo and M. Tamagno, and was completed five years later, after the death of the king. Galileo Chini, whose work the king had admired at the Venice Biennale, was commissioned in 1911–13 to decorate the vault with huge frescoes of notable events in Thai history. For a time following the end of the absolute monarchy the building served as the National Parliament. The square in front of the Ananda Samakhom is decorated with a large equestrian statue of Rama V, modeled by Georges Saulo when the king visited Paris. The statue was cast in parts and assembled in Bangkok, and was unveiled on November 11, 1908, the 40th anniversary of his coronation. Every year, on October 23, the anniversary of King Rama V's death, many people visit the statue and pay homage to his memory.

VIMARN MEK PALACE. This palace is an 81-room structure of golden teak and was originally intended to serve as a residence of King Rama V on the island of Si Chang in the Gulf of Thailand. Due to conflicts with the French over Cambodia, however, he decided to move the structure to Bangkok, and to use it as a residence during the construction of the nearby Dusit Palace. Long neglected after King Rama V's death, it was beautifully restored and furnished with fifth-reign royal treasures by Queen Sirikit as part of the 1982 Bangkok bicentennial celebrations. Queen Sirikit selected the furnishings, which include such curiosities as Thailand's first shower bath as well as historic photographs of the late 19th century.

"BIRTHDAY BRIDGES". During the latter part of his reign, King Rama V started an annual tradition of opening a new bridge on the occasion of his birthday. A number of these "birthday bridges" have been lost to progress, but several remain in all their ornate beauty.

WAT BENCHAMABOPIT. Popularly known as the Marble Temple, this wat was built at the turn of the century by King Rama V ● 48. It was designed by his brother, Prince Naris, with the help of Italian architect Hercules Manfredi. The temple is a blend of architectural styles and decoration: gray marble from Italy, for example, was imported to sheathe the bot and pave the surrounding cloisters, while inside there are stained-glass windows as well as a replica of the famous Phra Buddha Chinaraj image. Around the cloister are fifty-three bronze Buddha showing every style of Thai religious art and some from neighboring cultures. Also in the compound is a building in which King Rama V lived as a monk, the interior decorated with murals showing major events of his reign, and an ancient Bodhi tree.

VIMARN MEK PALACE
This was the first Siamese house to have electricity.

PHYA THAI PALACE
Following King Rama V's death in 1910, Phya Thai Palace served as the residence of Queen Sowabha Phongsri, having previously been occupied by Crown Prince Vajiravudh. The Victorian-style buildings were later a luxury hotel then became the Phra Mongkut Military Hospital. It is now open to the public as a museum.

◣ MODERN BANGKOK

«IN ASIA, A SILVER KEY CAN OPEN ANY LOCK.»
CARL BOCK, 1883

The three-wheeled vehicle known as a tuk-tuk (right) is still a cooler, cleaner, cheaper and popular form of transportation in the city, although it has been largely replaced by metered taxis.

BANGKOK TRAFFIC
With about the least road surface of any world city, Bangkok has failed to keep pace with the relentless increase in vehicle numbers, causing legendary traffic congestion. The speed of traffic flow on main streets fell from 8-9 miles per hour in 1984 to 5 miles per hour in 1991 and hasn't changed much since, despite a decade of construction of elevated expressways and new flyovers. Since 1999, an elevated SkyTrain has linked some central areas and the opening of the Subway in 2004 has helped further. A big reduction in congestion, however, awaits completion of a total of 180 miles of mass transit on seven lines.

No map can keep pace with modern Bangkok given the speed with which new suburban developments spring up as well as the rapid changes in older districts. The present skyline of towering condominiums, hotels, offices and shopping complexes is actually only a few decades old. Elderly residents can recall a time when now-crowded areas were serene ricefields and "downtown" meant the shops along New Road and Lower Surawong. Today, work, place of residence or particular interests are more likely to determine what one regards as the "center" of Bangkok. Sometimes such places overlap. More often they involve long trips through congested traffic; thus quite a number of

residents have never even seen such older landmarks as Wat Po and the National Museum. If some visitors enjoy strolling about at random, savoring the animated street life that can be found almost anywhere, others, for whom time is limited, will probably prefer to plan each day's activities based on one area per day.

SILOM ROAD, COMMERCIAL HUB

Silom Road, extending from Rama IV Road to New Road (also called Charoen Krung Road), has become an important commercial area. Many leading banks, advertising agencies, airline offices and handicraft shops are located along its length, as well as several large hotels and popular centers of nightlife such as Patpong and Thaniya Road. Lower Silom is a center of the booming Thai gems and jewelry industry, with numerous shops and wholesale outlets. Day and night the sidewalks near the Rama IV Road end are also crowded with vendors offering locally made copies of brand-name clothing and accessories, watches, cassettes and videos, as well as locally designed clothing and décor.
NIGHTLIFE IN PATPONG. Despite official disapproval, feminist protest, and the looming shadow of AIDS, Bangkok's anything-goes nightlife remains a major attraction for many visitors. The center of activity is Patpong Road, between Silom and Surawong, and several nearby

side streets; Thaniya Road, further up Silom, caters to a Japanese clientele. The attractions range from small bars with go-go dancers, sex shows and massage parlors to discos, trendy bars and restaurants, which are as popular with younger Thais and expatriates as with tourists. A smaller but similar concentra-tion can be found on Soi Cowboy, off Sukhumvit Soi 23. Though the reputation of Patpong derives mainly from sex tourism, prostitution remains an accepted part of life. Sex education for males often starts with a visit to a brothel, despite the natural shyness and puritanism of the Thais.

"As Calcutta smells of death and Bombay of money, Bangkok smells of sex, but this sexual aroma is mingled with the sharper whiffs of death and money."
Paul Theroux

LUMPINI PARK

Across from the Dusit Thani Hotel, Lumpini (right) is the original and largest park in central Bangkok. It was presented to the city by King Rama VI in the 1920's. Vehicular traffic is banned in the park, thus enhancing its appeal to joggers and others who come to exercise in the early morning and late afternoon. Many elderly Chinese who are early risers use the park as a venue for their *tai chi* exercises and folk-dance sessions.

Paddle boats await customers at the lake in Lumpini Park.

ERAWAN SHRINE

During the construction of the Erawan Hotel in the 1950's, work was plagued by a series of mysterious accidents that included the death of several laborers. The Erawan Shrine, containing an image of Brahma, was erected near the site in an effort to stop these mishaps. Large crowds now visit the shrine and present wooden elephants, garlands and other offerings in the hope of having their wishes granted; many successful supplicants hire resident dancers to perform in the courtyard as a way of showing their gratitude.

The ever-busy Erawan Shrine receives various forms of offerings from devotees throughout the day until late evening.

«NOT ONLY DO YOU HAVE BEAUTIFUL THINGS, BUT WHAT IS RARE
YOU HAVE ARRANGED THEM WITH FAULTLESS TASTE.»
SOMERSET MAUGHAM, IN A LETTER TO JIM THOMPSON

MISSING JIM
The disappearance of Jim Thompson, "the Silk King of Thailand," is one of the enduring mysteries of modern Asia. In March 1967, shortly after his 61st birthday, he went with friends for a holiday in the Cameron Highlands, a resort in northern Malaysia. There he went for a walk alone on Easter Sunday afternoon and never returned. Despite an exhaustive search – not to mention advice offered by experts in the supernatural – no trace of him has been found. There are plenty of theories, however, ranging from a kidnap that went wrong to misadventures in the jungle. Interest has been maintained through factual accounts, several novels, and hundreds of newspaper and magazine articles.

COLLECTOR'S HOUSE
Produced in pre-fabricated sections, the various structures were brought to the site by river barges. Carpenters skilled in traditional methods rebuilt the house.

JIM THOMPSON'S HOUSE. Located on Soi Kasemsan 2, off Rama I Road, is the Thai-style house built by Jim Thompson, an American who came to Thailand at the end of World War Two and stayed to revive the Thai silk industry.

On the bank of a klong, he assembled a group of old teak houses from several places into a multi-room house that became the template for conversion of old Thai houses for modern living. Thompson filled them with his collec-tion of art from Thailand and other Asian countries, including paintings, porcelain, statuary and antique furniture. The house is now a museum open to the public daily, and has a restaurant, shop and gallery focusing on textiles of past and modern usage.

SUAN PAKKARD PALACE. The former home of Prince and Princess Chumbhot stands in a large, landscaped tropical garden on Si Ayutthaya Road. It consists of five traditional Thai houses assembled in the 1950's as well as the Lacquer Pavilion, an elegant structure found in Ayutthaya and probably from the early Bangkok period. The interior walls of the pavilion are covered with fine gold-and-black lacquer paintings. The art collection displayed in the houses covers a wide range, from prehistoric bronze jewelry and pottery found in the northeast to furniture and other items that belonged to Prince Chumbhot's family. The grounds also contain a Khon Museum, about the traditional masked dance ● *34*, and Marsi Gallery, which exhibits contemporary art. The palace is open daily except Sundays.

THE KAMTHIENG HOUSE.
Bangkok's only real ethnological collection – fish traps, stoves, cook-ing pots and implements used by Thai farmers – is displayed with audio-visual commentaries at Kamthieng House, in the compound of the Siam Society on Sukhumwit Soi 21. The northern-style teak house, over 200 years old, came from Chiang Mai to Bangkok in sections. Also in the compound is a fine example of a Central Plains house ● *45*, thus offering visitors a comparison of the two styles. Both are open daily except Mondays.

KUKRIT PRAMOJ'S HISTORICAL HOUSE
The traditional Thai teak home of the late cultural scholar and former Prime Minister has been turned into a museum. This former hub of political culture displays Mom Rajawong Kukrit Pramoj's collection of Thai, Khmer and literary artefacts. Located on quiet Soi Phra Phinit, off Soi Suan Plu, the large grounds and terrace of potted plants are a trove of Thai gardening history. This museum is open on weekends and public holidays.

SIAM SOCIETY
The Siam Society was founded by a group of Thais and foreign residents in 1904 for research and investi-gation in matters appertaining to Siam. Placed under royal patronage during the reign of King Rama VI, it moved to its present location in 1933. The Society has an extensive library of books and other publications on Thailand and the rest of Asia, issues a journal for members, and organizes frequent lectures and exhibitions.

CHATUCHAK MARKET

From early Saturday morning until Sunday evening, one of the busiest places in Bangkok is the great Weekend Market at Chatuchak Park, just off Phahonyothin Road. Almost everything the country produces is on sale somewhere in this huge network of several thousand stalls: fruit trees, garden plants, clothing, antiques, handicrafts, fresh and preserved foods, fruit, furniture, porcelain, army surplus goods and pets of all kinds. Many stalls now also showcase contemporary Thai décor from emerging designers. Most of the prices are negotiable, as they are at all Thai markets, and for visitors who mind the heat the early morning hours are the best time to go.

PERMANENT PLANT MARKET. Between the end of the Kamphaengphet Road and Chatuchak Market is a daily market devoted to plants. Any true garden-lover should devote at least a few hours to strolling along the long row of shops displaying the full range of ornamental trees, shrubs and creepers available to local enthusiasts, in addition to pots and gardening tools. Of special interest are the shops and sidewalk vendors who offer dazzling displays of flowering orchids at prices that will seem ridiculously low to visitors from more temperate countries.

PRATUNAM MARKET

Pratunam, literally translated, means "water gate," and the market by that name is located near the locks of Klong Saen Saeb, at the intersection of Phetchaburi and Rajaprarop roads. It offers a huge covered area selling cloth and ready-made clothing, attended by seamstresses who are ready to make on-the-spot alterations or even produce a complete outfit. Low prices and an almost limitless choice make this highly popular place, particularly on weekends, so be prepared for crowds as well as some shrewd bargaining.

SIDEWALK VENDORS. Just about every Bangkok governor, at some point in his term of office, has made a determined effort to tidy the city's streets of sidewalk vendors. None has succeeded, for the simple reason that Thais (and most foreign visitors, too) enjoy coming across unexpected bargains as they walk here and there and don't mind whatever hazards the vendors might create. Sidewalk shopping is a city-wide affair, but certain areas are more crowded than others. Upper Silom Road, for instance, caters more to tourist tastes, merging with

GEMS AND JEWELRY
Export of gems and jewelry now ranks as one of Thailand's largest earners of foreign exchange. Gems such as sapphires, rubies, zircons, garnets and cat's-eyes are brought into the country from all over the world to be cut and polished by a growing force of skilled workers, while the quality of locally crafted jewelry has acquired an international reputation. Many of the gem and jewelry stores are located at the Jewelry Trade Center at Silom Road, where much of the industry is focused.

stalls filling Patpong after dark, and so does the stretch of Sukhumvit Road extending from Ploenchit to Soi 11, no doubt because both areas are convenient to numerous hotels. Rajadamri Road from the Rajprasong intersection to Pratunam is another popular gathering place for vendors, as are many streets in Chinatown, Banglamphu and countless other side streets citywide.

SHOPPING CENTERS

Modern shopping centers and department stores are a relatively new phenomenon in Bangkok, but the city has more than made up for lost time in the past two decades. The Ploenchit branch of the locally owned Central Department Store was originally one of the largest in Southeast Asia and there are numerous others, both Thai and Japanese, in almost every district. The goods are of high quality and, rather surprisingly in view of the luxurious surroundings, the fixed prices are not all that much higher than those at the markets. Popular department stores besides Central Department Store include Robinson's, Sogo, Isetan and Thai Daimaru. Shopping centers are also ubiquitous and most contain restaurants and fast-food outlets as well as smart boutiques selling ready-to-wear clothing, jewelry, leather goods and other items. Among those frequented by visitors are Amarin Plaza, Emporium, Peninsula Plaza, Rajadamri Arcade, River City, Mahboon Krong, Siam Center and World Trade Center.

THAI SILK
Probably the most sought-after product is Thai silk. The material is believed to have originated from the village folk of northeastern Thailand, who weaved it using primitive handlooms. The silk remained popular until its decline at the end of the 19th century, when Chinese and Japanese silk imports flooded the local market. The silk industry was revived by entrepreneur Jim Thompson after World War Two. The pioneer company he established remains one of the best and biggest silk producers in the country today. The main shop, open 12 hours daily to accommodate the endless flow of customers, is located at the intersection of Surawong and Rama IV roads. There are silk clothes and scarfs as well as the material itself, which can be bought by the yard.

THE FLOATING MARKET

Floating markets, consisting of hundreds of vendors congregating by boat, usually in the early morning, at some point on a river or canal, have long fascinated visitors to Bangkok and other parts of Thailand. A few decades ago, the most popular place to view this colorful phenomenon was the canal outside Wat Sai in Thonburi; eventually however this market became overcrowded with tourists.

DAMNERN SADUAK. Today the best of such markets convenient to Bangkok is on Klong Damnern Saduak in Ratchaburi province, a trip most itineraries combine with a visit to Nakhon Pathom. The floating market here takes place somewhat later than at other places – between 8am and 10am – and offers a busy, photogenic scene of boats laden with fruit, vegetables, cooked foods and other produce, sold principally by women wearing the broad straw hats and dressed in the blue cotton clothing favored by rural Thai people. For food lovers there are also many restaurants lined along the banks.

SAMUT SONGKHRAM

The intact canals and periodic floating markets in Amphawa, in Samut Songkhram province near the Gulf of Thailand, can be seen on tours or during canal homestays. In the charming riverside provincial capital, the Rama II Memorial Park features one of the most well preserved traditional Thai house complexes in Thailand.

NAKHON PATHOM

One of the oldest cultural centers in Thailand, Nakhon Pathom is believed to date from several centuries before the beginning of the Christian era and was an important Mon capital. It was deserted for long stretches at various times in its history, and the present town dates from the middle of the 19th century, when King Rama IV ordered restoration work to be done on its chedi.

PHRA PATHOM CHEDI. Dominating the town of Nakhon Pathom, and visible from many miles away, is the impressive Phra Pathom Chedi, which, at 352 feet, is the tallest Buddhist monument in the world and the oldest in Thailand ● 50. It was originally built about a thousand years ago but had fallen into a pile of rubble by the middle of the 19th century, when the future King Rama IV, then a Buddhist monk, came on a pilgrimage. Restoration work, which involved covering the old ruins with an entirely new chedi, began in 1853 but – due to numerous technical difficulties – was not completed until the reign of King Rama V. The base of

RIVER RITUAL
One of the most memorable sights along the canals of Ratchaburi and other provinces is that of Buddhist monks collecting their early-morning alms by boat from waterside houses. Strict rules apply not only to the type of boat used for this ritual but also the seemingly effortless manner in which it is paddled.

the chedi is surrounded by a circular cloister, with chapels containing Buddha images from various periods situated at the four cardinal points. A museum houses early religious objects that were found in the area, among them the Wheel of the Law and terra cotta bas-reliefs of the Dvaravati period (7th–11th century). A popular festival is held on the temple grounds each November, when the great chedi is beautifully illuminated.

SANAM CHAN PALACE. One of the beautiful wooden palace complexes built by King Rama VI stands around a park in central Nakhon Pathom town. Museums about his life and times now occupy several of the buildings, which vary in style from traditional Thai to tropical European. It also includes a theater reminiscent of a temple building.

RATCHABURI'S WATER JARS
Ratchaburi province is noted for its production of huge, glazed water jars, often decorated with swirling Chinese dragons and floral motifs, which are sent to many parts of Thailand. A recent industry using similar skills is producing fine reproductions of Chinese blue-and-white porcelain.

DVARAVATI STUCCOES
Nakhon Pathom was an important town of the Dvaravati Mon kingdom (6th–10th century). Excavations at the Chedi Chula Pathom, on the outskirts of the modern town, have led to the discovery of an interesting series of bas-reliefs in stucco. Other terracottas were found at Ku Bua and U Thong. These are now displayed in the museums of Nakhon Pathom, U Thong and Bangkok ▲ 81. They throw light on the ancient Mon aristocratic life of the elegantly dressed court ladies. Mon society was evidently refined and cosmopolitan, in touch with India, Indonesia and perhaps the Mediterranean.

«THE JAPANESE DID NOT CONSIDER HUMAN LIFE OF ANY VALUE WHEN VIEWED IN THE LIGHT THAT THE RAILWAY MUST BE PUSHED ON REGARDLESS OF COST.»

C. A. MCEACHERN, PRISONER OF WAR

CURING SNAKEBITES
Here is Ernest Young's recipe, from his book, *The Kingdom of the Yellow Robe*, for a mixture that could help cure snakebites in the event of an encounter with poisonous reptiles in the parks or rivers:
a piece of the jaw of a wild hog;
a piece of the jaw of a tame hog;
a piece of the bone of a goose;
a piece of the bone of a peacock;
the tail of a fish;
and the head of a venomous snake.

Lush jungles and winding rivers lie but a short distance away from the modern town of Kanchanaburi, which is also haunted by a modern epic of heroism and tragedy.

RIVER RESORTS

In recent years, the Kanchanaburi area – particularly the Kwai Noi and Kwai Yai rivers – has become a popular vacation spot for Bangkok residents in search of lush natural scenery. By boat along one of the rivers, or by road, one can travel to rural resorts, some built on floating rafts and others substantial structures with modern conveniences. The Kwai Yai leads to a large, scenic lake formed by the Srinakharin Dam, while the Kwai Noi, the more developed of the two in terms of resorts, winds through Saiyok National Park to a beautiful expanse of water created by the Khao Laem Dam.

ERAWAN NATIONAL PARK

Established in 1975, this 220-square-mile National Park is protected on the west by Saiyok National Park, on the south by Salak Phra Wildlife Sanctuary, on the east by the Kwai Yai River, and on the north by the Srinakharin National Park. Its most celebrated feature is the spectacular Erawan Waterfalls, a 4,950-foot cascade that is broken up into seven tiers; according to popular belief, the rock above the top level resembles the three-headed elephant Erawan of Hindu mythology. The park is a sanctuary to a wide variety of wildlife, including 80 species of birds, gibbons, barking deer and rhesus monkeys, as well as a profusion of flora; also within its area are two impressive caves, Phrathat

and Wang Badang, both adorned with huge stalactites and stalagmites. Bungalows and dormitories are available for visitors who want to stay overnight in the park.

THE DEATH RAILWAY

In June 1942, six months after the start of its conquest of Southeast Asia, Japan ordered the construction of a railway from Thailand to Burma as a substitute for the long sea route to Rangoon; it was meant to play a major role in the trans-portation of men and material for the planned invasion of British India. The task was formidable, the track leading through dense malarial rainforest, over rocky mountains, and across swift rivers. For labor, the Japanese deployed about 61,000 Allied prisoners-of-war (POWs) captured in Malaya, Singapore and the Dutch East Indies, plus an estimated 270,000 conscripted Asian workers. Slowly, painfully, over the next three years, the almost impossible task was completed, but at a horrifying cost in human life: over 12,000 POWs and 240,000 Asians died during the ordeal – or 393 men for every mile of the eventually useless Death Railway, as it came to be called by survivors. The bodies of 6,982 victims lie in a tranquil Allied War Cemetery near Kanchanaburi, where the railway began, and a museum displays other grim reminders of what one writer has called a "supreme monument to folly." A new Australian-funded museum stands at Hell Fire Pass, a particularly poignant cutting excavated through rock by hand. In Kanchanaburi town, the JEATH Museum recreates tableaux of the conditions faced by POWs, with artefacts and

artwork recording the human spirit that survived. The track itself was dismantled after the war but a length still runs along the Kwai Yai River and several of the bridges have been rebuilt. Toward the end of November, an annual fair is held in Kanchanaburi under the auspices of the Tourism Authority of Thailand, featuring a sound and light show at the so-called *Bridge On The River Kwai* and displays of prehistoric artifacts found in the region.

THREE PAGODAS PASS
The pass lies on the frontier between Thailand and Burma, and was the historic crossing point for Burmese armies who invaded Ayutthaya. It was also the place where the Death Railway led into Burma, though the tracks were dismantled by the British at the end of the war.

RIVER KWAI
Kanchanaburi gained its fame from the popular film *The Bridge on the River Kwai* – actually filmed in Sri Lanka – which in turn was based on the novel of the same name by Pierre Boulle. Local entrepreneurs cash in on this fame but the story is entirely fictional.

ชาวพัทยายินดีต้อนรับ
WELCOME TO PATTAYA

THE OLD ROAD TO PATTAYA

The old Sukhumwit Road, once the only route to Pattaya and other resorts on the eastern gulf coast, leads through Samut Prakarn Province and passes a number of popular tourist attractions before it joins a newer, more modern highway.

THE ANCIENT CITY. Muang Boran, or the Ancient City, started by a late art-loving millionaire in the early 1970's, contains numerous buildings and monuments – some replicas, others genuine – from Thailand's past, on a 200-acre site roughly shaped like the country itself. One enters from the far south, passing such attractions as the Phra Mahathat stupa of Nakhon Si Thammarat and another from the Srivijaya city of Chaiya ● 50, and then moves upward to the north through the splendors of Ayutthaya and Sukhothai. The idea might sound contrived, but it is executed with considerable taste, and expert advice from various authorities – among them a former director of the National Museum – which have been consulted throughout to ensure authenticity of detail. The replicas are one-third the original size, but there are also many original buildings. The village stilt-houses around the

"floating market" and the so-called "Market of Yesteryear" were once Thai houses that have been completely dismantled and moved to the site and then refurbished with original antiques and objects of everyday use. Two northern buildings of significance, a Lanna-style temple from Chiang Rai ● 49 and the Shan-Burmese temple from Ngao, have been salvaged from destruction and carefully restored in the Ancient City.

THE CROCODILE FARM. This popular tourist attraction is believed to be the largest of its kind in the world, containing more than 30,000 crocodiles, of both local and foreign species. The reptiles are bred not only to amuse visitors but also as a source of hides for belts, wallets, handbags, shoes and other items. (A brochure described the farm as "a happy compromise between wildlife conservation and commercial enterprise.") Starting daily at 9am, a show features fearless handlers who "tame" some of the larger and fiercer specimens. There is also a zoo with other animals.

PATTAYA

The fast road to Pattaya – and the world's longest elevated expressway – passes through Chonburi, a charmless provincial capital, Si Racha, noted for a locally made chili pepper sauce that bears its name, and Bang Saen, a seaside resort popular with Thai families, before reaching the string of beaches further down the Eastern Seaboard. Pattaya began attracting visitors from Bangkok in the 1950's, thanks to the ease with which its long white-sand beaches could be reached. Accommodation was a few simple bungalows, and the first hotel did not open until 1965. Development accelerated during the Vietnam War, when thousands of American soldiers went there on leave, and by the mid-1970's it had become a major resort, with hotels, restaurants and night-clubs extending the entire length of the main beach. The environmental cost of such rapid expansion has been high, and most of Pattaya's natural charms are gone, though the water has improved greatly in recent years. The free-wheeling nightlife has been cleaned up slightly in response to foreign media criticism, and the town's new status as a residential and educa-tional hub for the industrialising Eastern Seaboard means there are now malls and family attractions too, such as Ripley's Believe It Or Not and Pattaya Aquarium. Many visitors still enjoy its rowdy, laid-back atmosphere, however, and continue to come in large numbers. Those who prefer a quieter atmosphere and more privacy, at least after nightfall, can go further to less developed beaches like Jomtien or to offshore islands such as Koh Larn and Koh Sak. There are several golf courses in the area, as well as shooting ranges and other land-based sports facilities.

▲ BEYOND PATTAYA

❝On the 4th of January, at 8 o'clock in the morning, we arrived in the city of Chantaboon. It is built along the river, six or seven miles away from the mountains. About one third of the population is composed of Christian Annamites. The rest is mostly composed of Chinese merchants, some pagan Annamites as well as Siamese. The latter are all fishermen of Annamese descent. Their ancestors sailed all the way from Cochin-China hoping to fish in the northern waters of the Gulf of Siam. Little by little they settled in Chantaboon.❞

Henri Mouhot

CHANTABURI

Known in old travel accounts as Chantaboon, Chantaburi has been a center of gem-mining since the early 1400's. Mainly sapphires and rubies are mined in privately owned pits in the countryside. Gem trading is concentrated in a few blocks of the downtown area, where nearly all the shops are devoted to this, particularly on 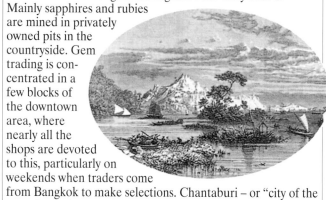 weekends when traders come from Bangkok to make selections. Chantaburi – or "city of the moon" – is also noted for the its tropical fruits.

KOH CHANG

The second largest island after Phuket lies off the coast of Trat Province, near the Cambodian border. Along with fifty nearby islands, Koh Chang is a beautiful marine national park, with numerous beaches and coral reefs. However, the government has targeted the islands for development, and the subsequent construction now threatens the ecosystem. Ferries leave several times daily for the island from Laem Ngob on the mainland, and an airport at Trat now serves the islands.

KOH SAMET

A long, narrow island 45 minutes by boat off the coast at Ban Phe near Rayong, it has since 1981 been part of a national park that also includes Khao Laem Ya on the mainland, a move that has limited the tourist facilities overlooking the beaches on its eastern side, popular with Bangkok residents. Some resorts are becoming more upmarket.

RAYONG'S GREAT POET
Sunthorn Phu (1786–1856), one of Thailand's greatest poets, was a native of Rayong. He was a particular favorite of King Rama II, with whom he collaborated on a number of works, and wrote the still-popular romantic epic *Phra Apaimani*. A statue has been erected in his memory at Amphur Klaeng, his birthplace.

RAYONG

Rayong is a busy fishing port known for the high-quality fish sauce, *nam pla*, which is produced in many small local factories and sold throughout Thailand. Along the coast are several peaceful resorts. Boats can be hired for visits to the various scenic offshore islands.

THE SOUTH

PHETCHABURI, *100*
HUA HIN TO SURAT THANI, *102*
KOH SAMUI, *104*
NAKHON SI THAMMARAT, *106*
SONGKHLA, HAADYAI AND PATTANI, *107*
PHUKET, *108*
PHANGNGA BAY, *112*
PHI PHI ISLANDS, *114*
KRABI AND OFFSHORE ISLANDS, *115*
ISLANDS OF THE ANDAMAN SEA, *116*

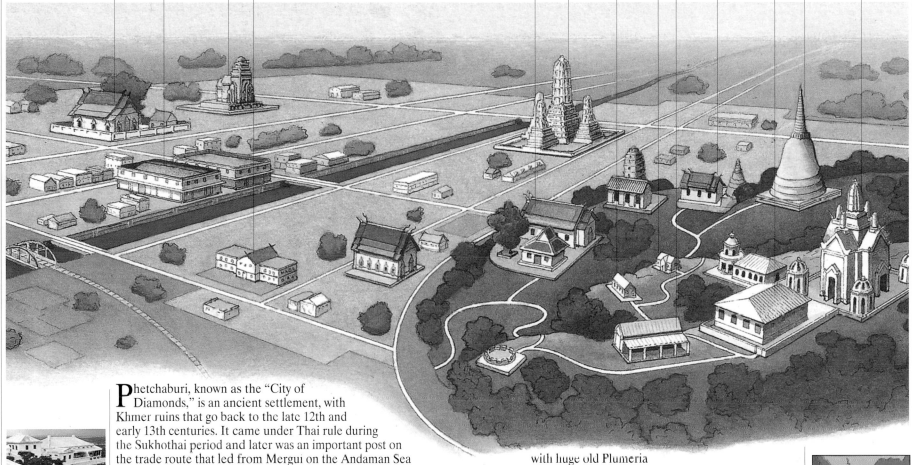

WAT YAI SUWANNARAM · MARKET · WAT KHAMPHAENG LAENG · CITY HALL · WAT MAHA SAMANARAM · WAT MAHATHAT · SALA YEN · PHIMAN PHETMAHET HALLS · PHRA THINANG SANTHA KAM · SATHAN · WAT PHRA KEO · PHRA THINANG PHET · PHUM PHAIROT · PHRA THAT CHOM PHET · PHRA THINANG WECHAYAN · WICHIEN PRASAT

Phetchaburi, known as the "City of Diamonds," is an ancient settlement, with Khmer ruins that go back to the late 12th and early 13th centuries. It came under Thai rule during the Sukhothai period and later was an important post on the trade route that led from Mergui on the Andaman Sea to Ayutthaya. Numerous traditional Thai crafts flourished in the town, among them woodcarving, silk-weaving and ornamental work on gold and silver, some of which still survive today. More than most provincial Thai cities, modern Phetchaburi has preserved its old temples, several of which contain important mural paintings, as well as traditional wooden houses in the Central Plains Thai style.

KHAO WANG

Khao Wang, the "Mountain Palace," was built by King Rama IV in the middle of the 19th century as a place where he could escape the pressures of the capital and also spend more time on astronomy, one of his favorite hobbies. Consisting of several European-style buildings, an observatory, and a Buddhist chapel, the palace complex is located on one of the shoulders of a hill just outside Phetchaburi; other buildings are scattered around the hill at lower levels, and a stairway leading to the top is lined with huge old Plumeria trees that fill the area with their fragrance. Sarah Coffman, an American missionary who visited the palace toward the end of the fourth reign, described the audience hall as "a long, low room, almost completely bare, with a semi-circular throne, consisting of four stone steps, at one end." Two large impressive Siamese paintings – *The Reception of the French Ambassadors at Court* and *Bronze Worshiping Gautama* – decorate the side walls. About a decade after Rama IV's death, another visitor, Carl Bock, found the palace "in a sad state of neglect." However, the palace has been restored by the Fine Arts Department, and its original charms are once more apparent.

A VIEW FROM KHAO WANG
Henri Mouhot, on the view from Khao Wang in 1858: "About 25 miles off stretches from north to south a chain of mountains called Deng...Beyond these rises a number of still higher peaks. On the low ground are forests, palm-trees, and rice-fields, the whole rich and varied in color. Lastly, to the south and east, and beyond another plain, lies the gulf, on whose waters...a few scattered sails are just distinguishable."

🕐 One day

The Buddhist chapel of Khao Wang.

«PHETCHABURI IS A VERY PRETTY PLACE…JUSTLY POPULAR WITH
EUROPEANS RESIDENT AT BANGKOK AS A SUMMER RESORT FOR A
CHANGE OF AIR OR A LITTLE BIT OF RUSTICATION.»

FRANK VINCENT

KHRUA IN KHONG
Khrua In Khong, one of King Rama IV's favorite painters, responded to the ruler's keen interest in Western culture by including European buildings and landscapes in his murals. At Wat Bowornivet in Bangkok, for example, he incorporated a building similar to that of Mount Vernon, George Washington's home, along with such contemporary subjects as an operation for cataracts.

WAT MAHA SAMANARAM

Located at the foot of the hill near the king's palace, Wat Maha Samanaram was built by King Rama IV. The chapel contains a beautiful Ayutthaya-style Buddha image and is decorated with murals by Khrua In Khong, a famous priest-painter of the fourth reign ● 55. The main scene in the murals depicts the pilgrimage of the Buddhist followers to the Buddha's Footprint at Saraburi.

WAT YAI SUWANNARAM

Dating from the 17th century, Wat Yai Suwannaram is one of Phetchaburi's most beautiful temples. The interior walls of the bot are decorated with some of the oldest surviving mural paintings in Thailand, dating from the late 17th or early 18th century; these show two rows of celestial beings facing the principal Buddha image, a large bronze statue in Ayutthaya style. Within the compound are also several wooden buildings adorned with fine carvings that attest to the high quality of Phetchaburi artisans. The *sala* ● 46, in front of the bot, has superbly carved doors, one of which has a gash supposedly made by Burmese invaders; inside are painted panels, one of which shows a rhinoceros, at that time found near the city. Except for this particular *sala* and the bot, the other buildings date from the reign of Rama V, who ardently supported the extensive renovations to the monastery.

WAT MAHATHAT

The most visible feature of Wat Mahathat is its towering central prang, surrounded by a cloister lined with Buddha images. Also noteworthy are the stucco decorations on one of the sanctuaries, which contains a number of Buddha images of the Ayutthaya period as well as several recently restored mural paintings.

WAT KO KEO SUTHARAM ★

Wat Ko Keo Sutharam, popularly called Wat Ko, lies on the bank of the Phetchaburi River. Inside one of the chapels are some well-preserved murals dating from 1740; one of the figures depicted on the side walls is believed to be that of a Jesuit priest in the robes of a Buddhist monk, possibly recalling an earlier French mission that came through Phetchaburi in the reign of King Narai of Ayutthaya, while another panel shows the conversion of foreigners to Buddhism. The monastic buildings of the temple, raised on posts around a courtyard, have been little altered over the years; one of the buildings contains a small collection of items that have been donated to the monastery.

FOREIGNERS IN WAT KO KEO SUTHARAM
Foreigners first began to appear in temple murals in the latter part of the Ayutthaya period. The earliest were Chinese, Persians and Indians, who came to trade in the capital; later, Europeans were seen, some obviously inspired by the French embassies who came to the court of King Narai in the late 17th century and others by various adventurers of the time.

WAT KHAMPHAENG LAENG

Wat Khamphaeng Laeng is a relatively modern temple that contains within its precincts a very important Khmer ruin dating from the 11th century. Remains of a massive stone wall (*khamphaeng laeng* in Thai), once encircled by moats, and a prang built in laterite can still be seen. The monument is of historical interest as it marks the southernmost point of expansion of the Khmer empire.

KHAO LUANG ★

This famous cave temple, in a hill just outside Phetchaburi, has long been one of the town's major attractions; it reminded Henri Mouhot, who arrived in 1860, of "the beautiful fairy scenes represented at Christmas in the London theaters." Light from a hole at the top of the main chamber dramatically illuminates a display of enormous stalactites along with numerous Buddha images that have been placed in the cave and that are presented with regular offerings. The late morning hours are the best time to view the effective natural lighting. Monkeys rush out from among the bushes to greet visitors to the cave.

HUA HIN

Credit for "discovering" the resort possibilities of Hua Hin, a scenic seaside village on the west coast of the Gulf, usually goes to Prince Chakrabongse, a brother of King Rama VI, who in 1911 took a visiting group of European royalty there for a holiday. The prince built a bungalow by the sea, other members of the royal family soon built houses nearby and eventually a king's palace called Klai Klangwan, "far from care." The entire court moved to Hua Hin for several months of the year, thus giving it a fashionable atmosphere still apparent in some of the spacious old bungalows visible from the beach. Completion of the southern railway line in the 1920's made Hua Hin easily accessible to the capital, leading to the Railway Hotel, a golf course and holiday homes of prominent Bangkok families. Even today, despite the addition of condominiums and hotels, Hua Hin retains a more sedate atmosphere than Pattaya, its boisterous competitor across the gulf. At Wat Hua Hin, the temple on top of the hill, visitors can enjoy charming views of the town.

A STAR PERFORMANCE
The Railway Hotel played a prominent role in the award-winning film, *The Killing Fields*, about Cambodia's trials under Khmer Rouge rule. The producers used the picturesque old building in place of the Royal Hotel, where many journalists who covered the war stayed in Phnom Penh.

MARUKHATHAYAWAN PALACE. Late in his reign, King Rama VI built this enchanting pastel wooden palace on stilts. Restored and open to the public, it stands in Rama VI Army Camp near Hua Hin Airport, just south of the resort town Cha-am.
FISHING PORT. One of the most colourful sights near Hua Hin town is the fishing port, where the daily is brought in by fishermen in the early hours of the morning.
RAILWAY HOTEL. A rambling colonial style structure, built in 1923, with broad verandas and a garden of topiary shrubs, the old Railway Hotel fell on hard times when the mass tourist trade shifted to Pattaya in the late 1960's. It has been beautifully restored today as the Central Sofitel Resort without sacrificing its spacious, airy charm.
GOLF COURSE. The golf course at Hua Hin was the country's first, with "a stock of golf requisites and the loan of clubs" available through the Railway Hotel, according to a 1929 guidebook. The 18-hole course overlooking the sea is still one of the most popular in the area, and the fact that it contains a temple and a topiary gives it a special Thai flavor.

KHAO SAM ROI YOT NATIONAL PARK ★

Covering 39 square miles, Khao Sam Roi Yot – literally, "the mountain of three hundred peaks" – was established as a park in 1966. Conveniently situated just a few miles south of Hua Hin, the park boasts numerous picturesque limestone peaks, the highest rising to 1,997 feet, as well as caves, and unspoiled beaches fringed by casuarina trees. It was formerly famous for its marshes, waterfalls and wading birds. However, recent encroachment by private shrimp farmers has seriously affected the state of the natural habitat. Several scenes in *The Killing Fields* were filmed within the boundaries of the national park. Bird life is especially varied in this park, with more than 275 identified species, 60 of which – painted storks, grey herons, egrets and rare imperial eagles among them – are found mainly in the marsh areas. Monkeys and deer are particularly common. Other mammals include crab-eating macaques, Malayan porcupines, leopard cats and, in the offshore waters, Irrawaddy dolphins.

PHRAYA NAKHON CAVE. The largest cave in the park is Phraya Nakhon, named after a ruler of Nakhon Si Thammarat who discovered it two centuries ago when he came ashore in a violent storm; a pavilion in the cave was built for a visit by King Rama V in 1896.

PRACHUAB KHIRI KHAN

Prachuab Khiri Khan is approximately 54 miles south of Hua Hin. Off the main southern highway, it is a tiny port overlooked by Khao Chang Krachok ("mirror mountain"), on top of which sits a temple offering panoramic views of the sea. There are bungalows to rent and seafood restaurants down at the beach near the town.

PINEAPPLES
A common sight around Hua Hin and along much of the southern peninsula are vast plantations of pineapples, which thrive in the sandy soil. Today, Thailand is one of the world's largest producers of canned and fresh pineapples for export, having long ago surpassed Hawaii. Southern pineapples are especially noted for their sweetness and succulence.

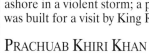

FAR FROM CARE
Although Klai Klangwan, the name of the royal palace at Hua Hin, means "far from care," it hardly proved so for King Rama VII. He was in residence there when he received word in June 1932 of the coup d'état that ended Thailand's absolute monarchy. Though he agreed to grant a constitution, he later abdicated in 1935 and died in England in 1941.

▲ THE SOUTH
HUA HIN TO SURAT THANI

«AT LOW WATER IMMENSE TRACTS OF MUD AND SAND
ARE LAID BARE, FOR THE EDIFICATION OF FLOCKS OF
PELICANS, CORMORANTS AND HERONS.»

H. WARRINGTON SMYTH

SRIVIJAYA
The Srivijaya kingdom ● 18, which originated in Sumatra, dominated the southern peninsula of Thailand between the 8th and 13th centuries. Though historians disagree over its extent, it was a Hindu culture that also practiced Mahayana Buddhism and produced some of Thailand's finest art in stone and bronze. This bronze Bodhisattva was found by Prince Damrong at Wat Mahathat, Chaiya, together with a number of other excellent pieces, and is now preserved in the National Museum in Bangkok ● 82.

CHUMPHON

Despite the construction of a sizeable seaside hotel some years ago, Chumphon has never really found popularity as a resort. It is noted, however, for its supply of edible birds' nests ■ 15, gathered from the offshore island of Koh Lanka Chiu. This island (and Koh Tao ▲ 106) can be visited by boat from the port of Paknam Chumphon.

KRA ISTHMUS

Just below Chumphon is the Kra Isthmus, only 15 miles wide and the narrowest point on peninsular Thailand, an area of rocky limestone precipices and breathtaking scenery. For many generations, this spot has been envisioned as the site of a Suez-type canal, which would cut nearly a thousand miles off shipping routes between ports on the Indian Ocean and the Gulf of Thailand. Several plans have been drawn up for such an undertaking – one proposer even suggested the use of nuclear weapons to ease the task – but thus far none has been successful, doubtless to the great relief of Singapore further south.

RANONG

Ranong, located on a river of the same name that empties into the sea across from Victoria Point, the southernmost tip of Burma, is a quiet provincial capital whose prosperity is mainly based on tin from nearby mines and a fishing fleet that sails far out into the Indian Ocean. The older houses, like those of Phuket and Songkhla further south, are built in the Sino-Portuguese style of Malacca and some of the downtown streets have covered arcades to shelter pedestrians from monsoon rains. The town is noted for a number of hot mineral-water springs, one of which supplies the Jansom Thara Hotel, picturesquely situated at the foot of a mountain just outside the town. Boat trips can be arranged from the port to visit off-shore islands, among them Koh Pa Yam where a company produces cultured pearls. (Entry into Burma is limited to Victoria Point and its casino). More hot springs – one of which produces 130 gallons of hot (158°F) water a minute – and tin mines can be found at Hat Sompin, about an hour away from Ranong by car. Another sight is Nam Tok Ngao, a waterfall on the highway southward. It is at its most impressive after a heavy rain.

CHAIYA

An ancient town, Chaiya is believed by some scholars to have been the capital of the great Srivijaya kingdom (8th–13th century) ● 18, which ruled most of peninsular Thailand from its base in Sumatra. The only remaining traces of this former glory are the ruins of several once-impressive temples. Wat Phra Boromathat is surrounded by walls and contains a chedi restored by King Rama V in 1901, but dating from the 8th century and considered the best example of Srivijayan archi-tecture ● 50, while Wat Keo, which was discovered in 1978, has a crumbled brick prang of the Srivijaya period (below left). A small museum displays antiquities found in the area, mostly within Wat Phra Boromathat itself, with reproductions of important pieces that are now displayed in the National Museum in Bangkok.

WAT SUAN MOK

This modern temple, popular with foreigners as a place for retreat and study, is renowned for teaching meditation in English on the first ten days of the month to anyone ready to accept its extremely strict and spartan rules. Notably, half of the places are for women. Otherwise, its most notable feature is a collection of colorful murals left by visiting foreigners depicting a bewildering variety of subjects, ranging from Zen to compositions inspired by Egypt.

SURAT THANI

Surat Thani is an important southern railway and highway center as well as a busy seaport. Although it has a number of excellent seafood restaurants serving dishes and offers attractive views along the water-front, Surat Thani is of interest to most travelers today mainly as an embarkation point from which ferries leave for Koh Samui, and the islands that lie beyond it.

TEN VOWS
A novice monk takes these ten vows:
"I take the vow not to destroy life."
"I take the vow not to steal."
"I take the vow to abstain from impurity."
"I take the vow not to lie."
"I take the vow not to eat at forbidden times."
"I take the vow to abstain from dancing, singing, music and stage plays."
"I take the vow not to use garlands, scents, unguents, or ornaments."
"I take the vow not to use a broad or high bed."
"I take the vow not to receive gold or silver."

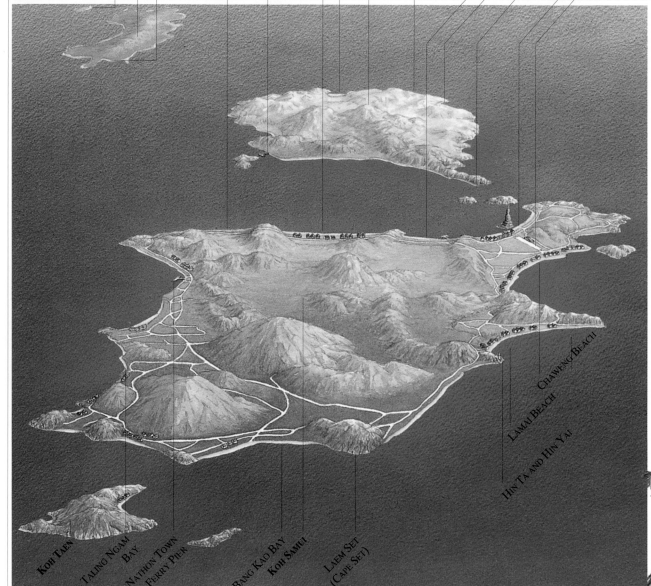

KOH NANG YUAN — KOH TAO — BAAN MAE HAAD — BANG PO BAY — THONG SALA — MAENAM BEACH — CHOLOKLAM BAY — KOH PHA-NGAN — KHUAT BEACH — BOPHUT BEACH — THONG NAI PAN BAY — RIN BEACH — BIG BUDDHA BEACH — AIRPORT

CHAWENG BEACH — LAMAI BEACH — HIN TA AND HIN YAI

KOH TAEN — TALING NGAM BAY — NATHON TOWN — FERRY PIER — BANG KAO BAY — KOH SAMUI — LAEM SET (CAPE SET)

Koh Samui islanders dry squid in the sun.

KOH SAMUI SEASHELLS

Cassis cornuta is very solid and heavy and has a short spine with about seven whorls.

Casum ceramicum is also solid and heavy, with a high spine.

Spondylus regius is a striking thorny oyster with seven elevated ribs bearing pointed spines.

Mitra mitra This is the largest of the mitra family.

some of the best coconuts in Thailand. Thousands of coconuts are sent to Bangkok and other parts of the country annually, and there is also a factory producing coconut fiber. Until the late 1970's the physical charms of Koh Samui were a closely guarded secret among backpackers in search of budget accommodation, long, virtually empty beaches, and a laid-back atmosphere. All that has changed. The island has seen a tremendous amount of development over the last decade with new five-star resorts introduced, massive property development and outstanding restaurants opened. Koh Samui now rivals nearby Phuket as an international destination, though with a mellow, New Age vibe reflected by the rapid growth of spas and alternative healing establishments. The two island resorts also complement each other in climate, since Phuket's season of

⏱ Two days

Thailand's third-largest island, about the size of Penang, Koh Samui is one of a group of islands lying 18 miles off the coast of Surat Thani. Ferries from the mainland call at the port of Tong Yang, while express boats berth at Nathon, Koh Samui's administrative capital. Covering 100 square miles, the hilly island has a thinly scattered population of about 50,000, most of whom traditionally derive a livelihood from huge inland plantations that produce

heaviest rain (July through September) runs concurrently with one of Koh Samui's sunniest times; the latter island's wettest months are toward the end of the year.

BUFFALO FIGHTING. One of the favorite pastimes of the islanders used to be buffalo fighting. To discourage gambling, the fights that were held every weekend are now restricted to festive occasions such as the Lunar New Year or the Thai New Year. A long ritual is performed before the fight. The brightly decorated buffaloes are splashed with holy water and kept apart by a curtain that is lifted at the very moment the two animals clash against each other. The fight ends when one of the buffaloes is pushed out of the arena.

BIG BUDDHA
The Big Buddha of Wat Phra Yai towers above the shrine of Koh Fan and is dedicated to the Parinirvana (reclining) Buddha. At the entrance of the temple, a figure of Maitreya, the Buddha of the Future, welcomes monks and visitors before they ascend to the colossal hilltop figure.

NORTHERN BEACHES

BIG BUDDHA BEACH (HAT PHRA YAI). This beach derives its name from a 40-foot-high image of the meditating Buddha at a monastery on a small islet called Koh Fan, connected by a causeway. The beach boasts a smooth stretch of sand, calm waters and a generally restful atmosphere. A boat ferries passengers daily over to Hat Rin on Koh Pha-ngan.

BOPHUT BEACH. East of Maenam is Ban Bophut, one of Samui's oldest settlements, with wooden shophouses lining the main street. The nearby beach is about a mile long, and the placid water, while not as clear as some others, is ideal for water-skiing. Boats ply the route from the village pier to Koh Phan-gan and a trip on one of these takes about 40 minutes.

MAENAM BEACH. This beach, near a village of the same name and with easy access to Nathon, is a 2½-mile stretch of white sand on a picturesque bay with a great view of Koh Pha-ngan offshore. Bungalows are available at a wide range of prices and boats can be hired for excursions to other beaches.

BANG PO BAY. This beach is still relatively undeveloped, mainly because the rocks and corals break the surface during the low tide. It is, however, one of the best locations for snorkeling and scuba-diving.

WHEELS FOR RENT
Motorbikes and automobiles are easily available for rent to those who want to tour the island on their own.

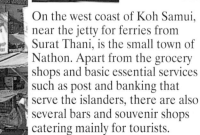

NATHON TOWN

On the west coast of Koh Samui, near the jetty for ferries from Surat Thani, is the small town of Nathon. Apart from the grocery shops and basic essential services such as post and banking that serve the islanders, there are also several bars and souvenir shops catering mainly for tourists.

CHAWENG BEACH

The most developed of Koh Samui's beaches, Chaweng is a 4-mile crescent with white sand and clear water. Tourist facilities and nightlife are concentrated in the central section, which also overlooks the best part of the beach. The bars, discos and restaurants are patronized heavily by vacationers from Bangkok, backpackers and rave partygoers from neighboring island Koh Pha-ngan. The few sleazier bars are located in Lamai. Equipment for windsurfing, para-sailing and scuba-diving are available. Water scooters have also invaded the beaches, robbing Koh Samui of its little-island charm.

OVERLAP STONE
This stone is a popular Samui landmark, a huge boulder balanced on a promontory above Lower Lamai Beach, where there are a few bungalows for rent and a refreshment stall. Another mile further up is a point of land that affords impressive views of the island's interior scenery.

LAMAI BEACH

After Chaweng, Lamai is probably the most popular beach, appealing to budget-conscious visitors. Besides the wide choice of accommodation and spas, there is nightlife with numerous restaurants and discos. Lower Lamai offers good swimming even when the seas elsewhere are too rough.

COCONUT PLANTATIONS

Until the advent of tourism, and to a large extent even today, Koh Samui's economy has been based on the graceful coconut palms that cover most of the interior, even extending up the mountain sides; an average of two million coconuts are transported to Bangkok monthly, a sizeable part of the national production. The sweet juice of young coconuts is a favorite drink, while coconut cream plays a bigger role in the local cuisine than it does elsewhere in the south. Some growers have trained monkeys who scamper nimbly up the lofty trunks, select only those coconuts ready for picking, and drop them to the ground.

HIN TA AND HIN YAI
Hin Ta and Hin Yai, or "Grandfather Stone and Grandmother Stone," are a pair of much-photographed rock formations suggesting genitals at the tip of a headland that separates Central Lamai and Lower Lamai. Hin Ta points toward the sky, while his companion is a wave-splashed cleft about 132 feet away.

WATERFALLS

For those who enjoy waterfalls, the interior of Samui offers a number of scenic opportunities. The two most popular are Hin Lat, which spills over several levels and has a pool good for bathing, and Na Muang, which cascades for over 130 feet down a slab of yellow limestone.

KOH PHA-NGAN ★

Less developed than Koh Samui – at least for the time being – is Koh Pha-ngan, the largest of its neighboring islands, 9 miles away. Covering about 76 square miles, it has a small population of about 8,000, mostly concentrated in the main town of Thong Sala. Tourist accommodation is simple and the atmosphere appeals to backpackers drawn to the health and meditation retreats. There are dozens of beautiful, unspoiled beaches, among the most popular being Hat Rin, which hosts the famous Full Moon Party every month and has direct boat services to and from Samui. Other highlights include Hat Khuat ("Bottle Beach"), in a secluded cove on the northern coast; and Choloklam Bay, on which there are several stretches of sand. There are daily express boats from Nathon pier to Thong Sala, as well as boats from Bophut Pier and Big Buddha Beach to Hat Rin; all boat services are subject to weather conditions.

KOH TAO

The "Turtle Island", so called because of its shape, covers only 8½ square miles, and takes two hours to reach by express boat from Thong Sala on Koh Pha-ngan, or three to four hours by the regular ferry. Although increasingly developed, the island offers a tranquil ambience. Clear waters and extensive offshore coral reefs make it Thailand's top location to learn diving. Most of the bungalow facilities are on the western and southern coasts of the island. A principal landmark is the triangular beach on Koh Nang Yuan, off the north coast.

ANG THONG NATIONAL MARINE PARK ★

Lying 19 miles northwest of Koh Samui, this archipelago of forty islands is characterized by impressive limestone outcrops and blue lagoons. Koh Tao is one of the larger islands in the group; the others vary greatly in size and many have hidden coves with white-sand beaches. Koh Wua Ta Lap ("Isle of the Sleeping Cow") has bungalow facilities, while Koh Mae ("Mother Island") has a beautiful beach surrounded by towering cliffs. There is a daily boat to the park from Nathon, leaving in the morning and returning in the afternoon.

WATER BABIES
"Little children, long before they can walk, are thrown into the water by their mothers, who fasten under their arms a tin float that always keeps the head above water. The wee brown dots splash and splutter about in the luke-warm current of the river, involuntarily learning the correct action of the limbs in swimming, and gaining an acquaint-ance with this element that ever afterwards prevents any feeling of fear. In this way many children learn to swim almost as soon as, if not before, they can walk."
Ernest Young

HISTORY

One of the oldest settlements in Thailand, Nakhon Si Thammarat was known to ancient travelers as Ligor and was an important center during both the Srivijaya and Dvaravati periods, over a thousand years ago. Many notable works of art – both Hindu and Buddhist – have been found in and around the city, testifying to the variety of cultures that influenced its development even before the Thais appeared on the scene. King Ramkhamhaeng of Sukhothai is popularly believed to have visited Nakhon Si Thammarat in the 13th century and to have been so impressed by the teachings of the city's Buddhist monks that he brought a group of them back to the first independent Thai capital.

The resplendent Viharn Luang of Wat Mahathat.

NIELLOWARE
One of Nakhon Si Thammarat's outstanding traditional arts is niello, which arrived before the 12th century, probably from India. An amalgam of dark metals is applied to etched portions of silver or gold to create intricate designs covering trays, boxes, vases and other objects. A 15th-century law in Ayutthaya decreed that high-ranking nobles could proclaim their position through the possession of a nielloware pedestal and tray, while in 1687, King Narai is recorded as having sent a nielloware bowl to King Louis XIV of France. Bangkok rulers have also traditionally presented the ware as gifts to foreign heads of state.

MUSEUM. The Nakhon Si Thammarat branch of the National Museum ▲ 81-2 is the most important in the country after Bangkok's. Among the items on display is an impressive collection of early Hindu images and some of the earliest Buddhist sculpture. The Hindu figures, found at Takua Pa, include a beautiful Vishnu once wrapped in the roots of a tree. It was decapitated by vandals and when the roots were cut away to move the figure, the missing head was discovered to have been a fake; the original one, now restored to its proper place on the body, was buried beneath the statue.

WAT MAHATHAT. The most revered of Nakhon Si Thammarat's Buddhist monuments is Wat Mahathat, founded during the Srivijaya period (8th–13th century). The temple's dominant feature is a towering 254-foot-high chedi, the spire of which is covered with gold leaf and studded with precious stones. The chedi stands in an immense cloister covered with colored tiles and surrounding it is a gallery lined with numerous Buddha images. A standing Sukhothai-style Buddha image is enshrined in one of the temple's two chapels while on the altar of the other there are bas-reliefs that show West-erners among the various figures. Outside the cloister of Wat Mahathat is the Viharn Luang, with columns that lean inward in the Ayutthaya style and a richly decorated ceiling.

LAKAWN WALLS.

«IT WAS WITH NO SMALL PLEASURE THAT WE RATTLED DOWN THE ANCHOR IN SONGKHLA, AND CONTEMPLATED THE BEAUTIFUL HILL-GIRDLED HARBOR THAT LAY BEFORE US.»
H. WARRINGTON SMYTH, 1898

SONGKHLA

Songkhla, once known as Singora, is the only natural port on the lower Gulf of Thailand side of the southern isthmus and as such has long been an important center of trade, founded and largely developed by Chinese. Much of the trade, along with the money it brought, moved to Haadyai, more conveniently located at a railway junction, with the result that Songkhla has been able to retain some degree of its old atmosphere and crumbling Sino-Portuguese architecture. A hill behind the Samila Beach Hotel, surmounted by an ancient chedi, offers scenic views. Boats can be hired for trips around an inland sea or Thale Sap, which empties into the gulf, or to nearby Muslim fishing villages.

SAMILA BEACH. Few foreign tourists visit the nearby Samila Beach, an attractive strand on the gulf lined with casuarina trees and stalls selling freshly cooked seafood, though visitors from Malaysia still come during the hot season. At its southern end, intricately painted Khorlae boats bring in their catches.

NANG TALUNG
A form of shadow play called *nang talung*, closely resembling the Indonesian *wayang kulit*, is frequently staged at festivals in the far south. The buffalo-hide figures have movable parts – arms, legs, or chin – and their concealed manipulators accompany their actions with songs and often ribald repartee. ● 36.

WAT MACHI MAWAT. This temple boasts several interesting murals showing life around the port in the late 1800's and early 1900's.
SONGKHLA MUSEUM. A beautiful old Chinese mansion dating from the late 19th century, once the residence of a provincial governor, has been restored as a museum (below). Chinese porcelain, statuary and objects from the excavations of nearby Sating Phra are displayed.
KOH YOH. Spread over a hillside on this island is an open-air ethnographic museum reached by the Tinsulanonda Bridge.

THALE NOI BIRD SANCTUARY

Just a few miles north of Songkhla is an 11-square-mile region of freshwater and swamp ecosystem known as Thale Noi. Several canals flow through the area, making it accessible to nature-lovers and bird-watchers.
BIRD-WATCHING. Nearly 200 species of birds – including several rare ones such as the lesser adjutant stork, white ibis, spot-billed pelican and gray heron – have been recorded in this nature reserve. Egrets, cormorants, terns and jacanas are also common here. The best period to observe the birds is between January and April. Boats can be hired for a three-hour trip from the nature reserve headquarters to Sala Nang Riam on the other side of the lake. The fishing village offers visitors to Thale Noi a peek at life in this typical southern community.

HAADYAI

Strategically situated at the junction of major railways and roads, Haadyai has become one of the most prosperous cities in the south in recent decades, of little architectural or cultural distinction but with a definite boom-town air of excitement. A considerable part of the money derived from such major southern industries as tin, rubber and seafood processing passes through Haadyai's bankers and businessmen and to this can be added a possibly even greater amount from tourism. Malaysians come in large numbers – around 600,000 a year, according to a recent estimate – across the border just 36 miles away, drawn partly by lower prices for luxury goods and partly by an uninhibited nightlife not available in their own country. Haadyai has more than 5,000 hotel rooms, most of them filled on weekends, plus hundreds of discos, bars and massage parlors.

FISHING BOATS
The fishing boats of southern Thailand have intricate colorful motifs similar to those of the northwestern coast of peninsular Malaysia – proof of the cultural link existing in this region. The decorations are to please the spirits and invoke them to bless the boats and protect the occupants from hazards at sea. When boats are launched a shaman is called to perform an ancient animistic ritual during which prayers are recited and offerings made to the spirits.

PATTANI AND ANCIENT MUSLIM KINGDOMS

Muslims comprise Thailand's largest religious minority, about two million in all, mostly Malay living in the southernmost provinces. Pattani and Pattalung have been in fact prosperous, independent kingdoms and active trading posts since the end of the first millennium. This prosperity came to an end when the Siamese invaded and destroyed Pattani, bringing the entire area under the rule of the Kingdom of Siam. Since then, there has always been friction between the Muslims and the Thai government, most evident during the 1960's and 1970's, when many Muslims fled to the jungles to join the communists. Today the southern provinces are relatively quiet but sporadic incidents are sufficient to dissuade tourists from coming. Although Muslim traditions are deep-rooted, there is little architectural evidence of the long history of these ancient Malay states. Most of the villagers are simple people, accustomed to a subsistence livelihood and spending their days fishing and mending nets.

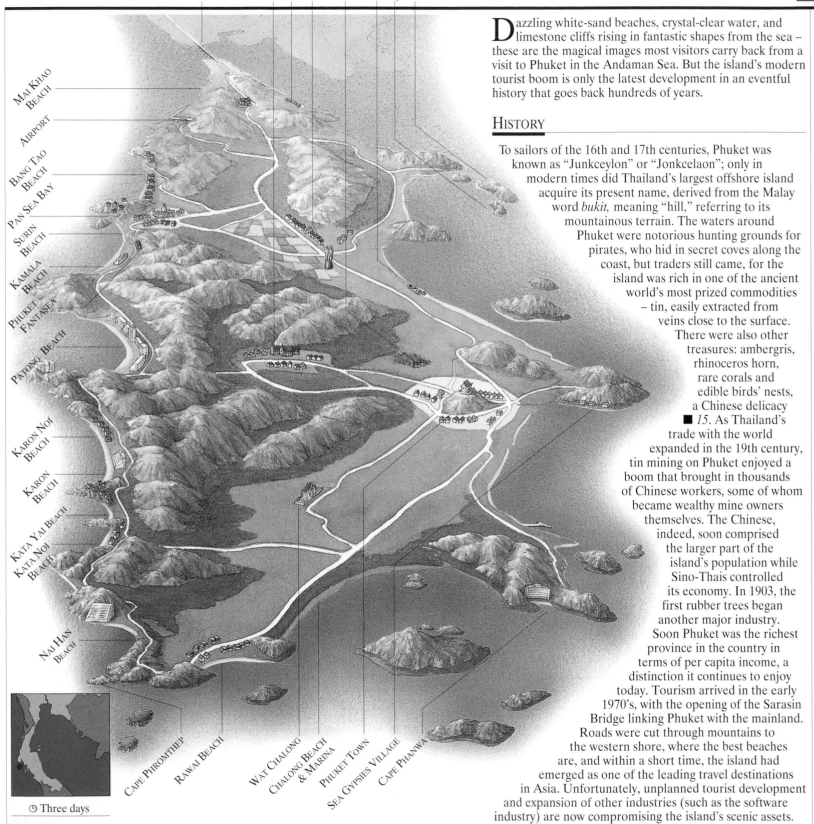

SARASIN BRIDGE
KATU VILLAGE
YACHT MARINA
MONUMENT TO
PHUKET'S HEROINES
AQUARIUM &
BUTTERFLY FARM
BOAT LAGOON
KOH NAKHA NOI
KOH NAKHA YAI

MAI KHAO BEACH
AIRPORT
BANG TAO BEACH
PAN SEA BAY
SURIN BEACH
KAMALA BEACH
PHUKET FANTASEA
PATONG BEACH
KARON NOI BEACH
KARON BEACH
KATA YAI BEACH
KATA NOI BEACH
NAI HAN BEACH

CAPE PHROMTHEP
RAWAI BEACH
WAT CHALONG
CHALONG BEACH & MARINA
PHUKET TOWN
SEA GYPSIES VILLAGE
CAPE PHANWA

⏱ Three days

Dazzling white-sand beaches, crystal-clear water, and limestone cliffs rising in fantastic shapes from the sea – these are the magical images most visitors carry back from a visit to Phuket in the Andaman Sea. But the island's modern tourist boom is only the latest development in an eventful history that goes back hundreds of years.

HISTORY

To sailors of the 16th and 17th centuries, Phuket was known as "Junkceylon" or "Jonkcelaon"; only in modern times did Thailand's largest offshore island acquire its present name, derived from the Malay word *bukit,* meaning "hill," referring to its mountainous terrain. The waters around Phuket were notorious hunting grounds for pirates, who hid in secret coves along the coast, but traders still came, for the island was rich in one of the ancient world's most prized commodities – tin, easily extracted from veins close to the surface. There were also other treasures: ambergris, rhinoceros horn, rare corals and edible birds' nests, a Chinese delicacy ■ 15. As Thailand's trade with the world expanded in the 19th century, tin mining on Phuket enjoyed a boom that brought in thousands of Chinese workers, some of whom became wealthy mine owners themselves. The Chinese, indeed, soon comprised the larger part of the island's population while Sino-Thais controlled its economy. In 1903, the first rubber trees began another major industry. Soon Phuket was the richest province in the country in terms of per capita income, a distinction it continues to enjoy today. Tourism arrived in the early 1970's, with the opening of the Sarasin Bridge linking Phuket with the mainland. Roads were cut through mountains to the western shore, where the best beaches are, and within a short time, the island had emerged as one of the leading travel destinations in Asia. Unfortunately, unplanned tourist development and expansion of other industries (such as the software industry) are now compromising the island's scenic assets.

PHUKET'S HEROINES
On the road from the airport leading toward Phuket Town stands a memorial to two Phuket heroines. In 1785, the brave pair rallied the residents of Thalang (then the island's main town) to defend it successfully against the Burmese invaders, in reward for which the two ladies were given noble titles by King Rama I of Bangkok.

OLD HOUSES
Adding considerably to the charm of Phuket Town are its surviving old Chinese houses (above), built in the Sino-Portuguese style also found in Malacca. Many of these houses belong to families whose ancestors first came to the island as laborers in the 19th-century tin mines.

MOVIE-MAKERS
The scenic beauties of Phuket and neighboring Phangnga Bay have attracted numerous moviemakers, foreign as well as Thai. Part of the movie *The Man with the Golden Gun* was filmed at Phangnga, while Phuket's interior was used in Brian De Palma's *Casualties of War* and the old District Office appeared as the French embassy in *The Killing Fields*.

THE PLEASURES OF PHUKET
Phuket has a wide range of attractions for visitors. Most are still centered around its renowned beaches: para-sailing, surfing, water-skiing, deep-sea fishing and romantic cruises on chartered boats. Dive trips vary from half and full day trips to overnight cruises to distant reserves like the Similan Islands ▲ *110*. In addition, shops sell handicrafts from all parts of Thailand, countless restaurants offer Thai or foreign cuisine, and attractions such as butterfly farms and orchid nurseries cater to the tourist trade.

PHUKET TOWN TODAY

Phuket Town, the bustling provincial capital, has a population of around 60,000. A recent boom in real estate has spurred developers to build countless shophouses, hotels and condominiums, with an inevitable loss of atmosphere, though many of the elegant old millionaires' mansions remain. Particularly colorful is the public market on Rasada Street, across from the minibus terminus, where all the local produce is piled in tempting abundance amid busy vendors and haggling customers. Close to the center of town is the hill known as Khao Rang, on top of which are a landscaped "fitness park" and a restaurant offering splendid views of the town itself and harbor, the sea and distant offshore islands.

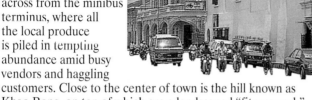

PHUKET AQUARIUM & BUTTERFLY FARM

Overlooking the sea on Chalong Bay, not very far from Phuket Town, the aquarium is part of the Marine Biology Research Center and rears a variety of sea creatures from local waters. It also serves as a hatchery for the eggs of huge sea turtles that come ashore to lay between October and February. The Butterfly Farm and Aquarium both lie two miles north of Phuket Town.

PHUKET PORT

A visit to Phuket's main port, east of the town, reveals the importance of deep-sea fishing. About 350 industrially equipped boats fish the waters around the island and all the way to the Indian Ocean, hauling in about 40,000 tons of seafood annually. The port scene is most colorful when the boats return to unload in the early morning. Further east a road connects to Koh Siray, where a Sea Gypsy village shows a fast disappearing way of life ▲ *110*.

CHINESE TEMPLES

Phuket's Chinese character is reflected in a number of temples. The principal ones are at Kathu, where the Vegetarian Festival originated in the 19th century, and Put Jaw Temple in town, both lavishly adorned with red and gold carvings and images of various gods and goddesses.

VEGETARIAN FESTIVAL. Held annually in October, this is another manifestation of the strong Chinese flavor that pervades the island. The festival was started by immigrants who flocked in large numbers from China and nearby Malaya to work in the tin mines, supposedly in response to a mysterious fever that was afflicting them. It now lasts for ten days and, in addition to abstinence from meat and rituals held at various Chinese temples, features gala processions that attract crowds of visitors as well as local believers. Many of the participants go into deep trances, enabling them to endure a wide range of self-inflicted ordeals, from walking over beds of red-hot charcoal to piercing their cheeks with long metal skewers; such practices are not a part of traditional vegetarian festivals in China and were most probably assimilated over the years from India.

BUDDHIST TEMPLES

Although Phuket has a sizeable number of Muslim residents, about 60 percent of the population are Buddhists, who attend

one or another of the island's twenty-nine temples. The largest and best-known is Wat Chalong, which contains images of two revered monks who helped put down a rebellion of Chinese immigrants in 1876; the images are kept supplied with offerings of flowers and incense. Another important temple is Wat Phra Thong (above), on the airport road, where the main attraction is a large Buddha image supposedly made of gold, half buried in the earth; after its discovery by a farmer, the image was left as it was and the temple built to shelter it.

LAK MUANG. In most old Thai cities, a shrine, or the *lak muang*, was erected at the "central axis," usually around a wood or stone pillar that marked the center of the settlement and provided a home for the spirit who guarded it. In the case of Phuket, the pillar is near the monument to two heroines in the sleepy district of Tha Rua ▲ *108*, where the island's principal community once thrived.

A HEAVY SMOKER
In Phuket, at the end of the last century, a monk who was a heavy smoker became famous. An image was erected in Wat Chalong and ever since has been kept supplied with offerings. These offerings commonly take the form of lighted cigarettes, placed in the mouth. A gentle draft causes the cigarettes to continue to burn. The image of the monk, therefore appears to be smoking.

«THE LAPPING OF THE WAVES IS ALL TOO OFTEN DROWNED OUT BY
THE RUMBLE OF CONCRETE MIXERS.»

ALISTAIR SHEARER

A LOCAL DELICACY
Prawns are skewered and arranged between lengths of bamboo and left to dry in the sun before they are eaten.

SOUTHERN CUISINE
Southern food has a reputation for being the hottest in Thailand. As well as standard dishes found in most parts of the country – often with lashings of extra chillies – many local restaurants also offer Malay-style fare that reflects Indian influence in its use of curry powder and turmeric.

PATONG BEACH

Stretching for 2½ miles around a bay, Patong was the first of Phuket's beaches to be developed and is still the only one to offer a really varied Bangkok-style nightlife. Hotels large and small, restaurants, shops, bars, even a towering new condominium, line its main street, overlooking a turquoise sea that, so far at least, remains remarkably clean. All sorts of water sports are available, from windsurfing to para-sailing, and boats can be hired for trips to less crowded swimming areas along the coast. The seabed shelves gently and, with usually calm waters and the natural grandeur of the forested backdrop, swimming and other water activities are very popular. Visitors staying elsewhere, on the other hand, often come to Patong to enjoy its rich seafood and after-dark activities.

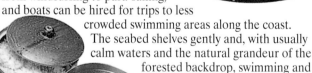

OTHER BEACHES

All of Phuket's best beaches are located on the western side of the island, facing the Andaman Sea, and range from strands several miles long to smaller crescents. There are thirteen major ones, starting at Mai Khao near the airport and extending down to Rawai at the southern tip, each with a distinctive character of its own. A narrow road connects the string of beaches and cuts down travel time along the coast considerably.

MAI KHAO AND NAI YANG. The northernmost of Phuket's west-coast beaches, Mai Khao and Nai Yang are still relatively undeveloped and therefore quiet. They stretch for more than 10 miles altogether. The water, however, is not as clear as at other beaches, especially at low tide.

KARON. This stretch actually consists of two beaches, one an idyllic little cove popularly known as Relax Bay and occupied by Le Méridien Hotel, and the other much longer and now lined with a variety of tourist accommodation large and small.

PAN SEA. Scenically, Pan Sea is one of the most enchanting beaches, with very good opportunities for snorkeling and swimming during the dry season.

KATA. Like Karon, Kata is divided into Kata Yai (Big Kata) and Kata Noi (Little Kata). The former, a long stretch of fine beach, is the site of the Club Méditerranée and several smaller facilities; the latter is further south and has a hotel, the Kata Thani, and several bungalow complexes.

SURIN. A picturesque strand with steep hills that rise sharply at the back, this is especially popular with Thai day-trippers on weekends and holidays. The spectacular Thai-style Amanpuri Hotel overlooks one end of the beach.

NAI HAN ★. Site of the Phuket Yacht Club, Nai Han is an otherwise undeveloped beach with white sand, clear water and a scenic view of Phrom Thep at the southern tip of the island.

RAWAI. An attractive strand fringed by coconut palms, Rawai is located on a shallow, silty bay and is therefore less popular with swimmers than some other beaches. Boats can be hired here for trips to the offshore islands.

LAEM PHROM THEP. This is an elevation at the far southern tip of Phuket, attracting crowds of tourists and many local people because of its panoramic views of the sea and often spectacular sunsets. As a result, traffic jams in the vicinity are a common sight. The visitor in search of solitude should look elsewhere. Among the picturesque islands worth a trip offshore is Koh Keo, where there are meditation cells for Buddhist monks and a graceful chedi.

SEA GYPSIES
The historically itinerant Chao Ley are probably Phuket's oldest inhabitants. While some still live on board their boats in other parts of the Andaman Sea, most have now settled in Phuket in small coastal villages such as Rawai and Koh Siray ▲ 109. The Sea Gypsies earn their living by fishing, diving for oysters and other shells, and harvesting edible birds' nests deposited on lofty limestone cliffs and in caves ■ 15, ▲ 114, 116.

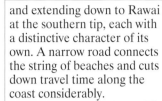

BEAUTIFUL BEACHES
Kata, Nai Han and Laem Phrom Thep (below) are just three of the beautiful beaches that make up the main tourist attraction on Phuket.

RUBBER TREES
"Beyond the forest the level of the land was higher and there were more rubber plantations – nothing but rubber. Thousands and thousands of acres were planted with the dark, dull green heveas. The trees stood in straight rows, and by the side of each was a stick. On the top of each stick was a porcelain cup upside down. In some places the cup was attached to the tree by a bit of wire below the tin spout through which the latex flowed when the tree was tapped. Coolies passed barefoot and soundlessly among the trees and turned the cups out into large zinc churns similar to European milk churns."

M.H. Lulofs

RUBBER PLANTATIONS

The first rubber trees, brought from Malaysia, were planted on Phuket in 1903, only a decade after they were first acclimatized to Southeast Asia at Singapore's Botanical Gardens. Thus began the vast plantations that are now scattered over the island, producing around 14,000 tons of dry latex annually. Thanks to these plantations and others on the mainland, Thailand is today a major exporter of rubber.

KHAO PHRA THAEO NATIONAL PARK

Located just off the airport road, Khao Phra Thaeo National Park contains the last remnants of the tropical rain forest that once covered Phuket. Near the entrance to the jungle is Tone Sai Waterfall, an attractive site popular with local day-trippers on weekends but virtually deserted at other times.

OFFSHORE ISLANDS

A number of Phuket's smaller offshore islands can be easily reached by boat on short trips. The most popular with visitors, especially snorkelers and scuba divers, is probably Koh Hi, also called Coral Island because of the extensive reefs that surround it, just east of the tip of Phuket. Koh Mai Thong, a little further, has fine beaches on the far side, while up the eastern coast are Koh Nakha Yai and Koh Nakha Noi. The latter has a cultured-pearl farm, where oysters are seeded and carefully tended for two years, the amount of time required for a pearl to form inside. Yet another attractive island is Koh Lawa Yai, located at the southern extremity of Phang-nga Bay.

SHELLS
The waters around Phuket are a rich source of shells, both rare and common for sale in the numerous shops. Some of the more serious dealers employ divers to search for the rarest specimens at great depths and sell their finds to international collectors at high prices.

KOH SIMILAN NATIONAL PARK ★

Approximately 60 miles northwest of Phuket in the Andaman Sea, the Similan group covers 51 square miles and consists of nine small islands, the name being derived from the Malay word *sembilan*, meaning "nine." Designated a national park in 1982, the islands have long been uninhabited except for Sea Gypsies ▲ 110 who come to fish the rich coral reefs around them. Tour groups have been coming in large numbers, attracted by the unspoiled beaches and the remarkable variety of underwater life, especially off Koh Miang. The Similans have over two hundred species of hard coral, hundreds of colorful fish and other sea creatures such as huge sea fans and barrel sponges, manta rays and whale sharks. Sea turtles come to lay their eggs on some of the beaches ■ 16, and wildlife on land ■ 10 includes macaques, langurs, bats and about thirty species of birds.

VANISHING TURTLES
Visitors to Similans at night should not disturb the endangered huge black turtles, which sometimes come ashore for a breath of air. They can lay as many as 150 eggs in 20 inch-deep sand-pits. After 50–60 days of incubation, the hatchlings break out of the eggs and waddle to the sea, guided only by the reflection of moonlight. They are easily distracted by artificial light such as camera flashes or lamps.

KHAO LAK

An hour north of Phuket, a rainforested headland opens out onto Khao Lak and Bang Niang beach. Despite unremarkable sand or water, this coast was growing fast thanks to its charm and national park ecology until devastated by the Tsunami. Rebuilding took over two years. Diving excursions reach reefs at the Similans, Koh Surin and Richelieu Rock.

KHAO SOK NATIONAL PARK

The road to Surat Thani passes Thailand's largest remaining tropical rainforest. Stretching from the coast to a reservoir rimmed by karst cliffs, this nature reserve protects many large species including tiger. Kayak trips and hikes can be arranged.

MANGROVE SWAMPS · KOH HONG · LIGHTHOUSE · KOH PHING KAN · KOH PANNYI · KOH KHIEN · KOH NOM SAO · PARK HEADQUARTERS · MANGROVE SWAMPS · PHANG-NGA BAY RESORT HOTEL · KOH TALU

KOH MAK · KOH YAO NOI

🕐 One day

Millennia ago, Phang-nga Bay was dry land with scattered limestone mountains; the sea invaded as glaciers melted, around 10,000 years before the beginning of the Christian era, leaving only a spectacular profusion of mountain peaks rising from the water to form one of the world's greatest natural attractions. The upheaval also led to the formation of several sea caves, some of which lie below sea level while others rise high above the rocks and remain mostly unexplored even to this day. Thirty-eight miles from Phuket by road, or about three hours by boat, the bay and surrounding areas it were declared a marine national park in 1981. More than forty islands are included, several reaching an altitude of 1,000 feet and shaped like animals, with dramatic sea caves and sheltered, pristine beaches. On the mainland around the bay are canals threading through dense mangrove swamps and

caves. Wildlife in the national park includes dolphins, crab-eating macaques and huge fruit-eating bats (also known as flying foxes) and numerous species of birds, of which the most easily seen are kingfishers, sea eagles and white egrets. Mudskippers, that queer breed of fish that use their flapping fins to move about on land, thrive among the mangroves ■ 12. Most visitors come on day trips from Phuket or Krabi, though excellent food and accommodation are provided by the Phang-nga Bay Resort Hotel.

LIMESTONE BEAUTIES
Much of the attraction of Phang-nga's countless caves, both on the mainland and on many of the islands in the bay, lies in their limestone formations. Intricate stalactites and stalagmites and the atmospheric lighting from cave openings produce a theatrical effect.

«THE UNIQUENESS OF PONGA DEPENDS UPON ITS LIMESTONE PEAKS, WHICH STAND IN SHARP POINTS AND STEEP PRECIPICES OUT OF ITS WATERS, SOME MORE THAN 1,500 FEET IN HEIGHT.»

H. WARRINGTON SMYTH

PHANG-NGA NATIONAL PARK

The headquarters of Phang-nga National Park are located on Highway 4144, near one of the estuaries leading to the bay. This is also a good point from which to explore by boat the park's fascinating mangrove swamps. The trees have strange root systems that protrude from the water and provide shelter for such creatures as mudskippers, fiddler crabs, lizards and numerous colorful birds. Some places in the mangroves allow for excellent swimming.

KOH KHIEN

Koh Khien ("Writing Island") has a large cave, on the walls of which are ancient paintings of men and such animals as sharks, dolphins and crocodiles. These paintings are believed to have been the work of people who inhabited the region 3,000–4,000 years ago and are visible from the sea.

GLOSSARY OF MARINE TERMS
koh = island
khao = mountain
hat = beach
tham = cave
laem = cape
hin = stone
ao = bay
thale = sea

KOH PANNYI

On Koh Pannyi, a picturesque little Muslim fishing village of about 400 people nestles in the shadow of an immense limestone slab that protects it from the monsoons. The houses are built above the water on stout piles of mangrove wood obtained from the mainland and most of the people earn their living by fishing and making shrimp paste. Additional revenue comes from the many tourists who visit Phang-nga Bay to photograph its quaint scenery and enjoy a sumptuous seafood lunch at one of the numerous restaurants.

KOH MAK

A flat round island with coconut palms, a Muslim village and beautiful beaches, Koh Mak makes an ideal picnic spot.

KOH HONG

"Hong" in Thai means "room," and this curiously shaped island – part of a group of the same name – contains an extraordinary enclosed waterway lit by an opening above and accessible to small boats. The chamber offers wonderful opportunities for swimming and photography.

THAM KEO

Tham Keo means "Glass Cave," and a shimmering grotto, hung with dazzling white stalactites, is the principal attraction of this island. Small boats enter the cave, which leads to an adjacent cavern with views of the sea below.

KOH PHING KAN

Consisting of two separate rock formations leaning one against another, Koh Phing Kan is also popularly known as James Bond Island, thanks to the fact that several scenes from the film *The Man with the Golden Gun* were shot there. The island has now become a tourist trap, its natural beauties obscured by boatloads of visitors and others trying to profit from them.

ORIGIN OF PHANG-NGA
The name of Phang-nga originates from a legend linked to a limestone mountain with dramatic slopes that loom over the provincial capital. Some farmers in remote times had attacked and killed by mistake an elephant god which at once turned into stone. The massive cliff in Phang-nga Bay is said to be the petrified form of the pachyderm with its butchered tusks leaning on its flanks.

LANAH BAY · PHI PHI VILLAGE · YONGKASEM BAY · **KOH PHI PHI DON** · LODALAM BAY · TON SAI BAY · WANG LONG BAY · LONG BEACH · VIKING CAVE · **KOH PHI PHI LE** · MAYA BAY

🕐 One day

About two hours from Phuket, Krabi, or Koh Lanta by fast boat, the Phi Phi Islands offer breathtakingly beautiful scenery and a number of good beaches for swimming and snorkeling. The two islands, together with Hat Nopparat in Krabi on the mainland, have been designated by the government as a national park.

KOH PHI PHI DON

The larger of the two islands, Koh Phi Phi Don is also the most developed in terms of tourism. Boats generally unload their passengers at a fishing village on Ton Sai Bay, protected by steep, jungled limestone cliffs on one side and by low hills on the other. Thanks to all the day-trippers, however, plus the numerous restaurants and other tourist facilities, the main beach there has lost much of its former tranquility and serious swimmers go to a series of quieter ones on the west side of the bay, culminating in Hat Yao, or Long Beach. Several other resorts have been built on serene beaches at the northern end of the island on the west coast, while across a narrow strip of land behind Ton Sai village is Lodalam Bay, a shallow lagoon with a wealth of crabs and other shellfish.

KOH PHI PHI LE ★

In terms of scenery, the smaller Koh Phi Phi Le is by far the more spectacular, with limestone cliffs that plunge hundreds of feet down to the sea and numerous secret coves with small crescents of white sand and crystal-clear water; a particularly beautiful spot is Maya Bay, surrounded by soaring cliffs and harboring three beaches where filming of *The Beach* took place. The controversial replanting of vegetation during filming and the increased tourism after that has damaged the ecology. A popular attraction is an immense, cathedral-like cave, festooned with stalactites and stalagmites, where edible birds' nests are harvested ■ *15*. It is dubbed Viking Cave because of some ancient rock paintings that do vaguely resemble Viking boats, though their origin is unknown.

EDIBLE BIRDS' NESTS. The main ingredient of birds' nest soup is produced by a tiny, fork-tailed swift known as *Callocalia esculenta*, which favors lofty caves and cliffs. The small cup-shaped nests, about 1½ inches in diameter, are composed of a gluey secretion discharged by the birds in long strands that harden after exposure to the air. As they are harvested at specified times – by Sea Gypsies ■ *110*, who fearlessly climb tall spindly bamboo ladders (right), often in total darkness – the swiftlets may have to build the nests up to three times between February and July. The birds' nests can be eaten raw or poached in soup, and are an expensive delicacy highly regarded for their nutritional value by Chinese gourmets.

PHI PHI EXCURSIONS
Most excursions to the Phi Phi Islands are in large boats, leaving Phuket either from Chalong or Rawai Beach around 8am and starting back around 3.30pm. When hiring smaller fishing craft be sure to check on the weather since the crossing can be rough during the monsoon season.

▲ THE SOUTH
KRABI AND OFFSHORE ISLANDS

OIL PALMS
Extensive oil palm plantations can be seen on the mainland around Krabi, forming an important local industry. The palms, which yield an oil used in both cooking and food processing, originated in Africa and were first acclimatized to Southeast Asia by the Dutch during their rule of Indonesia.

Known for its stunning karst scenery, Krabi has become a major destination since its airport opened. Like Phuket and Koh Samui in the early 1970's, it was accidentally "discovered" by intrepid backpackers and cruising yachts only in the 1980's. Shops, accommodation and restaurants are going upscale and spreading along the coast. Krabi's popularity with escapist travelers is not difficult to understand. It has several beautiful beaches with clear water ideal for snorkeling and diving, towering limestone cliffs, a pre-historic shell cemetery, atmospheric caves, mangrove forests ■ 12, rubber plantations, a national park (Khao Phanom Bencha) full of interesting wildlife, and access by boat to more than eighty scenic offshore islands. Krabi has suffered less from the sort of rapid, uncontrolled development that has disfigured so many beaches on Phuket and other southern island resorts, partly due to the efforts of newly aware Thai environmentalists.

BEACHES ★

Krabi's beaches, though less numerous than those of Phuket, are relatively unspoiled and exceptionally beautiful. The most easily accessible beach from Krabi town is Ao Nang, on a wide, shallow bay, where there are dozens of resorts, large and small, with many amenities. The town can be reached either by road or, more quickly, by the local long-tail boat down the mangrove-lined river and along the coast. About a mile further on is Nopparat Thara Beach, a casuarina-lined strand that is part of the national park including the Phi Phi Islands. Far more spectacular in terms of scenery, however, are several others that are only accessible

by boat around the sheer limestone cliffs of Laem Phra Nang. Rai Leh's two beaches sandwich all the lodgings, framed by mammoth rocks on the north and south, with an extensive coral reef at the southern end of Rai Leh West beach. Around another headland and facing the picturesque, lofty island of Koh Nang is a long, palm-fringed strand that many visitors regard as the most beautiful in the region. Between the beach and Koh Nang, a coral reef offers some limited snorkeling and diving.

CAVES AND CLIFFS

The limestone mountains around Krabi contain a large variety of splendid caves, several of them popular tourist attractions. Sua (Tiger) Cave, down a jungle trail about 2 miles from Krabi town, is a noted Buddhist monastery for meditation. Along Highway 4, leading to Ao Luk, is a small cavern called Tham Sadet, while two unspoiled caves, Tham Lot and Tham Phi Hua To, can be reached by boat from Tao Than village in Ao Luk. The so-called Princess Cave in the cliffside of Cape Phra Nang contains a shrine where fishermen leave phallic offerings. The surrounding cliffs offer Thailand's best rock climbing; climbing schools dot the cape.

OFFSHORE ISLANDS

Boats can be hired for trips to the Phi Phi Islands from both Ao Nang Beach and Krabi town, but there are many closer offshore islands that are good for swimming and diving. Koh Poda, 30 minutes by long-tail boat

from Ao Nang, has a large coral reef teeming with colorful fish. Further out, but even more alluring, is the Koh Dam group of two large islands and a number of smaller ones. A good beach, shaded by casuarina trees, surrounds Koh Dam Hok, which also has a few simple bungalows and a restaurant, while Koh Dam Khwan boasts a superb expanse of reef that extends from the island to a group of rocky islets off the north end.

SHELL CEMETERY BEACH
Hat Su San Hoi, or the Shell Cemetery Beach, is located in Ban Laem Pho, about 10 miles from Krabi town. Countless petrified shells, some of which are about 75 million years old, have formed immense slabs of rock along the beach. Japan and the United States are the only other countries where this phenomenon can be seen.

DISAPPEARING REEFS
The coral reefs that abound close to the beaches provide exciting underwater seascapes thriving with marine plants, sea anemones and reef fishes. However, easy access to these reefs and ongoing exploitation may well destroy the beautiful ecosystem within the next decade.

THE NORTHEAST

THE NORTHEAST (ISAN), 117
KHMER TEMPLES, 118
ALONG THE MEKONG, 121
NATIONAL PARKS, 122

KOH LANTA

TROPICAL FISH
Filled with much marine life, the Andaman Sea shelters a great variety of fish. Among the most beautiful are:

the squirrel fish (*Myripristis adustus*), which usually hides among the corals;

the sweetlips – such as the striped grunt (*P. diagrammus*), which tastes as good as it looks;

the snub-nosed *Chaetodon ephippium*, a butterfly fish known for its changing colors;

and the surgeon fish (*Acanthurus glaucopareius*) whose colors blend with those of the coral.

The latest island candidate to be the 'new Samui' is Koh Lanta Yai, with new investment only mildly denting its sleepy, local character. Reached from Krabi or Trang airports by road and boat via the nondescript Koh Lanta Noi, it is a 15 mile-long sliver. Dotting the sheltered east coast mangroves are destructive prawn farms and quaint fishing villages of Muslims and Sea Gypsies. The rugged west has a string of fine beaches, from the busy Hat Khlong Dao, where backpackers gather to party, down progressively tortuous roads to the relatively uninteresting national park headquarters at the southern tip. On the long, swimmable beaches in between, new resorts have earned plaudits for their sleek designs.

ISLANDS OF TRANG

One of the last of the archetypal desert islands left in Thailand, the islands off Trang province offer simple accommodation, which often gets booked up. Least isolated is Koh Hai which has some fine beaches and snorkeling, while acting as a base for excursions to Koh Mook, where the spectacular Emerald Cave, an inland beach, is accessed only by boat and a guided hundred-yard swim, partly through darkness. Koh Mook also features good swimming, snorkeling and sunsets. Koh Kradan has the finest scenery in the archipelago, while Koh Libong is famous for its migratory birds, wildlife and refuge of the endangered dugong.

TARUTAO NATIONAL PARK

Established as Thailand's first national marine park in 1974, Tarutao consists of fifty-one mountainous islands in the Indian Ocean near Malaysia. The largest of the group is Koh Tarutao, about 16 miles off the mainland and 3 miles from the Malaysian island of Langkawi, while the most beautiful is Koh Adang, which has fine beaches, clear water and coral reefs. Dolphins, sea turtles, and rare whales and dugongs are occasionally spotted in the area. Government bungalows and tents are available on both Koh Adang and Koh Tarutao. The best time to visit the park is between December and March, when the sea is usually calm.

▲ THE NORTHEAST (ISAN)

NAKHON RATCHASIMA GATE
Nakhon Ratchasima is the most populous town in the northeast of Thailand.

The northeast – or Isan as it is called by Thais – makes up a third of the country's total area, contains seven of its most populous provinces, and offers both varied scenery and numerous ancient sites. However, it remains the least known of Thailand's regions among tourists for many reasons. One was its long isolation. Though a railway linked Bangkok with Nakhon Ratchasima (Korat), the region's commercial center in 1900, it was not extended to the large city of Ubon Ratchathani until 1926 and reached Nongkhai on the Mekong River only in 1955. An extension to the Lao capital of Vientiane is now being built. Even as late as the 1950's, there were few all-weather roads in the region, and northeastern Thais did not receive a personal visit from their ruler until the mid-1950's, when the present king and queen made a pioneering tour. Another probable reason was social prejudice. The northeast has long been Thailand's "problem" region, afflicted by drought and hampered by infertile soil, its people often driven to seek a livelihood in Bangkok as taxi drivers, laborers or domestic servants. To other Thais, Isan hardly seemed a place to spend a holiday, nor were foreigners encouraged to do so. Many of these obstacles have now been overcome. Sharing borders with Laos and Cambodia, the northeast suddenly assumed a strategic importance during the Indo-Chinese war and an excellent network of highways was built. Now in peacetime, new bridges and roads connect Isan with the Vietnamese coast. Government concern has brought greater prosperity to its cities, and more outsiders are beginning to discover the region's attractions.

TOOLS OF THE TRADE
Traditional silk spinning wheel and implements (above).

"MUDMEE"
Mudmee is a kind of handwoven silk material (*ikat*) in which the threads are dyed before weaving. Popularized by Queen Sirikit, *mudmee* is now fashionable among Thai women.

THAI SILK PRODUCTION

Silk is undoubtedly the most famous of northeastern crafts. Even in the early 20th century, when production declined in other regions due to competition from foreign textiles, the family loom remained a part of most Isan village households and so kept the skill alive. The booming industry of today depends to a large extent on silk production from the northeast, particularly around Nakhon Ratchasima; at nearby Pakthongchai, for example, the Jim Thomp-son Company ▲ 94 has the largest handwoven silk facility in the world. Other notable weaving centers are Surin and Roi Et.

BAN CHIANG

In the early 1960's, during the construction of a road, some extraordinary fragments of painted pottery were unearthed near a small hamlet called Ban Chiang in Udon Thani Province. Subsequent excavations led to the discovery of a major prehistoric culture going back to 4000 BC and numbering among its achievements not only the painted pots but also the art of bronze metallurgy, at a period far earlier than any scholars had previously believed. A museum at Ban Chiang displays some of the remarkable items that have made the name world famous among archeologists and one of the excavations has also been preserved to show the different levels at which they were found. The discoveries at Ban Chiang are still very much a controversial subject; on the other hand, the site has undeniably shaken the traditional view of Southeast Asia as a "cultural backwater" that received its influences entirely from outside sources like China and India ● *18*.

ELEPHANT ROUNDUP

Each year in November the provincial capital of Surin holds a gala elephant roundup in which up to 150 of the huge animals take part, demonstrating their ability to haul logs and serve as mounts in warfare ● *28*. The Tourism Authority of Thailand organizes special tours from Bangkok by train or bus for this popular event. These often include visits to the nearby elephant village of Baan Ta Klang.

ARCHEOLOGICAL REMAINS
This vase was found at a dig in Ban Chiang, and is now on display in a Bangkok museum. Genuine pieces should not be confused with "discoveries" that are in fact manufactured in neighboring villages.

SHOW ANIMALS
No longer used for logging or warfare, elephants now entertain tourists and star in spectacles promoted by Thailand's tourist authority.

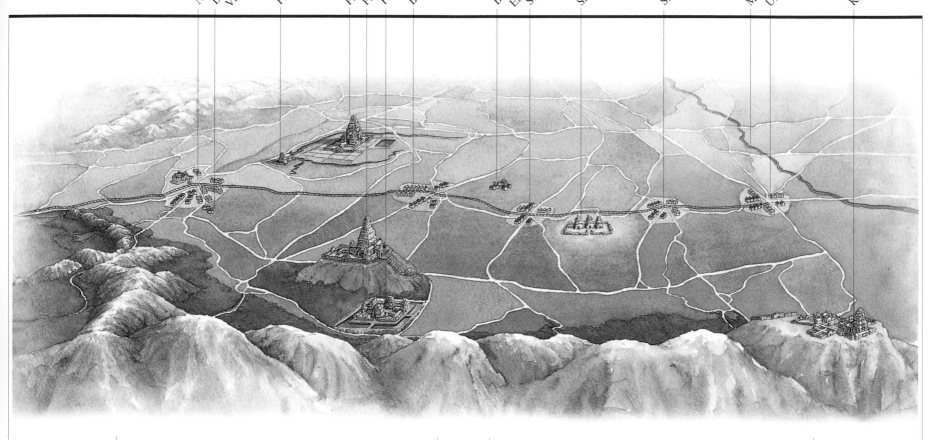

NAKHON RATCHASIMA
DAN KWIAN POTTERY VILLAGE
PRASAT PHANOM WAN
PHIMAI
PRASAT PHANOM RUNG
PRASAT MUANG THAM
BURI RAM
BAAN TA KLANG
ELEPHANT VILLAGE
SURIN
SIKHORAPHUM
SISAKET
MEKONG RIVER
UBON RATCHATANI
KHAO PHRA VIHARN

🕒 Four days

The Prasat Phanom Wan, viewed from the outside.

THE KHMER LEGACY

For almost 400 years, from the 9th century onward, much of the northeast was dominated by the Khmer civilization, which was centered around the famous temples of Angkor, in Cambodia. Khmer power extended much further at its peak during the 11th and 12th centuries, covering much of the Chao Phraya River valley and reaching down into the southern peninsula; not until the 13th century did it begin to wane and eventually give way to the rising Thais. The growth of the Khmer empire ● 18 began with the reign of King Jayavarman II (AD 802–50), who removed the capital to Angkor, but the great period of building in Thailand came under King Suriyavarman I (AD 1002–50), whose father had seized the throne of Lopburi from a Mon king and who himself captured the Cambodian throne at Angkor. Northeastern Thailand lay in the path of Khmer expansion and was thus regarded as a natural part of the empire, while the central region was an outlying province. Several monuments were built during this period in Nakhon Ratchasima, Surin and Buri

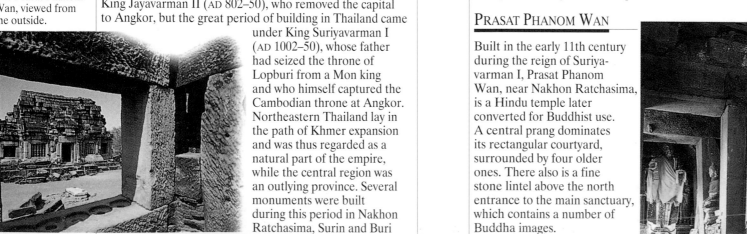

Ram provinces, splendid earthly abodes in stone and brick, and laterite for Hindu deities; temples with rounded prangs that represented the 33 levels of heaven, the highest being occupied by the god Indra. Suriyavarman II (AD 1113–50), who built Angkor Wat, was also responsible for edifices in Isan, among them Phimai in Nakhon Ratchasima. By the late 12th century, Mahayana Buddhism had replaced Hinduism and the last great Khmer builder-king, Jayavarman VII (AD 1181–1218), adapted many of the older structures, including Phimai, to suit the new religion. After his death, the empire collapsed, leaving several temples still unfinished ● 18.

PRASAT PHANOM WAN

Built in the early 11th century during the reign of Suriya-varman I, Prasat Phanom Wan, near Nakhon Ratchasima, is a Hindu temple later converted for Buddhist use. A central prang dominates its rectangular courtyard, surrounded by four older ones. There also is a fine stone lintel above the north entrance to the main sanctuary, which contains a number of Buddha images.

PRASAT PHANOM WAN
The interior of the 11th-century Prasat Phanom Wan, with several Buddha images still venerated by local people.

JAYAVARMAN VII
(AD 1181–1218),
the last of the great
Khmer builder-
kings, adapted many
Hindu temples in
northeast Thailand
built by earlier kings.
Jayavarman VII is
considered the last
great Khmer ruler of
the Angkor period.
In less than 15
years, the borders of
the kingdom were
extended further
to the south and
to the north into
neighboring Malaya,
Burma, Annam and
Champa. Under
his rule Mahayana
Buddhism was
declared the state
religion, thus
replacing Hinduism.

PRASAT HIN PHIMAI

Located about 30 miles from Nakhon Ratchasima, off the
road to Khon Kaen, Prasat Hin Phimai dates from the
end of the 11th century and is one of the finest examples
of early Angkorian art, which was later modified to
suit the needs of Mahayana Buddhism. The temple
has been restored by the Thai Fine Arts Department in
cooperation with Bernard Groslier, who had previously
been in charge of the restoration work at Angkor.

THE TEMPLE COMPLEX. The complex of buildings
stands in a large quadrangle that once also included
a town and was surrounded by a fortified wall. The
complex was originally an artificial island, surrounded
by the Mun River, two other natural waterways, and
a man-made canal, the last trace of which has now
disappeared.

GATEWAYS. The imposing southern gate, known as Pratu Chai,
or Victory Gate, is a pavilion-like structure with walls of pink
sandstone. It faces in the direction of Angkor, with which
Phimai was linked by a straight road; traces remain of three
other gateways at the other cardinal points.

ROYAL RESIDENCES. Among the notable structures within the
walls are a group of royal residences added by Jayavarman
VII; a laterite prang called Meru Baromathat (supposedly
where the cremation of King Baromathat took place) that
once enshrined a statue of Jayavarman VII, now in Bangkok's
National Museum; the remains of a pink sandstone prang
known as the Hin Daeng; and a central sanctuary, topped by a
lotus-bud finial.

THE CENTRAL SANCTUARY. The sanctuary predates the
construction of Angkor and was modified when Phimai
was converted into a Buddhist structure in the 12th or 13th
century. It is the best-preserved part of the complex.

It stands on a square base and has four entrances,
each guarded by five-headed *naga*, or sacred
serpents; the main door, a major projection, is to the
south. The lintels inside are particularly fine, and are
richly carved with scenes from the Buddha's life and
with Tantric deities that
rank among the finest in
Khmer art.

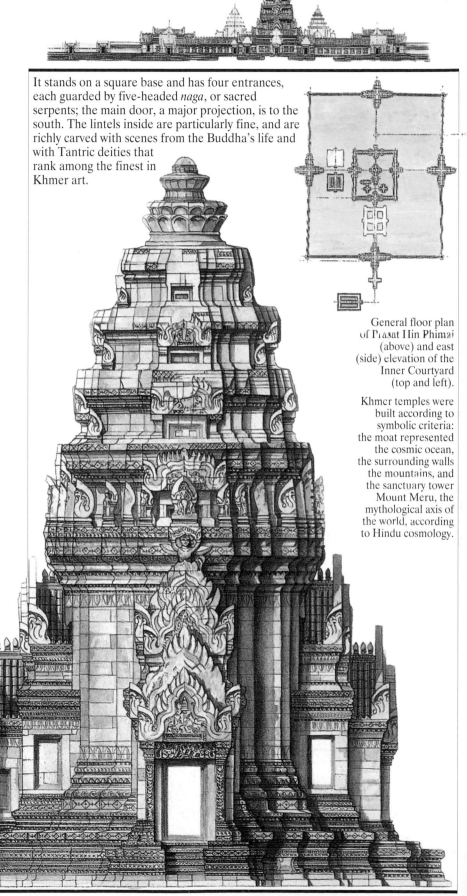

General floor plan
of Prasat Hin Phimai
(above) and east
(side) elevation of the
Inner Courtyard
(top and left).

Khmer temples were
built according to
symbolic criteria:
the moat represented
the cosmic ocean,
the surrounding walls
the mountains, and
the sanctuary tower
Mount Meru, the
mythological axis of
the world, according
to Hindu cosmology.

FEMALE DEITY
This small sandstone figure, found at Phanom Rung and now relocated at the National Museum of Bangkok, is believed to be Uma, Siva's consort, but since none of her attributes are preserved, her identification is uncertain. She wears a pleated sarong with a twist at the waist and a belt, indicating that she can be attributed to the Baphuon style (AD 1010–80).

STOLEN LINTELS
In the early 1960's, one of Prasat Phanom Rung's most beautiful lintels vanished, only to reappear some 25 years later in the collection of

Boston Museum in the United States. After protracted negotiations, the museum agreed to return the piece, which has now been restored to its proper place over one of the temple doorways. A famous lintel carving of Vishnu was also reinstated after it was retrieved from the Art Institute of Chicago, to which the stolen artefact had been donated.

PRASAT PHANOM RUNG ★

Scenically situated on a small hill in Buri Ram Province and facing the Dongrek Mountains that mark the frontier with Cambodia, Prasat Phanom Rung was built over a long period of time. Three of its brick prangs date from the early 10th century, while the main sanctuary was started in the 11th century but was never completed. The temple has since been restored by the Fine Arts Department with the help of several French experts, and with the same techniques as those used at Phimai. An impressive avenue built by Jayavarman VII, 600 feet long and 36 feet wide, leads to the main building atop a series of terraces, the lowest of which has a balustrade of *naga* (sacred serpents). Situated on an east-west axis, the main sanctuary consists of a prang on a square base with antechambers at the four compass points, the main entrance facing east. Beautifully carved lintels adorn the doorways, and there are friezes of very fine quality on the walls and columns.

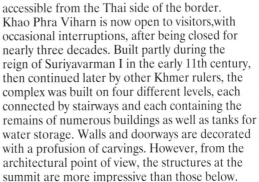

PRASAT MUANG THAM ★

About 3 miles from Prasat Phanom Rung is Prasat Muang Tham (below right). Construction of the temple began in the second half of the 10th century and was completed by Jayavarman V. Consisting of an outer and an inner courtyard surrounded by a laterite wall, Prasat Muang Tham is notable for the well-preserved bas-reliefs on small prangs at the four corners of the outer courtyard and for a large variety of beautifully carved lintels, doorway decorations and stone mullions, all rich in Hindu deities. To the north of the temple is one of the reservoirs built during the period to provide a constant source of water.

KHAO PHRA VIHARN ★

The imposing sanctuary of Khao Phra Viharn perches on a spur of the Dongrek mountain range, 1,800 feet above sea level. After a long dispute between Thailand and Cambodia over the ownership of the temple, international law in 1962 adjudged it to lie in Cambodian territory, even though it is quite easily accessible from the Thai side of the border. Khao Phra Viharn is now open to visitors, with occasional interruptions, after being closed for nearly three decades. Built partly during the reign of Suriyavarman I in the early 11th century, then continued later by other Khmer rulers, the complex was built on four different levels, each connected by stairways and each containing the remains of numerous buildings as well as tanks for water storage. Walls and doorways are decorated with a profusion of carvings. However, from the architectural point of view, the structures at the summit are more impressive than those below.

PRASAT HIN SIKHORAPHUM

Prasat Hin Sikhoraphum (right), in Surin Province, dates from the late 11th century and is built in the Angkor Wat style. It consists of a central brick prang and four smaller prangs at the corners of a laterite platform; the lintels and pillars of the entrance to the main prang are intricately carved with guardians, *apsara* (female divinities) and scenes from Hindu mythology.

OTHER KHMER RUINS

Besides major Khmer ruins, such as those mentioned in these and preceding pages, the northeast has thirty other smaller sites. Among the most interesting are Prasat Hin Non Ku in Nakhon Ratchasima Province and Prasat Thamuen Thom in Surin, both in the Baphuon style of the late 10th and 11th centuries; Prasat Ban Phluang in Surin, on the road from Angkor to Phimai; and Prang Ku in Chaiya-phum, which boasts several carved lintels.

❝There is no doubt that the Khmer art created in Thailand contains foreign elements beyond the style which evolved in the metropolitan area. However, the local differences are but variations upon a theme; the guiding analytic principle is that such provincial Khmer art was made with the standard technology and within the esthetic context of Khmer civilization.❞

Piriya Krairiksh

CHIANG KHONG

NAM NAO NATIONAL PARK
ERAWAN CAVE
VIENTIANE AIRPORT
NONGKHAI
UDON THANI
KHON KAEN

LAMPAO DAM
PHU PAN NATIONAL PARK
PADDY FIELDS
LAMPAO
SAKHON NAKHON
NAKHON PHANOM
THAT PHANOM
MUKDAHAN
UBON RATCHATHANI
SUWANNAKHET
WARIN CHAMRAP
KHONG CHIAM
KAENG TANA NATIONAL PARK

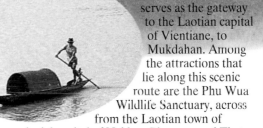

🕙 One week

MEKONG MOSAIC
Two scenes (right) of daily life by the Mekong in the 19th century and fishing boats (below) at the confluence of the Mekong and Mun rivers.

The world's twelfth-longest river, the Mekong originates on the Tibetan plateau and winds across 2,500 miles and six countries before emptying into the South China Sea.

It serves as the border between Thailand and Laos for more than 500 miles in the north and the east before flowing on through Cambodia and Vietnam. The most fertile areas of the northeast lie along its the banks, where rich alluvial silt nourishes mulberry and tobacco plantations, gardens and orchards. Sadly, rock blasting for commercial shipping, dams and other developments are reducing the Mekong's once steady supply of fish, including the nearly extinct gigantic catfish (*pla duk* in Thai), which can weigh up to one ton. For nearly 20 years after the end of the Indo-Chinese War, the Laotian side of the Mekong was closed to most tourists. Recently, however, relations between Thailand and its neighbor have improved and traffic across and along the river is steadily increasing, bringing greater prosperity to old Thai ports of entry such as Nakhon Phanom, Nongkhai and the northern ports of Chiang Saen and Chiang Khong.

FROM NONGKHAI TO KHONG CHIAM

A road runs along the Mekong from Nongkhai, a port that

serves as the gateway to the Laotian capital of Vientiane, to Mukdahan. Among the attractions that lie along this scenic route are the Phu Wua Wildlife Sanctuary, across from the Laotian town of Pakse, the provincial capital of Nakhon Phanom, and That Phanom with its famous chedi. A national park at Mukdahan contains unusual rock formations and Buddhist sites. At Mukdahan, the main highway moves away from the river and leads to Ubon Ratchathani, where each year in July, on the eve of the three-month Buddhist Lent period, there is a procession of enormous carved candles and figures carried on floats through the city streets. A boat can be hired here for the short trip along the Mun River to Khong Chiam, a picturesque confluence of waterways at the point where the Mekong curves and heads toward Cambodia and Vietnam on its journey to the sea.

WAT PHRA THAT PHANOM. Overlooking the Mekong, Wat Phra That Phanom is the most famous of all northeastern Buddhist temples. Its central chedi, originally built in the 9th century and containing a sacred relic, was modeled after the well-known That Luang in Vientiane. When the spire collapsed during a monsoon storm in 1975, it was regarded as a dire omen and was immediately reconstructed; the present one was inaugurated four years later by the Thai king.

THE MEKONG'S OTHER NAMES
The Mekong probably has as many names as the countries it passes through. Also called Lancang Jiang in the province of Yunnan, the river first flows into Burma at an altitude of 8,250 feet and continues through Thailand and into Laos (Kingdom of a Thousand Elephants). The river then meanders towards Thailand and Laos again, then into Cambodia and Vietnam, assuming the names Han Giang, Co Chien, Cua Dai and Bassal respectively.

FOREST TYPES

In Khao Yai National Park some of the last remaining Thai rainforests can still be observed ■ 10. Most of the forests of the dry northeast, however, are deciduous, including teak trees and deciduous dipterocarps, so called because of their two-winged seeds. Found in both types of forest are more than 70 species of bamboo. The acidic soil of the northeast also supports pine trees at an altitude of between 1,980 feet and 4,620 feet. The Phu Kradung National Park is famous for its pine trees. Flowering trees thrive in the dry northeast and, after long spells of drought, spectacular blooms appear. Khao Yai's pride are the thousands of species of orchid ■ 11 that cling to the trees in the wetter parts of the forest.

The northeast was once a densely forested region, teeming with wildlife. Logging, together with the demands of an expanding population, has denuded vast areas and its former natural wealth can be found mainly in those designated national parks.

KHAO YAI

Covering 869 square miles in four provinces – Nakhon Ratchasima, Saraburi, Nakhon Nayok and Prachinburi – Khao Yai was established in 1962 as the first of Thailand's national parks. It is also the most popular, thanks to its ease of accessibility from Bangkok, 120 miles away. Largely because of the number of visitors (more than one million in 2003), the government has been unable to resist building resorts and golf courses on the fringes of the park. Visitors with permission may also camp overnight in the park. There are picturesque trails through lush forests and a rich variety of wildlife ■ 9-10, including elephants, clouded leopards, gibbons, mouse deer, Malayan sun bears, and such birds as the great hornbill, the Siamese fireback pheasant, the silver pheasant and the brown needle-tail, allegedly the fastest bird in the world.

NAM NAO

Established as Thailand's fifth national park in 1972, Nam Nao covers 387 square miles of rolling hills and pine forests in Chaiyaphum and Petchabun. It was once a stronghold of communist insurgents but has been made safe for visitors since the early 1980's. Thanks to the adjacent Phu Khieo Wildlife Sanctuary, the park is unusually rich in animal life ■ 9-10, including elephants, Asiatic black bears and clouded leopards. In 1979 rhinoceros tracks were found in the park. Over 200 species of birds have been confirmed. A popular attraction in the park is Yai Nam Nao Cave, home to hundreds of thousands of bats.

KAENG TANA

Located near Ubon Ratchathani, where the rivers Mekong and Mun meet, the Kaeng Tana National Park covers a sprawling 32-square-mile expanse of land. Although not ranked as one of the popular ones in Thailand's northeastern region, the scenic park boasts features such as giant sandstone slabs, a cave and a waterfall with rapids.

PHU KRADUNG ★

Phu Kradung is a bell-shaped mountain in Loei Province, crowned with a 24-square-mile plateau of exceptional natural beauty. The climb to the top involves a 5-mile trek, sometimes up steep areas, but there are benches and shelters along the way. Plant life on the cool plateau includes many temperate-zone specimens such as rhododendrons, pines and oaks, and among the existing wildlife are elephants, sambar deer, gibbons and 130 bird species. The park is closed from June to August to allow for environmental recovery from the damage caused by visitors.

BIRD-WATCHING

The majority of Thailand's wild mammals tend to be shy creatures and sightings are rare. Birds, on the other hand, are plentiful, and visitors to any of the national parks will easily spot several of the estimated 928 species that live in the country.

HORNBILLS

Easily spotted because of their size and their noisy flappings, hornbills are among the largest jungle birds, distinguished by a huge beak often surmounted by a casque. After laying her eggs the female immures herself inside a tree cavity.

GIBBONS

Gibbons are among the most endearing of Thailand's native wildlife, swinging like gymnasts from the upper heights of the trees and hooting mournfully at daybreak. They are the subject of continuing research at Khao Yai, where both the white-handed (or lar) and the pileated species live in considerable numbers.

ENDANGERED SPECIES

The national parks of the northeast provide sanctuary for several once-common animals that are now endangered species. Just under 200 wild elephants, for example, live within the boundaries of Khao Yai, the largest population of any park in the country. A handful of Thailand's estimated 200 remaining tigers may possibly still live there. Thailand signed the international CITES treaty, and increasing attention and resources are dedicated to conserving the country's natural heritage.

LEOPARDS. Though rare today, leopards and clouded leopards may still be sighted in Khao Yai and Nam Nao. Prized for their skin, these beasts have been the target of persistent poachers who flout wildlife preservation laws.

BEARS. The Malayan sun bear is a smallish jungle bear that eats mostly fallen fruit, fish and carrion. It has the misfortune of being highly regarded as a medicinal ingredient by certain groups like the Koreans, who come on special tours just to

FURS
Up to the early 1980's, tiger and leopard skins were openly sold at souvenir shops in Bangkok. Today, they are sold secretly in small border villages.

eat grilled bear meat. The Asiatic black bear, still existing at Khao Yai and Nam Nao, is a much bigger animal, distinguished by its long hair and a wide V-mark from the upper breast to the shoulders.

THE KOUPREY. A recent discovery by Western zoologists, the kouprey is a bovine distinguished by huge lyre-shaped horns and a long dewlap drooping from the neck. Once commonly found along the Dangrek range near the Cambodian border, the beast was slaughtered for meat during the Cambodian conflict and is probably now an extinct species.

THE GAUR. This is a huge ox up to 10 feet long and 6 feet tall at the shoulder. Black with scimitar-like horns and white legs, they inhabit open forests in herds of six to 20, although one will see only their tracks. Nocturnal browsers, they feed in open spaces and are the prey of tigers, leopards and humans, who have reduced their numbers to under 500 and put them on the endangered species list.

EXTINCT SPECIES
During the 19th century, Thailand exported about 8,000 rhinoceros horns a year to China, where they were much prized for their supposed medicinal qualities, including that of high male potency. The number of rhinoceros was so drastically reduced that by 1977 it was estimated that not more than ten Sumatran rhinos and perhaps only a few of the Javanese species remained in the country. Today, none are left; rhinoceros-horn powder, however, is still sold at exorbitant prices in the markets of Bangkok's Chinatown.

THE CENTRAL PLAINS

AYUTTHAYA, *124*

LOPBURI, *127*

KAMPHAENG PHET, *128*

SUKHOTHAI, *129*

SI SATCHANALAI, *131*

PHITSANULOK, *132*

WAT PHRA SI SANPHET · VIHARA PHRA MONGKOK BOPIT · WAT NA PHRA MERU · KHUN PHAN'S HOUSE · NATIONAL MUSEUM · WAT PHRA RAM · AYUTTHAYA HISTORICAL STUDY CENTER · WAT RAJA BURANA · WAT PHRA MAHATHAT · MARKET · ELEPHANT CORRAL · CHANTARAKASEM PALACE · WAT PHANAN CHOENG · RAILWAY STATION · WAT YAI CHAI MONGKOL

WAT CHAI WATTANARAM · WAT PHUKAOTHONG

🕒 One day

HISTORY

TREASURES OF GOLD
In a crypt beneath Wat Raja Burana's central prang King Boromaraja II once hid a collection of gold objects in memory of his two dead brothers. They are now housed at the National Museum at Ayutthaya.

Founded in 1350 by King Ramathibodi I, Ayutthaya grew from a small town with mud walls on an artificial island on the Chao Phraya River into one of the largest, most cosmopolitan cities in Southeast Asia. With only one interruption, when it fell to the Burmese in the mid-16th century, it was the center of Thai power for more than 400 years, its rule extending over the entire Central Plains as well as many areas of the far east and south. The 33 rulers of Ayutthaya adopted the Khmer concept of divine kingship, complete with Brahminic rituals, and built spectacular palaces as well as great Buddhist monuments; most of the major remains visitors see today were constructed in the city's first 150 years. The peak of opulence came in the 17th century, when ships from all over the world sailed up the Chao Phraya to trade and Ayutthaya had a population of more than a million. During the reign of King Narai (1657–88), two French embassies came from the court of Louis XIV and a Thai embassy was sent to Paris. Ayutthayan power began to decline after the death of Narai, and a series of wars ensued with Burma. In 1767, after a 15-month siege, the city fell to an invading army that burned almost every building. Led by the future King Taksin, the Thais finally expelled the Burmese, but Ayutthaya was so thoroughly destroyed that the capital was moved further downriver to Thonburi, then Bangkok. The Ayutthaya Historical Study Center offers an overview of ancient Ayutthaya through models, dioramas and multimedia descriptions of life, culture and buildings. A branch of the Center stands in the former Japanese quarter.

THE RUINS OF AYUTTHAYA

WAT RAJA BURANA. Among the best known of Ayutthaya's monuments, Wat Raja Burana was constructed in 1424 by King Boromaraja II, on the site where two princes had killed one another in a duel on elephant-back. The king first built two chedis and later a far more imposing temple surrounded by a wall, with monumental gateways, a towering prang on a stepped platform and numerous smaller prangs and chedis ● 50.

Thailand's oldest paintings decorate the vault of the crypt of Wat Raja Burana.

«THE CITY OF AYUTTHAYA, AT THE PERIOD OF OUR VISIT,
CONSISTED OF SOME SIX FISHERMAN'S HUTS AND
A BETELNUT VENDOR'S STALL.»

FREDERICK A. NEALE

WAT PHRA SI SANPHET. Dating from 1491, Wat Phra Si Sanphet (left) was located inside the compound of the king's palace – the foundations of which are still visible – and served as the royal chapel, as Wat Phra Keo does in Bangkok. The three main chedis, although poorly restored, contain the ashes of three Ayutthaya kings, and the extent of the temple's ruins attests to its former splendor.

VIHARN PHRA MONGKOL BOPIT. Near Wat Phra Si Sanphet, this modern building houses a huge seated Buddha image from the 15th century and originally intended to stand in the open air. Restored several times, the image is highly revered by Buddhist visitors. In front stands a fine traditional teak house named after Khun Phan, hero of the epic *Khun Chang Khun Phan*, from which we have learned much about daily life of that period ● *66.*

WAT PHRA MAHATHAT is believed to be one of Ayutthaya's oldest temples, possibly built by King Boromaraja I (1370–88). Its central prang, of which only the base remains, was once 165 feet tall. Traces of the original stucco can still be seen on some of the surrounding chedis.

WAT PHRA RAM. Though founded in 1369, the ruins of Wat Phra Ram (right) date mostly from its restoration in the 15th century. Its main feature is a well-proportioned prang that stands on a stepped terrace adorned with chedis. Some of the prang's stucco decorations of walking and standing Buddhas still remain.

WAT MAHEYONG. This temple is unique as its main feature is a chedi supported by a base with stucco elephants, similar in style to those seen in Sukhothai and Si Satchanalai.

An engraving of the ruins of Wat Phra Si Sanphet.

ISLAND CAPITAL
Ayutthaya, like Bangkok later, was conceived as an island fortress, formed by digging a canal at a point where the Lopburi River curved sharply. Later shunts were dug linking the city with the Chao Phraya and Pasak rivers and these in time became the main courses of the two rivers. Canals also provided avenues of communication within the walled city as well as out into the surrounding countryside. Huge water gates blocked the access to the city when necessary.

NATIONAL MUSEUM

Also known as Chao Sam Phraya Museum, this remarkable collection of Buddhist art, mostly Ayutthayan, is located on Rojana Road and is open Wednesdays to Sundays. A highlight of the collection is the treasure found in Wat Raja Burana, which, besides the famed gold objects, comprises a collection of small, intact Buddha images of exquisite workmanship. Worthy of mention also are a set of painted banners with religious subjects and a lacquered book cabinet decorated with a representation of the Buddhist cosmos.

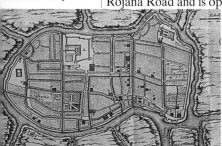

TEMPLES ALONG THE RIVERSIDE

WAT CHAI WATTANARAM. Built in 1630 by King Prasat Thong, Wat Chai Wattanaram (left) was conceived as a replica of an Angkorian temple, with a huge prang surrounded by smaller ones, symbolizing Mount Meru, the abode of the heavenly gods. Now restored, the temple has lost much of its former charm.

WAT YAI CHAI MONGKOL. A lofty chedi dominates Wat Yai Chai Mongkol (right) on the opposite side of the river. It was given its name by King Naresuan to commemorate a battle fought against the Crown Prince of Burma in 1592. Naresuan's victory brought independence to Ayutthaya after 15 years as a Burmese vassal. In the complex is also a huge image of a reclining Buddha in brick and stucco ● *50.*

WAT NA PHRA MERU. Located across the river north of the palace, this temple ● *47* was the only wat in the city not razed by the Burmese. It has been restored a number of times but still has a finely proportioned bot and a viharn. The viharn contains a large Dvaravati stone Buddha seated in European style, his hands on his knees, which some scholars think originated in Nakhon Pathom. The bot has a large gilded image in distinctively regal attire.

WAT PHANAN CHOENG. Facing the main city from across the river, this landmark with five prangs has been tidily restored. Built shortly before Ayutthaya became capital, it is now a major stop on boat cruises. The main building enshrines a huge seated Buddha image, 57 feet tall, the object of particular devotion to Thais of Chinese descent.

ELEPHANT CORRAL

Off the road from Ayutthaya to Ang Thong is the Elephant Corral. Repaired by King Rama I of Bangkok and restored by his successors, it was once the place where wild elephants were rounded up, sorted, and eventually trained for work and use in warfare.

CHANTARAKASEM PALACE

Originally built for King Naresuan (1590–1605) when he was Crown Prince, Chantarakasem Palace was reconstructed in the 19th century by King Rama IV of Bangkok, who used it as a summer retreat. Overlooking a main street now in the modern town, one of its elegant buildings contains a small but interesting collection of objects found in Ayutthaya.

MONUMENT PRESERVATION
The Fine Arts Department is gradually restoring all the monuments in Ayutthaya. However, the nature of the brick monuments is such that they cannot be stabilized without complete reconstruction. Buddhists generally frown upon damaged Buddha images, so statues found among the ruins are being replaced with replicas in cement, often made by unskilled craftsmen, while the original pieces are treasured by discerning collectors.

ELEPHANT SHOWS
Although the Elephant Corral was not used for its original purpose after the destruction of Ayutthaya, later Bangkok kings staged spectacular roundups there as a form of entertainment for distinguished visitors from abroad. One of the last great shows was recorded by photographer Robert Lenz in 1890.

LIFE ALONG THE KLONGS

Leading off the river in this area are numerous klongs, or canals, all dug centuries ago to facilitate communications. Cruising along these, one can catch glimpses of a lifestyle that has largely vanished in most other parts of the country: elegant wooden houses in the Central Plains style, raised above the ground on tall posts; huge hump-backed barges loaded with rice, being towed to the markets and warehouses of Bangkok; vendor boats supplying waterside houses with various necessities; the spires of Buddhist temples rising above feathery bamboo groves; and stretching away on either side, all the way to the horizon, the vast ricefields ■ *13* that have traditionally nourished and enriched the kingdom.

RICE FARMING. The majority of rural Thais are rice farmers, following an ancient cycle that begins with plowing the fields in April or May just before the rains; the young seedlings are then planted and carefully tended until harvest time, usually in late November or early December.

TRADITIONAL HOUSE PRODUCTION. In Ang Thong Province, a short drive from Ayutthaya, many skilled craftsmen earn their livelihood by prefabricating the components of traditional Thai-style houses: paneled walls, gables, roof beams, and the characteristic curving bargeboards. These are then transported elsewhere, mainly to Bangkok, and assembled on a framework of pillars in private compounds ● *45*.

THE THAI HOUSE
The classic Central Plains house is raised off the ground on stout pillars, with a veranda in front where most family activities take place. The walls lean slightly inward and the roofs are steep; traditionally, it has bargeboards that curve gracefully at the end, adding to the general effect of lightness and airiness ● *45*.

BANG PA-IN

A few miles down the Chao Phraya River from Ayutthaya is the Bang Pa-In Summer Palace. The site was first used by the royal court as a retreat from the hot weather in the 17th century but fell into ruin after the fall of Ayutthaya; it was restored by King Rama IV in the mid-19th century, though most of the buildings that exist today date from the reign of King Rama

V, who regularly spent his summers there. Typically of the fifth reign, the structures represent a variety of architectural styles, set in a large park around ponds and waterways. The only one of the royal residences open to the public is the Chinese-style Vehat Chamroon Palace, constructed entirely of materials imported from China. In addition, there is an Italian-style palace, a circular pavilion with steps leading down to a pool, the graceful Thai-style Aisawan Tippaya Asna pavilion in the middle of a lake, and, across one of the waterways, a Buddhist chapel in neo-Gothic style with stained-glass windows. Scattered around the extensive gardens are European statues as well as monuments erected by King Rama V in memory of members of his family, one of them to a much-loved Queen who was drowned in a boating accident.

WAT PHAI RONG RUA

Located on the river near Bang Pa-In, Wat Phai Rong Rua is worth visiting mainly as a curiosity, since its grounds are filled with large, rather garish statues depicting scenes from Buddhist hell and the grim fate that awaits those unlucky enough to go there.

BANG SAI

Bang Sai, also near Bang Pa-In, is a small riverside village established in 1982 by Queen Sirikit as a place where farmers are given the opportunity to learn the traditional crafts and thus acquire a supplementary source of income. There are regular demonstrations of basket making, cloth weaving, and leatherworking. A souvenir shop markets the finished products.

WAT PHAI LOM

Located on the riverbank below Bang Pa-In is Wat Phai Lom, famous as a bird sanctuary. Each December, thousands of rare open-billed storks fly over the temple from Bangladesh and head for their nests among the treetops to raise their young before departing in June.

RICE BARGES
For many centuries, the Chao Phraya has been the main highway for transporting rice and other produce to Bangkok and the outside world, usually in long processions of huge teakwood barges pulled by tugboats. Filled with heavy rice sacks, the round-bottomed barges appear to be almost submerged in the water.

The Aisawan Tippaya Asna pavilion at Bang Pa-In.

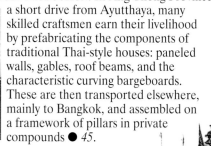

«LOUVO STANDS MOST PLEASANTLY AND IN A MOST WHOLESOME AIR; THE COMPASS OF IT IS VERY LARGE AND IT IS BECOME VERY POPULOUS SINCE THE KING HATH BEEN PLEASED TO LIVE THERE.»

FATHER GUY TACHARD

The fortifications of Lopburi were built with the help of the French engineer Monsieur de la Marre, who came to Siam with the mission of the Chevalier de Chaumont.

Once known as Louvo, Lopburi served as an important city during the Dvaravati period and also as an outpost of the Khmer empire. King Narai of Ayutthaya (1656–88) began using it as a summer retreat and eventually spent so much of his time there that it became virtually a second capital.

KING NARAI'S PALACE. Known as Phra Narai Raja-nivet, this palace was built by King Narai between 1665 and 1677 and was the scene of most of the important events during his reign. High crenellated walls with imposing gateways surround the large compound, which was divided into separate areas for government offices, ceremonial buildings and the king's private residence. French architects assisted in the design of part of the palace, particularly the Dusit Sawan Thanya Maha Prasat, where the king often received foreign ambassadors. Here, King Narai spent the winter months going out in search of wild elephants, often hoping to find an auspicious white one; walked through gardens described by Simon de la Loubère as "delightful,"; discussed affairs of state with his chief minister, the Greek adventurer Constantine Phaulkon; and, in a hall said to have been ablaze with mirrors brought from France, met with the envoys of Louis XIV. It was here too, in the spring of 1688, that he fell ill and died. The palace was restored and used again as a residence by King Rama IV in the 19th century. The buildings from the latter period are now used to display the finds from excavations of prehistoric sites in the Central Plains as well as items from King Rama IV's reign, including giant shadow puppets and various pieces of furniture. A collection of Lopburi-style Buddha images is displayed in the throne hall. The King Narai Fair every February reenacts scenes from his reign, with spectacular parades and shows.

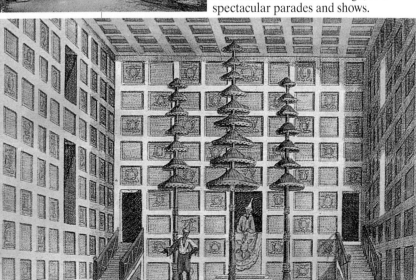

PHAULKON'S RESIDENCE. "One of the most amazing of the adventurers who have made the east the scene of their exploits" is how Somerset Maugham described Constantine Phaulkon, and many other writers and historians have agreed. Born in 1647 on the island of Cephalonia, then under Greek rule, he came to Asia as a cabin boy on an English merchant ship and after a series of adventures turned up at King Narai's court in Ayutthaya. A natural talent for politics, together with a gift for languages and what must have been considerable charm, led him to the highest echelons of power; by 1685, he was in charge of Ayutthaya's foreign trade and was one of the king's closest confidants, with the royal title of Chao Phraya Wichayen. The remains of Phaulkon's Lopburi residence – he had another, much grander one in Ayutthaya – stand in a compound with those of a Catholic church and a house built for members of a French embassy that came in 1685, all in a blend of European and Thai styles. Though the French mission was regarded as a success, it increased opposition to Phaulkon among conservative courtiers. When King Narai fell mortally ill in 1688, one of them, Phra Petchara, staged a revolt; Phaulkon was arrested, tortured for several days, and finally beheaded near a lake outside Lopburi.

WAT PHRA SAM YOT. Built in the 13th century and located in the center of old Lopburi, this Khmer temple has three laterite prangs, two containing damaged Buddha images. The laterite blocks were once covered with elaborate stucco decorations, of which little remains. The temple hosts a banquet each November for the many feral monkeys in the area that make the town famous among Thais.

WAT PHRA SI RATANA MAHATHAT. Lopburi's most important religious structure, Wat Phra Si Ratana Mahathat dates from the period of Khmer rule but was restored and enlarged by King Narai. It contains a large laterite prang as well as a brick viharn, added by King Narai, with the Persian-style pointed arch windows seen throughout Lopburi.

PHRA PHUTTHABAT

Phra Phutthabat, more commonly known as the Temple of Buddha's Footprint, is a much-revered shrine about 17 miles from the town of Saraburi. The sacred footprint – measuring 5 feet long – was discovered during the Ayutthaya period, but the buildings that enshrine it today were built by King Rama I of Bangkok and his successors. Many hermits still live in caves in the surrounding hills.

FRENCH EMBASSIES When King Narai reigned, two French embassies from the court of King Louis XIV were received by him in Ayutthaya (1685) and Lopburi, (1687); a Thai embassy bearing royal gifts returned with the first group and was received by the French king at Versailles in 1686. The French were encouraged by reports from Jesuit missionaries, who believed that Narai might be converted to Christianity; the king, however, was more interested in countering increased pressure from the Dutch and the British. After Narai's death, his conservative successor expelled nearly all foreigners from Ayutthaya ● 32, 52, 61.

K hamphaeng Phet, on the left bank of the Ping River, was one of the most important centers of the Sukhothai kingdom, although its principal monuments were built somewhat later than those of the other satellite city of Si Satchanalai. It was in Khamphaeng Phet that the last ruler of Sukhothai submitted to King Boramathat of Ayutthaya in 1378.

INSIDE THE "DIAMOND WALL"

A WESTERN VISITOR
In 1882, traveler Carl Bock spent a night in Khamphaeng Phet on his way to the far north. He dined with the governor of the province, an occasion he described as follows: "The menu was a good one, and the dinner was served in a style that would have done credit to a first-class hotel... Soon after I returned from the hospitable table of the governor, I was disturbed by the noise of drums and gongs, accompanied by the desultory discharge of firearms in all directions. Hastily getting up, I crossed over to a temple which stood opposite to my *sala*, where I found the priests assembled in full force, surrounded by an excited multitude of natives gazing at the great dragon swallowing the moon, and endeavoring by dreadful clamor to avert the calamity. In other words there was an eclipse of the moon."

Khamphaeng Phet ("Diamond Wall") was surrounded by massive ramparts of earth topped with laterite. The two principal temples are Wat Phra Keo (top and right), which has two large seated Buddha images, and Wat Phra That, which has a chedi surrounded by columns. Also of interest is the *lak muang*, the city's foundation stone pillar.

OUTSIDE THE WALLS OF KHAMPHAENG PHET

The finest of Khamphaeng Phet's ruins lie outside the city walls, where the surroundings were more conducive to prayer and meditation. Wat Phra Non enshrines the remains of a reclining Buddha, while Wat Phra Si Iriyabot (above left) has images of the Buddha in four attitudes – standing, walking, seated and reclining. Wat Chang Rob, "Temple Surrounded by Elephants," is notable for the remains of a large chedi surrounded by imposing elephant buttresses made of laterite covered with stucco, a decorative motif that originated from Sri Lanka.

TWO FORTS. At the southern and northern corners of Khamphaeng Phet's walls are the remains of two forts (above): Phom Chao Indra and Phom Phet. The latter has been excavated, is well preserved and suggests the impressive scale of ancient fortifications.

SUKHOTHAI

Sukhothai was the northernmost citadel of the Khmer empire and had flourished for centuries before the Thais began emigrating from the north in increasing numbers. During the first half of the 13th century, when Khmer influence was waning, a Thai chieftain later known as King Intradit united various groups, overthrew their Khmer overlord, and founded the kingdom of Sukhothai, the Pali version of which means "Dawn of Happiness." Sukhothai's power lasted less than two centuries before it became a vassal of Ayutthaya in 1378, but it enjoyed a brilliant flowering in both politics and culture. Under its third and most famous ruler, King Ramkhamhaeng (1279–98), direct or indirect rule was extended over much of present-day Thailand, and a Thai alphabet was devised. Most impressive of all were the remarkable achievements in art and architecture. Drawing from a variety of cultures – not only Khmer but also Mon, Indian and Sinhalese – Sukhothai artisans created superb temples, Buddha images and ceramics that were also distinctively Thai and are generally regarded as the finest examples of the country's cultural heritage ● *19*.

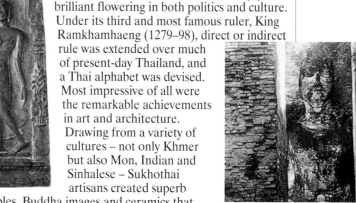

One of Sukhothai's many chedis, photographed in 1910.

The Sitting Buddha at Wat Si Chum ▲ *130*.

RESTORATION OF SUKHOTHAI

Declared a national historical park by the Thai government, Sukhothai has also received international attention in the form of aid from UNESCO. Over the past decade, many of the ancient capital's principal monuments have been carefully restored and villagers who had settled in the ruins were moved elsewhere. The original layout of the city was revealed and enhanced by dredging the moats and ponds, which had filled with silt over the centuries.

LOY KRATHONG
According to legend, the beautiful Loy Krathong festival held at the end of the rainy season to honor the water spirits originated at Sukhothai. The festival has been revived under the auspices of the Tourism Authority with a gala event that includes spectacular illuminations, colorful parades and thousands of lotus-shaped floats set adrift on ponds and waterways ● *38*.

Map labels (top): RAMKHAMHAENG NATIONAL MUSEUM · WAT MAHATHAT · WAT SRI SAWAI · STATUE OF RAMKHAMHAENG · WAT TRAPANG NGERN · WAT TRAPANG THONG LANG · WAT SA SRI · WAT PHRA PHAI LUANG · WAT SI CHUM · WAT SAPHAN HIN

Map labels (bottom): WAT TRAPANG THONG · WAT CHETUPON · SAN THA PHA DAENG

⏱ 1 day

RAMKHAMHAENG INSCRIPTION

"This Sukhothai is good. In the water there are fish. In the fields there is rice." Every Thai school-child learns these lines taken from a stone inscription dealing with life in the ancient capital, usually dated 1292 and attributed to King Ramkham-haeng. Of late, some scholars have questioned the authenticity of the inscription and even suggested that it might have been produced by King Rama IV in the mid-19th century.

RAMKHAMHAENG NATIONAL MUSEUM

The Ramkhamhaeng National Museum of Sukhothai, one of the richest in Thailand, is the best introduction to a visit to the ruins of the ancient capital. Located in a garden to the east of Wat Mahathat, the museum houses a large collection of Sukhothai Buddha images (among them a magnificent bronze Walking Buddha), Khmer statues, stucco decorations, ceramics, and a copy of the famous 1292 stone inscription attributed to King Ramkhamhaeng. In front of the museum, the Fine Arts Department has reconstructed an open Sukhothai-style viharn.

WAT MAHATHAT

Sukhothai's main Buddhist monastery, Wat Mahathat was adjacent to the former royal palace and covers a square measuring 660 feet each side.

Construction of the temple, started by King Intradit, Sukhothai's founder, continued under several other rulers before its completion by King Li Thai in 1345.

THE LOTUS CHEDI. The dominant structure is a central chedi, covering an old Khmer tower, with a lotus-bud finial, a distinctive feature of Sukhothai architecture. A fine stucco frieze showing Buddhist disciples adorns the base of the main chedi.

OTHER BUILDINGS. On two sides are towering standing Buddha images enclosed in a *mondop* (open image-house). There are also nearly 200 other chedis and the remains of 10 viharns, among other structures, all axially aligned with the rising and setting sun. Noteworthy is a stepped chedi that resembles the one in Polonnaruwa, and which acts as an important link between Sri Lankan and Thai art. Its unusual shape was replicated in several northern Thai temples, the most famous of which is at Wat Ku Kut, Lamphun ▲ 141. Sukhothai was a center of influence for Sinhalese culture, which spread to the northern mountains in Thailand ● 47, 60.

SUKHOTHAI BUDDHA
The Sukhothai Buddha image (below), particularly when cast in bronze, is regarded as the most beautiful in all Thai art ▲ 81. Depicted in seated, standing, reclining and walking attitudes, the images are not meant to be realistic. Rather, they emphasize the Buddha's supernatural qualities.

OTHER TEMPLES WITHIN THE WALLS

WAT SRI SAWAI. A Khmer-style temple southwest of Wat Mahathat, Wat Sri Sawai (left) was probably dedicated to the Hindu god Siva in pre-Thai times before it became a Buddhist shrine. Three well-restored prangs adorned with some of their original stucco decorations stand behind the remains of the principal sanctuary, which was added in the 15th century.

WAT SA SRI. Picturesquely sited on an island in a pond northwest of Wat Mahathat, Wat Sa Sri (right) shows the refinement of Sukhothai architecture. Roofless columns rise from the base of the main sanctuary, which also contains a large stucco Buddha image; behind are two elegant chedis, one of them in rounded Sinhalese style.

WAT TRAPANG THONG LANG. This temple has some remarkable stucco decorations (left) on the outer walls of a square chapel. Perhaps the most famous is the southern panel, which shows the descent of the Buddha from heaven surrounded by celestial attendants and which is regarded as one of the masterpieces of Sukhothai art.

WAT TRAPANG THONG. Situated on an island set in a peaceful pond, this temple (below) is marked by a bell-shaped chedi. The viharn has been reconstructed and the temple reconsecrated.

WAT TRAPANG NGERN. Located just behind Wat Mahathat, this temple comprises a number of buildings sited around a big pond. The main feature is an elegant lotus-bud chedi. Many visitors enjoy walking across the wooden bridge to the islet that once housed a viharn.

SAN THA PHA DAENG. East of Wat Sa Sri, inside the city walls, San Tha Pha Daeng is a Khmer laterite sanctuary consisting of a square cell and an antechamber. It is believed to be the the oldest building in the Sukhothai area, dating from the first half of the 12th century.

WAT CHETUPON

Located south of Sukhothai's city walls, Wat Chetupon is notable for an interesting, partially ruined chedi with images of the Buddha in the four ritual attitudes in stucco bas-relief; the tall standing Buddha is particularly fine. A wall of gray stone surrounds the compound.

WAT SAPHAN HIN

Situated west of the city on a small hill, Wat Saphan Hin derives its name (Stone Bridge) from the stone stairway leading up to it. Within the columns that remain of the viharn is a 41-foot-tall standing Buddha built against a thick brick wall that provides support for the huge image. In the groves and on the surrounding hills there are ruins of monasteries once inhabited by forest-dwelling ascetic monks.

WAT SI CHUM

This temple, southwest of the walled city, is one of the most impressive religious monuments in the area ● 47. It is dominated by a huge structure, 50 feet tall, enclosing a seated Buddha of stucco-covered brick almost the same height and 37 feet wide at the lap; the image is referred to as Phra Achana in the 1292 stone inscription attributed to King Ramkhamhaeng. Within the wall is an enclosed stairway, the ceiling of which is lined with engraved slabs of stone. The reason for the construction of the stairway, which leads to the top of the structure, is not known. Some have suggested that it may be linked with a legend that the image could speak to supplicants below.

WAT PHRA PHAI LUANG

North of Sukhothai's walls and partially surrounded by ponds are the extensive ruins of Wat Phra Phai Luang (below), which rivaled Wat Mahathat in size and importance. Originally, three concentric moats surrounded the main religious complex, consisting of a group of buildings. The complex, besides the religious symbolism related to the representation of the Primordial Ocean, undoubtedly served a practical purpose, similar to the one in Angkor. It is thus evident that the original layout of the city of Sukhothai was set out by the Khmers according to their religious beliefs. The temple originally had three Khmer-style prangs, only one of which remained when it was converted into a Buddhist temple by the Thais. On the same terrace are the remains of a viharn and a chedi, decorated with Buddha images in stucco. A nearby structure enshrines the Buddha in walking, standing, sitting and reclining attitudes.

SUKHOTHAI KINGS
Between 1238 and 1488, Sukhothai was ruled by nine kings, the last three of whom served mainly under the control of Ayutthaya. The most famous was King Ramkhamhaeng, under whom the kingdom achieved its greatest power, though the scholarly King Li Thai (1347–74) is remembered as the author of the *Tribhumikatha* (the Three Worlds of Buddhism), the oldest Thai literary work.
● 19.

LOTUS CAPITAL
The lotus capital is one of Sukhothai's unique contributions to religious architecture. Though possibly inspired by finials from the Mon period at Pagan in Burma, it is original enough in design to be called Thai
● 47.

STONE SLABS OF SI CHUM
Perhaps the earliest examples of graphic expression found at Sukhothai are the incised drawings above the stairway of Wat Si Chum.

Each of the 100 engravings depicts a self-contained scene from the Jataka tales, moralistic stories dealing with the Buddha's previous lives. The slabs may have been made for Wat Mahathat and later moved to Wat Si Chum for safekeeping.

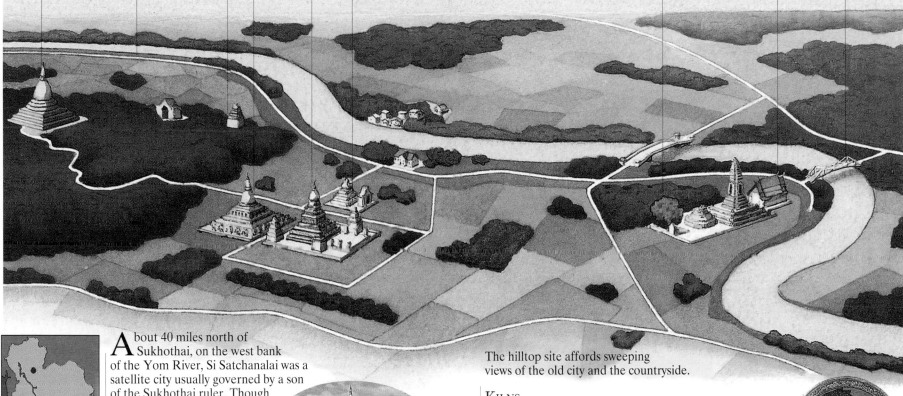

WAT KHAO SUWAN KIRI · ROAD TO POTTERY KILNS · WAT KHAO PHANOM PLOENG · WAT CHANG LOM · WAT CHEDI CHET THAEW · WAT SUAN KEOW UTAYAN NOI · CHALIENG VILLAGE · WAT PHRA SI RATANA MAHATHAT · SUSPENSION BRIDGE

⏱ Half a day

BAN KO NOI
EXCAVATIONS
Anyone interested in ceramics should visit an ancient kiln site at Ban Ko Noi, a few miles north of Si Satchanalai. Here a Thai-Australian project headed by Don Hein has uncovered more than 200 kilns and evidence of more, many of them predating those of Sukhothai by four centuries.

About 40 miles north of Sukhothai, on the west bank of the Yom River, Si Satchanalai was a satellite city usually governed by a son of the Sukhothai ruler. Though smaller than the capital, it was similar in plan and has a more picturesque location overlooking the river and rural scenery; the two cities were linked by the Phra Ruang Highway. A number of impressive Buddhist temples were built in Si Satchanalai, some as beautiful as those at Sukhothai, and a nearby district to the north became famous for kilns that produced superb ceramics known as Sawankhalok, the name given to the area during the early Ayutthaya period.

WAT CHANG LOM. Located in the center of the old city, Wat Chang Lom was built in the late 13th century. Its main feature is a large bell-shaped chedi that enshrines relics placed there by King Ramkhamhaeng; around the base of the chedi are several elephant buttresses, hence the name "Temple Surrounded by Elephants."

WAT CHEDI CHET THAEW. Covering a large area, this temple consists of a sanctuary and seven rows of chedis, which probably contain the ashes of Si Satchanalai rulers. Adorning one of the chedis is an impressive stucco image of a seated Buddha protected by the hood of a *naga*, or sacred serpent ● *50*.

WAT KHAO PHANOM PLOENG. Wat Khao Phanom Ploeng, "Temple of the Mountain of Fire," is located on a hill within the city, accessible by a steep flight of steps. The laterite columns of the temple remain, along with a restored seated Buddha image and a tall chedi.

The hilltop site affords sweeping views of the old city and the countryside.

KILNS

The popular legend that the art of making ceramics came to Sukhothai through Chinese potters brought back from a mission during the reign of King Ramkhamhaeng has been disproven. Nevertheless, ceramics were certainly a thriving export of the kingdom since the early 14th century. The first flask-shaped kilns were built in Sukhothai itself, outside the city wall, but around 1350 the craft moved to three main sites near Si Satchanalai, where superior clay was available. Water jars, bowls, jarlets, covered boxes and numerous other items were produced in bulk, mostly for export to the Philippines, Indonesia and Borneo; the glazes were equally varied, ranging from dark brown to sea-green celadon.

WAT PHRA SI RATANA MAHATHAT ★

Located just a mile from Si Satchanalai, in the village of Chalieng, Wat Phra Si Ratana Mahathat is one of the most remarkable Sukhothai-style temples, believed to date from the 13th century but restored and altered during the Ayutthaya period. The temple complex is aligned on an east-west axis and consists of several ruined buildings, a large Sinhalese-style chedi, and a magnificent prang showing Khmer influence. Among the images are a large seated Buddha and a standing Buddha partially imbedded in the ground; the walls of a sanctuary near the prang are decorated with very fine stucco reliefs that include a beautiful walking Buddha.

FISH MOTIF
One of the characteristic motifs on bowls and dishes produced during the Sukhothai period is that of a gracefully curving fish, drawn in profile. Sometimes surrounded by flower and leaf patterns, the fish has an appealing light-hearted quality, appealing to the eyes.

131

About 35 miles away, Phitsanulok is often used as a meeting base for visitors to Sukhothai. It is an almost entirely new provincial capital, as much of the old town burned down in the 1970's.

PHRA BUDDHA CHINARAJ
Such is the fame of Wat Mahathat's Phra Buddha Chinaraj that many replicas have been made for other temples in the country. The most noted was enshrined by King Rama V at Wat Benchamabopit (the Marble Temple), the last royal monastery to be built in Bangkok at the beginning of the present century ● 48.

FLOATING HOUSES

Along the Nan River that flows through Phitsanulok, there can still be seen many of the floating houses and shops that were once characteristic of all Thai towns on waterways, including Bangkok. Some of the floating houses have been converted by their enterprising owners into restaurants where visitors can enjoy their meals and watch life go by on the river ● 45.

WAT MAHATHAT

Wat Mahathat, more formally known as Wat Phra Si Ratana Mahathat, is the most important temple in Phitsanulok and well known throughout the country; thanks to its large compound, it escaped serious damage from the fire that destroyed many buildings nearby. Its dominant feature is a gilded, Khmer-style prang, built during the Ayutthaya period, and the doors of the main sanctuary are beautifully decorated with inlaid mother-of-pearl designs. Surrounding the prang is a cloister that also contains the main sanctuary flanked by two chapels. The principal Buddha image, a majestic seated bronze figure known as Phra Buddha Chinaraj and dating from the late Sukhothai period, is one of the most revered in Thailand. On either side of the altar where the majestic bronze image sits are numerous other Buddhas, while the wall behind is beautifully decorated with paintings of gilded angels and floral motifs.

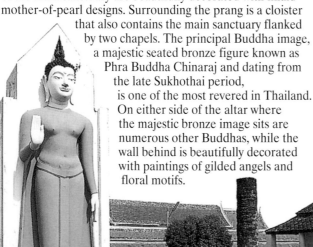

THE NORTH

CHIANG MAI MAP, *133*
CHIANG MAI, *134*
TEMPLES OF CHIANG MAI, *136*
CHIANG MAI CRAFTS, *138*
CHIANG MAI EXCURSIONS, *140*
LAMPHUN, *141*
LAMPANG, *142*
TEMPLES OF LAMPANG, *143*
WAT PHRA THAT LAMPANG LUANG, *14*
NAN VALLEY, *146*
MAE HONG SON, *148*
MAE RIM AND FANG, *150*
CHIANG RAI, *151*
HILL TRIBES, *152*
CRAFTS OF THE HILL TRIBES, *153*
CHIANG SAEN AND THE
GOLDEN TRIANGLE, *156*

1. WAT SUAN DOK
2. SUAN DOK GATE
3. WAT PHRA SINGH
4. WAT MENGRAI
5. WAT MUNYONGKON
6. WAT PUAK HONG

7. SUAN PRUNG GATE
8. CHIANG MAI GATE
9. BANYEN FOLK ART MUSEUM
10. WAT CHEDI LUANG
11. WAT PAN TAO
12. MENGRAI SHRINE

13. CHIANG PUAK GATE
14. WAT CHIANG MAN
15. BUS STATION
16. WAT KUTAO
17. TAPAE GATE
18. WAT BUPPARAM

19. WAT SAEN FANG
20. NIGHT BAZAAR
21. OLD MOAT
22. CHIANG MAI ART &
    CULTURE MUSEUM
23. THREE KINGS MONUMENT

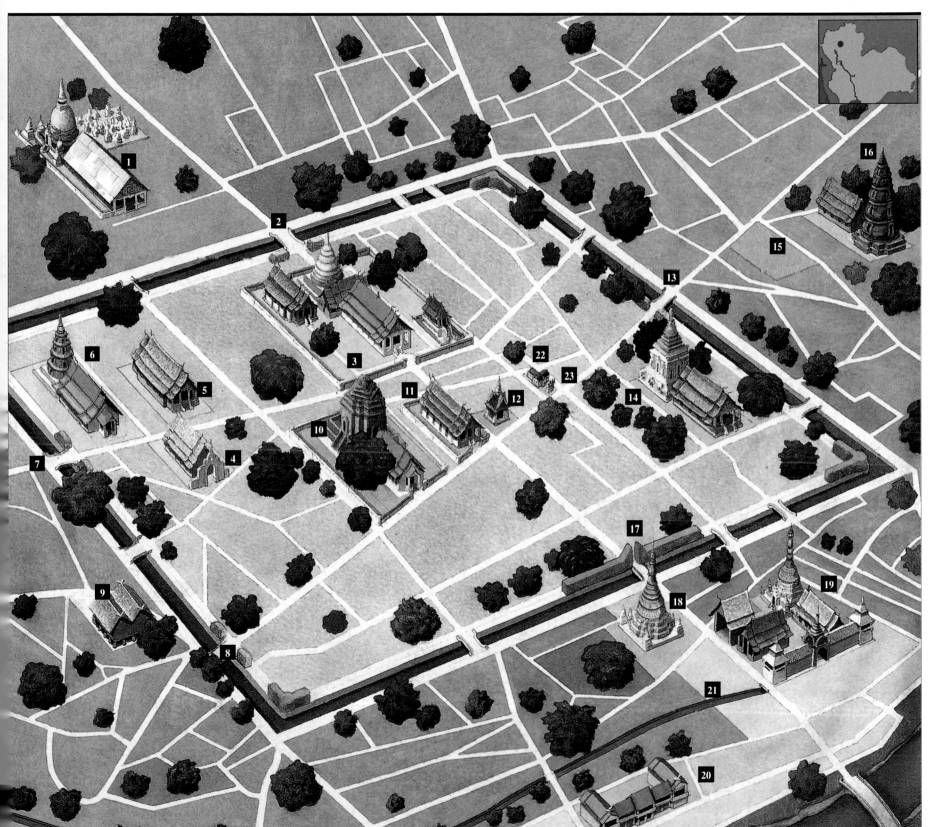

▲ THE NORTH
CHIANG MAI

«THERE IS AN EXCELLENT PATH TO CHIANG MAI WHICH ELEPHANTS
CAN FOLLOW, ARRIVING THERE IN NINE MARCHES.»
AN ENGLISHMAN'S SIAMESE JOURNALS, 1890–93

"The city of Zimmé, which lies 430 yards to the west of the river, is divided into two parts, the one embracing the other, like a letter L, on the south and east sides. The inner city faces the cardinal points, and is walled and moated all round. The inner city contains the palace of the head king, the residences of many of the nobility and wealthy men, and numerous religious buildings. In the outer city, which is peopled chiefly by the descendants of captives, the houses are packed closer together than in the inner one, the gardens are smaller, the religious buildings are fewer, and the population is more dense. The roads in both cities are laid out at right angles to each other; no rubbish is allowed to be placed outside the gardens of the houses, which are palisaded; water is led into the town from a stream flowing from Loi Soo Tayp (Doi Suthep); the floors of the houses are all raised six or eight feet from the ground; and the whole place has an air of trim neatness about it."
Holt S. Hallett,
A Thousand Miles on an Elephant,
1890.

Appealing in both culture and scenery, the Chiang Mai valley is one of the most popular Thai destinations. It may no longer be the remote Shangri-La described by early visitors – who had to journey for weeks by river and elephant to reach it – but it still possesses a beguiling blend of ancient ruins, local crafts and continuing traditions.

HISTORY

Once the cultural, religious and political center of a northern kingdom known as Lanna Thai, Chiang Mai (once known as Zimmé) was founded in 1297 by King Mengrai, who had previously established the city of Chiang Rai and also conquered the old Mon capital of Haripunchai (Lamphun today) ● 20. A northern legend says Mengrai had the assistance of two allies, King Ramkhamhaeng of Sukhothai and King Ngam Muang of Phayao, and that the site was selected because an auspicious assembly of rare animals had been seen there: two white sambar deer, two white barking deer, and a white mouse with a family of five. Over 90,000 laborers were supposedly involved in the construction of the city. By the time of Mengrai's death in 1317, he had set up a well-organized kingdom that extended from the northern frontiers of Sukhothai to the southern provinces of China, as well as a dynasty which would rule the north for another 200 years. The original walled city of Chiang Mai, containing the royal palace, noble houses and several important temples, was modified often by subsequent rulers. Chiang Mai's golden age came in the reign of King Tilokaraja (1441–87), during which a major Buddhist conference was held there in 1455 and numerous splendid temples were built. A period of instability followed, marked by wars with Ayutthaya and Burma. By 1558 Chiang Mai had fallen to the King of Pegu, and most of Lanna Thai remained under Burmese control for the next two centuries. King Taksin of Thonburi ● 20, who expelled the Burmese after the fall of Ayutthaya, recaptured Chiang Mai in 1776 but shortly afterward the impoverished city was abandoned for 20 years, its population being moved to Lampang. It was revived by King Rama I in 1796, with a son of the Prince of Lampang as ruler, and remained semi-autonomous until the late 19th century. The last Prince of Chiang Mai died in 1939, by which time the city was merely a provincial capital under control of the central government.

CHIANG MAI TODAY

Modern Chiang Mai, with a population of around 200,000, is Thailand's second-largest city after Bangkok, and is growing fast. The government increasingly earmarks Chiang Mai for development. Its airport is becoming a regional and international hub and the tourist season is being extended year-round with attractions like the Night Safari, golf courses and the Chiang Mai Zoo. Increasing numbers of Bangkok residents fly up to the cooler 'Northern Capital' to visit and even to live. Luxury hotel chains have recently opened

here, including Mandarin Oriental, Sheraton, and the Four Seasons. These and smaller boutique hotels on the river and within the moated old town reflect the resurgence of traditional architecture and design.
The city's handicraft heritage has spawned not only a huge industry of traditional crafts, textiles and souvenirs, but also of cutting-edge contemporary interior designs exported worldwide. Chiang Mai has also become a major center for New Age therapies, following renewed interest in traditional Thai remedies. Proud of this cultural legacy, *khon meuang* ('townsfolk') have supported a revival in Lanna pride after a century of modernization. This regional sensibility is not political, but expressed in new festivals, design, music, dance and a reappearance of northern fabrics in clothing. While progress has come in the form of unsightly high-rise buildings, traffic congestion and air pollution, numerous Buddhist temples and shady side streets offer ample opportunities to discover the city's fabled charms.

THE OLD AND THE NEW
Chiang Mai in the 1940's (left), and the city today (above). If some of the main streets have lost their charm due to modern construction, many smaller ones still to recall a more leisurely past, with picturesque temples and bungalows set in shady compounds among fruit trees.

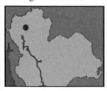

🕐 Five days

ROAD TRAFFIC
Dodge through the cars on a bicycle, a motocycle or a tuk-tuk, which can all be hired by the day.

NAWARAT BRIDGE
The first bridge built across the Ping River in Chiang Mai was the Nawarat, which leads into Tapae Road. Originally a covered structure made of wood, it was replaced by the present one in the 1950's. Five other bridges now span the river in the city area.

A restored section of the walls near Suan Prung Gate (top) and the banks of the Ping River (above).

THE OLD TOWN

The original layout of Chiang Mai was altered by several of King Mengrai's successors. The walls and surrounding moat, which today form a square around the old town, date only from the early 19th century, though the ruined gates and bastions have been rebuilt in recent decades. This square precinct contains many of the most important temples, which are best appreciated by walking from one tranquil, shady compound to the next. Chiang Mai's main artery, Rajadamnoen Road, is pedestrianized on Sundays when it becomes a huge market.

THREE KINGS MONUMENT & CITY MUSEUM. The central meeting point of the old town is the plaza where three bronze statues depict the pact between King Mengrai of Chiang Mai, King Ramkhamhaeng of Sukhothai and King Ngam Muang of Phayao to establish the city. Behind it stands the Western classical edifice of the former provincial authority. It now contains a museum describing the city from prehistoric times to the present day. Rather than focusing on artifacts, it features easily comprehensible models, dioramas, photographs and film clips.

THE COMMERCIAL DISTRICT

The town center lies between the Ping River and the reconstructed Thapae Gate, a plaza in front of which hosts events and entertainments. Around Tapae, Charoen Prathet and Chang Klan roads congregate many hotels, guest houses, travel agencies, shops and restaurants.

The Three Kings Monument.

NIGHT BAZAAR. Originating as a cluster of stalls on Chang Klan Road and conveniently located near several hotels, the night bazaar now includes modern shopping centers and a galleria where antiques and traditional crafts and fabrics predominate. All around, shops and sidewalk vendors offer a variety of souvenirs and practical items. Most of the local specialties are here: woodcraft, lacquerware, silverware, sausages, fruits, clothes, accessories, home decorations and hill tribe products. Bars, restaurants and traditional dance shows keep the bazaar district vibrant until at least midnight.

PING RIVER

The Ping River, which was once a considerable distance away, changed its course over the centuries and now flows through the town. One of the four main northern waterways, it stretches for over 350 miles. Until the Bhumibol Dam was built near the town of Tak in 1964, it was possible to go most of the way by boat from Chiang Mai to Nakhon Sawan and then on down the Chao Phraya to Bangkok. The dam is one of Thailand's biggest hydroelectric projects.

EAST BANK RIVERSIDE. Though concrete embankments blight the city's side, the verdant east bank between Naowarat Bridge and Wat Kate has become the hottest place to socialize at night. Several tree-shaded restaurant-bars provide food, music and river views from rustic buildings or conserved historic structures. This was a teak shipping district and several wooden buildings surviving along Charoenrat Road house galleries or boutiques. A riverside walk runs north of Wat Kate, while boats embark for tours from just north of Naowarat Bridge, passing handsome mansions, restaurants, waterwheels and a herb garden. South of Naowarat Bridge on Charoenrat Road stands the tourist office.

WESTERN CHIANG MAI

The most fashionable residential area is along Huay Kaeo Road, which leads to Doi Suthep, the mountain that overlooks the city. Starting at Kad Suan Kaew, a shopping center housing a theater, the road is flanked by hotels, bars, shops, condominiums and Chiang Mai University, one of the most favored places to study outside of Bangkok.

CHIANG MAI NATIONAL MUSEUM. With labels in English, this two-storey collection traces northern Thai history. Exhibits range from archeological finds and ceramics to items related to trade, health and the rise of the handicraft industry. Buddhist art forms the bulk of the artifacts. Located on the Superhighway ring-road just northeast of Wat Chet Yod, this building with Northern crossed *kalae* finials typifies many mid-20th century local edifices, with its Thai-style roof capping a concrete block.

CHIANG MAI UNIVERSITY ART MUSEUM. Thailand's first contemporary art gallery not only explains the development of traditional and modern art in the north, but also offers a major space for temporary exhibitions. Many of these shows are curated to international standards. The grounds, at the southern end of the university on the corner of Suthep and Nimmanhaemin Roads, feature large sculptures and the Hobby Hut puppet theater, which performs folk tales on weekends.

CENTER FOR THE PROMOTION OF ARTS & CULTURE. On the western side of the University Art Museum compound, five exquisite northern buildings have been reconstructed: three Lanna houses, a rice granary and a Thai Lue house. These form a living museum; Origin runs short courses here in English on authentic Lanna arts. Under renowned master Vithi Phanichphant, experts lead participants in dance, music, martial arts, flower offerings and other skills to impart a unique insight into Thai culture.

The building that once housed the provincial authority is now the Chiang Mai City Museum.

Wooden sculpture on the grounds of the Chiang Mai University Art Museum.

15th-century Lanna-style bronze Buddha head known as the Phra Saen Sae Buddha, on display at the Chiang Mai National Museum.

An aerial view of Wat Phra Singh in about 1930.

WAT PHRA SINGH

One of Chiang Mai's most important sanctuaries, Wat Phra Singh was founded in 1345 by King Pha Yu of the Mengrai Dynasty to enshrine the ashes of his father, King Kham Fu. The lofty main viharn, however, was built in 1925 and has recently been restored. Of greater interest is the older Viharn Laikam on the left, perhaps the finest building that survives in Chiang Mai, built in late Lanna style in 1806 or 1811 ● *49, 51*. This structure houses the famous Phra Buddha Singh, an early Lanna bronze image brought from Chiang Rai in 1400; the head of the original image was stolen in 1922 and the present one is a replica. The walls of the viharn are decorated with some fine murals painted in the late 19th century. Also notable in the compound is a wooden bot with beautiful stucco decorations and a graceful, elevated library adorned with carved wood and glass mosaics.

WAT PHRA SINGH PAINTINGS
The late-19th-century mural paintings at Wat Phra Singh, believed to be the work of a local artist named Jek Seng, are the best-preserved in Chiang Mai. In addition to scenes from Jataka stories, they vividly depict everyday northern life a century ago, from children's games to interior decoration ● *54*.

OTHER TEMPLES WITHIN THE WALLS

WAT CHEDI LUANG. Located on Phra Pokklao Road, Wat Chedi Luang is noted for its enormous ruined chedi. The structure was originally built in 1401, enlarged and raised to a height of 300 feet by King Tilokaraja, and destroyed by an earthquake in 1545. What remains has remnants of beautiful stucco figures flanking the steps and a seated Buddha in a niche. Also in the compound, to the left of the entrance, is an ancient gum tree, below which a small building shelters Chiang Mai's City Pillar; according to local legend, King Mengrai, founder of the city, was killed by a bolt of lightning near this spot in 1317.

WAT PAN TAO. Near Wat Chedi Luang on Phra Pokklao Road, Wat Pan Tao has one of the most beautiful Lanna-style viharns, with walls made wholly of wood panels and a roof resting entirely on wooden columns. The doors and windows of the viharn are decorated with exceptionally fine gilded stucco work.

MENGRAI SHRINE. Located across from Wat Pan Tao, at the corner of the Ratchadamnoen intersection, the Mengrai Shrine honors the founder of Chiang Mai and the dynasty that ruled the Lanna kingdom for 600 years. Local devotees regularly bring offerings to the shrine.

WAT PUAK HONG. Not far from Suan Prung Gate, on a lane off Samlan Road, Wat Puak Hong has an unusual chedi in the form of a round, stepped pyramid dating from the 16th or 17th century. Decorated niches on the chedi shelter images of meditating Buddhas.

WAT CHIANG MAN. Located on Ratchaphanikai Road, in the northeastern corner of the old city, Wat Chiang Man is believed to be the first temple built by King Mengrai ● *20* ▲ *134* on the spot where he camped when Chiang Mai was being constructed. Most of its buildings, however, are of more recent date, the chedi itself probably being a 15th-century reconstruction of the first one ● *51*. A 19th-century wooden bot contains an interesting collection of bronze images, while two more recent viharns enshrine a number of revered images, among them the tiny crystal Phra Buddha Setang Khamanai, which probably dates from the 7th century and is believed to have the power to bring rain.

TEMPLES ALONG TAPAE ROAD

WAT SAEN FANG. Just off Tapae Road, at the intersection with Kamphaengdin Road, a lane flanked with *naga* (sacred serpents) leads to Wat Saen Fang. Burmese influence is strong in its tall chedi, adorned with golden parasols, a large building where the monks reside, and a recently restored viharn resplendent in fresh red and gold paint.

PUAK HONG, THE "WHITE SWAN"
The seven-story chedi was built in the 16th and 17th centuries.

The shape of the chedi of Wat Puak Hong is probably inspired by that of Chinese pagodas. Although unusual, it is not the only one in the north; a similar one can be seen at Wat Rampoeng, just outside Chiang Mai.

MENGRAI IMAGE
Though a modern temple made entirely of cement, Wat Mengrai, off Ratchamanka Road, Lane 6, is of interest because of its ornate stuccoed entrance gate and a Buddha image cast during King Mengrai's reign and believed to resemble the first ruler.

WAT BUPPARAM Facing Wat Saen Fang on Tapae Road, Wat Bupparam is a blend of Burmese and Lanna styles. The facade of the main viharn, for example, has Burmese-style arches under a Lanna roof, while another small wooden viharn with stucco decorations is classic Lanna and enshrines three large Buddha images ▲ 82.

WAT MAHARAM. This temple contains a chedi and a viharn in Burmese style while the bot is Lanna. Of particular interest are the witty caricatured figurines of mythological beasts that stand on the wall facing the road.

NEW YEAR FLAGS
During the celebration of Songkran, the traditional Thai New Year ● 38, held in mid-April, devout Buddhists build small piles of sand in temple grounds to represent chedis. On each they place a little flag of colored paper as an auspicious adornment.

WAT BUA KROK LUANG

Across the Ping River, on a side lane off the road to San Khamphaeng, Wat Bua Krok Luang has a viharn containing the second most important mural paintings in Chiang Mai, after those in Wat Phra Singh. These were painted more than a century ago and show the life of the Buddha and scenes from the Jataka tales.

WAT UMONG

PAPER LANTERNS
During the festival of Loy Krathong ● 38, houses and temples in Chiang Mai are decorated with colorful paper lanterns. These lanterns are hung outside the doors, framed by arches of banana leaves and branches of the tree.

Wat Umong, at the end of a long, winding lane off Suthep Road, contains underground cells for meditation and is one of Chiang Mai's oldest monasteries. Of the original stucco decorations, only a few fragments of *naga* and the guardian giants known as *yaksa* remain. The chedi, which rises above the old meditation cells, is a recently built monument, though the cells themselves contain faint traces of the oldest surviving paintings in early Lanna style, dating from the 15th century. The new monastery in the compound is popular with Western Buddhists, who are welcome to join in the retreat and meditation.

WAT CHED YOD

Also known as Wat Potharam Maha Viharn, Wat Ched Yod is located outside the city walls on the highway near the Chiang Mai branch of the National Museum. Its principal feature is a chedi unlike any other in the north, composed of seven chedis on a laterite base with a barrel-vaulted chamber inside. The shape was possibly inspired by the Indian Mahabodhi temple of Bodhgaya or by Mon replicas in Burma. Most

northerners are convinced of the former source and claim that it was built by King Tilokaraja in 1455 for a major Buddhist gathering. The fine stucco decorations on the walls represent 70 celestial deities.

WAT KUTAO

Wat Kutao's unusual chedi is probably the main reason for visiting the temple, which is not very far from the National Stadium. Showing Chinese influence ● 48, it consists of a series of hemispheres superimposed in descending order of size. Wat Kutao was supposedly built in 1613 to hold the ashes of a Burmese ruler of Chiang Mai.

WAT SUAN DOK

About half a mile west of Suan Dok Gate is Wat Suan Dok, the "Flower Garden Temple," which was built on the site of a royal garden. The temple's huge, bell-shaped chedi, similar to those in Sukhothai, was erected at the end of the 14th century by King Ku Na in honor of a well-known monk named Maha Tera Sumana. The latter had come from Sri Lanka to teach in Chiang Mai and supposedly lived in the garden. Near the chedi is a complex of tombs and other structures containing the remains of Chiang Mai's royal family. Wat Suan Dok is the scene of a major religious ceremony during Songkran ● 38, which is the traditional Thai New Year's celebration in mid-April.

BURMESE INFLUENCE
Many temples in Chiang Mai reflect traces of Burmese influence. This is due to the immigrant carpenters and craftsmen from Burma who, in the late 19th century, came to work for British timber firms and also took part in temple construction. The use of Burmese clothing in murals reflects a tradition of idealizing heroes and other noble characters by using the attire of rulers, who were Burmese at the time ● 51.

A ROYAL CEMETERY
Behind Wat Suan Dok are the funeral chedis of the royal family of Chiang Mai.

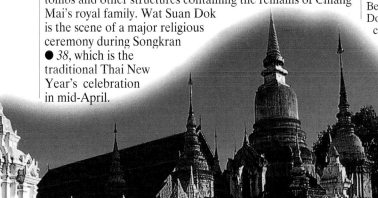

The themes of traditional Thai woodcarving were more often than not religious. In the early 1980's a ban on the

export of religious Thai items was enforced. Woodcarvers turned to Burma as a source of inspiration, since Burmese religious items were not included in the official ban.

Partly because of skills handed down from generation to generation and partly because of its long relative isolation from the changing fashions of Bangkok, Chiang Mai has preserved its strong crafts tradition, with skills that have remained unchanged for centuries. These constitute an important aspect of its attraction for modern visitors as well as a profitable export industry for many local producers.

WOODCARVING

Considering the extensive forests of teak and other hardwoods that once covered the northern mountains, it is not surprising that woodcarving ranks high among the local skills, as can be clearly seen in the splendid gables, panels and roof supports that decorate almost every temple in the region. Though wood is scarcer today, craftsmen still produce a wide range of furniture, animal figures, trays and other wooden items. The largest concentration of dealers is at Ban Tawai, off the highway, south to Mae Hong Son.

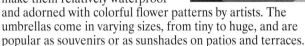

POTTERY

Local potters make a handsome array of lightly glazed earthenware water jars and pots used in most households; according to northern tradition, jars of cool water were placed outside gates for the relief of thirsty strangers who passed by. Celadon pottery production – which moved to the northern town of San Khamphaeng after the collapse of Sukhothai and eventually died out there – has also been revived by several local companies whose handsome tableware, vases and lamp bases are being exported and sold throughout the world.

CELADON WARE
Pale blue-green celadon is one of Chiang Mai's most popular crafts. The Mengrai Kilns, started by a former British consul who settled in the city, produce fine replicas of old designs, both Thai and Chinese, which are now being exported and sold in leading shops all over the world.

LACQUERWARE

Lacquerware, which probably came to Thailand from Burma, is made by applying successive coats of translucent colored lacquer to a wood or bamboo base, then embellishing it with designs. The most popular decorations are gold-and-black lacquer paintings, either figures or traditional motifs. Many household objects, from simple bowls to large cabinets, are made by this ancient process, which can be observed at the cottage factories in the Chiang

Mai area, especially on the road to San Khamphaeng.

UMBRELLAS

The small village of Bor Sang ▲ *135*, on the San Khamphaeng Road, is almost entirely devoted to the production of umbrellas. These are made of handmade paper stretched over a frame of bamboo, then lightly lacquered to make them relatively waterproof and adorned with colorful flower patterns by artists. The umbrellas come in varying sizes, from tiny to huge, and are popular as souvenirs or as sunshades on patios and terraces.

TEXTILES

Northern weavers are noted for the quality of their silks and cottons, as well as for their skill at embroidering them with bands of brocade and woven designs. These are traditionally produced in sarong-length pieces for women, the silk being reserved for special occasions and the cotton for everyday wear; a cotton sarong for men, called a *phakoma* ● *30*, comes in plaid patterns. The villages of San Khamphaeng and Pasang, near Chiang Mai, are noted for their weaving, and a wide selection is also available at the night bazaar.

SILVERWARE

Even though silver is not mined in Thailand, silverware has long been a Chiang Mai specialty, particularly bowls with intricate *repoussée* designs that are used in numerous ceremonies. The main community of silversmiths is based at Wualai Road, near Chiang Mai Gate, where one of the characteristic sounds is the constant clangor of hammer on metal. In addition to the classic bowls, more contemporary items like trays, teapots and tableware are also produced. In former days, the silver was generally obtained by melting down old coins from British India and Burma. Some of the hill tribes still produce their distinctive silver jewelry by this method, but the Chiang Mai artisans now import their silver from abroad. The price of a silver item is based not so much on the workmanship as on the quality of the metal.

BETEL BOXES
A set of beautifully crafted betel-nut boxes was an accessory found in every aristocratic household and many ordinary ones as well, consisting of a lacquerware tray and assorted containers used in the once-universal ritual of betel chewing.

«THE WOODWORK OF THE TEMPLES IS BEAUTIFULLY CARVED
AND GILDED, AND RICHLY INLAID WITH GLASS AND TINSEL
OF VARIOUS COLOURS.»

HOLT S. HALLETT

Chiang Mai not only celebrates more festivals than anywhere else in Thailand, but does so with an enthusiasm that attracts tourists and native visitors from all over the country. Dates of the festivals may vary from year to year since some celebrations are based on the lunar calendar, so it is best to check beforehand when planning a trip. The Chiang Mai Flower Festival, replete with colorful parades of blossom-covered floats, takes place in February. Since the 1990s, April now starts with a celebration of Lanna culture, with dance and music performances, and a *gad muang*, a traditional fair with stalls under red umbrellas, local produce in traditional containers, and most vendors and visitors dressed in Lanna clothing. Also in early April, the Shan community holds a Poi Sang Long ordination festival over three days to rival the equivalent in Mae Hong Son, with costumes and parades around Wat Pha Pao on the outer northeast edge of the moat. Soon after, Songkran ● *38*, the traditional Thai New Year, is celebrated for a full three days beginning April 13 and blends solemn religious ceremonies with riotous throwing of water on passers-by. Late October or November brings Loy Krathong ● *26, 38*, the magical water festival, when by the light of a full moon thousands of little lotus-shaped boats are set adrift on the Ping River and all sorts of activities take place on land. The year ends with the Winter Fair, three days of shows, sports and competitions, and a popular beauty pageant to select Miss Chiang Mai. Every alternate cool season, the city's streets and temple grounds become an open air gallery of contemporary artworks and performance art for the Chiang Mai Social Installation, lasting several weeks.

FESTIVALS AROUND CHIANG MAI. In addition to these major city functions, innumerable smaller ones that are equally high-spirited are held in surrounding towns. In January, for instance, the little umbrella village of Bor Sang, which is approximately 3 miles from San Khamphaeng, stages a festive fair along its main street, while in August the annual harvest of longan – a highly prized lychee-like fruit known in Thai as *lamyai* – is celebrated by the people of Lamphun. The paper umbrellas made in Bor Sang are waxed and painted in vivid colors with flowers and scenes from folk tales. Beauty contests are an essential element of any northern Thai festival, large or small, resulting sometimes in such singularly colorful events as the selection of a Miss Garlic.

The traditional way of entertaining guests in Chiang Mai is with a *khantoke* dinner – *khan* meaning "bowl" and *toke* being a low round table made of lacquer or rattan. Guests sit on the floor around the table and help themselves to various dishes, generally eaten with glutinous rice, a specialty of the northern region.

CONTEMPORARY NORTHERN DESIGN. Since the mid-1990s, Chiang Mai has become the focus of a major export industry in modern interior decorations and furnishings with a northern Thai character. A host of young designers simplify classic forms using minimalist lines and materials like ceramic, wood, rattan, water hyacinths, candles, incense, fabric and *saa* paper, which is handmade from mulberry pulp. They sparingly apply Lanna decoration inspired by textiles, stencils, carvings, lacquerware and gold leaf appliqués. Widely exported, the resulting style influences interiors and products seen across Thailand, though the focus in Chiang Mai are several shops, galleries and boutiques around the Huay Kaew Road end of Nimmanhaemin Road.

THAI TEMPLE DÉCOR
Nowhere has the Thai penchant for elaborate decoration been more abundantly realized than in Chiang Mai, where it is still supported by a wide variety of traditional skills. Most temples ● *49, 50* and many homes are adorned by wood carvings on gables, lintels, doorways, windows, columns and roof eaves, often further embellished by gilding and colored-glass mosaic. In addition, there are murals depicting both religious and secular subjects, intricate designs in gold and black lacquer, stucco decorations and figures of mythological creatures and divinities. Techniques brought by Burmese artisans, such as gilded metal filigree and embossed lacquer panels, add to the overall richness that distinguishes even lesser-known temples. Relatively few fall into disrepair; the desire to earn merit through donation and other forms of assistance ensures that most undergo frequent renovations.

«FINE FRUIT TREES, AND BEAUTIFUL BAMBOO CLUMPS
IN THE GARDENS BORDERING THE ROAD,
FORM A MAGNIFICENT AND SHADY AVENUE.»
HOLT S. HALLETT

DOI SUTHEP

Overlooking Chiang Mai, the 5,283-foot mountain called Doi Suthep is part of the twin-peaked Doi Suthep–Doi Pui National Park. There was no proper road up the mountain until the mid-1930's, when a monk named Phra Khruba Srivijaya initiated the construction of one, mainly with volunteer labor, to help pilgrims who wanted to visit the famous Wat Phra That Doi Suthep near the summit. It offers spectacular views and much lower temperatures even in the hottest months. The National Park headquarters are just beyond the temple car park.

GOLDEN CHEDI
The famous golden chedi of Wat Phra That Doi Suthep, 79 feet high and 39 feet across at its base, is covered with engraved gold plates; on the platform around it are four ornamental umbrellas, brightly gilded and adorned with beautiful filigree decorations, while the walls of the surrounding cloister are painted with murals from the life of the Buddha.

WAT PHRA THAT DOI SUTHEP. According to legend, holy relics discovered during the reign of King Ku Na (1355–85) were placed on the back of a white elephant, which carried them to Wat Suan Dok. The elephant was then set free to wander and it climbed Doi Suthep to the site of Wat Phra That, where it dropped dead. The present complex dates from the 16th century and was expanded or restored several times. A flight of 290 steps, bordered by a *naga* balustrade, leads up from the parking area to the temple, which has beautifully decorated buildings and a Lanna-style chedi covered with engraved gold plates, flanked by four ornamental umbrellas.

PHUPING PALACE. Built in 1972, Phuping Palace is about 2½ miles beyond Wat Phra That Doi Suthep and serves as the royal family's northern residence. The buildings are closed to the public, but when the royal family is not present the extensive gardens are open. January is the best month to see the numerous temperate-zone plants and trees in flower.

CHIANG MAI ZOO & NIGHT SAFARI

The Chiang Mai Zoological Park, near the foot of Doi Suthep, began as the private collection of Harold Young, an American working in Chiang Mai, and was taken over by the government in 1965 after his death. It has more than 500 animals in an attractively landscaped setting. Two pandas from China have brought many new visitors, while a Night Safari and elephant park expect to become major tourist draws.

SAN KHAMPHAENG

The 8-mile road from Chiang Mai to the village of San Khamphaeng passes the Bor Sang umbrella village ▲ 138 and is lined with shops selling various handicrafts. San Khamphaeng is famous for its handwoven silks and cottons, sold at many shops along the main street.

HANDICRAFT VILLAGES

Several villages devoted to handicraft production lie on or just off the Chiang Mai-Chom Thong highway. In Muang Kung the people make household pottery, while Hang Dong specializes in woven bamboo baskets ● 39. In Ban Tawai, there are hundreds of woodcarvers, and modern facilities for shipping their products around the world.

DOI INTHANON NATIONAL PARK

Covering 193 square miles, the only temperate rainforest in Thailand is a popular day trip from Chiang Mai. The park includes the 8,465-foot Doi Inthanon, Thailand's highest mountain. At the top is a chedi containing the ashes of the last ruler of Chiang Mai. Pilgrims paying homage once had to go up on foot or on ponies. During the 1970's, despite protests, the army built a 28-mile road to the summit, opening it to more visitors. However, the park still has many unspoiled trails, waterfalls (such as the Mae Ya falls in the southern part), mountain butterflies and 383 species of birds. The road passes twin chedi dedicated to King Bhumibol and Queen Sirikit, as well as Royal Projects of temperate flowers and fruit, all open to the public.

WAT SI CHOM THONG

Less than a mile beyond the turn-off to Doi Inthanon is Wat Si Chom Thong. It contains a Lanna-style chedi ● 51 from the 15th century and sheathed in brass plates, as well as a more recent Burmese-style chedi. The viharn, built in 1516 and restored in 1817, is beautifully decorated with intricate woodcarvings.

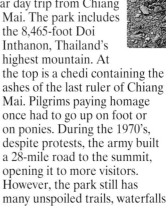

WOODCRAFT
❝Woodcarving is a favorite occupation, in which some technical artistic skill is displayed, and the native chiefs and some of the princes constantly employ men to make ornaments. Carved scroll work for doors, posts, household articles, is in much request.❞
Carl Bock

CATTLE MARKET
About a mile beyond the village of San Pa Thong on the Chiang Mai-Chom Thong highway, a colorful *kadwua*, or cattle market, is held on Saturday mornings, perhaps the largest of its kind in the north. Besides cattle and buffaloes, a wide range of other items are on sale, from exotic foods to herbal medicines.

A new expressway can now be used for the trip to Lamphun, 16 miles south of Chiang Mai, although the old road is still the more attractive of the two; some people, indeed, regard it as the most beautiful in the north, lined as it is with stately trees growing to 66 feet tall and meeting at the top to form a cool canopy. On the way, it passes large plantations of *lamyai*, a fruit much prized in the north, and the basket-weaving village of Saraphi.

HISTORY

Lamphun, now a quiet town on the Kwang River, was once an important cultural center. Founded in AD 660, it was the capital of the Mon kingdom of Haripunchai and remained independent until it was incorporated into the Lanna kingdom by King Mengrai in 1281. The walls and moat that can be seen today date only from the early 19th century, but a number of fine temples attest to the city's ancient glory ● *20*.

WAT PHRA THAT HARIPUNCHAI

One of the major temples in the north, both historically and architecturally, Wat Phra That Haripunchai, facing the Kwang River, was founded in 1044 by King Athitayaraj of Haripunchai on the site of a former royal palace. A modern viharn, built in 1925 to replace the original, houses the Phra Chao Thongthip, a Chiang Saen-style bronze Buddha image; to the right of the viharn is an enormous bronze gong, while to the left is a Lanna-style repository for religious scriptures built in the early 19th century. The most prominent feature of the temple complex – and the most sacred part – is a 165-foot-tall Lanna-style chedi built in 1467, sheathed in copper and adorned with a gold umbrella. Slightly behind this monument is the Suwanna Chedi, a stepped-pyramid form of chedi, dating from 1418 and a replica of

one in Wat Chamadevi, also in Lamphun. Elsewhere in the compound are a viharn enshrining a standing Buddha known as Phra Chao Tan Jai and a pavilion containing four Buddha footprints, one inside another. **MUSEUMS.** Some of the many Buddha images presented to Wat Phra That Haripunchai have been been placed in a small museum within the temple grounds. Opposite Wat Phra That Haripunchai is a small branch of the National Museum. It contains a fine collection of bronze Buddha images, together with stucco and terracotta figures of the early Haripunchai period found during archeological excavations in the area.

WAT CHAMADEVI

Also known as Wat Ku Kut, Wat Chamadevi contains Lamphun's oldest monuments: two brick chedis decorated with stucco figures of the Buddha. According to the noted authority Jean Boisselier, these ruins date from 1218 and are among the last surviving examples of Dvaravati-period (7th–11th century) architecture. The larger chedi, Sat Mahal Pasada, is in the form of a stepped pyramid 69 feet high and 51 feet wide and was possibly inspired by a similar monument at Polonnaruwa in Sri Lanka; it served as the model for similar structures elsewhere in the region. The other small chedi is octagonal and dates from the same period.

WIANG KUM KAM

Wiang Kum Kam, which can be visited on an excursion or on a trip to Lamphun, is a recently unearthed old city built by King Mengrai shortly before he founded Chiang Mai. He lived there for six years before the site was destroyed when the Ping River changed its course. Among the temples in the area, Wat Chedi Liem has a tall chedi – it is similar to the one at Wat Chamadevi – which was restored at the turn of this century with the addition of Burmese-style decorations. Wat Chan Kham has a spirit house where the soul of King Mengrai himself is believed to reside.

MCKEAN INSTITUTE

Not far from Wiang Kum Kam, on a small island in the Ping River, is the McKean Institute, where leprosy patients are treated. It was founded in 1908 by Dr James W. McKean, a Presbyterian missionary, and has become internationally recognized for its approach to the once-dreaded disease.

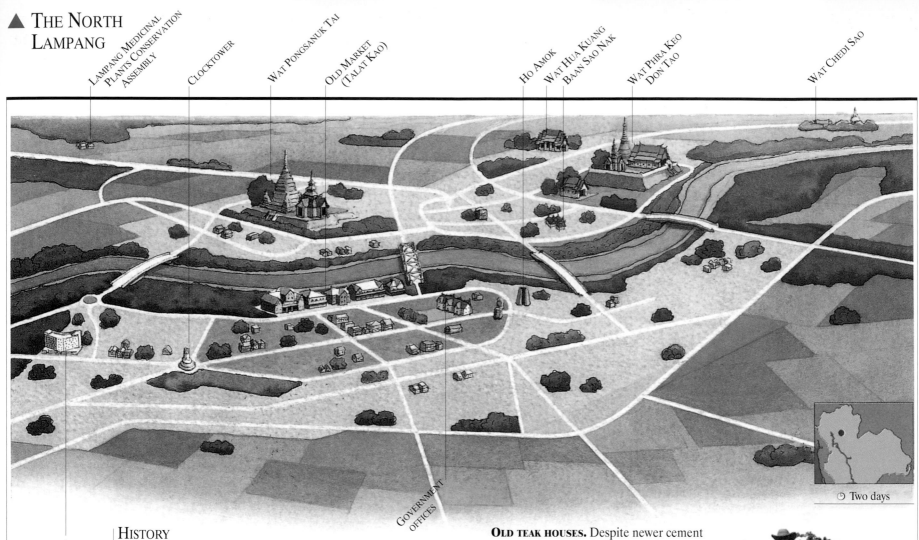

LAMPANG MEDICINAL
PLANTS CONSERVATION
ASSEMBLY

CLOCKTOWER

WAT PONGSANUK TAI

OLD MARKET
(TALAT KAO)

HO AMOK

WAT HUA KUANG
BAAN SAO NAK

WAT PHRA KEO
DON TAO

WAT CHEDI SAO

GOVERNMENT
OFFICES

TIP CHANG
HOTEL

⏲ Two days

HISTORY

Located in the valley of the Wang River, a tributary of
the Ping, Lampang is the second-largest town in northern
Thailand. Its long history goes back to the 7th century, when
it was supposedly founded by a son of the Haripunchai queen,
Chamadevi ▲ 141, who had established a Mon
kingdom in the north. Originally known as
Kelang Nakhon, it had four outlying
fortified satellite settlements,
of which only Wat Phra That
Lampang Luang still exists ● 49.
Lampang theoretically became
part of the Lanna kingdom under
Mengrai, though in many ways it was
ruled autonomously; like Chiang Mai, it
was occupied by the Burmese for three centuries.
The specific location of Kelang Nakhon is unknown, but the
town was on the opposite bank of the river from the main part
of today's city. In the early 20th century, Lampang was a center
of the northern teak industry,
with a population of more than
20,000 and some 4,000 working
elephants; it was also visited
yearly by ten caravans from the
Shan states of Burma, bringing
goods that ranged from
lacquerware to opium.

The
distinctive
style of Lanna
temples ● 49 is
captured in this old
engraving based on a
sketch by Carl Bock,
who visited the town
in the early 1880's.

Lampang women
during a local
festival.

OLD TEAK HOUSES. Despite newer cement
constructions being built, many fine old teak
mansions survive along the river.
OLD MARKET. Known as *talat kao*, this
market district along the river retains much
of its charm. The shophouses display a
mixture of Chinese, Burmese and Western
influences, and many are adorned with
Victorian fretwork imported by Burmese
carpenters. Some have been converted into
houses and restaurants.
BAAN SAO NAK. An extensive neighborhood
of wooden houses north of the river includes
this
restored
'many pillar house',
with displays of teak,
lacquer, ceramics
and old photos of
its noble family
owners.

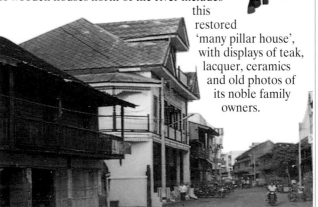

**HORSE-
DRAWN
CARTS**
The symbol of
Lampang, at least
to Thai visitors, is
the horse-drawn
cart. Such carts were
originally imported
from England in the
early years of the
present century and,
while they are no
longer as common
as they once were,
enough remain
to give the town a
leisurely ambience
and offer a pleasant
way to explore it.

«THIS COUNTRY OF LANNA…MAKES THE STRANGER FEEL THAT, IF
HE MUST BE EXILED FROM HIS NATIVE SHORES, HE COULD NOT FIND
A LAND OF GREATER CHARM AND SYMPATHY TO SPEND HIS DAYS.»

REGINALD LE MAY

MOSAIC CEILING
"The only note of incongruity," wrote Reginald Le May in 1926, "was a series of small gilt angel figures (of the Raphael type), pendent from the ceiling. How easily and only too well they learn from the West!" Such figures of cupids as well as horses and soldiers of Victorian inspiration had been widely used by Mandalay artists since the early days of the British occupation of Burma.

WIANG LUANG LAKON
Each year, usually in February, a festive parade called *Wiang Luang Lakon* is staged in Lampang. This celebrates the splendors of Queen Chamadevi's 7th-century court, with hundreds of participants in colorful period dress.

WAT PHRA KEO DON TAO

The most important temple in Lampang, Wat Phra Keo Don Tao supposedly once enshrined the famous Emerald Buddha, which is now housed at Wat Phra Keo in Bangkok ▲ 76, 88. This image, according to legend, was being brought from its place of discovery in Chiang Rai to Chiang Mai in 1436 when the elephant bearing it stopped in Lampang and refused to proceed; it therefore remained in the town until 1468, when King Tilokaraja finally took it to Chiang Mai. The name of the temple, however, comes from another image, the Phra Keo Don Tao, which was housed there before it was moved to Wat Phra That Lampang Luang. The only original structure remaining in the temple is a 165-foot chedi, reputed to enshrine a hair of the Buddha, while the most interesting building is a Burmese-style structure built in 1909 as a donation by a Thai prince. The latter has a three-tier roof, elaborate mirror mosaics and superb woodcarvings. The principal viharn, Phra Chao Thong Tip, was constructed in 1930 by the venerated northern monk Khruba Srivijaya and contains a fine Buddha image. A small museum in the temple compound displays a collection of Lanna-style furniture.

WAT SUCHADA. Adjacent to Wat Phra Keo Don Tao, Wat Suchada is regarded as part of the same monastery. Built by residents of Chiang Saen who were forcibly resettled after their hometown was destroyed at the beginning of the 19th century, it has a chedi and two viharns in late Lanna style; the main viharn houses a large brick and stucco Buddha and has some beautiful lacquer decorations.

OTHER OLD LANNA TEMPLES

WAT SENG MUANG MA ★. Also one of the Chiang Saen temples, Wat Seng Muang Ma is located on Thamma Oo Road. It contains a small but well-proportioned chedi, as well as a viharn that enshrines a large Buddha image and has some interesting paintings on wood panels dating from the turn of the century (above).

WAT HUA KUANG. Like Wat Suchada, this was built by resettled Chiang Saen people and has an interesting old viharn in late Lanna style, as well as Chiang Saen images and manuscripts on the art of casting bronze that the displaced people brought with them.

WAT PONGSANUK TAI ★. Located on Pongsanuk Road in Wiang Neua, the area occupied by the old Lanna town of Lampang, Wat Pongsanuk Tai is regarded by many as the most charming temple in the town. Within a tree-filled new monastery is an old one, almost intact, in Lanna style on a high platform that can be reached by flights of steps on each side. A Lanna chedi ● 49, 51 is covered with copper sheets and also on the platform is a splendid open-sided structure with a tiered roof and a mondop (right) in old Lanna style and a newer viharn containing a reclining Buddha image. All the buildings are gracefully proportioned and elegantly decorated.

KU YA SUDHA ★. "The Grotto of Grandmother Sudha" is the local name of the gatehouse of a now-destroyed monastery on Wiang Neua Road. Decorated with deities in stucco, it dates from the 15th century and is one of the oldest examples of Lanna art.

HO AMOK. The Octagonal Tower is one of the few parts of Lampang's ancient fortifications that remain today. Located in the modern part of the new town, on the west bank of the Wang river, it served as a lookout and is today a venue of a grand shamanistic ceremony in honor of the spirits of the town.

CHIANG SAEN REFUGEES
At the beginning of the 19th century, with the support of King Rama I of Bangkok, the Chiang Mai ruler, Kawila

● 20, launched a determined effort to increase the population of Lampang and Chiang Mai, depleted by so many years of war. In 1804, he destroyed Chiang Saen and resettled the inhabitants in Lampang. This group was responsible for the construction of a number of temples and the casting of major Buddha images in the city.

CEREMONIAL GATES
Monasteries in the north usually had very imposing ceremonial gates, richly adorned with stucco figures. With the disappearance of the wooden temple buildings over the years, these are the only structures that now survive ● 49.

WAT PRATU PONG ★ Not far from the Ho Amok and near a remaining part of the old city wall is Wat Pratu Pong, which, although slightly restored, is still one of the best examples of classic northern style. The gable is decorated with a fine woodcarving of a mythological creature with a serpent emerging from its mouth, while the doors of the temple are also exquisitely carved.

BURMESE TEMPLES

After the Burmese Occupation, many Burmese came to the north in the late 19th century to work in the timber trade and some became prosperous resident businessmen. The latter built or restored numerous temples ▲ 149, which partly accounts for the strong Burmese element in northern architecture ● 49, 51.

EARLY TOURISTS IN LAMPANG
Unfortunately destroyed by fire early in 1991, Wat Sri Chum, one of Lampang's Burmese-style temples, contained some fine lacquered wall paintings. Among the subjects depicted were foreigners, shown traveling by automobile through the forest to visit the temple and pausing at a local refreshment stand.

WAT PHA FANG Located opposite the office of Thai Airways on Airport Road, Wat Pha Fang is one of several temples in Lampang that show a strong Burmese influence, even though it has been recently restored. Its chedi, for example, is typically Burmese, while each of the surrounding chapels contains an image in Mandalay style. The bot, which is located near the chedi, is more elaborately decorated than the viharn.

WAT CHEDI SAO. Located a few miles to the left off the road to Jae Hom, this "Temple of the Twenty Chedis" is a charming country monastery. The whitewashed chedis are a blend of Thai and Burmese styles, and the compound also contains a remarkable collection of fanciful statues added in recent years. These include the twelve animals of the Chinese calendar as well as figures from Buddhist legends. The principal image in the viharn is a Lanna Buddha made of brick and stucco.

Some of the twenty chedis of Wat Chedi Sao.

TEMPLES OF LAMPANG LUANG

Located about 12 miles west of Lampang in the Kokha district, Lampang Luang was once a *wiang* (citadel) established during the early Haripunchai period. Protected by three earthen ramparts separated by moats, the site was part of a group of satellite fortresses associated with the ancient city of Kelang Nakorn.

WAT LAI HIN ★. The first temple in the Kokha district, Wat Lai Hin ● 51, is located on high ground overlooking a stream and ricefields. The main viharn, in old Lanna style, has elaborate stucco decorations on the gable and fine lacquer-work inside, both possibly 200 years old, while the gatehouse dates probably from the 15th or 16th century.

WAT PONG YANG KOK ★. Just past Wat Phra That Lampang Luang on the road to Hang Chat, Wat Pong Yang Kok has a beautiful open wooden viharn in the old Lanna style. Inside are some famous lacquer decorations featuring a motif of the bodhi tree repeated throughout.

THAI ELEPHANT CONSERVATION CENTER ★

One of the most natural ways to encounter Thai elephants is this large wooded complex 23 miles northwest of Lampang on the main road to Chiang Mai, route 11. Developed from a training center for young elephants, it offers shelter for pachyderms left unemployed by the 1988 logging ban and an elephant hospital, some of whose patients can be visited. Courses at the mahout school are also open to foreigners. Most daytrippers come in time to see the animals bathing in the lake before watching the non-exploitative shows at 10am and 11am daily and at 1.30pm on weekends. Elephant rides are also available. Displays explain elephants' lives, history, cultural importance and current predicament. To help raise funds for the center's huge expenses, a gift shop sells paper made from elephant dung, music with elephant accompaniment and abstract paintings by the pachyderms, which have been regarded seriously by some international art critics and auction houses ▲ 28.

THE PHRA KEO DON TAO
A small jasper image believed to have magical powers, the Phra Keo Don Tao, now housed at Wat Phrathat Lampang Luang, was much coveted by northern rulers of the 15th century.

THUNG KWIAN MARKET
Thirteen miles from Lampang, near the Thai Elephant Conservation Center, Thung Kwian Market makes for a fascinating stop on route 11 to Chiang Mai. It sells a breadth of traditional forest products from herbs and honeycombs to boar meat and edible insects. A foundry produces elaborate ceremonial blades. Another section stocks a huge range of the Lampang pottery tableware bearing a distinctive painted motif of the town symbol, the chicken.

1. PHRA TAT – CHEDI WITH BUDDHA RELICS
2. PRINCIPAL VIHARN
3. VIHARN BUILT IN 1802
4. VIHARN (CONTEMPORARY)
5. VIHARN NAM TAM (EARLY 16TH CENTURY)
6. VIHARN RECONSTRUCTED IN 1967
7. BOT BUILT IN 1924
8. *MONDOP* HOUSING BUDDHA'S FOOTPRINT
9. CEREMONIAL GATEHOUSE LEADING TO PORTICOED ENCLOSURE
10. STAIRWAYS FLANKED BY *NAGA*
11. BODHI TREE
12. VIHARN WITH PHRA KEO DON TAO BUDDHA
13. BODHI TREE WITH DECORATED CRUTCHES

WAT PHRA THAT LAMPANG LUANG ★

Many an enchanted traveler has called Wat Phra That Lampang Luang the most beautiful temple in Thailand. Showing a spectacular display of Lanna religious architecture ● 49 and decorative skills, the temple was founded in early Haripunchai times, and contains a 165-foot chedi believed to contain genuine relics of the Buddha. This and all the most important buildings are located within a porticoed enclosure, situated on top of a hillock; the main entrance is a monumental gatehouse adorned with stucco-work. Lions and *naga* (sacred serpents) guard the steps. The main viharn behind the gate-house is an open-sided structure built in 1496 and restored several times. The painting on the wooden panels below the roof eaves date from the late 19th century, but the building was actually reconstructed by Phra Khruba Srivijaya in the 1930's. Also in the enclosure are a bot, three viharns and a *mondop* containing a camera obscura image of the chedi. The Viharn Nam Tam is probably the oldest surviving Lanna building, and has been beautifully restored to its original form. Paintings from the 16th century were revealed during the restoration. In an enclosure to the side stands a simple viharn housing the Phra Keo Don Tao Buddha image. Beside it, hundreds of decorated carved wooden crutches rest against a vast multi-trunk bodhi tree. Lampang Luang is the main surviving example of a fortified settlement, which was built around a citadel, or *wiang*. This type of stronghold was once very common in northern Thailand, and was used for military purposes until the 18th century, when it was occupied by the Burmese. In 1736, Lampang Luang became the scene of a famous duel between the Burmese general and the Thai hero, Tip Chang, who had cleverly sneaked inside the walls through a drain to confront the enemy. Today the farming community is still clustered around the temple, which was built on high ground, though its fortifications have been dismantled. Traces of three parallel earthen ramparts – separated by two moats filled with water – can still be seen in the village.

GILDED KU
The main viharn enshrines a gilded *ku* ● 49 (pagoda-like structure inside the temple) containing the presiding Buddha image (below).

Wat Phumin (above) is undoubtedly the most famous wat in Nan.

Nan can be reached from Chiang Mai by road in four hours or by air in 45 minutes. The road trip is worthwhile since it offers the opportunity to enjoy some pleasant rural scenery and also to visit interesting attractions along the way.

PHRAE

Coal mining and, until recently, logging have traditionally been the sources of Phrae's prosperity, still evident in some fine old wooden mansions and a thriving local furniture industry. Baan Vongburi is an authentic old mansion with its teak fretwork, old furniture, documents and decorations preserved and open to the public. Phrae's biggest teak house, Baan Pra Tab Jai, was built in 1976 from 130 ancient logs to house an eclectic display of objects for tourists to see local craftwork. Burmese influences can be seen in Wat Chom Sawan, while the most famous temple is Wat Phra That Cho Hae, atop a teak-covered hill just outside the town.

PHAE MUANG PHI

Phae Muang Phi, the "Ghost City," is located off Highway 101 on the way to Nan. This is actually not a town but a shallow depression where soil erosion has resulted in a number of strange rock-like formations that do indeed resemble the deserted dwellings of some mysterious race.

NAN TOWN ★

As late as the 1910's, Nan was capital of a semi-autonomous principality, founded in 1368. Until around 1450, the city had a close relationship with Sukhothai, then came under the indirect control of the Lanna kingdom. It was ruled by the Burmese from 1558 to 1788, before it pledged allegiance to

HILL TRIBES
The Phi Thong Luang, "Spirits of the Yellow Leaves," who live in the Nan area, are among the most elusive of the hill tribe groups, still following a virtually prehistoric lifestyle ● 17. Only in the 1960's was their existence confirmed by an expedition that came across some of them in their jungle hiding place.
In the Nan Valley are also several hundreds of Khamus, an Austro-Asiatic tribe that inhabited the region before the arrival of the Thais.

Bangkok, but the local ruling dynasty retained considerable authority until the central government finally assumed full control in 1931. Spread out along the west bank of the Nan River, the modern town has a prosperous air, with many shops selling luxury goods.

TEMPLES

WAT PHUMIN. This temple is the leading landmark of Nan, established in 1596 by a ruler named Phra Chao Chetabutra Phromin and extensively renovated in 1867. The cruciform viharn has steps leading up to splendidly carved doors on each of the four sides, while the interior is dominated by four large Buddha images facing the cardinal points ● 49. Of special interest are the murals probably painted at the turn of the century by Tai Lue artists. These mainly depict the Khatta Kumara and Nimi Jataka tales and contain a wealth of detailed visual information about the dress, tattoos and hairstyles of the period.
WAT PHRA THAT CHAE HAENG. Located southeast of the town on the opposite bank of the Nan River, this temple is noted for the enormous *naga* (serpent) stairway that leads to the entrance. Inside the courtyard is a 180-foot-high golden chedi with four smaller chedis, while the viharn is a beautiful structure showing Laotian influence.
WAT CHANG KHAM VORA VIHARN. This temple, directly opposite the local branch of the National Museum, dates from 1406 but has been restored several times; it once contained five Buddha images commissioned in 1426 by a Nan ruler, only one of which – a 5-foot walking Buddha in solid gold – is kept at the temple in the monks' residence.
WAT PHRAYA PHU. This houses two of the other images, both made of bronze in the Sukhothai style. Wat Suan Tan, on the western side of town, enshrines the important Buddha image known as Phra Chan Thong Thip, a fine example of Sukhothai style, while Wat Satharos on the northern outskirts has an unusual chedi mounted on a high square base.

NAN BOAT RACES
Held to celebrate the end of Buddhist Lent in late October or early November, the Nan boat races take place along a stretch of river near the Governor's residence. Over 40 *naga*-prowed boats, each with up to 50 oarsmen, participate in this colorful event, one of Thailand's most exciting festivals. Ernest Young wrote in his book, *The Kingdom of the Yellow Robe,* "In these races no consideration is paid to 'fouls.' The object of each crew is to reach the winning-post first, and any crew is allowed to prevent its opponents attaining that desirable end, by any means they care to employ. The consequence is that the first part of the race revolves itself into a series of 'ramming' manoeuvres. There is a fierce struggle between the rival crews who try to upset each other. The intense excitement prevails amongst the spectators as two boats near each other."

One of the most scenically stunning trips in Thailand is the loop west from Chiang Mai that takes in the little provincial capital of Mae Hong Son ▲ *148*. The clockwise southern and anti-clockwise northern routes each take a full day's driving to reach Mae Hong Son. Since there is much to see en route, many travellers break overnight on each leg of the trip to make a jaunt lasting several days, though a new road via Mae Chaem shortens the southern route. If there is time for only half the loop, travellers can fly to or from Mae Hong Son.

SOUTHERN ROUTE VIA CHOM THONG AND HOT

Continuing south on the Chiang Mai-Chom Thong road past Hot leads to the first metalled road to reach Mae Hong Son. It was opened in 1965 and has been extensively improved in recent years. It winds through some of Thailand's most beautiful scenery, with misty mountains, verdant valleys and forests of pine trees planted to replace those cut down by the hill tribes. The view is at its most spectacular as the road descends steeply into the narrow valley of the Pai River where Mae Hong Son is located.

OB LUANG GORGE. A narrow defile with steep walls, the Ob Luang Gorge is one of Thailand's most celebrated beauty spots. Nearby is a nature park, where trails lead 650 feet down to the bottom of the gorge.

MAE SARIANG. A small town 62 miles from Hot on the road from Chiang Mai to Mae Hong Son, Mae Sariang has wooden shophouses and a rickety bridge that spans the Yuam River and leads to the mountain range bordering Burma. Two local temples are worth visiting for their Burmese-style architecture ● *51*. Wat Utthayarom, which dates from 1896, has three chedis, one of which has nine spires, while nearby Wat Boonruang is much more elaborately decorated and has the monks' quarters in a longhouse raised on stilts. A dirt track leads south from Mae Sariang along the Burmese border all the way to Tak, but as it is known to be unsafe, the route is seldom used by foreigners.

SOUTHERN ROUTE VIA MAE CHAEM

An old Shan-style teak mansion in Pai.

A newly metalled road quickens the southern route slightly, but is worth taking in its own right. Just before Chom Thong ▲ *140*, take the road up into Doi Inthanon National Park, then take a left onto route 1192, which crosses the mountain's shoulder and drops precipitously into the Mae Chaem valley, before heading north up the valley on route 1088 and east on route 1263 to join the southern route at Khun Yuam, passing Mae Surin Waterfall and some of the sunflower fields for which Mae Hong Son province is famed.

MAE CHAEM. Long isolated, this valley retains many traditions lost elsewhere. It is renowned for the *teen chok* weaving used in Lanna skirt hems, particularly in the settlements of Ban Tha Pha and Ban Thong Fai. Near Ban Tha Pha are two of the valley's well-preserved rural temples, Wat Pa Daet, and Wat Yang Luang, both of which have charming murals.

NORTHERN ROUTE VIA PAI

If anything, the later northern route via Pai is even more dramatic. Taking the Chiang Mai-Fang road north past Mae Sa ▲ *150* and Mae Rim, turn left at Mae Malai onto route 1095, which follows a route that Japanese occupiers in World War II forced local people to build as a link into Burma. As the elevation increases, the road passes Mok Fa Waterfall, Pong Duet Hot Springs and a viewpoint. Shortly afterwards, a turning to Huay Nam Dang National Park offers an even greater lookout over ranges of mountains, with a view most magical at sunrise. Continuing past Pai, the road offers a side-trip to Tham Lot, an enormous cave with a river running through it that can be explored with a guide. Before the road drops into Mae Hong Son, a viewpoint presents an awesome vista of forested hills marching off west into Burma, with the border less than 13 miles away.

PAI. Until a decade ago, this quaint village on the Pai River was a quiet community farming rice on terraced fields. Originally populated by Shan, it is home to many minorities, including a large Muslim-Thai presence. Backpackers discovered its charms as a place to relax, but it developed in an culturally rich way. Not only were old buildings retained, but many of the guesthouses and small hotels feature painting studios, cooking schools, jewelry workshops, massage training centers, herb gardens, art galleries and surprisingly cosmopolitan food. Five miles south of Pai, the Tha Pai Hot Springs bubble in a forested setting. The same distance south but on the west side of the river, Pai Gorge features small eroded canyons. Pai is a good base from which to trek to hill tribe villages, visit nearby waterfalls or go whitewater rafting. Things will likely change faster with the planned opening of a small airport.

Rice paddy fields around Pai.

HOT SPRINGS
The mountainous Thai border with Burma follows a geological fault line. Though there is little seismic activity, superheated water surges to the surface at steaming springs. Accessible springs include Pong Duet, on the road to Pai, and Tha Pai Hot Springs, five miles south of Pai. Downstream from the scalding sulphurous outlets, where Thai tourists like to boil eggs, it is possible to bathe in the warmed stream. This is more comfortable at a couple of nearby resorts that tap the medicinal hot waters for outdoor spa baths.

WAT DON JADEE

WAT PHRA THAT DOI KONG MU

WAT HUA WIANG

MARKET

WAT PANG LOR

WAT PHRA NON

WAT KHAM KHO

JONGKHUM LAKE

WAT KRANG TUNG

WAT CHONG KAM

🕐 Four days

M ae Hong Son is the closest place in Thailand to a Shangri-La. Though it has certainly been discovered by the outside world, it retains an allure through its remoteness, beauty, tribal folk and natural setting within a narrow forested valley. Initially popularized by trekkers looking for less disturbed hill tribe villages to visit, the town has become a tourist base for urbanites wanting a retreat and adventure-seekers seeking thrills like mountain biking, horse riding and whitewater rafting. Mae Hong Son is known to Thais as the "town of three mists". In the rainy season, misty clouds swirl through the surrounding peaks. During the cool season, light fog cossets the lake and temple spires in the morning. By the hot season, temperatures rise to 100ºF, and the burning of rice stubble and forest underbrush for cultivation creates the third mist: smoke. From February through April, smoke can at times cause respiratory problems and force flights to be cancelled, though most of the time the area is a delight to visit.

HISTORY

Though constituted as a city by the ruler of Chiang Mai in 1874 and as a province under the Ministry of Interior in 1893, Mae Hong Son is regarded as the back of beyond by most people in Thailand. It remained isolated from the rest of Thailand until 1965 when the metalled road was opened. Mae Hong Son is in fact so remote that it was a favored place of exile for government officials charged with serious offenses against the State. Today, however, a regular domestic air service links the city with Chiang Mai, thus opening up the valley to tourism.

SHANS
Shans, who belong to the same ethnic group as the Thais, began visiting the Mae Hong Son valley from northern Burma centuries ago, and worked seasonally in the forests. By the mid-19th century increasing numbers were settling permanently, and one group built an elephant-trapping corral on the site that eventually became Mae Hong Son. The Shans still constitute nearly 50 percent of the province's population.

Wat Chong Kam and Wat Chong Klang are situated beside a small lake (above).

MAE HONG SON TODAY ★

Nestled amid forested, mist-shrouded mountains, Mae Hong Son still has a tranquil feeling of remoteness, a leisurely ambience that comes as a welcome contrast to the bustle of most other modern northern towns. The liveliest time of day is between 6am and 8am, when a busy market springs up behind the Mae Tee Hotel, with stalls selling food, clothing and household goods, and colorful hill tribe people mingle with the local populace. Otherwise the chief charm of Mae Hong Son is strolling about scenic Jongkhum Lake, visiting various temples in the area, and enjoying its cool climate during the winter months.

WAT PHRA THAT DOI KONG MU ★

Doi Kong Mu is the name of the small hill that dominates Mae Hong Son, often covered with mist in the morning. A road leads to Wat Phra That Doi Kong Mu at the summit, where there are a number of Buddha images and two chedis – one built in 1860, the other in 1874. The

SHAN ORDINATION CEREMONY
Each year in early April the Shans of Mae Hong Son observe a colorful ritual known as Poi Sang Long. This marks the initiation of young boys into the monkhood ● 25 and involves a gala procession in which the novices are carried to the monastery with dances performed by participants dressed in animal costumes.

mist clears in the afternoon, giving visitors spectacular panoramic views of the valley and the surrounding mountains; the wonderful experience is enhanced by the tinkle of bells from the tops of the chedis, which are quite dramatically illuminated after dark.

LOY KRATHONG. The water festival ● 38 is celebrated in Burmese fashion in Mae Hong Son. Instead of being set adrift on rivers and ponds, as in the rest of the country, the lotus-shaped *krathong* are attached to paper lanterns and released into the air from the top of Doi Kong Mu overlooking the town.

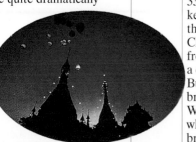

OTHER TEMPLES

WAT HUA WIANG. Located near the morning market, Wat Hua Wiang is a dilapidated wooden temple that houses an exceptionally fine brass seated Buddha, a replica of the one in Mandalay. Sections of the image were cast in Burma, then transported overland and by river and assembled in Mae Hong Son.

WAT KHAM KHO. Across the road from Wat Phra Non, Wat Kham Kho was built in 1890; the covered walkway from the main gate and the viharn have elegant filigree work on the eaves. The viharn contains five principal Buddha images, the central one being Burmese in style. In front of the altar there is a beautiful 80-year-old peacock throne inlaid with colored glass.

WAT PHRA NON. Located at the foot of Doi Kong Mu is Wat Phra Non, a rebuilt temple that houses two large Buddha images made of plaster over brick. One, 40 feet long, is in the reclining position, and the other is seated; both have realistic, painted faces in the Burmese fashion. Just behind this temple are two huge stone lion statues carved in Burmese fashion. They guard the entrance to the old deserted footpath up Doi Kong Mu. A few steps further on is a row of six chedis built on an elevated platform – all that remains of Wat Muay Toh.

WAT CHONG KAM AND WAT CHONG KLANG ★. These are two Burmese-style temples in the same compound, picturesquely sited beside a small lake and surrounded by a palm grove. Of special interest is a collection of 33 wooden figures. These figures are kept in a small barred room just inside the entrance to the viharn of Wat Chong Klang. Representing figures from the Vessantara Jataka – one of a collection of stories dealing with the Buddha's previous lives – these were brought from Burma in 1857. Near Wat Chong Kam is Luang Pho To, which enshrines a revered 16-foot-tall brick and plaster Buddha image.

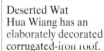

Deserted Wat Hua Wiang has an elaborately decorated corrugated-iron roof.

Detailed filigree work is a feature of Shan temples.

O ne of the most scenic drives in the Chiang Mai area is through the Mae Sa Valley, an increasingly developed area that begins with a left turn at Mae Rim, about 7 miles out of Chiang Mai on the road to Fang. Several resorts have appeared in the valley over the past few years, with terraces on the mountain slopes and neat, landscaped gardens of mostly temperate-zone plants. There are also rustic cottages that attract city-dwellers longing for a change of scene and a taste of country life without the usual discomforts. The winding road eventually slopes down to the Chiang Mai–Chom Thong Highway. The scenery, however, is most attractive along this least developed section.

"The road to Tatong lay through a somewhat open forest, with a high mountain-chain, running north and south, rising abruptly to the left. The trees were literally covered with orchids, which were just past their prime, the dry season being the time for flowering. Many other varieties of flowers, of most gorgeous colours and often of gigantic size, flourished in the open patches between the trees. I do not remember to have seen anywhere such a profusion of flowers as when travelling through Lao and in this particular district they seemed more abundant than ever."
Carl Bock

ORCHID FARMS

There are several orchid nurseries in the Mae Sa Valley, all open to visitors for a nominal entrance fee. In addition to dazzling displays of blooming plants ● *11*, both native and hybrid, most of the nurseries also have demonstrations of orchid propagation and shops selling such souvenirs as orchid blossoms coated with gold.
FA MUI ORCHID. One of the most beautiful of northern Thailand's indigenous orchids is *Vanda coerulea*, known in Thai as *Fa Mui*, the natural color of which is a heavenly blue that comes in a variety of subtle shades. This is prized by foreign orchid growers for hybridization and was used to produce the famous *Vanda rothschildiana* (right) ● *11*.

ELEPHANT-TRAINING CAMP

One of the most popular tourist stops along the Mae Sa Valley road is an elephant-training camp near the Mae Sa Waterfall. The animals and their trainers give a performance

at around 9am every day. Elephant rides through the jungle to the Mae Sa Valley Resort can also be arranged.

CHIANG DAO CAVES

Doi Chiang Dao, at 7,540 feet Thailand's third-highest mountain, is 45 miles from Chiang Mai. Nestling at the foot of the mountain are the Chiang Dao Caves, accessible through a narrow entrance at the top of a covered stairway. They consist of several chambers (above), the first of which receives some light from an opening above and is the most impressive. Shan Buddhists have long venerated the caves and have placed a number of large Buddha images there. Further in, more steps flanked by a long *naga* lead down to a large reclining Buddha carved out of the limestone and a life-sized statue of one of the Buddha's disciples.

FANG

Founded by King Mengrai ● *20* in 1268 and once a prosperous, independent city, Fang was destroyed by the Burmese at the beginning of the 19th century and deserted until 1880. The present town is mainly of interest because of its proximity to Burma and the colorful tribal people who come to its market to sell their goods.

TO CHIANG RAI BY BOAT

Tha Thon is a small village on the bank of the Kok River, about 14 miles north of Fang. From a landing near Wat Tha Ton, long-tail boats leave at 12.30pm daily for a three-hour trip down the river to Chiang Rai, which offers exciting rapids and exceptionally beautiful natural scenery. A three-day trip can be made by bamboo raft. Booking for the trip should be made 10 days in advance.

PHI POB PEOPLE
Legend has it that the little town of Chiang Dao was once inhabited by people possessed by *phi pob*, spirits ● *27* who ate the entrails of their victims. Like lepers, such people were sent to live in remote communities far away from others.

FARMHOUSES
The Fang valley, is peppered with picturesque farming communities made up of simple native huts with thatched roofs, reflecting a timeless way of life in striking contrast to the bustling, modern ways of larger northern towns and cities.

HILL TRIBE TREKS
Treks into the northern mountains to enjoy the scenery and visit remote and exotic hill tribe villages became an important part of Chiang Mai's appeal in the 1980's, especially with adventurous travelers. That area eventually became "overtrekked," at least among more dedicated enthusiasts, so the focus shifted to Chiang Rai, then to Pai and Mae Son. Dozens of agencies opened in these places, offering everything from daytrips and two day excursions to treks lasting a week or more, with a wide range of prices and amenities available. Look for an agency that meets your particular requirements, keeping in mind a few basic considerations. The best time for trekking is the cool, dry season from November through the end of February; March through May can be hot and hazy, while during the rainy season the mountain trails are often muddy and slippery. Most of the villages provide a place to sleep, and food is generally part of the trek package, but bring along snacks to supplement the limited variety of food available there.

Though relatively little remains of its past, Chiang Rai has an ancient history, having been founded by King Mengrai in 1262 ● *20*, on a site protected by the Kok River and by three small hills. Its strategic location near the border made it an important trading center but also ensured that it would suffer during the frequent wars between Thailand and Burma; for a long period during the 19th century it was more or less abandoned, with only a few hundred families remaining within the old city walls. Prosperity returned slowly – as late as 1970, it had a population of only around 10,000 and has had a strong visible effect only in recent years.

CHIANG RAI TODAY. Modern Chiang Rai has little to offer in the way of physical beauty or exotic atmosphere, being for the most part a typical Thai provincial capital full of nondescript rows of cement shops and drab, dusty streets. Nevertheless, it has enjoyed a considerable boom over the past decade, thanks to its proximity to the fabled Golden Triangle and its convenience as a base for trekking expeditions into the nearby hills. New hotels, including a large one on an island in the Kok River, have risen almost everywhere, along with restaurants and shops catering to foreign tourists and numerous agencies that organize visits to tribal villages.

CHIANG RAI TEMPLES. Wat Phra Singh, on Singhakai Road, once enshrined the revered image known as Phra Buddha Si Hing, now at the temple of the same name in Chiang Mai; a replica is kept at the Chiang Rai temple. Wat Phra Keo, on Ruang Nakorn Road, contains an early bronze Chiang Saen image and a reconstructed chedi, where in 1436 the famous Emerald Buddha was discovered. Wat Ngam Muang has an ancient chedi with the remains of King Mengrai. Wat Doi Tong is on a hill that commands a fine view of the Kok River.

CITY WALLS. In the late 1980's, the municipality of Chiang Rai became aware that the city's claims to an ancient and glorious past are not supported by an adequate amount of archeological and architectural evidence, and tourist attractions are somewhat wanting in the town. It was then decided to build them and sponsors, historians and artists were called in to help to restore the glory of the city. The first objective was the city walls. The original walls were pulled down in 1920 on the advice of Dr Briggs, an American missionary physician who argued that they were not only useless but were also a permanent source of all kinds of illnesses because they obstructed the flow of fresh air. Initially, it had been hoped that a complete city gate and a good part of the walls could be rebuilt, but no evidence whatsoever was found to help with the reconstruction except an engraving showing an elephant passing through a gate against the rays of the rising sun. The elephant was quickly taken as a yardstick, and assuming that its height may have been at least 8 feet, a stretch of cement wall covered with bricks was quickly built. It measured 330 feet long and 16 feet high, with an opening in the middle (no evidence upon which to reconstruct the gate was found). This "antiquity" now stands proudly in front of a shopping center.

CITY PILLAR. The second achievement was the construction of a city pillar, which Chiang Rai never had. This was erected on a hilltop – Doi Chomthong – on the outskirts of the town where a telephone exchange was about to be built. Pittaya Boonag, a lecturer from the Faculty of Architecture at the University of Chiang Mai, was called in to design a city pillar according to Thai cosmology, and he ended up with a complex of 108 granite pillars surrounding "the navel of the Universe," a larger column of phallic shape 5.5 feet high. The design represents major features of the universe as illustrated in various Thai murals in Bangkok, and therefore completely alien to the Lanna culture of old Chiang Rai. The complex was inaugurated on January 31, 1989 (six days after the date on the commemorative inscription), but has gone unnoticed since.

A MODERN ARTIST'S TEMPLE
New temples are rarely built in Thailand and most of those conform to a standard template based on the Bangkok formula, sometimes regardless of regional character. One exception, Wat Rong Khun, is among the most beautiful and unusual in the country. Located just south of Chiang Rai, it is the brainchild of Chalermchai Kositphiphat, a local painter who became a nationally known figure. Most famous for his murals at the Thai temple in Wimbledon, London, Chalermchai designed the Wat Rong Khun viharn and its causeway in a style combining Lanna aesthetics and a personal flair that reminds some of Antonio Gaudi's Sagrada Familia cathedral in Barcelona. The florid tracery and fantastical depictions of mythical creatures are familiar from his modern Buddhist paintings, only sculpted in all-white stucco. Featuring more of his murals inside, the temple became a destination for pilgrims and art lovers even before its completion.

«WHEREVER YOU GO…MAY YOUR FEET NOT STUMBLE,
YOUR ARMS NOT FALTER; MAY YOUR WORDS PROVE TRUE, YOUR
HOPES BE FULFILLED…AND ALL YOU UNDERTAKE FLOURISH.»
TRIBAL BLESSING

The mountains of Thailand's far north, along the borders of Burma and Laos, are home to a number of tribal groups, each with its own distinctive culture and traditions. Only one tribe, the Karens, has lived in the region since ancient times; others began migrating in the 19th century into what was then rugged hills, left unpopulated by the Thais, who are lowland farmers. Some have come only in relatively recent years, driven by the wars in Indo-China and the unrest in northern Burma. The total tribal population is estimated at about half a million, divided into two general ethnic groups. The Hmongs and the Miens (known to Thais as the Yao) belong to the Sino-Tibetan group, while the Karens, Akhas, Lisus and Lahus are members of the Tibeto-Burmese group.

HILL TRIBE SETTLEMENTS

The tribes ● 17 do not possess definite territories but live interspersed in a number of settlements, each at a preferred altitude. Traditionally all the tribes are semi-nomadic. They will settle on the hills, clear the land by fire, and cultivate it for a few years until the soil is impoverished.
They will then move on to another hill site. Slash-and-burn cultivation has caused considerable damage and efforts are being made to resettle them at lower altitudes where the land can be irrigated. However, tribesmen find difficulty adapting to the heat in the valleys and to new developments in rural life.

OPIUM CULTIVATION

With the exception of the Karens, the hill tribes were mainly opium cultivators. The practice of opium cultivation was originally forced upon the Hmongs by the French government in Indo-China, which was secretly selling opium to the Marseilles

**THE FIRST
HILL TRIBES**
The Lahus were the first hill tribes to migrate to northern Thailand in the last quarter of the 19th century.
The Akhas were the last to arrive and their first village was erected in 1905. The largest migration took place in the 1960's and 1970's, and by 1983 the total population was 416,000.

gangsters to finance the war against the communists. When the Hmongs migrated, they spread opium cultivation and trade in the region. Subsequently the Americans through the CIA encouraged opium cultivation to win the support of the Hmongs in the secret war against the Pathet Laos. Only when public opinion became concerned about drugs did the Western powers try to stop opium cultivation, forcing Third World countries to ban what had become a major source of income and a powerful political tool. While the military elites of many Indo-Chinese countries are still actively involved in the opium trade and drugs keep reaching the West, the big losers are the hill tribes, who see their only source of income under constant threat. Once addicted to opium, most tribesmen now turn to heroin, and cases are reported of children below school age who are already addicted. An interesting scheme to eradicate opium cultivation has been initiated by the King of Thailand, who has sought to introduce new commercial crops to replace the opium poppy as well as to bring better medical treatment and social welfare to the tribal groups. Among the crops introduced successfully thus far are coffee, vegetables, strawberries, peaches, lychees and apples. As a result of such efforts, opium production has dropped drastically in the country, many hill tribe children are receiving a basic education in settled villages, and their elders are more often seen mingling with the majority Thais in lowland towns and cities.

Old postcards from the early 20th century depicting typical Akha attire (left) and Karen dress.

THE KARENS
Numbering about 250,000, the Karens are the largest hill tribe group. They are skilled farmers and have become sedentary, living on irrigated land. Karen women are noted for their skill in weaving cotton, commonly red or orange, which they embroider and decorate with seeds.

"Hill tribes" is not an ideal term for these diverse peoples of Thailand. Though they each possess a strong ethnic identity, their communities are dispersed throughout northern Thailand, with no unifying "tribal" organization. These groups do share some characteristics that justify the name of hill tribe, differentiating them from the other ethnic groups of northern Thailand. One of these characteristics is a rich material culture. The Mien or Yao peoples are among the most "Chinese" of the hill tribes, probably originating from southern China about 2,000 years ago. There are large numbers of Mien in China, Laos and Vietnam. They first migrated to Thailand from Laos in the mid-19th century. They use Chinese script, their social organization is patriarchal, and their religion shows a strong Chinese influence. They share with other groups great skill in textile-making, specializing in cross-stitch embroidery work.

APPLIQUÉ
The appliqué technique allows women to adorn their textiles with shapes which are more organic than motifs on embroidered cloths. Though still symmetrical, the shapes are made of complex lobes and tendrils. The appliqué example shown above is from a saddlecloth, white braiding highlighting the appliqué shapes.

SILVER
Silver is a crucial part of hill tribe costume. These ornaments, to be suspended from a silver neck ring, are also decorated with cloisonné enamel.

MIEN TEXTILES
Homespun cotton cloth, dyed a deep indigo is the basic material for most Mien textiles. Today that cloth is purchased from Thai weavers of the lowlands. The patterns were originally embroidered with naturally dyed homespun silk, the embroidery stitches running in parallel with the warp or weft. Today Mien embroiderers buy threads, in new colors, and prefer the cross-stitch, in which the embroidered thread runs diagonally across the warp and weft. The turban, waistcloth and pants of a traditional woman's outfit are embroidered; the tunic with its red fur collar is not as fully adorned.

ANCESTOR FIGURES
The Mien traditionally practice forms of ancestor worship that owe much to Chinese ritual. Ancestors' names are recorded in a special book, and recited when offerings are made. Ancestor figures such as this one symbolize the generalized presence of the ancestors, who are informed of births and weddings, and who provide protection to their descendants.

RELIGIOUS PAINTINGS
Mien religion draws its visual expression from archaic forms of Chinese folk religion. These paintings depict figures in a large hierarchical pantheon of gods and spirits.

«A TINY NEEDLE, STRANDS OF BRIGHT THREAD, AND THE GENIUS OF A HMONG WOMAN – THESE ARE THE INGREDIENTS OF SOME OF THE MOST EXQUISITE NEEDLEWORK TO BE FOUND ANYWHERE.»

PAUL AND ELAINE LEWIS

Hmong women are particularly skilled in the production of textiles. Their traditional version of the backstrap loom is unique, equipped with foot treadles for shifting the warp threads. They are the only group among the hill tribes to use the batik resist-dyeing technique, producing designs in blue and white monochrome. These designs are often enhanced with a layer of embroidery. To a modern eye, the Hmongs' mastery of geometric designs is especially pleasing. Special clothes are worn by young women at New Year, but the Hmongs traditionally reserve their full repertoire of textile expression for ornate funerary costumes, as in this woman's set.

FUNERARY ELEGANCE
Burial clothes are made by the wife for her husband and herself. Made from hemp cloth, apart from the pants or skirt, there are three or more upper richly embroidered garments.

COLLARS
These collar pieces (right), made by the women of the White Hmong subgroup, demonstrate a range of embroidery and appliqué techniques. Measuring around 5 by 6 inches, they hang from a flap down the back.

CHILDREN'S JACKETS
The Chinese-style asymmetrical front fastening is highlighted with fine embroidery in this child's jacket. The abstract embroidery motifs are particularly attractive and even the smallest clothes are richly adorned.

SPIRIT LOCKS
This silver ornament, one of many kinds favored by Hmong men and women, is said to represent a lock, binding the soul to the body. It hangs from a neck ring. The incised patterning seems to be derived from the embroidery patterns used in women's collars.

The Lahu, Akha and Lisu peoples are distinguishd from the other hill tribes by their languages, all in the Yi subgroup of the Tibeto-Burmese family. These hill tribes migrated to Thailand from the Shan states of Burma and from Yunnan, China in this century. Though all the peoples of the Golden Triangle use silver ornaments, arguably the most dramatic use of the precious metal is by these three Tibeto-Burmese speaking groups. Silver is plentiful in Yunnan and the upper Irrawaddy in Burma, and has been used in mainland Southeast Asia for centuries. But it became even more popular in the region thanks to the influence of the Europeans, who brought in relatively cheap New World silver to trade for Asian goods. Today, silver is still used for exchange and as a currency. Aluminum is now replacing silver for some uses.

NECK RINGS
Plain flat silver neck rings are particularly favored by Akha women. Often they serve as a kind of a base for the many silver ornaments that may be dangled from them, in front or at the back. They are often covered by the ornaments that hang from the headdress. The omega shape, with the scrolls at each end, is a popular form in much Southeast Asian jewelry, though this is a particularly vigorous expression of the basic form. These rings are flat, but others may be hollow, with a similar shape but rounded in profile. Neck rings like these are often copied in aluminium, to deter robbers.

PIPES
Apart from opium, the hill tribes also use the more respectable tobacco. The two pipes pictured here are solid silver, the bottom one exhibiting some cloisonné decoration as well. They could have been used by any of the three groups considered here, or indeed by the Miens or Hmongs as well.

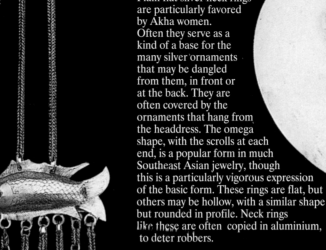

BANGLES
Many of these dramatic twisted wire bracelets are made by Chinese silversmiths. They are hollow and some feature engraved designs. They are worn predominantly by the Akha people.

AKHA HEADGEAR
Adorned with silver coins and hollow silver balls, beads and buttons, Akha headdresses show one of the most striking uses of silver by a hill tribe group. This piece (right), with a large trapezoidal silver plate at the back, is in the Loimi-Akha style, favored by recent migrants from Burma. It is worn by young girls on festive occasions.

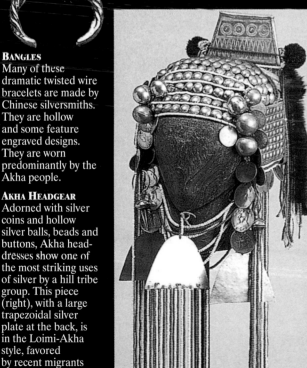

PENDANTS
The fish is a favorite motif in the pendants worn by many hill tribe groups. Such pendants, like the one shown above, can be worn around the neck in the front or hanging from a solid neck ring at the back, over a jacket. Elongated bell-shaped beads and a set of stylized grooming implements such as tweezer and ear cleaners, hangs below this fish.

CONTAINERS
Small silver containers like these are usually made by the Shan peoples who live mostly in Burma, and traded to the hill tribes. Used for betel nut paraphernalia and tobacco, they are collected as status objects, particularly by the Akhas.

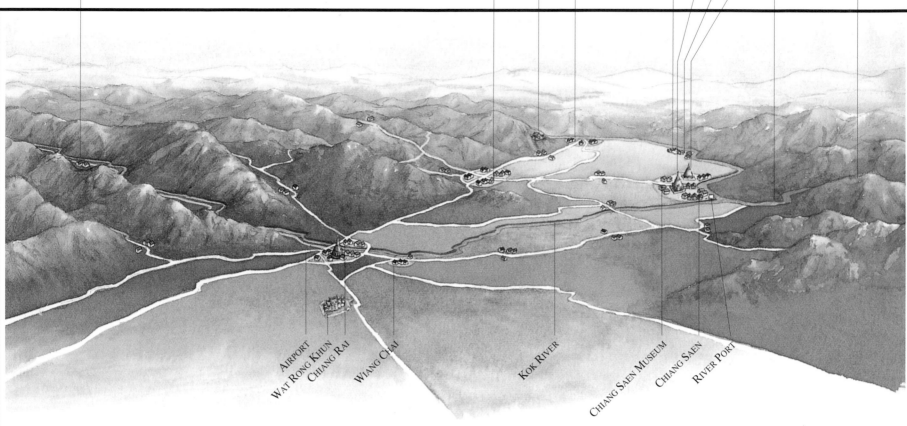

FANG

MAE CHAN · DOI TUNG · MAE SAI

OPIUM MUSEUM · WAT PA SAK · SOP RUAK · WAT PHRA THAT CHOM KITTI · MEKONG RIVER

CHIANG KHONG

AIRPORT · WAT RONG KHUN · CHIANG RAI · WIANG CHAI · KOK RIVER · CHIANG SAEN MUSEUM · CHIANG SAEN · RIVER PORT

⏱ Two days

Wat Phra That
Chom Kitti.

HISTORY

The origins of Chiang Saen ● *20* are obscure. However, most historians agree that a town of considerable influence probably existed earlier on the site before the city of Chiang Saen was founded in 1328 by Phra Chao Saen Pu, a grandson of King Mengrai ● *20*. Chiang Saen became associated with Chiang Mai and was ruled by Lanna kings until 1558, when it was invaded by the Burmese, who remained in control for more than two centuries. In 1804, forces loyal to King Rama I seized the city and burned it after which the city was abandoned. Chao Inta, an offspring of the Prince of Lamphun, brought back the descendants of its former population and rebuilt the town 70 years later.

CHIANG SAEN SIGHTS

Chiang Saen's former importance is underlined by the fact that the Fine Arts Department lists 66 ruined monuments within its once-fortified walls and 75 outside. Among these is Wat Pa Sak, the city's oldest chedi, built in 1295 and adorned with fine stucco decorations; the structure displays a number of influences, in particular that of the early

Haripunchai period. About half a mile away, atop a hill accessible by 350 ancient steps, is Wat Phra That Chom Kitti, which contains an 82-foot-high chedi (left) on a rectangular base. At Wat Chedi Luang, an octagonal chedi rises 190 feet, supposedly constructed in 1331 and rebuilt in 1515. Nearby is the Chiang Saen Museum, which displays several Chiang Saen bronze images as well as objects unearthed during excavations at Wat Chedi Luang. Along the road leading to the old town are several other ruined chedis, most notable among them being Wat Mung Muang and Wat Phra Buat.

THE GOLDEN TRIANGLE

The so-called Golden Triangle – a term coined by journalists and since then often used by novelists – is the area where Thailand's borders meet those of Burma and Laos. Its notoriety stemmed from the fact that over 50 percent of the world's opium supply was produced there. Converted into heroin by secret refineries, it eventually found its way to the streets of major Western cities, bringing "gold" to dealers who act as middlemen, but not

INLAND PORT

Chiang Saen is being transformed by an influx of ships from China. To ease their passage, many rapids in the Mekong have been blasted. With dams altering the water flow, this has serious consequences for fisherfolk, small boats, irrigation and biodiversity. Chiang Saen town has also changed through the physical presence of Chinese traders, products and traffic.

«THE MYSTERY OF OLD CHIANG SAEN STILL HAUNTED ME…LONG LINES OF WOMEN, PRIESTS, SOLDIERS AND PRINCES KEPT PASSING BEFORE ME, WHISPERING THEIR HISTORY FROM THE DEPTHS OF THE JUNGLES.» REGINALD LE MAY, 1926

THE LOST ARMY

When communists took over mainland China in 1949, the 93rd Army of the Kuomintang was cut off from the forces of Chiang Kai-shek, which were then retreating to Taiwan. The army settled on the Thai border, and sustained itself with opium cultivation and smuggling. They made Doi Mae Salong their stronghold for more than 20 years. Their presence was tolerated by the Thai government as it was felt that they were useful to keep communists at bay. The Kuomintang forces have since surrendered and the government accepted them as Thai citizens.

MAE SAI

Situated at the pinnacle of the Golden Triangle, the atmosphere in this frontier town is more Burmese than Thai.

AKHA VILLAGES

The Akha, while not major opium-poppy growers, still cultivate the crop on a small scale outside their villages.

to the tribal people who actually grow the poppies. Thailand's share of the market has dropped dramatically in recent years, thanks to a royal program to introduce new crops for the tribes; but sizeable quantities are still coming from beyond its borders. Although geographically inaccurate, a spot designated as the center of the triangle is located near Chiang Saen where the Kok River joins the Mekong, complete with a noticeboard and a picnic pavilion.

HALL OF OPIUM ★. Located a few minutes north of Sop Ruak, this museum explains the history and impact of the drug trade through reasoned expo-sition rather than preaching. Multimedia displays covering 60,000 square feet explore opium's former medicinal use, drug suppression efforts and the effects of heroin on the user. It also traces the origin of poppy growing in Thailand by hill tribes in recent decades. Most dramatically, a 150-yard tunnel simulates the coming down from a heroin high, illustrated by what has happened to famous addicts. It ends on a positive note in a Hall of Reflection.

ANANTARA MAHOUT SCHOOL. Located opposite the Hall of Opium, this opulent resort and spa includes an elephant camp on its grounds, where foreigners can learn the art of being a mahout. The course is run to standards of the Thai Elephant Conservation Centre in Lampang ▲ 144.

RIVER TRIP TO CHIANG KHONG

From Chiang Saen visitors can hire a boat down the Mekong River to the small town of Chiang Khong. The trip takes about two hours and offers some scenic views, particularly of the less developed Laotian side. With Thai-Laotian relations improving, Chiang Khong may once more become an important point for crossing the river.

MAE SAI

Thailand's northernmost town, Mae Sai is located on the Mae Sai River, which forms the border with Burma. Numerous shops on the Thai side of the border sell Burmese herbal medicines and everyday products, though most of the souvenirs originate in Chiang Mai. One exception is jade. Countless shops sell jade items created in local workshops, many of which can be seen in action. Except during occasional periods of military or political tension, the immigration checkpoint at the bridge is open to foreigners who wish to cross and spend the day in Takhilek town, though it is possible to continue on to Chiang Tung and the Chinese border. This new land route looks set to increase trade with China, and add a Chinese as well as Burmese character to Mae Sai's frontier feel.

DOI MAE SALONG ★. A popular excursion from Mae Sai, this mountain is inhabited by the Akhas and Miens. Most of the villages along the road set up bazaars, which attract tourists. At the end of the road is Santi Kiri, inhabited by the families of the former Kuomintang army. The village is now developing into a hill station with hotels and guest houses, but the town still looks very much like a typical Chinese settlement. Most of the products in the market are imported over the mountains from China. Many families here are Chinese Muslims from Yunnan.

DOI TUNG ★. The late Princess Mother lived the latter part of her life in this remote outpost, where she initiated civic projects such as crop-substitution schemes among opium-growing tribes. Her Mae Fah Luang Foundation runs several Royal Projects here, from crafts centers and a zoo to an arboretum right on the border. Most visitors tour her former home on Doi Tung, which means "Flag Mountain". She styled Doi Tung Royal Villa after both Lanna architecture and the chalets of Switzerland, where she spent much of her young life. The Mae Fah Luang Garden is probably Thailand's best ornamental park. Mae Fah Luang has also applied its wealth of local fabrics into an fashion brand of international acclaim.

OPIUM

Source of heroin, opium is prepared from the juice of *Papaver somniferum*, one of the more than 250 species of poppy, which requires very specific climatic and geographical conditions for commercial cultivation. The plant grows best at altitudes of 3,000 to 7,000 feet and prefers a relatively dry climate; crop production can vary 300 percent from year to year depending on the weather. When the petals fall, the seed pod is sliced to release the juice, which is milk-white at first but dries to a gummy brown substance that can be stored for years without losing its potency ▲ 152.

OPIUM EATER

"The vapors of opium fill up her empty head, Reclining her bust on the silky cushions; She follows in the ether the fanciful reverie, That phantasy unravels to her eyes."
Anonymous

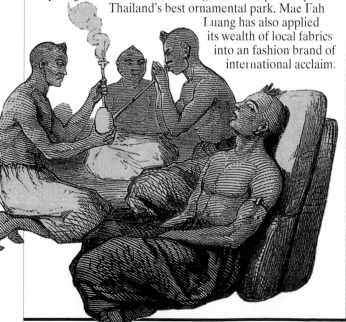

APPENDICES

BANGKOK

Where relevant, listings include the nearest Bangkok Mass Transit System (BTS) Skytrain station or Mass Rapid Transit Authority (MRTA) Subway station after the address.

PRACTICALITIES

AIRPORT
SUVARNABHUMI INTERNATIONAL AIRPORT
Tel 0 2132 1888
www.bangkokairportonline.com
All international flights and some connections to Phuket, Chiang Mai, Krabi and Had Yai.

DON MUANG INTERNATIONAL AIRPORT
Tel 0 2535 1111
Most domestic flights and some smaller international carriers are based out of here.

TOURIST INFORMATION
TOURISM AUTHORITY OF THAILAND (TAT)
1600 New Phetburi Rd, Makkasan
Phetburi Subway
Tel 0 2250 5500
info@tat.or.th
www.tat.or.th
Open Mon–Fri 8.30am–4.30pm
For national enquiries, try the tourism headquarters' building or TAT branches in Bangkok and major tourist regions of Thailand.

TAT BRANCH
4 Rajadamnoen Nok Ave
Tel 0 2283 1500 ext 1620
Open daily 8.30am–4.30pm

TAT BRANCH
Suvarnabhumi Airport
Tel 0 2132 1888/3888
Open daily 8am–10am

TAT CALL CENTER
Tel 1672
Open daily 8am–8pm

BANGKOK TOURIST BUREAU
17/1 Phra Arthit Rd, under Phra Pinklao Bridge
Tel 0 2225 7612–4
Fax 0 2225 7615/6
www.bangkoktourist.com
Open daily 9am–7pm
Has full information on Bangkok sights and tours, and organizes walking and cycling tours with qualified guides. Runs street booths at tourist centers around Bangkok.

TOURIST POLICE
TPI Tower Bldg, 23rd Fl, 26/56
Chan Rd
Tel 1155
tourist@police.go.th
www.touristpolice.net
Has booths and mobile units in tourist areas.

HOSPITALS
BNH HOSPITAL
9 Convent Rd
Sala Daeng BTS
Tel 0 2632 0560
Fax 0 2632 0577–9
www.bnhhospital.com

BUMRUNGRAD HOSPITAL
33 Sukhumvit Soi 3
Ploenchit/Nana BTS
Tel 0 2667 1000
Fax 0 2711 8000
www.bumrungrad.com

SAMITIVEJ HOSPITAL
133 Sukhumvit Soi 49
Tel 0 2392 0011–9
Fax 0 2391 1290
www.samitivej.co.th

POST OFFICE
CENTRAL POST OFFICE
Charoen Krung Rd
Open Mon–Fri 8am–8pm,
Sat–Sun 8am–1pm
All postal services, including Poste Restante. Each postal district has a post office.

CURRENCY
BANGKOK BANK (HEAD OFFICE)
333 Silom Rd
Sala Daeng BTS/Silom Subway
Tel 0 2231 4333
Fax 0 2231 4742
www.bangkokbank.com
The biggest commercial bank in Thailand. It has the largest network of branches and 24-hour ATMs in English, is part of the country's biggest ATM network, and is linked to thousands of banks worldwide.

SUPER RICH 1965
47/11-13 Ratchadamri Road
Tel 0 2655 2488
www.superrich1965.com
One of Thailand's best known money changers has nine outlets in Bangkok and always up-to-date exchange rates. See website.

CHURCHES
SANTA CRUZ CHURCH & CONVENT
112 Thetsaban Sai I Rd
Tel 0 2465 7930
Open daily 5pm–8pm

Services: Mon–Sat 6am and 7pm,
Sun 6am, 8.30am and 7pm

ST. FRANCIS XAVIER CHURCH
94 Samsen Soi 13
Tel 0 2243 0060–2
Services: Mon–Sat 6am and 7pm,
Sun 6.30am, 8.30am,
10am and 4pm
All Masses in Thai.

ACCOMMODATIONS

Rates quoted (in US dollars) are high season rack rates for a standard double room, though prices may be lower in the off-season. Restaurant prices are for dinner for two without alcohol, except where noted. All river hotels have their own ferries to Saphan Thaksin BTS and River City.

ANANTARA BANGKOK RIVERSIDE RESORT & SPA
257/1–3 Charoennakorn Rd
Saphan Taksin BTS
Tel 0 2476 0022
Fax 0 2476 1120
bangkokmarriott@minornet.com
www.marriotthotels.com/bkkth
Rates: Deluxe from $150
Presidential Suite $1800
Features: 407 rooms, swimming pool and spa in huge quiet garden, 10 riverside restaurants, adjacent shopping arcade.
This riverside resort in lush gardens is a serene hideaway and can be reached by hotel boat from the BTS. The spacious Thai-accented rooms have unobstructed views of the Chao Phraya river.

BANYAN TREE BANGKOK
21/100 South Sathorn Rd
Tel 0 2 679 1200
Fax 0 2 679 1199
www.banyantree.com
Rates: Premier $330–$1000
Presidential Suite $1,300
Features: Shopping companion service, ROM service (24 hrs IT support).
The tallest luxury hotel in the city, this all-suite address tops it all when it comes to wellness. Occupying six levels, the celebrated Banyan Tree spa is known for its pioneering signature treatments. On the 61st story is Vertigo (6,000 baht), the city's first rooftop al fresco restaurant, offering a 360˚ view of Bangkok – a must for dinner or cocktails at sunset.

CENTARA GRAND & BANGKOK CONVENTION CENTRE AT CENTRALWORLD
999/99 Rama I Road
Chidlom BTS
Tel 0 2100 1234
Fax 0 2100 1235
cgcw@chr.co.th
www.centarahotelsresorts.com
Located in the central business district and one of the largest hotels in Asia Pacific, this five-star accommodation features 505 luxurious rooms and suites. There are nine executive floors, including the World Executive Club, and nine restaurants and bars, including Fifty Five, an unforgettable outdoor rooftop venue.

CENTRE POINT
Located in nine downtown locations
Tel 0 2630 6345
Fax 0 2630 6354
reservations@centrepoint.com
www.centrepoint.com
Features: Leading provider of serviced apartments.
Offering hotel rooms and long-term accommodation, Centre Point has the highest quality apartments in outstanding locations throughout the city. All accommodations offer top amenities and are conveniently located to public transportation. For business travellers and tourists looking for the comforts of home, look no further than Centre Point. See website for locations and details.

CONRAD BANGKOK HOTEL
All Seasons Pl, 87 Witthayu Rd
Ploenchit BTS
Tel 0 2690 9999
Fax 0 2690 9980
info@conradbangkok.com
www.conradbangkok.com
Rates: 6,000–9,000 baht
Features: Secretarial services, ballroom, babysitting service, floodlit tennis courts, integrated with All Seasons Shopping Centre.
Well-priced chic hotel with Thai style interiors in the embassy district and close to corporate HQs. Diplomat Bar is a fashionable place to chill out to live jazz. Run a lap on the 240-yard long rooftop jogging track before taking it slow at the Seasons Spa.

THE DUSIT THANI
946 Rama IV Rd
Sala Daeng BTS/Silom Subway
Tel 0 2200 9000
Fax 0 2236 6400

booking@dusit.com
www.dusit.com
Rates: $200–$2,500
Features: Daily shuttles to Dusit Resort Hua-Hin and Dusit Resort Pattaya.
A long-time favourite given a modern renovation. Its beautiful Devarana Spa is built around the inner garden and has 14 lavish therapy suites. Its long-revered restaurants include Benjarong for sumptuous royal Thai cuisine (2,000 baht), while VIPs prize Hamilton's great steaks (3,000 baht). D'Sens is a stunning modern French restaurant (3,500 baht). This hip joint commands terrific city center views. The modish Mybar is off the lobby lounge.

FOUR SEASONS BANGKOK
155 Ratchadamri Rd
Ratchadamri BTS
Tel 0 2126 8866
Fax 0 2253 9195
reservations.bangkok@
fourseasons.com
www.fourseasons.com/bangkok
Rates: $250–$2,200
Features: Garden pool, children's amenities and babysitting service.
Formerly The Peninsula then Regent, this grand hotel near the business and shopping centers features some of the city's best restaurants. Cutting-edge Shintaro dishes out innovative Japanese cuisine (1,600 baht) while the Italian restaurant Biscotti is much loved by locals and is jam-packed every day (2,600 baht). Pond-side Aqua Bar is a trendy watering hole with surrounding boutiques.
The splendid Sunday brunch is one of the best in town. The hotel's lovely lobby is a habitual meeting place to do business or have tea. Book a Cabana suite for garden and poolside views. Very family-friendly.

GRAND HYATT ERAWAN
494 Ratchadamri Rd
Chidlom BTS
Tel 0 2254 1234
Fax 0 2253 6308
bangkok.grand@hyatt.com
www.bangkok.grand.hyatt.com
Rates: 11,600–17,200 baht, suites 19,400–72,000 baht
Features: i.sawan Residential Spa & Club, 25-metre pool, .
Beside the Erawan Shrine and main shopping and business districts. The lobby teems with shady plants and

serves charming afternoon tea. Party seekers should go to Spasso (2,000 baht), the Italian restaurant cum nightclub with live band, which is packed every night. Topnotch health club with a grass tennis court and rooftop pool. High-end shops at Erawan Shopping Center next door.

MANDARIN ORIENTAL BANGKOK
48 Oriental Ave
Tel 0 2659 9000
Fax 0 2238 0264
mobkk-reservations@mohg.com
www.mandarinoriental.com
Rates: $510–$2,550
Features: Thai cooking school, Thai Culture program, day care center for kids with babysitting, tennis coaches. Elite shops.
The grand dame of all Bangkok hotels. For more than 125 years, it has welcomed royally and dignitaries. Every room of this historic hotel is serviced by a private butler and has fantastic views of the Chao Phraya. Its Le Normandie restaurant has consistently been among the city's best and sees Michelin-starred guest chefs in its kitchen (8,000 baht). Bamboo Bar offers the best jazz experience. Don't miss the classes at the prestigious Thai Cooking School, afternoon tea at the Author's Lounge (900 baht) or treatments at the Oriental Spa, which is sheltered in a teakwood house on the other side of the river, reached by a teak hotel ferry. Beside the spa, khon dance performances entertain dancers at Sala Rim Nam Thai restaurant (4,000 baht set menu with khon show). Beside the main hotel, the Oriental's Chinese restaurant is in a revamped old wooden building, The China House (3,200 baht).

THE METROPOLITAN
27 South Sathorn Rd
Tel 0 2625 3333
Fax 0 2625 3300
res.met.bkk@comohotels.com
http://www.comohotels.com
Rates: $240 and up
Sleek hotel of minimalist design spawned from the original in London with rooms that come with their own yoga mat and prayer stool. Nahm, one of the best Thai restaurants in the country, features Thai delicacies from award-winning chef David Thompson (3,000 baht). The spa itself has several therapy rooms where guests can enjoy its distinctive list of treatments. There are also steam rooms, hydro pools and a yoga studio, plus spa foods at Glow restaurant. It is a fine urban retreat.

MILLENNIUM HILTON BANGKOK
123 Charoen Nakhon Rd
Tel 0 2442 2000
Fax 0 2442 2020
www.hilton.com
Rates: $230–$1,570
Features: Full business services, including office rental, notary and video conferencing. Sandy beach beside the pool.
A 32-storey landmark on the Chao Phraya opposite River City, this tower topped with a saucer-like venue houses the 543-room Hilton. Thai designs colour the contemporary Western décor by BARstudio and Tony Chi. Benefits include a spa surrounding a banyan tree, convention facilities and social outlets including Zeta Bar, Prime steakhouse (4,500 baht) and Flow café (2,000 baht), with its riverside deck.

NAI LERT PARK—A RAFFLES INTERNATIONAL HOTEL
2 Witthayu Rd
Tel 0 2253 0123
Fax 0 2253 6509
Bangkok-nailertpark
@swissotel.com
www.nailertpark.swissotel.com
Rates: $150–$1,500
Features: Tennis court, executive club, secretarial service.
Luxury Swissôtel on Wireless Road within the vicinity of embassies and offices. Its lush tropical garden bestows upon it a tranquility unlike any other in Bangkok. Ma Maison's French cuisine continues to impress (3,500 baht), while Genji imports most of its ingredients from Japan (4,000 baht).

THE OKURA PRESTIGE BANGKOK
Park Ventures Ecoplex
57 Wireless Road
Tel 0 2687 9000
Fax 0 2687 9001
reservations@okurabangkok.com
www.okurabangkok.com
Deluxe rooms from US$250
All rooms offer impressive views across the dynamic Bangkok skyline through triple-glazed tinted panoramic windows that insulate against both heat and noise. The rooms combine comfort and luxury with the very latest technological developments designed to impress business and leisure travellers. Among the dining outlets are Yamazato, a world-famous Japanese brand, gourmet restaurant Elements, and Up and Above Restaurant and Bar.

THE PENINSULA
333 Charoennakorn Rd,
Thonburi
Tel 0 2861 2888
Fax 0 2861 1112
pbk@peninsula.com
www.peninsula.com
Rates: $500–$3,000
Features: The Peninsula Academy for cultural insights, kids programs such as Junior chef, Diva for a day (girl only) and yoga for kids. Peninsula Spa run by ESPA in a colonial-style annex. Elite shops.
All the rooms of this 37-storey hotel have exceptional river views and are fitted with modern Asian interiors and one of the world's best contemporary Thai art collections. Mei Jiang has been one of the best addresses for Cantonese food, thanks in part to its resident Hong Kong chef (4,000 baht). Thiptara has superb Thai cuisine served in seven riverside teak pavilions from Ayutthaya (3,000 baht). Guests can arrive in style either by private boat or helicopter, with access to the penthouse heli-lounge. The pool cascades down several levels towards the river.

PLAZA ATHÉNÉE BANGKOK—A ROYAL MERIDIEN HOTEL
61 Wireless Rd
Ploenchit BTS
Tel 0 2650 8800
Fax 0 2650 8500
reservation.bangkok@lemeridien.com
www.plazaatheneebangkok.com
Rates: Deluxe Room $220,
Rattanakosin Suite $2,500
Features: Secretarial services, video conferencing, squash court, babysitting service.
Within a stone's throw of embassies and financial centers, this Royal Meridien hotel has very opulent suites. The Aspara relaxing therapy rooms are on the same spacious level as the pool deck. Glaz Bar's fine singers draw a lively crowd to the lobby lounge. The Thai restaurant Smooth Curry is renowned for its sumptuous food and décor (2,000 baht).

RENAISSANCE BANGKOK
518/8 Ploenchit Road
Ploenchit BTS
Tel 0 2125 5000
Fax 0 2125 5001
www.marriott.com
Guest rooms are expressive yet functional. Classically styled features include oversized windows and glass enclosed bathrooms. Located right in the heart of the city's premier shopping area, Renaissance hosts modern Chinese and Italian restaurants.

ROYAL ORCHID SHERATON
2 Captain Bush Lane,
Charoen Krung Rd
Tel 0 2266 0123
Fax 0 2236 8320
00172@sheraton.com
www.sheraton.com/bangkok
Rates: 5,400–63,000 baht
Features: Tennis courts, babysitting service.
A large riverside hotel with over 740 rooms. It stands right beside River City Shopping Center, the place for antiques and Thai curiosities. Only minutes away from Bangkok's main tourist attractions. Thai music and dance performances are held nightly at Thara Thong, its riverside Thai restaurant (2,000 baht).

SHANGRI-LA HOTEL
89 Soi Wat Suan Plu,
Charoen Krung Rd
Tel 0 2236 7777
Fax 0 2236 8579
slbk@Shangri-la.com
www.shangri-la.com
Rates: $200–$2500
Features: Shuttles to CBD, direct access to BTS, babysitting/child care, clinic.
Has nearly 800 rooms with great views of the Chao Phraya. Its two riverside swimming pools are shaded by palms and tropical plants, lending a resort-like appeal.

SHERATON GRANDE SUKHUMVIT
250 Sukhumvit Soi 12
Tel 0 2649 8888
Fax 0 2649 8000
Reservations.sgs
@luxurycollection.com
www.sheratongrandesukhumvit.com
Rates: 5,000–34,000 baht
Luxury Bangkok accommodation in the heart of the city with spacious, well-appointed and striking rooms, especially those facing Lake Ratchada. Two top-rate restaurants; Rossini's (2,000 baht) features fine, traditional Italian cuisine, and Basil (1,600 baht) serves daring, avant-garde Thai dishes. Advance booking is necessary for its immensely popular Sunday brunch, held at The Living Room (1,100 baht), which also stages world-class jazz and is full every night. Close to Queen Sirikit convention center and the shopping mall Terminal 21.

THE ST. REGIS BANGKOK
159 Ratchadamri Rd
Ratchadamri BTS
Tel 0 2207 7777
Fax 0 2207 7744
stregis.bangkok@stregis.com
www.starwoodhotels.com/stregis
Rates: US$300 and up
With an outstanding location and a reputation for luxury, this new five-star addition to the hotel scene is making its mark. Features 1,560 square-metre Elemis Spa and several sophisticated dining and bar outlets, including Japanese izakaya restaurant Zuma, Italian outlet JoJo and the New York City-inspired The St. Regis Bar.

THE SUKHOTHAI
13/3 Sathorn Tai Rd
Tel 0 2344 8888
Fax 0 2344 8889
info@sukhothai.com
www.sukhothai.com
Rates: 12,000–86,000 baht
Features: Satellite video link-up, squash and tennis court, 25m pool with swimming instructor.
Lotus ponds, pools with miniature chedis, and frangipani gardens surround this low-rise, high-class hotel designed with elegant restraint by Ed Tuttle of Amanpuri fame. Rooms are furnished in luxurious Thai silk and teak wood. Its attractive pool is a place to be seen, while the Sukhothai Spa is one of a kind. Thai island pavilions flanked by lily ponds make a meal at Celadon an unforgettable experience (2,500 baht). La Scala serves savoury Italian dishes amid sleek modernist décor (3,000 baht). Don't miss the weekend chocolate buffet at the Lobby Lounge (750 baht) or the gargantuan Sunday brunch in the Colonnade (1,850 baht).

DINING & NIGHTLIFE

Bangkok is a culinary paradise, with five-star quality dishes served by roadside vendors, markets galore, and excellent hotel restaurants that are popular with not only visitors but also residents. Most malls also have good dining options, not just fast food. The amount of choice in the city is breathtaking. The nightlife is similarly diverse. Sophisticated venues located in hotels include Club 87 Plus in the Conrad, MyBar in the Dusit Thani, BarSu in the Sheraton Grande, Vertigo/Moon Bar atop the Banyan Tree, and Zuk Bar in The Sukhothai, with top-notch jazz at the Bamboo Bar in The Oriental, The Living Room in the Sheraton Grande, and the Conrad's Diplomat Bar. Prices are for dinner for two without alcohol except where noted.

AOI
132/10–11 Silom Soi 6
Sala Daeng BTS/Silom Subway
Tel 0 2235 2321/2
Open daily noon–2.30pm, 6pm–10:30pm; www.aoi-bkk.com
Very good Japanese restaurant with comely interiors lined with paper and slate (1,600 baht). Additional branches at The Emporium and Siam Paragon malls.

BAAN KHANITHA
69 Sathorn Tai Rd
Tel 0 2675 4200
www.baan-khanita.com
Open daily 11am–11pm
This famous Thai brand attracts locals who flock to impress their guests with good Thai cuisine, fine service and free miang DIY-starter (2,200 baht).

LE BEAULIEU
Athénée Tower
63 Wireless Road
Tel 0 2168 8220
Open Tue–Sun 11.30am–3pm, 6:30pm–11pm
Consistently rated as one of the best fine dining restaurants, Le Beaulieu offers mouth-watering classic and rustic French dishes.

BED SUPPERCLUB
26 Sukhumvit Soi 11
Nana BTS
Tel 0 2651 3537
www.bedsupperclub.com
Open daily 7:30pm–2am
Chic, space-age pod on stilts where you dine on beds. Weekends see surprise set menus of fusion cuisine. The action later moves to the bar in the rear, where guest DJs and theme parties keep this unique space hip. Bring ID.

BISCOTTI
Four Seasons Bangkok
155 Ratchadamri Rd
Ratchadamri BTS
Tel 0 2254 9999
Located inside one of Bangkok's most popular hotels for food and drinks, Biscotti serves consistently outstanding Italian fare. The lunch-time salad bar and set meals are especially popular with local business people.

BLUE ELEPHANT COOKING SCHOOL & RESTAURANT
233 South Sathorn Rd
Surasak BTS
Tel 0 2673 9353–4
www.blueelephant.com
Open daily 11.30am–2.30pm, Sat 6.30pm–10:30pm
People come for the avant-garde Thai dishes as well as the distinctive ambience exuded by this stunning wooden building, which houses an elite cooking school (2,000 baht).

CRÊPES AND CO.
59/4 Langsuan Soi 1
Ploenchit BTS
Tel 0 2652 0208
www.crepesnco.com
Open daily 9am–11pm
Has delicious French crêpes and Mediterranean specialties such as couscous and feta cheese salad. Very busy during the legendary Sunday brunches (1,000 baht). There is a second branch in the Thonglor area.

LE DALAT
57 Soi Prasarnmitr, Sukhumvit Soi 23
Asoke BTS/Sukhumvit Subway
Tel 0 2664 0670
Open daily 11.30am–2.30pm, 5.30pm–10.30pm
Very charming Thai house adorned with lacquer paintings and Vietnamese antiques. The best address for Vietnamese food in Bangkok (2,000 baht).

EAT ME! ART RESTAURANT
2nd Fl, 1/6 Pipat Soi 2, Soi Convent, Silom Rd
Sala Daeng BTS/Silom Subway
Tel 0 2238 0931
www.eatmerestaurant.com
Open daily 3pm–1am
A magnet for the hip and arty, with constant exhibitions and impressively eclectic music. Dishes out experimental Pacific Rim cuisine (<2,000 baht).

FACE (HAZARA, LAN NA THAI, MISAKI, FACE BAR)
29 Sukhumvit Soi 38
Thonglor BTS
Tel 0 2713 6048–9
www.facebars.com
Open daily 11.30am–2.30pm, 6.30pm–11.30pm
Complex of newly-built teak houses decorated with Asian antiques and artifacts. Lan Na Thai serves local specialties while Hazara is known for fine Indian food. A vast gallery, raised terrace, ponds and twin massage pavilions make Face a true experience (2,700 baht).

GAGGAN
68/1 Soi Langsuan
Tel 0 2652 1700
Open daily 6pm–11pm
One of Bangkok's best restaurants, Gaggan serves contemporary Indian cuisine. Its tasting menu is a experience full of surprises and the a la carte menu is also outstanding. The restaurant is housed in a beautiful colonial-style house.

GIANNI'S RISTORANTE
34/1 Soi Tonson, Ploenchit Rd
Chidlom BTS
Tel 0 2252 1619
Open daily noon–2pm, 6pm–10.30pm
One of Bangkok's first fine dining Italian restaurants, with excellent food and service (2,400 baht).

GIUSTO
16 Sukhumvit Soi 23
Tel 0 2258 4321
www.giustobangkok.com
Open daily 11am–2.30pm, 6pm–10.30pm
Elegant modern Italian restaurant with subtly stylish décor and house specialties that taste just right (2,600 baht).

GREYHOUND CAFÉ
Floor 2, Emporium, Sukhumvit Rd at Soi 26
Tel 0 2632 4466
www.greyhoundcafe.co.th
Open daily 11am–10pm
Excellent café chain set up by a local fashion label whose minimalist interiors and innovative and affordable Euro-Thai fare continues to attract a fashionable young crowd. Its many branches include Emporium and Central Chidlom locations (<1,000 baht).

HARMONIQUE
22 Charoen Krung 34, Bangrak
Saphan Taksin BTS
Tel 0 2237 8175, 0 2630 6763
Open Mon–Sat 11am–10pm
Closed in Apr and Dec each year
Quaint century-old Chinese shophouse with courtyard tables frequented mostly by foreigners. The Chinese-Thai dishes are humbly priced and mildly spiced (1,000 baht). Book ahead.

KALPAPREUK
Pramuan Rd
Tel 0 2236 4335
Open daily 11am–10pm
This trendy home-grown restaurant with high-society origins is renowned for its split menu of Thai or Western fare, including a much-lauded bakery. Emporium branch has lovely views of Benjasiri Park (<800 baht). With branches at The Emporium, All Seasons Place and Siam Paragon.

KOI
26 Sukhumvit Soi 20
Tel 0 2258 1590
www.koirestaurantbkk.com
Open daily 6pm–midnight
In a sublime, tree-shaded compound, this Japanese restaurant (with a New York branch) serves modern but authentic Nipponese cuisine with visual panache. Red lights bathe the sleek, Zen-style structures, which include a separate bar (3,600 baht).

KUPPA
39 Sukhumvit Soi 16
Asoke BTS/Sukhumvit Subway
Tel 0 2259 1954
www.kuppa.co.th
Open Tue–Sun 10am–10pm
Though it feels more like a restaurant than a café, this yuppie hangout has created an all-day following for its tasty cakes, pleasurable atmosphere and excellent coffee. Good for families.

MAHANAGA
2 Sukhumvit Soi 29
Phrom Phong BTS
Tel 0 2662 3060
www.mahanaga.com
Open daily 11.30am–2.30pm, 5.30pm–11pm
Old teak house and pavilions styled in a dazzling Asian-Moroccan amalgam. Serves Thai fusion. Excellent choice for al fresco dining (1,600 baht).

Q BAR
34 Sukhumvit Soi 11
Nana BTS
Tel 0 2252 3274
www.qbarbangkok.com
Open daily 8pm–1am
Having started as a world-famous bar in Saigon, this posh New York-style club attracts top international DJs and has perhaps Bangkok's broadest range of drinks. Draws a crowd every night.

RANG MAHAL
26 Fl, Rembrandt Hotel, 19 Sukhumvit Soi 18
Asoke BTS/Sukhumvit Subway
Tel 0 2261 7100
www.rembrandtbkk.com
Open daily 11.30am–2.20pm, 6.30pm–10.10pm
Has the opulence of a Maharaja's palace, grand views of the capital and a superb Indian band. The rich North Indian cuisine is without rival. Topnotch service (1,400 baht).

SIROCCO, MEZZALUNA & DISTIL
The Dome, 63rd Fl, LeBua at State Tower, Silom Rd
Tel 0 2624 9555
www.lebua.com
6pm–1am daily; DJ 8pm–midnight daily at Distil
The city's highest open-air restaurant complex, known as The Dome, features the al fresco Sirocco, the Mediterranean restaurant Mezzaluna and the lounge bar Distil. Having been featured in the Hollywood film The Hangover Part 2, The Dome is drawing bigger crowds than ever. Can be windy at times.

SUPATRA RIVER HOUSE
266 Soi Wat Rakhang, Arun Amarin Rd
Tel 0 2411 0305
Open daily 11am–2pm, 5.30pm–11pm
Award-winning Thai restaurant with spectacular views of the Grand Palace from the terraces and pavilions. A museum explains that this was the home of the woman who founded the Chao Phraya River express boats. Its own retro boat shuttles to Maharaj Pier (<800 baht).

THOMPSON BAR & RESTAURANT
Jim Thompson's House, 6 Soi Kasemsan 2, Rama I Rd
National Stadium BTS
Tel 0 2612 3601
www.jimthompson.com/restaurant.asp
Open daily 9am–5pm and 7pm–11pm.
Smart international restaurant in the museum compound mixing Thai and Western dishes. Subtle

interior décor by Ou Baholyodhin echoes the original house, which the sheltered terrace faces across a lotus pond. Opening into the evening, the restaurant extends upstairs where there is also a bar and room for functions. Araya Hall upstairs holds cultural and social events.

UGOLINI

59 Soi Lang Suan, Ploenchit Rd
Chidlom BTS
Tel 0 2252 8108–10
Open daily 11.30am–2pm,
5:30pm–10.30am
This swank, easygoing restaurant turns out well-prepared Italian dishes including home-made pasta (2,500 baht).

ZANOTTI

1st Story, Sala Daeng Colonnade,
21/2 Soi Sala Daeng
Sala Daeng BTS/Silom Subway
Tel 0 2636 0002
www.zanotti-ristorante.com
Open daily 11.30am–2pm,
6pm–11pm
Classy Italian restaurant with Gilded Age interiors, a genial chef-patron and excellent selections from the grill. Don't pass on the desserts. Branches include Zanotti Vino across the soi and Limoncello Pizzeria on Sukhumvit Soi 11.

ZENSE

999/9 Rama I Road
17th Floor, ZEN, Central World
Chidlom BTS
Tel 0 2100 9898
Open daily 5:30pm–1am
With gorgeous panorama views of downtown and several options for indoor or outdoor dining (Japanese, Thai, Italian or Indian), this is a great destination for a date or special night out.

SHOPPING

ONE-STOP

ASIATIQUE THE RIVERFRONT

2194 Charoen Krung Road
Tel 0 2108 4488
Open daily 5pm–midnight
www.thaiasiatique.com
One of the biggest, outdoor lifestyle shopping complexes in Asia, this popular shopping and dining destination situated on the Chao Phraya River combines the ambience of Thai-style markets with upscale food and beverage in an outdoor plaza and promenade area.

CENTRAL CHIDLOM

1027 Ploenchit Rd, Pathumwan
Chidlom BTS
Tel 0 2793 7777
Open daily 10am–10pm
www.central.co.th
Thailand's leading department store with local and international outlets and one of the city's best supermarkets. Top story Food Loft boasts stylish but good value dining, as well as Asia Books, with its racks of international magazines and many Southeast Asian titles.

CENTRAL WORLD

4/1–2 Ratchadamri Rd
Chidlom BTS
Tel 0 2100 9999
Open daily 10am–10pm
Central has imaginatively expanded this landmark, which is anchored by two top department stores, Isetan and ZEN. It features huge cinemas, an event space and a glazed avenue leading to a central atrium beyond which a convention centre and hotel have recently opened.

CHATUCHAK WEEKEND MARKET

Phahonyothin Rd, corner of
Kamphaengphet Rd
Morchit BTS/Kamphaengphet
Subway
Tel 0 2272 4440–1
www.chatuchak.org
Open Sat–Sun 5am–6pm
Plants only daytime Wed 6am–6pm
Always sweltering hot and crowded, this vast market sells everything from pets and silverware to Thai furniture and antiques, all at extremely low prices. This is definitely a place to test your bargaining skills and to see some of the local colour. Areas along the Kamphaengphet Road side of the market showcase up-and-coming Thai designers.

THE EMPORIUM

622 Sukhumvit Soi 24, Klong Toei
Phrom Phong BTS
Tel 0 2269 1000
www.emporiumthailand.com
Open Mon–Fri 10.30am–10pm,
Sat–Sun 10am–10pm
Busy upscale department store sharing its name with a mall anchored by Paul Smith, Chanel and Hermès flagship stores. These plus other designer boutiques attract those with money to burn. Others come for the home-grown fashion labels, home furnishing, restaurants, food court and cinemas on the upper stories,

not to mention the monthly sales. Kinokuniya is one of Bangkok's most comprehensive bookshops.

ERAWAN BANGKOK

494 Rajdamri Rd
Chidlom BTS/Ratchadamri BTS
Tel 0 2250 7777
www.erawanbangkok.com
10am–9pm daily; Urban Kitchen floor 10am–11pm daily
Anchoring the corner of the Grand Hyatt Erawan behind the Erawan Shrine, this compact boutique mall specialises rather than generalises. Top end couture by Burberry and Club 21 set the designer tone, while a floor of high-tech health and beauty clinics looks after skin tone and wellness. Erawan Tea Room (which serves Thai) and a basement of excellent restaurants and dessert parlours enhance its handy meeting-point location.

GAYSORN PLAZA

999 Ploenchit Rd, corner of
Ratchadamri Rd
Chidlom BTS
Tel 0 2656 1149
www.gaysorn.com
Open daily 10am–8pm
This all-white temple of high fashion has one of Bangkok's most diverse lists of designer labels, with immense Louis Vuitton, Prada and Gucci boutiques forming the cornerstones. The third story has a range of shops selling the most refined Thai home décor. They include names like Artitude, Triphum, Ayodhya and Lamont Contemporary/Lamont Antiques.

OP PLACE

30/1 Charoen Krung Soi 38
(located behind the Mandarin Oriental Hotel)
Saphan Taksin BTS
Tel 0 2266 0186
Open daily 10:30am–6.30pm
Within a stone's throw of the Oriental Hotel, it attracts tourists who come in for high-end shops that sell quality Thai crafts, Asian fine art and outstanding antiques.

PENINSULA PLAZA

153 Ratchadamri Rd, Pathumwan
Ratchadamri BTS
Tel 0 2253 9791
Open daily 10am–8pm
A French-style shopping center frequented by an older affluent clientele, it is home to local and international designer boutiques like Dunhill, expensive tailors and airline offices. Noted for watch and

jewelry stores like high society favourite Frank's.

RIVER CITY

23 Trok Rongnamkhaeng, Yotha Rd
off Charoen Krung Rd
Saphan Taksin BTS
Tel 0 2237 0077–8
www.rivercity.co.th
Open daily 10am–9pm
Center for authentic Asian antiques as well as Thai handicrafts and collectibles. Hosts monthly auctions and regular fairs.

SIAM CENTER

989 Rama I Rd, Pathumwan
Siam BTS
Tel 0 2658 1000 ext 500
www.siamcenter.co.th
Open daily 10am–9pm
Remodeled on Japanese lines, Thailand's first mall remains an oasis for trendy youngsters who come in to cool off from Siam Square, have a quick cheap bite on the top food floor, or browse the shops, mostly selling mid-priced apparel. Local labels such as Jaspal, Chaps, Playhound, Aunurak, Soda and Theatre stand alongside international high street brands.

SIAM DISCOVERY CENTER

989 Rama I Rd, Pathumwan
Siam BTS
Tel 0 2658 1000/19
www.siamdiscovery.co.th
Open daily 10am–9pm
The younger, sleeker twin of Siam Center contains an array of shops targeting the young and the wealthy. Calvin Klein resides here and so too freestanding Shiseido and Shu Uemura beauty bars. Urban home furnishings can be found at Propaganda, anyroom, the Panta Shop, °2 Gilles Caffier, EGG and Habitat. Other pluses include the Mac Center, a large Asia Books and the deluxe EGV Cinemas.

SIAM PARAGON

Rama I Rd
Siam BTS
Tel 0 2610 9000
www.siamparagon.co.th
Open daily 10am–10pm
This top-of-the-line shopping and entertainment complex holds many flagship stores, from high street leaders like Zara to designers like Chloe or Zegna, plus Bangkok's biggest book shops, and Paragon department store. Among other attractions are gourmet dining outlets; a huge food hall; Royal Paragon Hall convention centre;

Siam Ocean World, Asia's largest aquarium; and the Siam Opera, 16 cinemas, an Imax 3-D theater and 52 bowling lanes.

TALAD ROT FAI

Kampaeng Phet Road, near
Chatuchak Weekend Market
Kampaeng Phet Subway, Exit 3 or
Morchit BTS
Open Sat–Sun 5pm–midnight
This new weekend market has taken the city's youth by storm. Specialising in vintage items, the outdoor market is expanding every week and is now packed with bargain-hunting crowds.

TERMINAL 21

2,88 Sukhumvit Soi 19
Tel 0 2108 0888
www.terminal21.com
Asok BTS/Sukhumvit Subway
Open daily 10am–10pm
This shopping mall recreates the ambience of different world cities on different levels, namely San Francisco, New York, London, Rome, Paris and Istanbul.

ZEN@CENTRAL WORLD

4, 4/5 Ratchadamri Rd
Chidlom BTS
Tel 0 2100 9999
www.zen.co.th
Open daily 10am–10pm
An amalgamation of all that is modern in today's multi-brand product retailing, ZEN prides itself on its uniqueness, individual style and merchandise that appeals to a wide range of shoppers. Set in a vast, theatrical space.

SHOPS

ART'S TAILORS

Four main branches, at Four Seasons Hotel Bangkok, Siam Paragon mall, Central Chidlom mall and The Emporium.
www.arttailorsbangkok.com
Established tailor where the rich and powerful have their suits made. Allot 2 weeks for orders.

ASIA BOOKS

Many branches throughout the city
Tel 0 2252 7277
www.asiabooks.com
Open daily 10am–7pm
Thailand's leading book chain, specializing in books on the country and Asia, magazines and paperbacks. Branches in several malls, including Central World, Siam Paragon and The Emporium.

JIM THOMPSON THAI SILK COMPANY

9 Surawong Rd, Bangrak
Sala Daeng BTS/Silom Subway
Tel 0 2632 8100
www.jimthompson.com
Open Mon–Fri 9am–9pm
This silk company's main store has racks of silk clothing, furnishings, pashminas and ties as well as the latest collection from Nagara, its couture label. Also sells furniture designed by Ou Baholyodhin and high end imported fabrics suitable for home décor.

KAI BOUTIQUE

Bangkok Cable Bldg,
Ratchadamri Rd
Ratchadamri BTS
Tel 0 2251 0728
Open Mon–Fri 9am–7.30pm
Prestigious women's outfits tailored for the customer by long-time Thai fashion master, Kai. Branch in Peninsula Plaza.

LOTUS ARTS DE VIVRE

www.lotusartsdevivre.com
With branches in the Four Seasons Hotel Bangkok and Mandarin Oriental Bangkok, this innovative design studio stocks fine jewelry and objets d'art with fantastic designs. It is renowned for employing gold, silver and precious stones with more exotic materials such as coconut shell, galuchat and buffalo horn.

MAE FAH LUANG FOUNDATION

1875 Rama IV Rd
Tel 0 2252 7114
www.doitung.org
Chic clothing and furnishings in hand-loomed fabrics from royally-initiated grassroots programs that provide an alternative source of income for villagers. Hotels such as the Metropolitan have purchased its ceramics, mulberry paper and hand-made carpets and textiles. Branch in Siam Discovery Center.

OTOP

Phahonyothin Rd, corner of Kamphaengphet Rd
Morchit BTS/Chatuchak Park Subway
Tel 0 2618 2620
(Head Office tel 0 2282 2922)
www.thaitambon.com
Open Sat–Sun 7am–6pm
The 'One Tambon, One Product' government project encourages each district to use local materials and manpower to produce a special commodity. Products include furnishings, gift items and textiles. Available in department stores and the OTOP shop in Chatuchak.

GALLERIES

100 TONSON GALLERY

100 Soi Tonson, Ploenchit Rd
Chidlom BTS
Tel 0 2684 1527
www.100tonsongallery.com
Open Thu–Sun 11am–7pm
Small art space that regularly exhibits works by high-caliber artists from abroad.

GALLERY 55

Unit 212, 2nd Fl, All Seasons Place Retail Center,
87/2 Witthayu Rd
Ploenchit BTS
Tel 0 2655 2588
Open Mon–Sat 10am–6pm
Renowned for the abstract paintings it carries and highlights works by Thai and regional artists.

H GALLERY

201 Sathorn Soi 12, Sathorn
Surasak BTS
Tel 08 1310 4428
www.hgallerybkk.com
Open daily except Tuesdays
10am–6pm
Charming wooden Thai house converted into an art space. Mostly features up-and-coming local names. Opening parties always on the social calendar.

NUMTHONG GALLERY AT AREE

72/3 Aree 5 (North),
Phahonyothin Soi 7
Tel 0 2617 2794
www.gallerynumthong.com
Open Mon–Sat 11am–6pm
Dealership for most of the leading mature Thai modern artists. The works are innovative and skillfully rendered.

TANG GALLERY

Unit B-28, Silom Galleria,
919/1 Silom Rd
Sala Daeng BTS/Silom Subway
Tel 0 2630 1114 ext 0
www.tangcontemporary.com
Open Mon–Sat 11am–7pm
The largest private gallery in Bangkok carries first-rate Chinese contemporary art.

THAVIBU GALLERY

Suite 308, 3rd Fl, Silom Galleria,
919/1 Silom Rd
Sala Daeng BTS/Silom Subway
Tel 0 2266 5454
www.thavibu.com
Open Mon–Sat 11am–7pm
Its name stands for Thailand, Vietnam and Burma (plus Laos) where most of its works are sourced. Archives of past and new exhibitions available online.

WTF GALLERY AND BAR

7 Sukhumvit Soi 51
Thonglor BTS
Tel 0 2662 6246
www.wtfbangkok.com
Open Tue–Sun 6pm–midnight
One of Bangkok alternative creative centres. The friendly downstairs bar is very popular with expats and the indie crowd, while the upstairs gallery hosts some of the most interesting exhibitions in town. Across the street, a space known as Opposite, under the same management, hosts poetry readings, pop-up dinners and other fun events.

WELLNESS

ABSOLUTE YOGA

www.absoluteyogabangkok.com
Probably the capital's leading yoga studio, with six locations, various teaching styles and tailored to different skill levels. Includes Hot yoga, Vinyasa, Astanga, Mysore and Yin traditions, as well as pilates.

CHIVA SOM INTERNATIONAL ACADEMY

11th Fl, Modern Town Bldg 87,
Sukhumvit Soi 63. Ekkamai BTS
Tel 0 2711 5270–3
info@chivasomacademy.com
www.chivasomacademy.com
Learn trade secrets from one of the world's best wellness resorts. The academy offers short courses on spa management, massages, Ayurveda, and holistic spa therapies.

DEVARANA SPA

Dusit Thani Hotel
946 Rama IV Road
www.devaranaspa.com
Open daily 9am–10pm
An oasis of tranquility at the centre of the city, this exceptional spa, whose name means "Garden of Heaven", will enchant you from start to end.

DIVANA SPA

7 Sukhumvit Soi 25
Asoke BTS/Sukhumvit Subway
Tel 0 2661 6784–5
www.divanaspa.com
Open 11am–11pm Mon–Fri;
10am–11pm Sat, Sun
One of the most prominent day spas, Divana offers a full range of treatments in a house setting with comfy rooms, wooden tub showers and a garden pavilion. An emphasis on modesty makes this suitable for first-time spa-goers. Divana produces a signature brand of spa products.

ATTRACTIONS

TOURS & RECREATION

ASIAN TRAILS

9th Fl, SG Tower,
161/1 Soi Mahadlek Luang 3,
Ratchadamri Rd
Ratchadamri BTS
Tel 0 2626 2000
www.asiantrails.com
The tour company not only has excellent tours within Thailand, but in destinations beyond, such as Bhutan and Indonesia.

BLUE ELEPHANT COOKING SCHOOL & RESTAURANT

233 South Sathorn Rd
Surasak BTS
Tel 0 2673 9353
www.blueelephant.com/bangkok
Its half-day courses are an excellent introduction to Thai cuisine. Students prepare four to five dishes on their own cooking stations. Morning classes include a trip to Bangrak market.

MANOHRA CRUISES

Anantara Riverside Resort & Spa,
257/1–3 Charoennakorn Soi 57
Tel 0 2476 0022
www.manohracruises.com
Take an overnight trip to Ayutthaya onboard a 100-year-old teak rice barge.

SIGHTS

Some landmarks that are normally closed to the public are open on Children's Day, which falls on the second Saturday in January. Such venues include the Ananta Samakhom Throne Hall, Parliament building, Government House, and the Defense Ministry. Other venues often have free admission.

AKSARA GRAND THEATRE

King Power Complex,
8 Rangnam Rd
Tel 0 2 677 8888 ext 5605
Fax 0 662 677 8877
Shows daily; times vary
Ticket prices vary by show
This intimate new theatre in Bangkok's duty free shopping centre has state-of-the-art facilities. A troupe of hun lakorn lek puppets (see Thai Puppet Theatre below) will be the permanent company (Mon–Thu), with diverse performances each weekend.

DECK @ BAIYOKE SKY HOTEL

77th Fl and 84 Fl,
222 Rajaprarop Rd
Tel 0 2656 3000
www.baiyokehotels.com
Open daily 10am–10pm
Admission: 300 baht before 6pm and 400 baht after 6pm
The highest point in the city provides an awesome panorama.

JOE LOUIS THEATRE

Located at Asiatique The Riverside
S193, 2194 Charoen Krung Road
Tel 0 2108 4488
www.joelouistheatre.com
This is the last remaining troupe of traditional Thai hun lakorn lek puppets, each of which is operated by three puppeteers. The troupe gives a fascinating behind-the-scenes show as well as a traditional drama performance. It makes for a rare and utterly charming experience. A branch of the troupe perform at Aksara Grand Theatre.

LAK MUANG (CITY PILLAR)

Sanam Luang
Open daily 6.30am–6pm
This monument marks the founding of Bangkok as the nation's capital.

NATIONAL GALLERY

5 Chao Fa Rd
Tel 0 2282 2639
Open Wed–Sun 9am–4pm
Admission: 30 baht
Thailand's most esteemed gallery of art houses exhibitions from abroad as well as those by important local artists.

NATIONAL LIBRARY

Tha Wasukri,
Samsen Rd
Tel 0 2281 5212
www.natlib.moe.go.th
Open daily 9am–7.30pm

OCTOBER 14TH MONUMENT

Rajadamnoen Ave
Tel 0 2622 1013–5
This monument is dedicated to

those who died in the name of Thai democracy on 14 October 1973.

PATPONG MARKET
Patpong Soi 1 and 2, Silom Rd
Sala Daeng BTS/ Silom Subway
Popular tourist-oriented night market backed by go-go bars.

PATRAVADI THEATER
69/1 Soi Wat Rakang,
Arun Amarin Rd
Tel 0 2412 7287/8
www.patraviditheatre.com
Set in a beautiful semi-open compound, the country's leading contemporary dance and drama company also showcases traditional Thai and foreign acts. Caters to English speakers. Riverside restaurants attached.

PHYA THAI PALACE
Phra Mongkut Army Hospital,
Rajawithi Rd
Tel 0 2245 7732
Open Sat 9am–4pm
Rama V-era palace contains strong collection of Thai antiques and artefacts.

QUEEN'S GALLERY
Phra Sumen Rd, Phan Fah Bridge,
Ratchadamnoen Ave
Tel 0 2281 5360/1
Open Thu–Tue 10am–7pm
This unique pentagonal building of Bangkok Bank has important exhibitions of contemporary art as well as collections from the royal family and Bangkok Bank's annual art competition.

ROYAL BANGKOK SPORTS CLUB (RBSC)
1 Henri Dunant Rd
Siam BTS
Tel 0 2652 5000
Horse Races every week
www.rbsc.org
Sun 12pm–6pm
Downtown horse-racing course in an otherwise private club. Check website for race schedule. A fun way to spend a weekend afternoon.

SIAM NIRAMIT (BANGKOK)
19 Tiamruammit Road
Tel 0 2649 9222
www.siamniramit.com
Shows at 8pm
Lavish stage production is a tribute to Thai cultural heritage featuring over 100 performers and special effects. A popular spectacle.

SIAM OCEAN WORLD
Ground floor, Siam Paragon

Rajawithi Rd
Tel 0 2254 7732
www.siamoceanworld.co.th
Open daily 9am–10pm
Bangkok's best aquarium.

SNAKE FARM
Queen Saovabha Memorial Institute, 1871 Rama IV Rd
Sala Daeng BTS/Silom Subway
Tel 0 2252 0161–4
www.saovabha.com
Open Mon–Fri 8.30am–4.30pm,
Sat–Sun 8.30am–12pm
Shows Mon–Fri 10.30am and 2.30pm, Sat–Sun 10.30am
Shows feature snake handling and milking of venom to make anti-venom.

TALING CHAN FLOATING MARKET
Office of Taling Chan District, 324 Chakphra Rd
Tel 0 2424 5448
Open Sat–Sun 9am–5pm
Touristed confluence of boats and canalside vendors.

THAILAND CREATIVE & DESIGN CENTER (TCDC)
6th Floor, Emporium Shopping Complex, 622 Sukhumvit Rd at Soi 24
Phrom Phong BTS
Tel 0 2664 8448
www.tcdc.or.th
Open Tue–Sun 10.30am–9pm
International exhibitions with a focus on creativity open every couple of months at this impressive centre with a mission to raise design awareness and quality. Not only does it show Thais the best in global products, it also presents Thai creativity abroad. Equipped with a permanent collection, an auditorium, online archives and a vast 15,000-volume library, this is also only the fourth place in the world (after New York, Milan and Berlin) to have Material ConneXion, a trailblazing tactile library of the latest design resources.

THAILAND CULTURAL CENTER
Thiem Ruam-mitr Rd,
Rajadaphisek Rd
Thailand Cultural Center Subway
Tel 0 2247 0028 ext 4103–4
This is a major venue for local and touring productions of international standard.

MUSEUMS
JIM THOMPSON'S HOUSE MUSEUM
6 Soi Kasemsan 2,

Rama I Rd
National Stadium BTS
Tel 0 2216 7368
www.jimthompsonhouse.com
Open daily 9am–5pm
Admission: 100 baht, under-25s 50 baht, under-10s 10 baht

M.R. KUKRIT PRAMOJ'S HERITAGE HOME
19 Soi Phra Phinij,
Sathorn Tai Rd
Tel 0 2286 8185
Open Sat–Sun 10am–5pm
Admission: 50 baht, students 20 baht

PRASART MUSEUM
9 Krung Thep Kreetha Soi 4A,
Krung Thep Kreetha Rd
Tel 0 2379 3601
Open by appointment
Tue–Sun 9am–3pm
Admission: 1,000 baht
(500 baht for two or more persons)

QUEEN SIRIKIT MUSEUM OF TEXTILES
Ratsadakorn-bhibhatana Building
The Grand Palace
Tel 0 2225 9405
Open daily 9am–4:30pm
This new museum displays the most outstanding examples of Thai textiles, from silk to other local handicrafts.

SIAM SOCIETY & BAAN KAMTHIENG
131 Sukhumvit Soi 21
Asoke BTS/Sukhumvit Subway
Tel 0 2661 6470–7
www.siam-society.org
Open Tue–Sat 9am–5pm
Admission: 100 baht
The library is open to members only, lectures are open to all, as is the Baan Kamthieng Northern anthropological museum.

SIRIRAJ HOSPITAL MUSEUMS
Phrannok Rd
Tel 0 2419 7000 ext 6363
Open Mon–Fri 8.30am–4.30pm

TEMPLES & SHRINES
ERAWAN SHRINE
494 Ratchadamri Rd
Chidlom BTS/
Ratchadamri BTS
Tel 0 2252 8754
Open daily 6am–10.30pm

MAHA UMA DEVI (WAT KHAEK)
2 Pan Rd
Surasak BTS
Tel 0 2238 4007
Open daily 6am–8pm

TUB TIM SHRINE
Soi Nai Lert, at service entrance of Nai Lert Hotel, off Ploenchit Rd
Chidlom BTS

WAT ARUN
34 Arun Amarin Rd
Tel 0 2891 1149
www.watarun.org
Open daily 8am–6pm
Admission: 20 baht

WAT BENCHAMABOPIT (MARBLE TEMPLE)
69 Rama V Rd
Tel 0 2282 7413
Open daily 8am–5.30pm
Admission: 20 baht

WAT INDRAWIHAAN (WAT IN)
144 Visut Kasat Rd
Tel 0 2281 1406
Open daily 7am–midnight

WAT KALAYANIMIT
371 Soi Wat Kalayanimit,
Thetsaban I Rd
Tel 0 2466 4665
Open daily 8am–5pm

WAT LENG NOI YEE (WAT MANGKON KAMALAWAT)
Charoen Krung Rd, between Mangkorn Rd and Soi Itsaranuphap
Tel 0 2222 3975
Open daily 6am–5.30pm

WAT PATHUM WANARAM
969 Rama I Rd
Siam BTS
Tel 0 2254 2545
Open daily 8.30am–6pm

WAT PO
2 Sanamchai Rd
Tel 0 2226 0335
Open daily 8.30am–6pm
Admission: 50 baht

WAT RAJA BURANA
119 Chakkaphet Rd
Tel 0 2221 9544
Open daily 8.30am–4.30pm

WAT RAJATHIWAT
3 Samsen Soi 9
Tel 0 2243 2125.
Open Sat, Sun 8am–11am,
1pm–4pm
www.watraja.org

WAT SUWANNARAM
33 Charan Sanitwong Soi 32
Tel 0 2433 8045
Open daily 8am–4.30pm

WAT TRAIMIT
661 Charoen Krung Rd

Tel 0 2225 9775
Open daily 9am–5pm
Admission to Golden Buddha:
20 baht

WAT YANNAWA
1648 Charoen Krung Rd
Saphan Taksin BTS
Tel 0 2672 3216
www.watyan.com
Temple open daily 5am–9pm
Ubosot open daily 8am–9am,
5pm–6pm

PALACES
CHITRALADA PALACE (ROYAL PROJECTS)
Rajawithi Rd
Tel 0 2283 9145
Booking 0 2282 8200
Open by special permission
Mon–Fri 8.30am–4pm

DUSIT PARK (VIMARN MEK PALACE)
16 Rajawithi Rd
Tel 0 2628 6300–9
www.vimarnmek.com
Open daily 9.30am–4pm
Admission: 100 baht (free with Grand Palace ticket)

SUAN PAKKARD PALACE & MARSI GALLERY
352 Sri Ayutthaya Rd
Phayathai BTS
Tel 0 2245 4934
www.suanpakkad.com
Open daily 9am–4pm
Admission: 100 baht, students 20 baht
Adjoining the museum, Marsi Gallery exhibits contemporary Thai art.

PARKS
BENJAKITTI PARK
New Ratchadaphisek Rd
Queen Sirikit Centre Subway
Tel 0 2229 3000
Open 5am–8pm
To commemorate HM the Queen's 72nd birthday, the section around Lake Ratchada was completed in 2004. The park provides undulating jogging and cycling tracks for exercisers.

BENJASIRI PARK
Sukhumvit, between Soi 22 and 24
Phrom Phong BTS
Tel 0 2262 0810
Open daily 5am–9pm

CHATUCHAK PARK & RAIL HALL OF FAME
Phahonyothin Rd
Morchit BTS/

Chatuchak Park Subway
Tel 0 2272 4575
Open daily 4.30am–9pm
Hall of Fame open Sat–Sun
7am–3pm

CHUVIT GARDEN
188 Sukhumvit Soi 10
Nana BTS
Open daily 6am–7pm
One of the most congested tourist areas of an under-greened city now relishes an expanse of lawns and flame trees the size of a London garden square.

LUMPINI PARK
192 Rama IV Rd
Lumpini Subway
Tel 0 2252 7006
Open daily 4.30am–9pm

SANTICHAIPRAKARN PARK
Phra Arthit Rd, Banglamphu
Open daily 5am–10pm

SOMDET PHRA SRINAGARINDA BOROMARAJAJONANI MEMORIAL PARK (PRINCESS MOTHER PARK)
Somdet Chao Phraya Soi 3,
Thonburi
Tel 0 2437 7799
Open daily 9am–4pm

CHIANG MAI

PRACTICALITIES

AIRPORT
CHIANG MAI AIRPORT
Tel 0 53 203 300–19

TOURIST INFORMATION
TAT CHIANG MAI
105/1 Chiang Mai-Lamphun Rd,
Amphoe Muang
Tel 0 53 248 604, 0 53 248 607
Fax 0 53 248 605
tatchmai@tat.or.th

CHIANG MAI TOURIST POLICE
606 Rimping Plaza, Charaonrat Rd
Tel 0 53 247 318, 0 53 249 806
(Emergencies 1155)
www.chiangmaitouristpolice.org

HOSPITAL
CHIANG MAI RAM HOSPITAL
8 Boonruangrit Rd
Tel 0 53 224 851–61
www.chiangmairam.com

POST OFFICE
POST OFFICE
Charoen Muang Rd
Tel 0 53 241 070

ACCOMMODATIONS

Rates quoted are high season rack rates for a standard double room, though prices may be lower in the off-season. Restaurant prices are for dinner for two without alcohol, except where noted.

THE CHEDI
123 Charoen Prathet Road
Tel 0 5325 3333
Fax 0 5325 3352
www.ghmhotels.com
Rates 11,440–17,200 baht
Features: Yoga/Aerobics room. Overlooking the river, this exemplar of discrete contemporary Asian architecture re-opened in March 2006 after the floods of 2005. Laden with teak, the 32 suites and 52 rooms, all with courtyard, daybed and top-notch equipment, provide privacy. A gym, spa, reflecting pond and riverbank pool surround the Thai-Indian-international restaurant in the century-old ex-British consular building.

D2 HOTEL CHIANG MAI
100 Chang Klan Rd
Tel 0 5399 9999
Fax 0 5399 9900
www.dusit.com
Rates: US$154–$513
Features: Outdoor pool, corporate lounge.
The first in Dusit Hotels' new boutique chain is beside the Night Bazaar and targets design-conscious urbanites. The brand's bold splash of orange pervades the minimalist reconditioned building, from the contemporary Thai furniture and the glowing lift to the Mix Bar lobby bar and Moxie restaurant, which serves impressive international cuisine at reasonable prices. Cheerful, practical rooms have glazed bathrooms, flat-screen TVs with DVD, windows that can be opened, and good desk amenities. Staff (which D2 calls 'agents') sport uniforms by Greyhound and change shift with a groovy dance at 2pm in the lobby. Includes the Dusit's serene Deverana spa concept.

FOUR SEASONS CHIANG MAI
Mae Rim-Samoeng Old Rd,
Mae Rim
Tel 0 53 298 181
Fax 0 53 298 190
reservations.chiangmai@fourseasons.com
www.fourseasons.com
Rates: $475–$2,100
Features: Tennis courts, children's program.
Often topping international polls of resorts, this spectacular enclave has 64 spacious northern Thai-style pavilions and 16 residences with private verandahs overlooking rice terraces and the Doi Suthep mountain range. The floors are teak, the interior decorated with Thai fabrics. The residences come with their own house-keeper. Also facing the rice paddies are Sala Mae Rim restaurant (2,000 baht), which offers northern Thai cuisine and Terraces (4,000 baht), with an international menu. The Four Seasons Chiang Mai Spa, consistently voted among the best in the world, has roomy private treatment suites. The cooking school offers a comprehensive program on Thai cuisine.

MANDARIN ORIENTAL DHARA DHEVI
51/4 Moo 1, Chiang Mai-San Kamphaeng Rd,
Tambon Tasala
Tel 0 53 888 888
Fax 0 53 888 999
www.mandarinoriental.com
Rates: $500–$2,900
Features: Golf at Chiang Mai Green Valley Country Club.
Spread over 52 majestic acres, the Oriental's first branch outside Bangkok has 142 Lanna-style villas and suites, furnished with Asian antiques and opulent Thai furniture. Some rooms feature plunge pools and private pavilions. Terraces have views of rice terraces, verdant gardens and northern architecture. The 33,000-square foot spa is a cluster of gilded buildings inspired by a Mandalay palace. Housed in a group of northern Thai-style buildings is the resplendent Le Grand Lanna (2,000 baht), a restaurant serving regional specialties.

RACHAMANKHA HOTEL
6 Rachamankha 9,
Tambon Phra Singh
Tel 0 53 904 111
Fax 0 53 904 114
info@rachamankha.com
www.rachamankha.com
Rates: $170–$200
Features: Outdoor pool.
Relaxing, small designer hotel in the old town which draws inspiration from history and tradition. Focused on a building inspired by one of Thailand's most beautiful temple chapels, the hotel has rooms decorated with Lanna and Chinese antiques and collectibles. The leafy perimeter is filled with palms, frangipani and bougainvillea.

TAMARIND VILLAGE
50/1 Rajadamnoen Rd
Tel 0 53 418 896–9
Fax 0 53 418 900
sales@tamarindvillage.com
www.tamarindvillage.com
Rates: 6,000–14,000 baht
Features: Lanna style restaurant.
The city's first boutique hotel. The 42 guest rooms and 3 suites have simple bathrooms and wooden terraces that overlook verdant courtyards, as if in a traditional village. Located inside the moat, it is very central; important temples are within walking distance.

DINING

Probably the most spectacular dining experience in town is at Le Grand Lanna, which came to prominence before the rest of the Mandarin Oriental Dhara Devi Hotel complex opened. Prices are for dinner for two without alcohol, except where noted.

BAAN SUAN
25 Moo 3, Sanphisua
Tel 0 53 854 169
Open daily 6pm–10pm
Lanna teak villas, decorated with northern artefacts, arranged in a garden along a river bend. Serves northern and traditional Thai food (<1,000 baht).

LE COQ D'OR
11 Soi 2 Koh Klang Rd
Tel 0 53 282 024
Open daily 12pm–2pm, 6pm–10pm
Serving first-rate French cuisine in an old teak house, this has for years been Chiang Mai's classiest restaurant (3,800 baht).

THE GALLERY
25–29 Charoenrat Rd
Tel 0 53 248 601/2
www.thegallery-restaurant.com
Open daily 12pm–12am
Specializing in northern Thai cuisine, the riverside garden restaurant is housed in a beautiful century-old teak building (1000 baht). The Gallery shop displays Lanna art.

HEUAN PHEN
112 Rachamankha Rd
Tel 053 277 103
Open daily 5pm–11pm
For long a leading specialist in northern dishes. The area towards the rear that is reserved for evening meals is most charming, being filled with antiques and bric-a-brac of bygone times (<800 baht).

THE HOUSE
199 Moonmuang Rd
Tel 0 53 419 011
www.thehousethailand.com
Open daily 11pm–2.30pm, 6pm–10.30pm
Restaurant and wine bar in a renovated colonial-style home serving delicious fusion cuisine, including tapas, Indian and Middle Eastern flavors. Dinner for two: 1,500 baht. Contains Ginger Shop (see below).

SHOPPING

MALLS
DHARA DHEVI SHOPPING VILLAGE (KAD DHARA)
Mandarin Oriental Dhara Dhevi,
51/4 Moo 1, Chiang Mai-San Kamphaeng Rd,
Tambon Tasala
Tel 0 53 888 888
Fax 0 53 888 999
Open daily 10am–9pm
The resort's traditional market "village" holds various boutiques selling local handicrafts.

KAD SUAN KAEW
Huay Kaeo Rd
Open daily 10am–9pm
Chiang Mai's first mall stands near the northwest corner of the moat. It offers the usual chain stores, a branch of Central Department Store, some craft shops, a theater of international standard, as well as cinemas.

NIGHT BAZAAR
Chang Klan Rd
Open daily from late afternoon to 11pm
The first stop for local handicrafts. Stalls carry a wide range, from jewelry and textiles to home furnishings and antiques. Shops of note include Under the Bo, specializing in artifacts sourced from Tibet to New Guinea, Chilli, and In the Oriental Spirit, respected providers of quality antiques.

SHOPS

Nimmanhaemin Road in and around Soi 1 and the Nimman Promenade at Soi 4 brim with boutiques selling upmarket interior décor items, artifacts and clothing of export quality. Catering often to large groups and wholesale buyers, huge craft workshops with showrooms line San Kamphaeng Road and the woodcarving village of Ban Tawai, on Chiang Mai's eastern and southwestern outskirts respectively.

AKA GALLERY & CAFÉ
35/1 Rattanakosin Rd
Tel 0 53 260 514
www.aka-aka.com
This glass-walled shop in quiet woodland has mock-up rooms of contemporary home furnishings by AKA, EGG and Earth+Fire intermingled with art exhibitions and tables for taking "high-tea".

ARNUT ASIA
35 Soi 12 Chotana Rd
Tel 0 53 409 134
info@arnutasia.com
www.arnutasia.com
Khun Arnut's extensive Indochinese collection includes collectibles and hard-to-find antiques like puppets, religious ornaments and Buddha heads.

BAN PHOR LIANG MUENS
36 Phra Pokklao Soi 2
Tel 0 53 278 187
Open daily 8am–5pm
Sells terra cotta murals, ceramic sculptures and stone statues.

GERARD COLLECTION
6/23–24 Nimmanhaemin Rd
Tel 0 53 220 604
info@gerardcollection.com
www.gerardcollection.com
Top of-the-line bamboo furniture fashioned in Thai and Asian styles. Inventory includes sofas, beds and home furnishings.

GINGER SHOP
THE HOUSE RESTAURANT
199 Moonmuang Road
Tel 0 5341 9014
Open daily 10am–10.30pm
contact@gingerfashion.com
An eclectic trove of whimsical, maximalist décor objects, clothing, jewelry and inspired one-off objects. Branches at 6/21 Nimmanhaemin Road (Tel 53 215 635).

GONG DEE GALLERY
30 Nimmanhaemin Soi 1
Tel 0 53 225 032
www.gongdeegallery.com
Open daily 8am–8pm

This gallery/café offers distinctive home and gift items, all in the signature Gong Dee style.

LOST HEAVENS
234 Tha Phae Rd
Tel 0 53 215 551–7
Open Mon–Sat 9.30am–6pm
Owner sources one-of-a-kind tribal pieces from the Yao and other minorities living in far-flung villages in Southeast Asia and Southern China.

MENGRAI KILNS
79/2 Arak Rd, Phra Singh
Tel 0 53 272 063
www.mengraikilns.com
Open daily 8am–5pm
Named after Chiang Mai's founder, it produces limited edition Lanna celadon and stoneware, which come in a variety of glazes.

NOVA COLLECTION
179 Tha Phae Rd
Tel 0 53 273 058
www.nova-collection.com
Open Mon–Sat 9am–8.30pm, Sun 11am–4.30pm
This shop and jewelry school has a selection of rings with very modern designs.

ORIENTAL STYLE & VILA CINI
36 Charoenrat Rd
Tel 0 53 243 156
enquiries@orientalstyle.co.th
Open daily 8.30am–10.30pm
This shop in a heritage building sells a variety of modern furniture and home items. The adjacent Vila Cini (tel 0 53 246 246) specializes in high-quality silk and cotton furnishings.

PAOTHONG'S PRIVATE COLLECTION
4 Nimmanhaemin Soi 1
Tel 0 5321 7715
Open daily 9.30am–6.30pm
Paothong_shop@hotmail.com
Textile specialist Paothong Thongchua fills his three-story shop with his hand-woven, authentically-dyed silk and cotton fashions, antiques and beetle-wing appliqué.

SOP MOEI ARTS
150/10 Chareonrajd Rd, Watgate
Tel 0 53 306 123
sma@sopmoeiarts.com
www.sopmoeiarts.com
Sells basketry and wall hangings by Pwo Karen villagers, who employ traditional techniques and modern designs. The showroom is in an old riverside teak house.

STUDIO NAENNA
138/8 Soi Changkhian, Huay Kaeo Rd
Tel 0 53 226 042
www.studio-naenna.com
Open Mon–Sat 8.30am–5pm
The eco-friendly shop has naturally dyed garments and home accessories, all spun by in-house Karen tribe weavers. Branch opposite the Four Seasons Resort.

SURAWONG BOOK CENTER
54/1–5 Sridonchai Rd
Tel 0 53 281 052–5
The north's leading bookstore, with a small branch in Chiang Mai Airport.

WELLNESS

BAN SABAI SPA VILLAGE
216 Moo 9, San Pee Sua
Tel 0 53 306 123
Fax 0 53 854 775
www.bansabaivillage.com
The spa village has four Lanna style teakwood villas with stylishly decorated rooms. Also has an open treatment sala, pool, sauna and four rooms to rent.

BAN SABAI SPA VILLAGE (BRANCH)
17/7 Charoen Prathet Rd
Tel 0 53 285 204–6
Open daily 10am–10pm

DAAN SAEN DOI RESORT & SPA
199/135 Moo 3, Baan Nai Fun 2 Kan Klong, Chanprathan Rd, Mae Hia, Chiang Mai
Tel 0 53 839 260
Fax 0 53 839 263
www.baansaendoi.com
Rates: 6,500–7,500 baht
Features: Gym, tennis, meeting rooms, golf tours, medical checkup.
This destination wellness retreat near Doi Suthep-Pui National Park envelops guests in luxurious surroundings with tribal accents to the contemporary Thai décor. The first northern spa to do the hot-stone massage, it also offers a full range of East-West therapy and pampering by staff trained at Chiva Som Academy. A garden pool and Saenkham restaurant – serving northern and central Thai dishes – add to the appeal. Those staying can choose from 4 rooms and 7 suites with neo-Lanna fittings.

OASIS BAAN SAEN DOI SPA RESORT
Phra Pokklao Rd

Tel 0 53 920 199
cs@oasisluxury.net
www.oasisluxury.net
Boutique retreat with Lanna architecture, great views and wonderful hospitality.

ATTRACTIONS

TOURS & RECREATION

CHIANG MAI SKY ADVENTURE CLUB
Tel 0 53 255 500
flying@skyadventures.info
www.skyadventures.info
Open daily 8am–11pm, 4.30pm–6pm
Get a view of the Chiang Mai countryside from above during 15- or 30-minute rides aboard a microlight plane.

BALLOON ADVENTURE THAILAND
Floraville, 9 Moo 4, Km 9, Doi Saket Hwy
Tel 08 4611 4128
flyingmedia@gmail.com
www.balloonadventurethailand.com
Take a slow journey over Chiang Mai on a one-hour balloon trip that begins at sunrise. Champagne celebration on landing.

ORIGIN CULTURAL COURSES
Center for Promotion of Arts & Culture, Contemporary Art Museum compound, Suthep Rd
Tel 0 2259 4896 (Bangkok Office)
origin@truemail.co.th
www.alex-kerr.com
Explore northern culture through hands-on courses in English covering several arts like dance, floral offerings, wai khru ceremony, cooking and northern fabrics. Led by Lanna expert Vithi Phanichphant, courses lasting from a day up to a week are held in a museum of protected northern teak buildings.

ACTIVE THAILAND
54/5 Moo 2, Soi 14, Tambol Tasala
Tel 0 53 850 160
Open mid-Jun to end-Jan
Mon–Sat 8am–6pm
info@activethailand.com
www.activethailand.com
Pioneer whitewater rafting organiser on the Pai river. Safety equipment provided.

SIGHTS
CHIANG MAI CITY ARTS & CULTURAL CENTER
Phra Pokklao Rd

Tel 0 53 217 793
Open Tue–Sun 8.30am–5pm
Admission: 90 baht, under-12s 40 baht

CHIANG MAI NIGHT SAFARI
33 Moo 12 Nong Kwai District, Hang Dong, Chiang Mai
Tel 0 5399 9000 ext 1063
www.chiangmainightsafari.com
Open daily 10am–5pm, 6pm–11pm
Tickets: Thais up to 250 baht; non-Thais up to 500 baht.
On the edge of Soi Suthep-Pui National Park, the world's third and largest night zoo presents mainly Thai, Kenyan and Australian creatures, lit as if under a full moon in three zones: cute small animals (walking trail, also open by day), large grazers (tram tour) and predators (tram tour). Each starts from a Lanna Village of shops and restaurants.

CHIANG MAI ZOO AND AQUARIUM
100 Huaykaew Rd
www.chiangmaizoo.com
Open daily 8am–5pm

DOI INTHANON NATIONAL PARK
119 Ban-Luang Amphur Chom Thong
Tel 0 53 286 728
inthanon_np@hotmail.com
www.dnp.go.th
Admission: 200 baht, children 100 baht

MAESA ELEPHANT CAMP
1119/9 Tapae Rd
Tel 0 53 206 247
www.maesaelephantcamp.com
Largest assembly of elephants in northern Thailand available for treks through the jungle.

OLD CHIANG MAI CULTURAL CENTER
185/3 Wualai Rd
Tel 0 53 202 993–5
info@oldchiangmai.com
www.oldchiangmai.com
Khantoke dinner 7pm–10pm, Shows 8pm–9.30pm
Khantoke Set Menu 320 baht

ROYAL FLORAL RATCHAPRUEK
2006 Mae Hia
www.royalparkrajapruek.com
Open daily 8am–6pm
Stunning and expansive gardens dedicated to Thailand's wildflowers and flora.

UMBRELLA MAKING CENTER
111/2 Bor Sang Village
borsang@hotmail.com

www.handmade-umbrella.com
Tel 0 53 338 324
Open daily 8am–5pm

MUSEUMS

CHIANG MAI ART MUSEUM
Phra Pokklao Rd,
Tumbon Sripoom
Tel 0 53 219 833
www.chiangmaicitymuseum.org
Open Tue–Sun 8.30am–5pm
Admission: 90 baht

CHIANG MAI NATIONAL MUSEUM
North along Chiang Mai-Lampang
Superhwy 11
Tel 0 53 221 308
Open Wed–Sun 9am–4pm
Admission: 30 baht

CHIANG MAI UNIVERSITY ART MUSEUM
239 Nimmanhaemin Rd.
Tel 0 53 218 280, 0 53 944 833
www.finearts.cmu.ac.th/cmu/
This art space at Chiang Mai
University regularly hosts visiting
exhibitions from Thailand and
across Southeast Asia.

TEMPLES & SHRINES

WAT KETKARAM
Charoenrat Rd
Tel 0 53 262 605
Open daily 10am–12pm, 2pm–4pm

WAT PHRATHAT DOI SUTHEP
Sivichai Rd, Route 1004
Tel 0 53 295 002
Open daily 8.30am–5pm

GOLF

ALPINE GOLF RESORT CHIANG MAI
336 Moo 4, San Kamphaeng,
Banthi Rd
Tel 0 53 880 880–4
www.alpinegolfresort.com
This 18-hole course is a favourite
for international tournaments and
events.

LANNA SPORTS CENTER & GOLF CLUB
Chotana Rd
Tel 0 53 221 911
www.golflannachiangmai.com
A long-time favourite of the locals,
the golf course has 27 holes
spread throughout the woods.
Amateurs can practice in the
driving range.

ROYAL CHIANG MAI GOLF RESORT
169 Moo 5,
Chaing Mai-Prao Rd
Tel 0 53 849 301–6

golf1@royalchiangmai.com
www.royalchiangmai.co.th
Five-time British Open winner Peter
Thomson and Michael Wolveridge
have designed an 18-hole golf
course that puts golfers to the test.

SUMMIT GREEN VALLEY COUNTRY CLUB
183/2 Chotana Rd
Tel 0 53 298 222
www.summitgreenvalleygolf.com
With tropical gardens, pools and
mountain views, the world-class
18-hole golf course is one of the
best in the area.

CHIANG RAI

PRACTICALITIES

AIRPORT
CHIANG RAI INTERNATIONAL AIRPORT
Chiang Rai Town
Tel 0 53 793 048–57

TOURIST INFORMATION
TAT CHIANG RAI
448/16 Singhaklai Rd,
Chiang Rai Town
Tel 0 53 717 433
Fax 0 53 717 434
tatchrai@tat.or.th

TOURIST POLICE
Tel 0 53 717 779/717 796

POST OFFICE
POST OFFICE
486/1 Utarakit Rd,
Chiang Rai Town
Open Mon–Fri 8.30am–4.30pm,
Sat–Sun 9am–12pm

ACCOMMODATIONS

*Rates quoted are high season
rack rates for a standard double
room, though prices may well be
lower in the off-season. Restaurant
prices are for dinner for two without
alcohol, except where noted.*

ANANTARA GOLDEN TRIANGLE
229 Moo 1, Wiang, Chiang Saen
Tel 0 53 784 084
Fax 0 53 784 090
goldentriangle@anantara.com
www.anantara.com
Rates: from $128–$255
Features: Elephant camp in
hotel area.
Low-rise resort perched on a quiet
hillside. Well-appointed rooms have
balconies overlooking Myanmar

and Laos. Guests can interact with
elephants or take a mahout course
at the nearby camp.

FOUR SEASONS TENTED CAMP
18 Chiang Saen, Chiang Rai
Tel 0 53 910 200
Fax 0 53 652 189
www.fourseasons.com/
goldentriangle
Rates: minimum stay 3 nights
$1,120–$1,557
Features: Elephant trekking, hiking,
15 tented accommodation.
Four Seasons has adapted the
luxury camping concept from
safaris to the bamboo forests of the
Golden Triangle. Reached by river,
the 15 sturdy canvas villas feature
amenities like hand-beaten copper
baths. Guests can learn to be a
mahout, trek, have campfire meals
and take drinks in the treetops on
3- or 4-day inclusive adventures.

LE MERIDIEN CHIANG RAI RESORT
221/2 Moo 20 Kwaewai Rd,
Tambon Robwieng
Tel 0 53 603 333
lemeridien.chiangrai
@lemeridien.com
www.starwoodhotels.com
Poised along the Mae Kok river and
spanning 26 rai of verdant beauty,
this 159-room resort encourages
guests to unwrap the mystery of
the surrounding area. Take an
excursion into nature through the
Golden Triangle or into the stunning
mountain ranges; trips can be
arranged by the hotel.

PHU CHAISAI RESORT & SPA
388 Moo 4, Ban Mae Salong Nai
Mae Chan
Tel 0 53 918 636/7
Fax 0 53 918 333
www.phu-chaisai.com
Rates: 5,000–6,000 baht
Features: Pottery, cooking and
umbrella painting classes, bamboo
handicraft workshop, hiking.
Hilltop resort with grand views of
verdant mountains. Thatched
roof bamboo rooms exude rustic
charm. Behind tropical trees and
flowering plants are secluded
areas, perfect for couples who
want to be away from it all.
Open-air spa uses natural
ingredients for treatments.

ATTRACTIONS

DOI TUNG ROYAL VILLA & MAE FAH LUANG GARDEN
Mae Fah Luang Foundation

Tel 0 53 767 015–7 (Bangkok
Office, tel 0 2252 7114)
Fax 0 53 767 077
tourism@doitung.org
www.doitung.org
Open daily 7am–5.30pm (Doi
Tung Royal Villa; daily 7am–5pm
Princess Mother Commemorative
Hall), 6.30am–6pm (Mae Fah
Luang Garden and Arboretum)
Admission: 70 baht Royal Villa;
30 baht Commemorative Hall;
80 baht (Garden only);
200 baht, children 50 baht
(Garden with Haw Kham and
Haw Kaew Pavilions)
Aside from the palace and formal
gardens of the late Princess
Mother, the Mae Fah Luang
Foundation runs a nearby Arts and
Crafts Center and an Arboretum
right on the Myanmar border. It also
produces clothing sold in Bangkok
and abroad.

HALL OF OPIUM
Golden Triangle Park, Chiang Saen
Tel 0 53 784 444
www.doitung.org
Open Tue–Sun 8:30am–4pm
Admission: 300 baht, 12s–18s,
50 baht
An outstanding museum
dedicated to the history of
opium, its harvesting, trade and
paraphernalia.

HUA HIN

PRACTICALITIES

TOURIST INFORMATION
TAT HUA HIN AND CHA-AM
500/51 Phetkasem Rd, Cha-am
Tel 0 32 471 005/6
Fax 0 32 471 502
tatphet@tat.or.th

TOURIST POLICE
Tel 0 32 515 995
(emergencies 1155)

HOSPITAL
SAN PAULO HUA HIN HOSPITAL
222 Petchakasem Rd
Tel 0 32 532 576

POST OFFICE
POST OFFICE
Damnoenkasem Rd
Tel 0 32 511 063

ACCOMMODATIONS

Rates quoted are high season

*rack rates for a standard double
room, though prices may well be
lower in the off-season. Restaurant
prices are for dinner for two without
alcohol, except where noted.*

ANANTARA HUA HIN
43/1 Phetkasem Beach Rd
Tel 0 32 511 890
Fax 0 32 520 259
huahin@anantara.com
www.anantara.com
Rates: $150–$350
Features: Golf, courses in flower
arrangement, fruit carving, takraw,
Thai boxing, cooking and Thai
language.
Clusters of Thai villas are arranged
like a small village with pools,
flower patches and tropical
gardens, appointed with modern,
Zen-like finishings and private
terraces.

CENTARA GRAND BEACH RESORT & VILLAS HUA HIN
1 Damnoen Kasem Rd
Tel 0 32 512 021
Fax 0 32 511 014
chbr@chr.co.th
www.centarahotelresorts.com
Rates: $200-$500
Features: 5 restaurants, 6 bars,
children's club.
The historic, colonial-style hotel has
more than 200 elegant rooms and
suites, some with terraces directly
facing the hotel's romantic topiary
gardens and the Gulf of Thailand.

CHIVA SOM
73/4 Petchkasem Rd,
Prachaub Khirikhan
Tel 0 32 536 536
Fax 0 32 511 154
reservation@chivasom.com
www.chivasom.com
Rates: 3 nights $1,650–$4,500
(minimum stay 3 nights)
Features: Aqua aerobics, muay
Thai, fruit carving, hydropools,
plunge pools, fitness areas.
This destination spa is world-
renowned for its diverse range
of therapies for body and mind.
Treatment salas and Thai-style
pavilions are set in acres of
tropical gardens fronting the
Gulf of Thailand. Celebrated spa
cuisine features healthy gourmet
specialties. Also runs a holistic
therapy school in Bangkok.

DUSIT RESORT & POLO CLUB
1349 Phetkasem Rd, Cha-am
Tel 0 32 520 009
Fax 0 32 520 296
drh@dusit.com

www.dusit.com
Rates: $229–$1,700
Features: Fitness centre, close to golf courses.
The oceanfront resort is located along Cha-am's powdery beach along the Gulf of Thailand. All rooms and suites are styled with Thai accents and appointed with modern comforts. Horseback riding classes are available on the polo grounds.

HUA HIN HILTON RESORT & SPA
33 Naresdamri Rd
Tel 0 32 538 999
Fax 0 32 538 990
www.huahin.hilton.com
Rates: 5,500–25,000 baht
Features: Huge children's pool, spa, fitness centre.
The rooms of this hotel tower provide grand views of Hua Hin and the ocean from their balconies. All come with modern comforts, with teak floors and Thai furnishings adding to the tropical ambience. World News Coffee is a popular place for a relaxed read while Hua Hin Brewing Company is a beerhouse that gets packed in the evening. Also has a popular Sunday brunch.

HYATT REGENCY HUA HIN
91 Hua Hin-Khao Takiap Rd
Tel 0 32 521 234
Fax 0 32 521 233
hotel.hrhuahin@hyattintl.com
http://huahin.regency.hyatt.com
Rates: 5,800–22,800 baht
Features: Camp Hyatt for 4–12s, Thai cooking class, tennis, watersports.
The beachfront resort has 204 rooms among landscaped gardens and pools. Its pool has cascading waterfalls, jacuzzi and a 72-foot long waterslide. Has all sorts of recreational activities for children including a children's club and a cyberzone.

LET'S SEA HUA HIN AL FRESCO RESORT
83/188 Soi Huathanon 23, Khaotakien, Hua Hin Rd
Tel 0 32 536 888
Fax 0 32 536 887
Info.huahin@letussea.com
www.letussea.com
Rates: $150–$300
Features: Horse riding, elephant trekking, wind surfing, fishing.
A distinctive boutique hotel with imposingly modernist architecture that takes its details of décor and ambiance from Thailand's

easygoing beachlife. Many rooms have direct access to the canal-like pool and a moonwatching deck. Its modern beachside restaurant Let's Sea (daily food service 6.30am–11pm; Beach Bar & Terrace 11am–midnight) offers Thai home cooking. Very casual, with a deck of sunloungers (1,000 baht).

PUTAHRACSA HUA HIN
22/65 Nahb Kaehat Rd
Hua Hin
Tel 0 32 531 470
www.putahracsa.com
Rates: $185–$450
Beautiful boutique hotel with wonderful furnishings, day spa, and accommodations set right on the beachfront.

SAILOM HOTEL HUA HIN
29 Phetkasem Highway
Hua Hin
Tel 0 32 520 250
www.sailomhotelhuahin.com
Rates: $100–$200
Excellent oceanfront restaurant offers succulent seafood, while the comfortable rooms are good value for money.

VERANDA RESORT & SPA HUA HIN
737/12 Mung Talay Rd, Cha-am
Tel 0 32 709 099
Fax 0 2513 6844
Rates: $130–$300
Features: Free form infinity pool, kid's club, in-room daybed
This is a medium-size boutique hotel. Rooms and pool villas with modern Thai-Western décor.

DINING
Prices quoted are for dinner for two without alcohol, except where noted.

BRASSERIE DE PARIS
3 Naresdamri Rd
Tel 0 32 530 637
Open daily 10.30am–5pm, 6pm–10pm
This classy French restaurant located right on the water has a strong selection of wines (1,200 baht).

PIER RESTAURANTS
Naresdamri Rd
Group of small seafood restaurants lining city pier with tables on the boardwalk. Not too fancy, but the dishes are delicious and the view in the evening is marvelous (<500 baht).

SUPATRA BY THE SEA
122/63 Takiab Rd, Nong–gae
Tel 0 32 536 561–2
www.supatra-bythesea.com
Open daily 11am–11pm
Seaside sister of the famed Bangkok restaurant serves Thai cuisine and seafood. Spectacular views of the ocean and neighbouring hills. Dine al fresco or inside rustic, tropical pavilions (<1,000 baht).

SHOPPING

BAAN KHOMMAPHAT
218 Phetkasem Rd
Tel 0 32 513 506
Open Thu–Tue 9am–5pm
Sells pha phim khommaphat or native cotton fabric made with Khommaphat prints.

JIM THOMPSON
33 Naresdamri Rd
Tel 0 32 512 888
www.jimthompson.com
Open daily 10am–8pm
Thai silk specialists. See website for additional branches of this famous fashion retailer.

ATTRACTIONS

TEMPLES & SHRINES
WAT HUA HIN
Phetkasem Rd
Open daily 8am–5pm

MAREUKATHAYAWAN PALACE
Rama VI Army Camp, 10km south of Cha-am
Tel 0 32 508 026
Open daily 8am–4pm,
Admission: 30 baht

PARKS
KHAO SAM ROI YOT NATIONAL PARK
Khao Daeng, Kui Buri
Tel 0 32 559 246
Open daily 6am–6pm
Admission: 400 baht, children under-14s 200 baht

GOLF
ROYAL HUA HIN GOLF CLUB
Damnoen Kasem Rd
Tel 0 32 512 475
Fax 0 32 513 038
www.golfhuahin.com/royalhuahin.htm
Repeatedly refurbished since its opening in 1924, the 18-hole course offers great views of the Gulf and the picturesque buildings on its grounds.

SPRINGFIELD ROYAL COUNTRY CLUB
Off Cha-Am 193 Moo 6, Huasai Nua, Cha-am
Tel 0 32 709 222
Fax 0 32 709 234
www.springfieldresort.com
A world-class resort designed by renowned golfer Jack Nicklaus.

PHUKET & ENVIRONS

PRACTICALITIES

AIRPORT
PHUKET INTERNATIONAL AIRPORT
Tel 0 76 327 230–7

TOURIST INFORMATION
TAT PHUKET, PHANG-NGA & KRABI
73 75 Phuket Rd, Amphoe Muang
Tel 0 76 212 213
Fax 0 76 213 582
tatphket@tat.or.th
www.phukettourism.org

PHUKET TOURIST POLICE
100/31–32 Chalermprakiat Rd
Tel 0 76 254 693
(emergencies 1155)
phukettouristpol@phuketpolice.com

HOSPITAL
BANGKOK PHUKET HOSPITAL
2/1 Hongyok Utis Rd
Tel 0 76 254 421
(emergencies 1719)
Fax 0 76 254 425
www.phukethospital.com
Open daily 8am–5pm

PHUKET INTERNATIONAL HOSPITAL
44 Chalermprakiat Rd
Tel 0 76 249 400
(emergencies 0 76 210 935)
Fax 0 76 210 936
www.phuket-inter-hospital.co.th
Open daily 8am–8pm Emergency 24 hours

PROPERTY AGENTS
ASIALAND LAND AND PROPERTY CONSULTANTS
74/8 Vichitsongkram Rd
Tel 0 76 249 215/6
www.realestatephuket.com
Broker with years of experience in the purchase and/or sale of big ticket houses, land and condos.

CB RICHARD ELLIS
12/9 Moo 4,
Thep Kasattri Rd, Koh Keo

Tel 0 76 239 967
Fax 0 76 239 970
phuket@cbre.com
www.cbre.co.th
An international real estate agent specializing in high-end properties.

ACCOMMODATIONS

Rates quoted are high season rack rates for a standard double room, though prices may well be lower in the off-season. Restaurant prices are for dinner for two without alcohol, except where noted.

AMANPURI
Pan Sea Beach Phuket
Tel 0 76 324 333
Fax 0 76 324 100
amanpuri@amanresorts.com
www.amanresorts.com
Rates: $700–$7,800
Features: Fleet of luxury boats for "Aman Cruises" excursions.
Perched on a headland, this influential resort designed by Ed Tuttle features opulent minimalist Thai pavilions and villas, coconut groves, fantastic ocean views and unparalleled privacy. The jet-set Aman Spa has spacious treatment rooms and open salas for relaxation. Thai pavilions housing restaurants and activity rooms flank the large pool. The amphitheater-like stairwell leads to the powdery sands of Pan Sea Beach.

BANYAN TREE PHUKET
33 Moo 4, Srisoonthorn Rd, Cherng Talay, Thalang
Tel 0 76 324 374
Fax 0 76 324 375
phuket@banyantree.com
www.banyantree.com
Rates: $580–$3,200
Features: Dining cruises, golf, library, diving class, sailing, and watersports.
This is a favourite destination for honeymooners and couples in search of romance. The award-winning spa resort has 123 ravishing villas with lovely tropical gardens and sunken open-air baths. Some have private swimming pools. The Banyan Tree Spa carries a full-range of signature treatments to soothe the body, mind and soul. Dining options are equally diverse.

THE CHEDI PHUKET
118 Moo 3, Cherng Talay, Thalang
Tel 0 76 324 017–20
Fax 0 76 324 252

hotel@chedi-phuket.com
www.ghmhotels.com
Rates: 16,200–38,600 baht
Features: Watersports,
children's club.
Enveloped by tropical palms and
frangipani trees, The Chedi has
89 thatched cottages, 16 suites
scattered on the hillside and
along the beachfront. Each has a
spacious, private verandah with
ocean vistas, teakwood floors
and angel beds. The resort has
an enormous hexagonal pool and
shares a powdery private beach
with the Amanpuri.

COSTA LANTA
212 Moo 1, Saladan, Koh Lanta
Yai, Krabi
Tel 0 2662 3550
Fax 0 2260 9067
info@costalanta.com
www.costalanta.com
Rates: 6,050–9,460 baht
Features: Massage service,
infinity pool.
Avant-garde, minimalist resort with
20 freestanding box bungalows
made from recycled timber and
polished concrete. Bedroom
walls retract to invite sea breezes,
ocean views and the lush tropical
surrounds.

DUSIT LAGUNA RESORT
390, Srisoonthorn Rd, Thalang
Tel 0 76 324 324
reservation 0 76 324 320
Fax 0 76 324 174
www.phuket.dusit.com
Rates: $385–$1,585
Features: Children's centre,
cooking classes, wind surfing,
kayak, sailing, and other
watersports, pool volleyball, pool
basketball, batik painting.
The low-rise beachside resort is
surrounded by indigo lagoons.
Spacious rooms are decorated with
local hardwood, ceramics, antiques
and Thai silk. All have private
balconies.

INDIGO PEARL
Nai Yang Beach, Phuket
Tel 0 76 327 006, 0 76 327 015
Fax 0 76 327 338–9
info@indigo-pearl.com
www.indigo-pearl.com
Rates: 3,655–25,806 baht
Features: Thai cooking school,
tennis court, library, diving,
kids club (Thai dance class, fruit
carving, batik painting).
Stunningly themed boutique hotel
near a coastal national park.
Created by the expert Bill Bensley,

the décor takes its metallic,
industrial-chic cue from the area's
tin mining heritage. The blue hues
even extend to the choice of plants
in the ground. The rooms have
unique characteristics, from walk-in
wardrobes and balcony baths to
villas with private pools or terraces.
There's a spa and six dining
outlets with evocative names like
Underground Café and Rivet Grill.

JW MARRIOTT PHUKET
231 Moo 3, Mai Khao, Thalang
Tel 0 76 338 000
Fax 0 76 348 348
www.marriott.com
Rates: 1,200–99,990 baht
Features: Conference facilities,
children's pavilion, Ginja cooking
school, watersports.
The beachfront resort sits on an
undeveloped stretch of northwest
Phuket, north of the airport. Lined
with flowering tropical gardens,
all rooms and suites command
romantic views of the ocean.
Guests can get some world-class
pampering at the award-winning
Mandara Spa.

LAGUNA BEACH RESORT
323 Srisoonthorn Rd,
Bang Tao Bay
Tel 0 76 324 352
Fax 0 76 324 353
www.lagunabeach-resort.com
Rates: $170–$950
Features: Golf at Laguna Phuket,
cooking and diving classes,
watersports, beach volleyball,
football.
Rooms of this low-rise resort
have views of the Andaman or
the lagoons. Each has a sunken
bath and Thai sitting area. Resort
has a strong activities program
for children and an outdoor
management training program for
corporate visitors.

LE MERIDIEN KHAO LAK BEACH &
SPA RESORT
9/9 Moo 1, Kuk Kak,
near Takua Pa, Phang-nga
Tel 0 76 427 500
Fax 0 76 427 575
www.starwoodhotels.com/
lemeridien
Rates: $350–$700
Features: Penguin kids club,
snorkeling, wind surfing,
sailing, kayaking.
Khao Lak's first resort neighbours
isolated beaches, two national
parks, waterfalls and rolling
mountains. It has 243 suites and
villas furnished in contemporary

Thai style. Pool villas enjoy butler
service. Lots of outdoor activities
nearby such as whitewater rafting,
elephant trekking, sea canoeing
and diving.

MOM TRI'S BOATHOUSE &
VILLA ROYALE
12 Kata Beach, Phuket
Tel 0 76 330 015
Fax 0 76 330 561
info@boathousephuket.com
www.phuket.com/villaroyale/
Rates: 11,500–23,000 baht
Features: Pool, massage service,
paintings and antiques gallery,
diving, cooking class every
weekend 10am–2pm.
Boutique hotel with 33 spacious
rooms, 3 suites that face Kata
Bay. Noted for its gourmet
restaurants (Mom Tri's Boathouse
Wine & Grill, Mom Tri's Kitchen
& Gung Cuisine Thaïe) which
feature great European and Thai
cuisine. Behind it is Villa Royale,
a very small boutique extension
also overlooking the Andaman.
Eighteen rooms and suites are
housed in Thai-style buildings and
surrounded by beautiful gardens. It
also has a superb restaurant.

PIMALAI RESORT & SPA
99 Moo 5, Ba Kan Tiang Beach,
Koh Lanta Yai, Krabi
Tel 0 75 607 999
Fax 0 75 607 998
reservation@pimalai.com
www.pimalai.com
Rates $340–$1,690
Features: Library, watersports,
Thai cooking class, squid boat
safari, sunset cruise (Nov–Apr),
diving.
Southern Thai-style houses have
contemporary rooms with teak
floors, silk fabrics and rattan
furniture. A spa designed like
a village with thatched huts is
located towards the forest.

RAYAVADEE
Laem Phra Nang Cape,
214 Moo 2, Ao Nang, Krabi
Tel 0 75 620 740
Fax 0 75 620 730
sales@rayavadee.com
www.rayavadee.com
Rates: 22,300–118,000 baht
Features: Watersports, diving,
rock climbing, trekking,
Thai cooking class.
Straddling three beaches and
sheltered by towering karst
formations and coconut trees,
this resort lies at the very end
of picturesque Laem Phra Nang

cape. Some 77 pavilions are styled
with authentic Thai décor and most
have private jacuzzis. The cape is
reached by boat, which the hotel
can provide.

LE ROYAL MERIDIEN PHUKET
YACHT CLUB
23/3 Viset Rd, Nai Harn Beach
Tel 0 76 380 200–19
Fax 0 76 380 280
www.phuket-yachtclub.com
Rates: $500–$2,020
Features: Watersports.
Suites and rooms have huge
private terraces up the hillside and
wide ocean vistas. Strong line-up of
sports and recreation-al activities
includes catamaran sailing,
mountain biking and windsurfing.
A glamorous motor yacht runs
sunset cruises between here and
Le Meridien.

SHERATON KRABI BEACH RESORT
155, Moo 2, Nong Talay, Krabi
Tel 0 75 628 000
Fax 0 75 628 028
sheraton.krabi@sheraton.com
www.sheraton.com
Rates $140–$350
Features: Diving center,
windsurfing, kayaks,
sailing, babysitting.
Set among natural mangroves a
20-minute drive from both Krabi
town and the star beaches at
Laem Phra Nang, this beach
resort has spacious rooms in
contemporary Thai style, with dark
hardwoods and brightly colored
silk furnishings. The relatively
undeveloped beach looks across
Phang-nga Bay.

SRI PANWA
88, Moo 8, Nong Talay, Sakdidej
Road, Vichit, Muang, Phuket
Tel 0 76 371 000
Fax 0 76 371 004
www.sripanwa.com
Features: Private cars available,
gym, world-class snorkelling and
scuba nearby, tennis and more.
Perched high above Cape Panwa
on 32 acres of gorgeous landscape,
this resort offers breathtaking views
of the Andaman ocean. More than
50 villas, many with their own pools,
offer the best in luxury. Consistently
rated as one of Phuket's best
resorts, Sri Panwa is an oasis of
calm in one of Thailand's most
beautiful holiday spots.

TRISARA
60/1 Moo 6, Srisoonthorn Rd,
Cherng Talay, Phuket

Tel 0 76 310 100
Fax 0 76 310 300
reservations@trisara.com
www.trisara.com
Rates: $780–$1,940,
residential villas $2,000–$3,250
Features: Library, tennis, diving,
plasma screens, wine cellar,
luxury yachts, golf club access.
Ensconced in a lush tropical forest,
the resort's 42 villas and have
fantastic views of its private beach
and the open ocean. Bedrooms
face a 30-foot long private infinity
pool and sundeck. Spacious en
suite bathroom, outdoor showers
and refined Thai interiors.
Residential villas come with live-in
maids and cooks. Hillside spa has
6 treatment suites and a separate
pavilion for yoga and meditation.

TWIN PALMS RESORT
106/46 Moo 3, Surin Beach Rd,
Cherng Talay
Tel 0 76 316 500
Fax 0 76 316 599
www.twinpalms-phuket.com
Rates 10,900–39,600 baht
Features: Library.
Modern boutique resort with
very spacious rooms and suites,
decorated either in Asian or
Western style. Private terraces
overlook tropical gardens and a
150-foot lap pool.

DINING & NIGHTLIFE

*Prices quoted are for dinner for
two without alcohol, except where
noted.*

BAAN KLUNG JINDA RESTAURANT
158 Yaowarat Rd
Tel 0 76 221 777
Fax 0 76 214 040
dining@baanklung.com
www.baanklung.com
Open daily 11.30am–2.30pm,
6pm–12am
Set in a marvelous Thai house,
this classy restaurant serves
authentic Thai dishes and sea-food
specialties (<1,000 baht).

BAAN RIM PA RESTAURANT
223 Kalim Beach Rd
Tel 0 76 34 0 789
Fax 0 76 342 460
www.baanrimpa.com
Open daily 12pm–11pm
Perched on a cliff, this elegant
restaurant offers great views of the
coast. But it is the careful pairing
of wines with exquisite Thai cuisine
that people come for (2,200 baht).

BLUE ELEPHANT PHUKET
96 Krabi Rd
Tel 0 76 354 355
Fax 0 76 354 393
phuket@blueelephant.com
www.blueelephant.com/phuket
Open daily 11:30am–2:30pm and
6:30pm–10:30pm
Blue Elephant presents Thai
cuisine with a mix of tradition and
novelty.

BRASSERIE PHUKET
18 Rassada Rd
Tel 0 76 210 511
Fax 0 76 383 452
info@brasseriephuket.com
www.brasseriephuket.com
Open daily 6pm–midnight
Lobster and oyster bar, fine wines,
Belgian beers all on offer at this
elegant and comfortable high-end
venue.

DA MAURIZIO BAR RISTORANTE
100/9 Kalim Beach Rd
Tel 0 76 344 079
info@damaurizio.com
www.damaurizio.com
Perfect oceanside venue for good
Italian cuisine and moonlit romance
(2,000 baht).

KAN EANG@PIER
44/1 Viset Road, Moo 5
Tel 0 76 381 212
Fax 0 76 381 715
sales@kaneang-pier.com
www.kaneang-pier.com
Open daily 10:30am–11:30pm
Kan Eang@pier's outdoor terrace
stretches 200 metres along
Chalong Bay, with a menu focused
on seafood.

LA GAETANA
352 Phuket Rd
Tel 0 76 250 523
Open Thu–Tue 6pm–12am, Mon,
Tue and Fri 12pm–2pm
Closed 19 July–19 August
Small cozy shophouse restaurant
offering fine Italian food
(1,100 baht).

GITANO MUSIC CAFÉ
Ong Sim Pai Rd
Tel 0 76 225 797
www.phuketwatch.com/Gitano.htm
Open Mon–Sat 4pm–12am
A restaurant-bar with European and
Thai food, where the atmosphere
is definitely Latino. Guests hang
out till late for the nightly themed
evenings, live acoustic music
and special events like stand-
up comedy and fashion shows.
Longtime favourite of Phuket

expatriates and visitors who want
to know what's happening locally.
Has a branch at Club Andaman
Beach Resort (<1,000 baht).

KA JOK SEE RESTAURANT
26 Takuapa Rd
Tel 0 76 217 903
Open Tue–Sat 7pm–10pm
Sizzlingly hot Thai restaurant-bar
cloistered in a Chinese shophouse.
Lounge music perfects the mood.
Gets lively as a bar later on
(1,000 baht).

NAKA FLAVOR'S RESTAURANT
6/23 Moo 6 T. Kamala,
Patong Beach
Tel/Fax 0 76 345 703
nakaflavors@yahoo.com
Open Wed–Mon 5pm–12am
Diners can enjoy French dishes
and Asian favorites in its nice
courtyard or underneath the Thai
sala (<1,500 baht).

ROCK FISH
33/6 Kamala Beach Rd,
Cherng Talay
Tel 0 76 279 732
Fax 0 76 278 020
Open daily 7.30am–2am
www.rockfishrestaurant.com
A stylishly quirky wooden
construction perched upon
forested rocks overlooking Kamala
Bay, with a deck for barbecues
and sundowner drinks. Fish is
the focus, and it's presented
delightfully and tastes even better
(2,000 baht).

SALVATORE'S RESTAURANT
15 Rasada Rd
Tel/Fax 0 76 225 958
info@salvatorestaurant.com
www.salvatorestaurant.com
Open Mon–Sat 12pm–2.30pm,
6.30pm–11pm
Homey but elegant, this restaurant
dishes out Sardinian specialties
such as spaghetti served with
Bottarga caviar. Choose from a
long wine list (2,000 baht).

WATERMARK BAR RESTAURANT
The Boat Lagoon Marina,
22/1 Moo 2, Thepkasattri Rd
Tel 0 76 239 730
Fax 0 76 239 078
info@watermarkphuket.com
www.watermarkphuket.com
Open daily 10am–10pm
Posh quayside restaurant featuring
innovative Australian and Pacific
Rim cuisine. Glass panels offer
views of beautiful yachts moored in
the marina (2,200 baht).

SHOPPING

*Phuket is turning into a shopping
island, with Central Festival,
followed by Jungceylon at Patong,
and a boutique mini-mall near
Surin Bay developed by Hong
Kong developer Alan Zeman,
and Horizons, a retail and villa
development at Royal Phuket
Marina, with a spa, top restaurants,
fitness center and promenade
attractions.*

MALLS
**CANAL VILLAGE SHOPPING
CENTER**
390/1 Moo 1, Srisoonthorn Rd,
Cherng Talay, Thalang
Tel 0 76 324 453–7
Fax 0 76 324 065
shopping@lagunaphuket.com
www.lagunaphuket.com
Complex of 40 small shops whose
range includes Jim Thompson silks
and lovely home spa amenities
from the Banyan Tree Gallery.

CENTRAL FESTIVAL
Chalermprakiat Rd, just west of
Phuket Town
Tel 0 76 249 000
www.central.co.th
Open daily 10am–10pm
Huge and modern shopping
mall on the successful model of
Central's other branches. Has
a Central department store,
bookstores, appliance shop,
office supplies, homebuilders'
square and SFX Coliseum cinema
complex, plus a craft and festival
area.

THE COURTYARD
90/4 Moo 2,
Chaofa Rd (West), Wichit
Tel 0 76 263 707
Fax 0 76 263 708
info.x@thecourtyard-phuket.com
www.thecourtyard-phuket.com
The island's first high-end home
furnishings center include shops
like Asian Gallery, which specializes in Asian silk fashions, a branch
of Azur and a ginseng shop.

JUNGCEYLON
Jungceylon Phuket Square,
181 Rat-U-Thit
200 Pee Rd,
Patong
Tel 0 76 600 111
Fax 0 76 292 111
info@jungceylon.com
www.jungceylon.com
This comprehensive lifestyle
center offers numerous shopping,

dining and entertainment facilities,
including an SF cineplex,
restaurants, bowling, micro-
brewery, jazz bar, dance clubs,
music bards, and recreation area
with a junk ship. It encompasses
both Burasari boutique hotel, and
the Millennium Resort Patong.

LAGUNA PHUKET ENTRANCE
382/45 Laguna Phuket Rd, Cherng
Talay
This is a cluster of antique and
home décor shops lined along the
entrance of Laguna Resort. Of note
are Art & Gift Gallery (tel 0 76 324
453), Heritage Collection, Soul of
Asia, and Oriental Antique City
(tel 0 76 324 312). Also
represented are Bangkok's Art of
Living (tel 0 76 325 148), renowned
for its ultramodern tropical
furniture.

SHOPS
AZUR
20 Ratsada Rd, Phuket
Tel 0 76 256 588
info@creationtamarino.com
Open Mon–Sat 9am–6pm
This shop features delicate silk
home furnishings created by a
French designer. Branch at The
Courtyard.

CERAMICS OF PHUKET
71/3 Vichit Songkram Rd, Kathu
Tel 0 76 321 917
Fax 0 76 202 087
info@ceramicsofphuket.com
www.ceramicsofphuket.com
Open Mon–Sat 8am–5pm
Sells tea and coffee sets, kitchen
pots, spa amenities and vases
made from local clay and then
blasted in a variety of glazes.
Branch at Clay House Gallery,
185/6–7 Moo 7, Srisoontorn Rd,
Talang (0 76 272 151–2)

JIM THOMPSON
office@jimthompson.com
www.jimthompson.com
Purchasing the famed silk
company's silk fashions and home
accessories is a must for every
traveller visiting Thailand.
Branches at hotels and in shopping
plazas throughout the island. See
website for locations.

SONGTIQUE
63/16 Moo 1 Cherng Talay, Talang,
Phuket
Bangkok office 0 2437 5555
sales@songtique.com
www.songtique.com
Open daily 9am–6pm

Phuket branch of the shop at
Bangkok's River City carries
antique Buddhas, Chinese
wedding cabinets and Vietnamese
lacquer paintings.

TAWEESUWAN
30–32 Montri Rd, Phuket
Tel 0 76 230 230
Fax 0 76 216 085
www.taweesuwan.com
Open Mon–Sat 8.30am–6pm
Sells all sorts of diamond jewelry,
pendants, necklaces, rings,
earrings, bangles and bracelets.

GALLERIES

**THE PALACE OF ART GALLERY
SHOP**
103/3 Moo 4 Banbangjoe,
Srisoonthon Rd, Thalang, Phuket
Tel 0 76 273 533
Fax 0 76 273 535
shahe@thaiart.com
www.thaiart.com
Open daily 8.30am–6pm
Three galleries containing an
impressive collection of antique
Thai, Burmese and Cambodian
Buddha images, some more than
200 years old. A treasure trove of
pieces made from lacquer, bronze,
sandstone or teak. Has a tropical
garden outside with Thai salas.

SARASIL ART GALLERY
121 Phang-nga Rd, Phuket City
Tel 0 76 224 532
Open daily 8am–10pm
Collection of oils, watercolors
and mixed media with abstract
and realist themes. All painted by
Phuket-based Thai artists.

SOUL OF ASIA
5/50 Moo 3, Cherngtalaya, Thalang
Tel 0 76 271 629
Fax 0 76 270 055
info@soulofasia.com
www.soulofasia.com
Open Mon–Sat 10.30am–8pm
This gallery holds fine Chinese
antique furniture, porcelain and
rugs, Asian antiques and a private
collection of Chagall, Dalí, Picasso
and Warhol pieces.

ATTRACTIONS

TOURS & RECREATION
FANTASEA DIVERS
Silvertip Co Ltd, 219 Rat-Uthit 200
Years Rd,
Patong Beach,
Phuket

Tel 0 76 281 388
Fax 0 76 281 389
info@oceanrover.com
www.fantasea.net
Offers luxury live-aboard dive cruises to the Andaman and Myanmar from Nov to May. Boats have cabins with en-suite bathrooms, provisions for diver safety and good facilities for underwater photography enthusiasts.

JOHN GRAY SEA CANOE
124 Soi 1, Yaowarat Rd,
Talad Yai,
Phuket City
Tel 0 76 254 505–7
Fax 0 76 226 077
info@johngray-seacanoe.com
www.johngray-seacanoe.com
This outfit was set up by the award-winning environmentalist who pioneered eco-tourism trips in southern Thailand. Adventure seekers paddle into lagoons and limestone grottos. A highlight is "Hongs by Starlight", an evening kayak trip through the karst formations.

PHUKET BOAT LAGOON
22/1 Moo 2, Thep Kasattri Rd,
Phuket
Tel 0 76 239 055
Fax 0 76 239 056
Full-service marina with great facilities. Houses yacht companies which charter all kinds of boats to the surrounding islands. Clubhouse has pools, restaurants and suites.

ROYAL PHUKET MARINA
68 Moo 2, Thep Kasattri Rd (Office)
Tel 0 76 239 755
Fax 0 76 239 756
paradise@royalphuketmarina.com
www.royalphuketmarina.com
The waterfront development has berths for 350 boats. Luxury residences include condos and villas with private pools. The Horizons development features all sorts of shops and services.

SEA CANOE
125/461 Moo 5, Baan Tung Ka–Baan Sapam Rd
Tel 0 76 528 839
Fax 0 76 528 841
info@seacanoe.net
www.seacanoe.net
A multiple award-winning eco-tourism company that organizes sea kayak trips to tidal caves and cliff-lined lagoons along Phang-nga and Krabi as well as national parks in Tarutao and Khao Sok.

SEE-BEE DIVING
1/3 Moo 9 Viset Rd, Ao Chalong,
Phuket
Tel. 0 76 381 765
Fax 0 76 280 467
info@sea-bees.com
www.sea-bees.com/eng/liveaboars_Thailand.htm
3 days trip: similan double $555, single $685
Luxury dive cruises to important spots in the area like the Similan and Surin Islands and the Mergui Archipelago, including on the renowned Genesis Liveaboards. Also conducts dive expeditions around Koh Samui.
Branch at Khao Lak 33/3 Moo 6, Petchkasem Rd-Khao Lak, Takuapa, Phang Nga (Tel 0 76 485 174 Fax 0 76 485 175)
Khaolak@sea-bees.com

THE YACHT HAVEN MARINA PHUKET
141/2 Moo 2,
Maikhao Thalang
Tel 0 76 206 704/5
Fax 0 76 206 706
info@yacht-haven-phuket.com
www.yacht-haven-phuket.com
This marina located on the north Phuket has more than 150 berths for boats of all sizes. Facilities open to charter companies and private boat owners.

SIGHTS
PHUKET BUTTERFLY GARDEN & INSECT WORLD
71/6 Moo 5, Soi Paneung,
Yaowarat Rd
Tel 0 76 210 861
Fax 0 76 523 609
phuketbutterfly@hotmail.com
www.phuketbutterfly.com
Open daily 9am–5pm
Admission: 300 baht, children 150 baht

PHUKET FANTASEA
99 Moo 3, Kamala Beach, Kathu
Tel 0 76 385 111
Fax 0 76 385 222
info@phuket-fantasea.com
www.phuket-fantasea.com
Open Mon–Wed, Fri–Sun 5.30pm–11.30pm
Shows Fri–Wed 9pm
Admission: 1,600 baht, children 4–12 years 1,300 baht (with pre-show buffet dinner); 1,100 baht (same price for children)
An entertainment and shopping complex that includes a huge Thai restaurant and theater. Las Vegas-style performance with dancers, fireworks and animals every night.

TEMPLES & SHRINES
PUT JAW TEMPLE
Ranong Rd, Soi Puthon

WAT CHALONG
Route 4022, between Chalong and Phuket Town
Open daily 8am–5pm

GOLF
BLUE CANYON COUNTRY CLUB
165 Moo 1,
Thep Kasattri Rd,
Thalang, Phuket
Tel 0 76 328 088
Fax 0 76 328 068
golf@bluecanyonclub.com
www.bluecanyonclub.com
The club houses two challenging 18-hole courses which are situated among lagoons and rubber plantations. It is the site of important international golf tournaments and also has a golfer's lodge and an academy for novices.

LAGUNA PHUKET GOLF CLUB
34 Moo 4, Srisoonthorn Rd,
Cherng Talay, Phuket
Tel 0 76 324 350
Fax 0 76 324 351
golf@lagunaphuket.com
www.lagunaphuketgolf.com
This challenging 18-hole golf course designed by Max Wexler has lots of water hazards and sand traps set amidst coconut palms. Among its facilities is a pitching green, a driving range, a large putting green and a clubhouse.

PHUKET COUNTRY CLUB
80/1 Vichit Songkram Rd,
Kathu, Phuket
Tel 0 76 321 038–41
Fax 0 76 321 721
info@phuketcountryclub.com
www.phuketcountryclub.com
One of the best in Thailand, this golf club has both an 18-hole course and a 9-hole course. It has hosted national and international golf tournaments.

KOH PHI PHI

ZEAVOLA
Koh Phi Phi, Krabi
Tel 0 75 627 000
Fax 0 75 627 023
reservation@zeavola.com
www.zeavola.com
Rates: 16,000–29,000 baht
Features: Beach games, diving, spa, open-air en-suite showers.

An exquitsite boutique hotel of 48 all-suite thatched villas made entirely of wood on the northern tip of Ko Phi Phi Don, backing the rustic luxury with high-technology and refined service. Stylish Thai dining, a beachfront bar and large pool add to the appeal. One hour by speedboat from Phuket.

KOH SAMUI

PRACTICALITIES

TOURIST INFORMATION
TAT SAMUI
Tel 0 77 420 504
tatsamui@tat.or.th

TOURIST POLICE
Nathon
Tel 0 77 421 281
(emergencies 1155)

HOSPITAL
SAMUI INTERNATIONAL HOSPITAL
North Beach Rd, Nathon
Tel 0 77 422 272

POST OFFICE
POST OFFICE
Seaside Rd, Nathon
Open Mon–Fri 8.30am–4.30pm,
Sat–Sun 9am–12pm

ACCOMMODATIONS

Rates quoted are high season rack rates for a standard double room, though prices may well be lower in the off-season. Restaurant prices are for dinner for two without alcohol, except where noted.

ANANTARA BOPHUT KOH SAMUI
99/9 Bophut Bay
Tel 0 77 428 300–9
Fax 0 77 428 310
bophutsamui@anantara.com
www.anantara.com
Rates: $320–$800
Features: Yacht charters, sea kayak excursions, catamarans, wind surf classes, cocktail mixing class, Thai cooking class, traditional crafts class.
Located on Bophut beach, the resort's modern rooms are placed among leafy gardens. Furnishings are very Zen in lines, but Thai in ornateness and opulence. The Anantara Spa has private, glass-walled treatment areas enveloped by tranquil water gardens.

CENTARA GRAND BEACH RESORT SAMUI
38/2 Moo 3, Bophut,
Chaweng Beach
Tel 0 77 230 500
Fax 0 77 422 385
csbr@chr.co.th
www.centarahotelresorts.com
Rates: 8,900–19,500 baht
Features: Massage service.
Beachfront resort with rooms providing modern comforts. Lots of activities for sporty types; amenities include watersports and a dive center. Good facilities for children. Centara Spa has exceptional treatments. Zico's, a popular Brazilian grill, is one of its many restaurants.

FOUR SEASONS SAMUI
219 Moo 5 Laem Yai,
Koh Samui
Tel 0 77 243 000
Fax 0 77 243 002
www.fourseasons.com/kohsamui
Rates: $600–$3,300
Features: Kids club, elephant trekking, hiking, fishing, sailing, wind surfing, kite board, diving and other watersports.
Nestled in a remote hillside coconut grove or just off the beach, this exquisitely designed resort has 63 villas and residences with their own infinity pools, sculpted-bath and open-air dining spaces as an alternative to the teak Thai seafood restaurant. The spa has individual treatment rooms set in the jungle and a Thai-style yoga sala.

THE LIBRARY KOH SAMUI
14/1 Moo 2, Bophut,
Chaweng Beach
Tel 0 77 422 767
Fax 0 77 422 344
rsvn@thelibrary.co.th
www.thelibrary.co.th
Rates: $300–$500
An elegant minimalist structure set in a lush environment, this coastal heritage property made a big splash when it opened for its outstanding design and ecological sensitivity.

KAMALAYA KOH SAMUI
102/9 Moo 3, Laem Set Road
Tel 0 77 429 800
Fax 0 77 429 899
www.kamalaya.com
Rates: $190–$600
Wellness retreat and resort offers detox programmes, yoga and more. Centred around a monk's cave, Kamalaya is perfect for rejuvenation.

NAPASAI SAMUI, SPA & PRIVATE VILLAS
65/10 Ban Tai, Maenam
Tel 0 77 429 200
Fax 0 77 429 201
napasai@orient-express.com
www.napasai.com
Rates: $235–$890
Features: Spa and in-room spa services, beach sport facilities. A recent addition to the Orient-Express Hotels' selection of distinctive travel experiences. Small but very beautiful boutique resort with special cottages and villas designed for families, spa lovers and couples in search of romance. The Thai-style villas feature interiors lined with opulent local fabrics and tropical hardwoods. Large free-form infinity-edged pool provides wide, unobstructed views of the Gulf. Tall coconut trees and lush flowering plants frame the picture perfect surroundings.

RENAISSANCE KOH SAMUI RESORT & SPA
208/1 Moo 4 Maret, Lamai
Tel 0 77 429 300
Fax 0 77 429 333
www.marriott.com
Rates: 5,120–19,000 baht
Features: Excellent restaurants and Quan Spa.
Set in lush tropical gardens on the Laem Nan peninsula of Lamai Bay. Offers luxurious villas and spacious deluxe rooms with sea views.

LE ROYAL MERIDIEN BAAN TALING NGAM
295 Moo 3, Taling Ngam Beach
Tel 0 77 429 100
Fax 0 77 423 220
reservations@baan-taling-ngam.com
www.baan-taling-ngam.com
Rates: $300, $500 villas
Features: PADI diving school, 7 pools, watersports, catamarans. The hillside resort has a 1.5-mile long private beach. The Thai-style rooms open to wonderful views of the green surrounds and the Gulf of Thailand.

SILA EVASON HIDEAWAY & SPA IN SAMUI
9/10 Moo, Baan Plai Laem, Bophut
Tel 0 77 245 678
Fax 0 77 245 671
Reservation-samui@evasonhideaways.com
www.evasonhideaways.com
Rates: 21,900–140,000 baht

Features: Wine cellar, watersports, activities such as sunrise yoga, pilates, tai chi, Tibetan yoga. The Evason's stunning 66 villas are fashioned from tropical hardwoods and have spectacular ocean panoramas. Most villas are split-level with private infinity-edged pools and sundeck, each coming with personal butlers. Other standard features include sunken bathtubs, outdoor showers and daybeds. Holistic treatments are offered at the spa, which has four outdoor treatment salas.

TAMARIND RETREAT TROPICAL VILLAS
205/7 Moo 4, Thang Takian, Maret, on headland between Chaweng and Lamai
Tel 0 77 424 221
Fax 0 77 424 311
www.tamarindretreat.com
Rates: 3,600–10,900 baht
Features: Outdoor showers, full kitchens, organic breakfast, herbal steam sauna
Garden villas built around Samui's trademark boulders. One of a kind back-to-nature retreat with most hotel amenities intentionally omitted: no room service, TV, air conditioning, or restaurant. But fans are drawn by the villas' seamless incorporation into the grounds. Tamarind Springs is the island's best independent spa.

TONGSAI BAY VILLAS
84 Moo 5, Bophut
Tel 0 77 245 480–500
Fax 0 77 425 462
www.tongsaibay.co.th
Rates: 11,0000–70,500 baht
Features: non motorized watersports, cocktail party, tennis, scuba diving.
At this long-established retreat, the 83 units include 15 villas of 870-square foot, with wooden terrace, sunken bathtub, bar and gazebo with grand sea vistas. The teak bedroom is decorated with Thai materials. One villa is furnished with antiques, another has 270° view of the sea

DINING & NIGHTLIFE

Prices quoted are for dinner for two without alcohol, except where noted.

BETELNUT RESTAURANT
43/4, Moo 3, Chaweng Blvd
Tel 0 77 413 370

Fax 0 77 413 782
betelnut@betelnutsamui.com
www.betelnutsamui.com
Open daily 6pm–11pm
Small restaurant run by a Californian chef who fuses West Coast cuisine with Thai (2,000 baht).

THE MANGROVE
32/6, Moo 4, Airport Rd, Big Buddha Beach
Tel 0 77 427 584
the_mangrove@hotmail.com
Open daily (except last 3 days of the month) 5.30pm–9.30pm
One of the best dining venues, this French riverside restaurant overlooks mangroves and plantations. A La Rochelle native works the stoves here (1,600 baht).

THE MINT BAR
Soi Green Mango, Chaweng Beach
Tel 08 1082 4030
Open daily 9am–2am
This is a great party venue which attracts many big name DJs. The two-level club is airy and usually flocked with beautiful young people in the mood for some serious partying.

NOORI INDIA RESTAURANT & PUB
38/39, Moo 3, Chaweng Beach Rd
Tel 0 77 413 600
Open daily 11.30am–11.30pm
An established Indian restaurant with a reputation for good food and service (1,700 baht).

POPPIES
28/1, Moo 3, Chaweng Beach Rd
Tel 0 77 422 419
Fax 0 77 422 420
info@poppiessamui.com
www.poppiessamui.com
Open daily 6.30am–midnight, breakfast 6.30am–noon, lunch noon–4pm, dinner last order 11pm
Popular hotel restaurant serving European and Thai food on the beach and under the stars (2,500 baht).

SHOPPING

MALLS
CENTRAL SAMUI BEACH RESORT SHOPPING ARCADE
38/2 Moo 3, Bophut, Chaweng Beach
Tel 0 77 230 500

Fax 0 77 422 385
Open daily 11am–8pm
Arcade featuring all kinds of shops selling everything from bikinis and surfwear to bespoke suits and jewelry.

SHOPS
BEAUTIFUL WORLD
252/20, Moo 1, Tambon Maenam
Tel/Fax 0 77 447 030
Mobile 08 1956 0331
info@beautifulworldthailand.com
www.beautifulworldthailand.com
Open daily 9am–7pm
The eco-friendly shop is one of Samui's best sources for furniture, mostly made from Indian rosewood, teak, water hyacinth and mahogany.

NAGA PEARL SHOP
81/1, Moo 5, Taling Ngam
Tel 0 77 334 038
Open daily 10am–8pm
Sells cultured South Sea pearls harvested from their pearl farm on Koh Matsum. Bookable only via tour agencies.

WELLNESS

CHEDI SPA
155/60 Moo 2 Bophut, Chaweng Beach
Tel 0 77 422 787/8
Fax 0 77 422 790
chedispa@kohsamui.com
Stunning full-range spa with Thai pavilions set among lush gardens. Special treatments for the sunbaked.

ATTRACTIONS

TOURS & RECREATION
EASY DIVERS
18/8 Maenam Beach
Tel/Fax 0 77 427 398
info@thaidive.com
www.thaidive.com
This is a reputable company offering dive training and

excursions to Koh Samui, Koh Pha-ngan, Koh Tao, Koh Nang Yuan, Krabi, Chumphon and Koh Lanta.

PLANET SCUBA KOH SAMUI
Seatran Pier, Bophut, Chaweng
Tel 0 77334 038
sam@planetscuba.net
www.planet-scuba.net
Prestigious diving school set up in Samui and Koh Tao. Conducts progressive courses for divers who want to improve skills underwater or become professional instructors.

SITCA—SAMUI INSTITUTE OF THAI CULINARY ARTS
46/6 Moo 3, Chaweng Beach
Tel 0 77 413 172
Fax 077 413 434
info@sitca.net
www.sitca.net
Good Thai cooking school with courses such as vegetarian or budget cooking and 12-day intensive training for professionals. Classes in the morning and evening. Each student has his own cooking station for a true hands-on experience.

SIGHTS
ANG THONG NATIONAL MARINE PARK
145/1 Talat Lang Rd
Tel 077 286 025, 0 77 280 222
reserve@dnp.go.th
Admission: 400 baht, under-14s 200 baht

HIN LAD WATERFALLS
Rd 4172, 1.2 miles south of Nathon
Open daily 8am–5pm

NA MUANG WATERFALLS
Rd 4169, Samui
Open daily 9am–5pm

TEMPLES & SHRINES
WAT PRA YAI
Moo 4, Bophut
Tel 0 77 425 158
Open daily 8am–5pm

Photographer: Luca Invernizzi Tettoni, unless stated otherwise.
1 Son of King Rama V, Robert Lenz, c. 1890.
2 Elephant hunt at Ayutthaya, Robert Lenz, c. 1890.
3 Chao Phraya River, Robert Lenz, c. 1890.
Wat Arun gate, Robert Lenz, c. 1890.
4 Floating houses, Bangkok, Robert Lenz, c. 1890.
5 Phra Mongkol Bopit, Ayutthaya, photogravure from photograph taken by Martin Hürliman, from *Burma, Ceylon, Indo-China*, 1930.
8–16 Illustrators: Osman Asari, Seah Kam Chuan, Cheong Yim Mui, Manfred Winkler, Soong Ching Yee, Anuar Bin Abdul Rahim.
15 All photographs, except nest collection, by Lawrence Lim.
16 Page from manuscript on Thai military art, National Museum, Bangkok.
17 Thai people at Si Satchanalai, old photograph, c. 1900.
Siamese People, from H. Mouhot, *Travels in Siam, Cambodia and Laos 1858–60*, London, 1862.
Siamese woman, from *Guide to Bangkok*, Royal Railways, 1927.
Siamese man (center), Robert Lenz, c. 1890.
Northern Thai women at Chiang Mai, old photograph c. 1900.
Laotian girls, from H. Mouhot, *Travels in Siam, Cambodia and Laos 1855–60*, London, 1862.
Shan women, old photograph from Milne and Cochrane, *The Shans at Home*, London, 1910.
Muslim traders, mural painting in Wat Bowornivet, Bangkok.
Karen, from C. Bock, *Temples and Elephants*, London, 1883.
Lawa, old photograph, from E. Seidenfaden, *The Thai Peoples*, Bangkok Siam Society, 1967.
18 Hunting scene, cave painting from Khao Chan-Ngam, from *The Stone and Metal Ages in Thailand*, Bangkok, 1988.
Three-legged pot, from Ban Kao 2000 B.C., National Museum, Bangkok.
Ban Chiang bronze bracelets, Suan Pakkard Palace collection, Bangkok.
Drawing of a Ban Chiang pot.
Vishnu from Wiang Sa, National Museum, Bangkok.
Srivijaya votive tablet, National Museum, Bangkok.
Wheel of the Law, Dvaravati period, 7th century, National Museum, Bangkok.
Phimai Temple.
19 Elephant and soldiers, celadon ware, National Museum, Bangkok.
Monument to Ramkhamhaeng, Sukhothai Archeological Park.
Illustration from *The Romance of the Rose* by King Rama VI.
Gold rings, Ayutthaya period, National Museum, Ayutthaya.
Miniature gold fan, Ayutthaya period, National Museum, Ayutthaya.
Louis XIV receiving Thai ambassadors in Paris, in Chakri Throne Hall, Bangkok.
Rama IV, from Sir J. Bowring, *The Kingdom and People of Siam*, London, 1857.
Rama V and family, painting by Edoardo Gelli, 1899, Royal Palace, Bangkok.
20 Bodhi tree, lacquer on wood from Wat Pong Yangkok, Lampang Luang.
Buddha images, Wat Chamadevi, Lamphun.
Wat Ched Yod, Chiang Mai.
A Burmese prince (center), painting on wood, Seng Muang Ma, Lampang.
Detail of Lanna woodcarving.
Old walls of Chiang Mai, old photograph.
Last king of Chiang Mai, old photograph.
21 Rama VII in state, old photograph.
Rama VII entering Chiang Mai on an elephant, old photograph.
Field Marshal Pibul (left), from *The Bangkok Post*.
Dr Pridi Panomyong (right), from *The Bangkok Post*.
Siamese flags.
Portrait of King Ananda (Rama VIII).
Early portrait of King Bhumibol.
22 Postcard of Ananda Samakhom Throne Hall, c. 1915.
Contemporary stamps.
State opening of Parliament.
Rama VIII Bridge, photograph by Robert McLeod.
Technopolis Science Museum, photograph by Robert McLeod.
23 Bangkok SkyTrain, © Charlotte Shalgosky.
Bangkok SkyTrain station, photograph by Robert McLeod.
Page from astrology manuscript, 19th century, William Warren collection.
24 Old map, Michael Sweet, Antiques of the Orient, Singapore.
Stone Buddha head, late 18th century, National Museum, Lopburi.
Wheel of Law and deer, Dvaravati period, 7th century, National Museum, Bangkok.
Mural depicting the Buddha cutting his hair, Buddhaisawan Chapel, Bangkok.
Gold Buddha, Chao Sam Phraya National Museum, Ayutthaya.
Stone bodhi tree, Ayutthaya,17th century, National Museum, Bangkok.
Bronze Padmapani bodhisattva, Chaiya, 9th–10th century, National Museum, Bangkok.
Sandstone eight-armed bodhisattva, Prasat Muang Singh in Kanchanaburi, late 12th–early 13th century, National Museum, Bangkok.
Detail of mural from Wat Thong Thammachat, Bangkok.
Detail of mural from the Lacquer Pavilion, Suan Pakkard Palace, Bangkok.
25 Monk contemplating death, Robert Lenz, c. 1890.
The Buddha collecting alms, lacquer panel, Suan Pakkard Palace.
The Buddha in meditation, contemporary sculpture in Wat Thammakai, Bangkok.
Serenity, painting by Surasit Souakong, oil on canvas, © Visual Dhamma Art Gallery.
26 Flower arrangements.
27 Offerings and spirit houses.
Spirit house (top right), photograph by Alberto Cassio.
28 Elephant, carving on bullock cart.
Ivory tusks carved with the Buddha and other Buddhist motifs, Robert Lenz, c. 1890.
Elephant hunt in Pattani, engraving from *De Bree Voyages*, Frankfurt, 1607.
Page from treatise on elephant training showing capture of wild elephants, manuscript from the Second Reign, National Library, Bangkok.
Detail from 19th-century manuscript (top), National Library.
Elephant parade, old postcard.
Page from treatise on elephant training showing mythical elephants, manuscript from the Second Reign, National Library, Bangkok.
Page from a treatise on elephants showing a hunting scene, 19th century, National Library, Bangkok.
Howdahs, from Father G. Tachard, *Voyages de Siam des Pères Jésuites envoyés par le Roi aux Indes et à la Chine*, Paris, 1686.
White elephant, engraving, 19th century.
29 Royal oarsman.
Royal barges (center), c. 1900.
From manuscript showing royal barge procession, 19th century, National Library, Bangkok.
Royal barge, old postcard.
Royal barges (right), engravings, from Father G. Tachard, *Voyage de Siam des Pères Jésuites envoyés par le Roi aux Indes et à la Chine*, Paris, 1686.
Royal barges used in fighting, S. de la Loubère, *Du Royaume de Siam*, Paris, 1691.
30 Woman going to a festival (top right), detail from mural, Wat Bowornivet, Bangkok.
Women adorning themselves (center), detail from mural, Wat Suthat, Bangkok.
Woman wearing a jongkrabane, Robert Lenz, c. 1890.
Group of men wearing loin cloth, from 19th-century manuscript *The Pilgrimage to Saraburi*, National Library, Bangkok.
Farmer wearing a *mor hom*, cigarette card, c. 1930.
Men with cropped hair, from mural from Wat Phumin, Nan, late 19th century.
Laotian woman, from E. Seidenfaden, *The Thai Peoples*, 1967.
Tattoos, from C. Bock, *Temples and Elephants*, 1883.
31 Chakri crest, embroidery on silk, Royal Palace, Bangkok.
Rama VI on throne, old photograph.
Son of King Rama V, old photograph.
Royal prince, Robert Lenz, c. 1890.
Tonsure ceremony, Robert Lenz, c. 1890.
A mandarin, chromolithograph, from Sir J. Bowring, *The Kingdoms and People of Siam*, London, 1857.
Rama IV and Queen, old photograph
Rama V, painting on ceramic, Royal Palace, Bangkok.
Royal regalia, c. 1920.
Two of the wives of the King of Siam, from H. Mouhot, *Travels in Siam, Cambodia and Laos, 1855–60*, London, 1862.
32 Portrait of a monk, Robert Lenz, c.1890.
Monk in full robes, from Father G. Tachard, *Voyage de Siam des Pères Jésuites envoyés par le Roi aux Indes et à La Chine*, Paris, 1686.
Military costume, cigarette card, 1920–30.
Ceremonial costume, cigarette card, 1920–30.
Thais wearing "ambassador's hat" 19th-century engraving, from G. Ferrario, *Mondo Antico Orientale*, 1817, © White Lotus,Bangkok.
A mandarin, from S. de la Loubère, *Du Royaume de Siam*, Paris, 1691.
Ambassador's hat, National Museum, Lopburi.
Thai Ambassador's attire, 17th-century engraving, © White Lotus, Bangkok.
Thai ambassadors at Versailles, from Father G. Tachard, *Voyage de Siam des Pères Jésuites envoyés par le Roi aux Indes et à la Chine*, Paris, 1686.
33 Group of musicians, from mural painting, Wat Phra Keo
Ranad, National Museum, Bangkok.
Group of musicians, stucco relief, Dvaravati period, National Museum, Bangkok.
Khong Wong (center), National Museum, Bangkok.
Gong, National Museum, Bangkok.
Phipat orchestra, from F. A. Neale, *Narrative of a Residence at the Capital of the Kingdom of Siam*, London, 1852.
Chakhay, National Museum, Bangkok.
34 Mask, Bangkok Dolls.
Khon actors (center), © White Lotus, Bangkok.
Performance of *Ramakien*, from mural in the ordination pavilion of Rama V, Wat Benchamabopit, Bangkok.
Masks, Bangkok Dolls, Bangkok theatre, © White Lotus, Bangkok.
35 Manora dancers, old photograph.
Siamese rope-dancer, from H. Mouhot, *Travels in Siam, Cambodia and Laos 1858–60*, London, 1862.
Manora dancer, cigarette card, 1920–30, two pictures.
Dancers (center), Robert Lenz, c. 1890.
Lakhon performance, detail from mural, Wat Bowornivet, Bangkok.
36 Thai puppets.
37 Takraw, from F.A. Neale, *Narrative of a Residence at the Capital of the Kingdom of Siam*, London, 1852.
Thai kites, detail from mural, Wat Phra Singh, Chiang Mai.
Thai boxing from manuscript on Thai martial arts, National Museum, Bangkok.
Thai boxing, woodcarving on ox cart.
38 Plowing ceremony, from mural at Wat Mongkut, 19th century, Bangkok.
Portrait of Rama IX realized in flowers.
Rocket festival, candle festival, Songkran festival and the making of miniature sand chedis, four paintings on wood, by Panya Vijinthanasarn, Thai pavilion at World Expo, Australia, 1988.
Loy Krathong festival, traditional Thai painting, © Visual Dhamma Art Gallery, Bangkok.
39 Illustrations by Paul Yip.
40 Food.
Dry spices (bottom right), photograph by Alberto Cassio.
41 Preparation of Thai meal.
Siamese ladies at dinner, from H. Mouhot, *Travels in Siam, Cambodia and Laos, 1855–60*, London, 1862.
42 Thai fruits and sweets.
43 Page from old manuscript, National Museum, Bangkok.
Wrapped manuscript, National Museum, Bangkok.
Ruins of a pagoda at Ayutthaya, from H. Mouhot, *Travels in Siam, Cambodia and Laos 1858–60*, London, 1862.
44–51 Illustrators: Bruce Granquist, Kittisak Nualvilai.
51 Royal barges, © White Lotus, Bangkok.
52 Royal barges, © White Lotus, Bangkok.
Royal Elephant, from S. de la Loubère, *Du Royaume de Siam*, Paris, 1691.
Map of Ayutthaya, © Cabinet des Estampes, Paris.
Views of the observatory (two), © Cabinet des Estampes, Paris.
53 All paintings by Arunothai, private collection, Bangkok.
54 From murals in Viharn Laikam, Wat Phra Singh, Bangkok.
55 From murals by Khrua In Khong, Wat Bowornivet, Bangkok.
56 Chromolithographs, by E. Hildebrandt, collection of A. Duchauffour, Paris.
57 All paintings, G. Chini, © Chini family.
58 Illustration from *Romance in the Harem*, A. Leonowens, 1870.
59 Map from *A Suma Oriental of Tomes Pires*, Hakluyt Society, London, 1944.
The French ambassadors received at Ayutthaya, from Father Guy Tachard, *Voyage de Siam des Pères Jésuites envoyés par le Roi aux Indes et à La Chine*, Paris, 1686.
Siamese woman, from S. de la Loubère, *Du Royaume de Siam*, Paris, 1691.
60 Temple layout, from S. de la Loubère, *Du Royaume de Siam*, Paris, 1691.
The Queen of Pattani, from *De Bree Voyages*, Frankfurt, 1607, © White Lotus, Bangkok.
61 Audience with the King of Siam, from Father G. Tachard, *Voyage de Siam des Pères Jésuites envoyés par le Roi aux Indes et à la Chine*, Paris, 1686.
Portraits of Thai ambassadors,17th-century engravings, © Cabinet des Estampes, Paris.
Map of Ayutthaya, collection of A. Duchauffour, Paris.
62 Sketches from C. Buls, *Croquis Siamois*, Brussels, 1901, (two).
Book cover of *An Asian Arcady*, R. Le May, Cambridge.
63 Illustration from F. A. Neale, *Narrative of a Residence at the Capital of the Kingdom of Siam*, London, 1852.
King Mongkut (Rama IV) receiving foreign ambassadors, oil on canvas, Royal Palace, Bangkok.
Floating houses, Bangkok, Robert Lenz, c. 1890.
64 Illustration from F. A. Neale, *Narrative of a Residence at the Capital of the Kingdom of Siam*, London, 1852.
Seals of the King of Siam, Sir J. Bowring, *The Kingdom and People of Siam*, London, 1857.
Wat Arun, Robert Lenz, c. 1890.
65 Book cover of *Rice without Rain*, Minfong Ho, Times Books International, Singapore, 1986.
Sketch from C. Buls, *Croquis Siamois*, Brussels, 1901.
66 Temple entrance, from C. Buls, *Croquis Siamois*, Brussels, 1901.
Mekong, watercolor from *Peeps at Many Lands – Siam*, London, 1910
67–70 All photographs © Photobank except for 67 top left (Jeff Hutchens), 67 middle left (Ben Simmons), and 67 middle right (Dow Wasiksiri).
68 Kata Yai beach, Alberto Cassio.
70 View across Bangkok to the Golden Mount.
71–157 Illustrators: Julian Davison, Bruce Granquist, Anuar Bin Abdul Rahim.
72 Detail of mural, from Wat Rajapradit, Bangkok, 1864.
Wat Arun, Robert Lenz, c. 1890.

Rama I, Royal Palace.
Floating house, old photogravure, Robert Lenz, c. 1890.
Floating house, Robert Lenz, c. 1890.
73 New Road, Bangkok, Robert Lenz, c. 1890.
River scene, painting by Khrua In Khong, Bangkok.
Rickshaw, old photograph, 1927.
Tram, painting by Arunothai, private collection.
Chinatown, old photograph, 1950.
74 Garuda, wood carving, early 19th century, Neold Collection.
Pavilion containing the ashes of the late King of Siam in the gardens attached to the palace at Bangkok, from H. Mouhot, *Travels in Siam, Cambodia and Laos 1858–60*, London, 1862.
Phra Thinang Aphonphimok Prasat, Grand Palace, Bangkok.
King Rama V alighting at the Phra Thinang Aphonphimok Prasat, old photograph, c. 1900.
Grand Palace walls.
Phra Thinang Busbok Mala throne, Grand Palace, Bangkok.
Topiary.
75 Royal Palace, from A. Leonowens, *The English Governess at the Siamese Court*, 1870.
Audience Hall of the Chakri Maha Prasat, Bangkok.
Queen Sowabha Phongsri, Robert Lenz, c. 1890.
Women guards of the Inner Palace, from Marquis de Beauvoir, *Java-Siam-Canton*, Paris, 1869.
Tonsure ceremony, from H. Mouhot, *Travels in Siam, Cambodia and Laos 1858–60*, London, 1862.
Chakri Throne Hall, Robert Lenz, c. 1900.
76 Emerald Buddha, Grand Palace, Bangkok.
Detail of a mural, Wat Phra Keo, Bangkok.
Statues of Chakri kings, Prasat Phra Thep Bidom, Grand Palace, Bangkok.
77 Mythological creatures: *yaksa, kinnon* and *kinnari* (top, bottom left and bottom right), Grand Palace, Bangkok.
Scene from a mural from Wat Phra Keo, showing

the army crossing the sea over Hanuman's body.
Replica of Angkor Wat, Wat Phra Keo, Bangkok.
78 Chinese stone figures (top left and bottom left), Wat Po, Bangkok.
Wat Po, Robert Lenz, c. 1890, two pictures.
Wat Po, chromo-lithograph, *Guide to Bangkok/Siam*, Royal State Railways of Siam, 1927.
Stone Rishi figure, Wat Po, Bangkok.
Massage techniques, detail from mural, Wat Po, Bangkok.
79 Reclining Buddha, from Marquis de Beauvoir, *Java-Siam-Canton*, Paris, 1869.
Marble engraved panels showing scenes from *Ramakien*, Wat Po, Bangkok.
Walking Buddha, Sukhothai period, 14th century, Wat Benchamabopit, Bangkok.
Buddha Maravijaya, Lanna School, 14th century.
Buddha in royal attire, Ayutthaya period, late 17th century.
Ivory Buddha, late 19th century.
Standing Buddha, bronze and enamel, early 19th century.
83 Wat Mahathat, Bangkok.
Pig statue, Bangkok.
Lak Muang, Bangkok.
Wat Rajapradit, Bangkok.
Detail from a mural, Wat Rajapradit, Bangkok.
84 All photographs by Robert McLeod.
Khao San Road.
The National Gallery.
Riverside walkway at Santichaiprakarn Park.
October 14th Monument.
King Prajadiphok Museum.
Phra Sumen Fort.
81 All images from the National Museum, Bangkok.
Stone Bodhisattva Avalokitesvara, 6th–7th century.
Stone Vishnu, 8th–9th century.
Bronze image of Siva, Sukhothai period.
Sukhothai horseman , 14th–15th century.
Mural painting (center), Bangkok School.
Stucco *yaksa* and head, 9th century.
Thepanom glazed stoneware, 14th–15th century.
Terra cotta praying deities, Sukhothai

period.
Detail from a mural, Bangkok School.
Duck-shaped water vessel, 14th–15th century.
Lanna bronze elephant, 1575.
82 All images from the National Museum, Bangkok, except where indicated otherwise.
Stone Buddha, Lopburi School.
Stucco Buddha head, 8th century.
Lacquered and gilded bronze Buddha, 14th century.
Buddha image from Lopburi, 7th–14th century.
Detail of mural showing casting of Buddha images, Wat Bowornivet, Bangkok.
80 Seal of the Second King, from Sir J. Bowring, *The Kingdom and People of Siam*, London, 1857.
Sanam Luang.
The Second King, from F. Vincent, *The Land of the White Elephant*, New York, 1874.
Palace of the Second King, now National Museum, Robert Lenz, c. 1890.
Watercolor of Sanam Luang with rickshaw, from *Peeps at Many Lands – Siam*, London, 1910.
Buddhaisawan Chapel, National Museum.
Amulets sold in the street.
Stone Buddha seated in Western fashion, Dvaravati period, National Museum.
Bronze image of Siva, Sukhothai period, National Museum.
85 Body left to the vultures, Wat Saket, old photograph, © White Lotus, Bangkok.
The Golden Mount, Robert Lenz, c. 1890.
Wat Saket, 19th-century engraving, © White Lotus, Bangkok.
Library window, Wat Saket, Bangkok.
City walls, Robert Lenz, c. 1890.
Lohaprasad, Wat Rajanadda, Bangkok.
86 Statue of sailor, Wat Suthat, Bangkok.
Statue of horse, Wat Suthat, Bangkok.
The giant swing, old

photograph, © White Lotus, Bangkok.
Wat Suthat.
Cemetery, Wat Rajabopit, Bangkok.
Wat Rajabopit, Robert Lenz, c. 1890.
Wat Rajabopit.
87 Floating houses, Chao Phraya, Bangkok, Robert Lenz, c. 1890.
Chao Phraya River, Bangkok, Robert Lenz, c. 1890.
Chao Phraya ferries, Bangkok.
88 Old guidebook to Wat Arun, 1920.
Wat Arun, Bangkok.
Memorial Bridge, Bangkok, old photograph.
Ho Phra Trai Pidok Library, Wat Rakhang, Bangkok.
Pak Klong Talaad market, Robert Lenz, c. 1890.
Wang Lee House, Bangkok
89 View of the port of Bangkok, from H. Mouhot, *Travels in Siam, Cambodia and Laos 1858–60*, London, 1862.
French Embassy, Bangkok, photograph by Robert McLeod.
Oriental Hotel, Bangkok, painting on canvas.
Robert Hunter's house, from F. A. Neale, *Narrative of a Residence at the Capital of the Kingdom of Siam*, London, 1852.
Church of the Immaculate Conception, Bangkok.
Detail from a mural in the Ordination Pavilion of King Rama V, Wat Benchamabopit, Bangkok.
Siamese twins, old photograph.
90 Boats along Bangkok klongs, watercolor by E. A. Norbury, from *Peeps at Many Lands – Siam*, London, 1910.
Hong yao boat, Bangkok.
Royal barges, Bangkok.
Klong vendor on boat, Bangkok.
Life along the klongs, Bangkok, old postcard.
Mural painting showing elephant, Wat Suwannaram, Bangkok.
91 Lion dance painting, Bangkok.
Vendor, Paul Bonnetain, *L'extrême Orient*, Paris, 1887.
Opium smoker, Paul Bonnetain, *L'extrême Orient*, Paris, 1887.

photograph, © White Lotus, Bangkok.
Wat Suthat.
Interior of bot, Wat Suthat, Bangkok.
Candles lighting a shrine, Wat Mangkon Malawat, Bangkok.
Vegetarian offerings.
92 Ceiling of Ananda Samakhom Throne Hall.
Ananda Samakhom Throne Hall.
Trooping the colors, Bangkok.
Vimarn Mek Palace, Bangkok.
Phya Thai Palace, Bangkok, old photograph.
Window of Wat Benchamabopit, Bangkok.
Wat Benchamabopit, Bangkok.
93 Tuk-tuk, three wheeled vehicle, Bangkok.
Baiyoke Tower, © Charlotte Shalgosky.
Baiyoke Tower from street level, photograph by Robert McLeod.
Night life in Patpong, Bangkok.
Paddle boats in Lumpini Park lake, Bangkok.
Erawan Shrine, Bangkok.
94 Drawing room of Jim Thompson's house, Bangkok.
Lacquered panel in Lacquer Pavilion, Bangkok.
Kukrit Pramoj's house, Bangkok, photograph by Robert McLeod.
Siam Society building, Bangkok, old photograph.
Kamthieng House, Bangkok.
95 Silver boxes.
Figure of market vendor with baskets.
Plant market, Bangkok.
Sidewalk vendor's stall, Bangkok.
Interior of Jim Thompson's Thai silk shop, Bangkok.
Market in Bangkok, old postcard, c. 1900.
96 Floating market boats, Bangkok.
Floating market, Damnern Saduak, Bangkok.
Dvaravati stucco head from Chula Pathon, Nakhon Pathom, 8th century, National Museum, Bangkok.
Water jars, Ratchaburi, photograph by Alberto Cassio.
Phra Pathom Chedi, Nakhon Pathom.
Mural painting from ordination pavilion

Yaowarat Road, Bangkok, photograph by Robert McLeod
97 River Kwai, Kanchanaburi.
Erawan Falls, Erawan National Park, Kanchanaburi.
Train on railway line to Burma, from H. V. Clarke, *A Life for Every Sleeper*, Allen and Unwin, 1986.
Tomb of the Unknown Soldier, Kanchanaburi.
River Kwai Bridge, from H. V. Clarke, *A Life for Every Sleeper*, Allen and Unwin, 1986.
98 Muang Boran Ancient City.
Temple garden, Ancient City.
Welcome sign, Pattaya.
Crocodile Farm, Samut Prakarn.
Pattaya beach (two).
99 Gemstones.
Chantaburi from H. Mouhot, *Travels in Siam, Cambodia and Laos 1858–60*, London, 1862.
Koh Chang Island.
Beach scene, Rayong
Kata beach.
100 Phetchaburi.
Mural painting of Khao Wang by Khrua In Khong, Wat Maha Samanaram, Phetchaburi.
101 Mural of Wat Maha Samanaram by Khrua In Khong, Wat Bowornivet, Bangkok
Mural painting, Wat Yai Suwannaram, Phetchaburi.
Wat Mahathat, Phetchaburi
Stone walls, Wat Khamphaeng Laeng.
Temple mural, Phetchaburi.
Khao Luang, from H. Mouhot, *Travels in Siam, Cambodia and Laos 1858–60*, London, 1862.
102 Hua Hin.
Railway Hotel, Hua Hin, old post card.
Pineapple harvest, Hua Hin.
Phraya Nakhon Cave, Khao Sam Roi Yot National Park, Hua Hin.
Rama VII in exile in England, old photograph.
Prachuab Khiri Khan temple, photograph by Alberto Cassio.
103 Bodhisattva Avalokitesvara, bronze, National Museum, Bangkok.
Wat Mahathat Chaiya, Chaiya (center).
Along the river at

of King Rama V, Wat Benchamabopit.
Ranong, from F. A. Neale, *Narrative of a Residence at the Capital of the Kingdom of Siam*, London, 1852.
Foreigner in meditition at Wat Suan Mok.
104 Fish at a market, Koh Samui.
Islanders, Koh Samui.
Seashells.
105 Big Buddha at Koh Fan Wat, Koh Samui.
Bophut beach.
Motor vehicles for hire, Nathon, Koh Samui.
Shells.
Overlap Stone, Koh Samui.
Chaweng beach, Koh Samui.
Monkey collecting coconuts, Koh Samui.
Hin Ta and Hin Yai, Koh Samui.
106 Koh Pha-ngan, photograph by Alberto Cassio.
Koh Tao, two photographs by Alberto Cassio.
Viharn Luang, Wat Mahathat, Nakhon Si Thammarat.
Detail from furnishings of a royal barge for King Rama V, Nakhon Si Thammarat, National Museum.
Vishnu figure from Takua Pa, Nakhon Si Thammarat, National Museum.
Vishnu figure from Takua Pa, Nakhon Si Thammarat, old photograph.
Scenes of Wat Mahathat, from H. Warrington Smyth, *Five Years in Siam, from 1891-6*, London, 1898.
107 Nang Talung, shadow puppet.
Old gate of Songkhla, old photograph.
Chinese mansion, Songkhla Museum.
Decorations from southern boats.
Southern coastline, from F. A. Neale, *Narrative of a Residence at the Capital of the Kingdom of Siam*, London, 1862.
Muslims in Pattani.
108 Door motif of old Chinese house, Phuket.
Front of old Chinese house, Phuket.
109 Fishing boats, Phuket.
Street scene, Phuket.
Fishing at Phuket.
Sailboat, Phuket.
Put Jaw Temple, Phuket.
Vegetarian festival, Phuket.
Wat Phra Thong, Phuket.
Statue of smoking monk, Wat Chalong.

110 Patong beach, Phuket.
Skewered prawns.
Patong night life, Phuket.
Seafood, Phuket.
Karon beach, Phuket.
Kata beach, Phuket.
Nai Han beach, Phuket.
Laem Phrom Thep, Phuket.
111 Rubber plantation, Phuket.
Tapping rubber, Phuket.
Shell, Phuket.
Pearl farm, Koh Nakha Noi, Phuket.
Koh Similan National Park, two photographs by Alberto Cassio.
Beach, Phuket.
112 Phang-nga Bay, two pictures.
Limestone cave, Phang-nga Bay.
113 Phang-nga National Park.
Koh Pannyi, Phang-nga Bay.
114 Phi Phi Islands.
Koh Phi Phi Le.
Ton Sai Bay, Koh Phi Phi Don.
Viking Cave, Koh Phi Phi Le.
Cave containing birds' nests, Koh Phi Phi Le.
115 Krabi, with traditional sailing boat.
Oil palm plantation, Krabi (center).
Beaches on Krabi and the offshore islands, five photographs by Alberto Cassio.
116 Ba Kan Tiang Beach, Koh Lanta, © Charlotte Shalgosky.
Shells.
Ban Chiang pottery, Suan Pakkard collection, Bangkok.
117 The gate of Korat.
Traditional implements used in making silk, from H. Hallett, *A Thousand Miles on an Elephant in the Shan States*, London, 1890.
Mudmee silk-making.
Northeastern ox cart, from *Peeps at Many Lands – Siam*, London, 1910.
Ban Chiang vase, Suan Pakkard Palace collection, Bangkok.
Elephant roundup, Surin.
118 Prasat Phanom Wan.
Buddha images, Prasat Phanom Wan.
119 Stone statue of Jayavarman VII, National Museum, Bangkok.
East elevation of Prasat Hin Phimai Temple (top and main drawing).
Floor plan of Prasat Hin Phimai Temple.
120 Sandstone figure of female deity, Baphuon

style, National Museum, Bangkok.
Prasat Phanom Rung.
Lintel detail from Prasat Phanom Rung.
Khao Phra Viharn, side elevation.
Prasat Hin Sikhoraphum.
Prasat Muang Tham.
121 Life along the Mekong river, 19th-century engravings (two), © White Lotus, Bangkok.
Mekong fishing boats.
Paddleboat.
Wat Phra That Phanom.
122 Khao Yai forest, photograph by Alberto Cassio.
Monkeys playing with a crocodile, from H. Mouhot, *Travels in Siam, Cambodia and Laos 1858–60*, London, 1862.
Khao Yai National Park landscape.
Elephants drinking, Nam Nao National Park.
Hornbill.
Gibbon.
Phu Kradung, © Photobank.
123 Leopard fur.
Attacking a rhinoceros, from H. Mouhot, *Travels in Siam, Cambodia and Laos 1858–60*, London, 1862.
Detail from manuscript on elephant training, 19th century, National Library, Bangkok.
Standing Buddha in *abhaya mudra* (absence of fear), 13th - 14th century, Chao Sam Phraya, National Museum, Ayutthaya.
124 Bracelets and sword in gold, National Museum, Ayutthaya.
Sitting Buddha, Phra Mongkol Bopit, Ayutthaya, Robert Lenz, c. 1890.
Paintings in the crypt of Wat Raja Burana.
125 Ruins of Ayutthaya (Wat Phra Si Sanphet), from H. Mouhot, *Travels in Siam, Cambodia and Laos 1858—60*, London, 1862.
Ruins of a pagoda at Ayutthaya (Wat Phra Ram), from H. Mouhot, *Travels in Siam, Cambodia and Laos 1858--60*, London, 1862.
Map of Ayutthaya, 17th century, © White Lotus, Bangkok.
Wat Chai Wattanaram.
Reclining Buddha, Wat Yai Chai Mongkol.
Elephant corral, Robert Lenz, c. 1890.
Gilded bronze Buddha in royal attire, late 17th

century, Chantarakasem Museum.
126 Klong scene.
Building a Thai house.
Rice barges, Chao Phraya.
Buddha, Wat Phai Rong Rua.
Aisawan Tippaya Asna pavilion at Bang Pa-In.
127 Map of Lopburi, © White Lotus, Bangkok.
Exterior of palace of King Narai, Lopburi.
Interior of palace of King Narai, Lopburi.
two views, from G. Ferrario, *Mondo Antico Orientale*, 1817, © White Lotus, Bangkok.
Receiving French Embassies, from Father G. Tachard, *Voyage de Siam des Pères Jésuites envoyés par le Roi aux Indes et à la Chine*, Paris, 1686.
Wat Phra Sam Yot.
Detail from a gilded cabinet showing the Buddha's footprint, early 19th century, National Museum, Bangkok.
128 Wat Phra Keo, Khamphaeng Phet.
Wat Phra Sri Iriyabot, old photograph.
Phom Phet Fort, Khamphaeng Phet.
Standing Buddha, Wat Phra Si Iriyabot, old photograph, c. 1950, National Library, Bangkok.
Chedi, Sukhothai, old photograph, c. 1910.
Votive tablet with image of the walking Buddha, National Museum, Bangkok.
Wat Si Chum, old photograph, c. 1950, National Library, Bangkok.
Loy Krathong Festival, Sukhothai.
129 Stucco decoration from Wat Mahathat, National Museum, Sukhothai.
Inscription of King Ramkhamhaeng, National Museum, Bangkok.
Wat Mahathat, Sukhothai.
Restoration of Wat Mahathat, Bangkok National Library.
Buddha Maravijaya, National Museum, Bangkok.
130 Wat Sri Sawai, Sukhothai.
Wat Sra Si, Sukhothai.
Panel showing the Buddha's descent from heaven, Wat Trapang Thong Lang, Sukhothai.

Lotus-bud chedi, Wat Trapang Ngern, Sukhothai.
Stucco decoration, Sukhothai, National Museum.
Engraving on stone slabs showing Jataka tales, Wat Si Chum, Sukhothai.
Wat Phra Phai Luang, Sukhothai.
131 Wat Chang Lom, Si Satchanalai.
Sukhothai pottery, private collection.
Plate with fish motif, private collection, Bangkok.
Wat Phra Si Ratana Mahathat, old photograph.
132 Replica of Phra Buddha Chinaraj, Wat Benchamabopit, Bangkok.
Temple in Phitsanulok, old photograph.
Floating houses, Phitsanulok.
Cloister of Wat Mahathat, Phitsanulok.
Ruins of viharn and main prang, Wat Mahathat, Phitsanulok.
Chiang Mai boy at Loy Krathong parade.
134 Chiang Mai princess, old photograph, late 19th century.
King Rama VII entering Chiang Mai.
Old market, Chiang Mai, from R. Le May, *An Asian Arcady*, White Lotus, Bangkok, 1986.
Chiang Mai today.
Chiang Mai in the 1940's, old photograph.
Street scene, Chiang Mai.
Nawarat Bridge, Chiang Mai, old photograph.
135 Ping river, Chiang Mai, two pictures.
Three Kings Monument, Chiang Mai, © EJ Haas. All Rights Reserved.
Akha women and other hilltribe vendors at the Night Bazaar, Chiang Mai, © EJ Haas. All Rights Reserved.
Chiang Mai City Arts and Cultural Center, Chiang Mai, © EJ Haas. All Rights Reserved.
Sculpture at the Chiang Mai University Art Museum, Chiang Mai, © EJ Haas, 2004. All Rights Reserved.
140 Golden Chedi, Wat Phra That Doi Suthep.
Doi Inthanon National Park (center).
A Red Lahu (Nahu Nyi) hilltribe man weaving a bamboo basket, Chiang Mai, © EJ Haas, 2004. All Rights Reserved.
West wing of Chiang Mai National Museum building, Chiang Mai,

© Oliver Hargreave.
136 Wat Phra Sing, aerial view, c.1930.
Wat Phra Sing, Chiang Mai.
Wat Phra Sing mural painting, Chiang Mai.
Phra Buddha Sing, Wat Phra Sing.
Wat Chedi Luang, Chiang Mai.
Ornate woodcarving.
Chedi of Wat Puak Hong.
Door of Wat Chiang Man.
Mengrai image, Wat Mengrai.
Singhas, Wat Saen Fang.
137 New Year flags, Chiang Mai.
Mural detail, Wat Bua Krok Luang, Chiang Mai.
Paper lanterns, Chiang Mai.
Detail of stucco deity, 15th century, Wat Ched Yod.
Mural detail, Wat Phra Sing, Chiang Mai.
Chedi of Wat Kutao, photogravure from an old photograph by Martin Hürliman from *Burma, Ceylon, Indo-China*, 1930.
Wat Suan Dok, Chiang Mai.
138 Detail of cloth.
Wooden statues, Chiang Mai crafts.
Animal woodcarvings, Chiang Mai crafts.
Potter, Chiang Mai.
Lacquerware, Chiang Mai.
Umbrellas, Bor Sang.
Detail of cloth.
Silversmiths, Chiang Mai.
Betel boxes, Banyen Folk Art Museum, Chiang Mai.
139 Thai festival.
Flower festival, Chiang Mai.
Lanna temple decorations, nine pictures.
Handmade lacquerware tray from Living Space, Chiang Mai, © EJ Haas, 2002. All Rights Reserved.
A modern take on old Lanna-style rooms, © Brent T. Madison / www. MadisonImages.com
141 Woodcarving from Wat Pratu Pong, Lampang.
Lacquer painting from Wat Sri Chum, Lampang.
Burmese girl, Robert Lenz, c. 1890.
Wat Chedi Sao, Lampang.
Decoration, Wat Phra That Lampang Luang.
Phra Keo Don Tao jasper image, Wat Phra That Lampang Luang, Lampang.
Elephant trekking at the Elephant Conservation Center, Lampang, ©

Mai Chom Thong Highway.
Chedi of Wat Si Chom Thong, 15th century.
141 Wat Phra That Haripunchai, aerial photograph.
Terra cotta, Lamphun Museum.
World's largest gong, Wat Phra That Haripunchai, photogravure from old photograph by Martin Hürliman, from *Burma, Ceylon, Indo-China*, 1930.
Chedi of Wat Phra That Haripunchai.
Wat Chamadevi (Ku Kut), Lamphun, photogravure from old photograph by Martin Hürliman, from *Burma, Ceylon, Indo-China*, 1930.
Wat Chedi Liem.
Ruins of Wiang Kum Kam.
142 Lampang temples, from C. Bock, *Temples and Elephants*, London, 1883.
Lampang women at festival.
Horse-drawn cart, Lampang.
Shophouses, Talat Kao, Lampang.
143 Mosaic ceiling, Lampang.
Wat Phra Keo Don Tao, Lampang.
Buddha image, Phra Chao Thong Tip, Wat Phra Keo Don Tao, Lampang.
Wiang Luang Lakon Festival parade, Lampang, two pictures.
Detail of mural, Wat Seng Muang Ma, Lampang.
Lanna-style viharn of Wat Hua Kuang, Lampang.
Mondop of Wat Pongsanuk Tai, Lampang.
Stucco deity, Ku Ya Sudha, Lampang, 15th century.
141 Woodcarving from Wat Pratu Pong, Lampang.
Lacquer painting from Wat Sri Chum, Lampang.
Burmese girl, Robert Lenz, c. 1890.
Wat Chedi Sao, Lampang.
Decoration, Wat Phra That Lampang Luang.
Phra Keo Don Tao jasper image, Wat Phra That Lampang Luang, Lampang.
Elephant trekking at the Elephant Conservation Center, Lampang, ©

Brent T. Madison / www. MadisonImages.com
Chedi of Wat Si Chom Thong, 15th century.
Tableware with distinctive chicken motif, Lampang.© EJ Haas, 2004. All Rights Reserved.
145 Bot of Wat Phra That Lampang Luang, Lampang.
Detail of gilded *ku*, Wat Phra That Lampang Luang, Lampang.
146 Wat Phumin, Nan.
Phrae Market, from R. Le May, *An Asian Arcady*, © White Lotus, Bangkok, 1966.
Khamu, from E. Seidenfaden, *The Thai Peoples*, Bangkok Siam Society, 1967.
Boat race, Nan.
Interior detail, Wat Phumin, Nan.
Naga Makara – serpent stairway, Wat Phra That Chae Haeng, Nan.
147 Karens, Mae Sariang.
Shan-style old teak mansion, Pai, Mae Hong Son, © Brent T. Madison / www.Madison Images.com
Lush hills and waterfalls in Doi Inthanon, two pictures © Rachot Visalarnkul.
Stalagmites at Tham Lot, Mae Hong Son, © Oliver Hargreave.
Rice paddies, Pai, © Brent T. Madison / www. MadisonImages.com
Pong Duet hot springs, Huay Nam Dang, © Oliver Hargreave.
Looking east towards Chiang Dao from Kup Kap, Chiang Mai, © EJ Haas, 2000. All Rights Reserved.
148 Stucco temple decoration, Mae Sariang.
Dawn view east over the Mae Taeng Valley from Huay Nam Dang, © Oliver Hargreave.
Giant Singha, Wat Phra That Doi Kong Mu.
Shan man, from C. Bock, *Temples and Elephants*, London, 1883.
149 Mae Hong Son.
Wat Phra That Doi Kong Mu, Mae Hong Son. Shan.
Loy Krathong Festival, Mae Hong Son.
Wat Phu Wiang, Mae Hong Son.
Wat Phra Non, Mae Hong Son.
Temple decoration.
Wat Chong Kam and Wat Chong Klang, Mae Hong Son.

150 Orchid farm, Mae Rim. *Vanda rothschildiana* orchid.
Elephant-training camp, Mae Sa Valley.
Stamps.
Buddha images in Chiang Dao Caves.
Northerner, and farmhouses, two pictures from C. Bock, *Temples and Elephants*, London, 1883.
151 Kok River, Chiang Rai.
Yao woman, Chiang Rai.
Northern landscape.
Wat Rong Khun, Chiang Rai, two pictures © Oliver Hargreave.
152 Lahus, from H. Hallett, *A Thousand Miles on an Elephant in the Shan States*, London, 1890.
Hmong child.
Akhas at New Year Festival.
Akha attire, old postcard.
Karen dress, old post-card. Karen.
153–155 Except where indicated, all photographs by Mayer-Lipton Hilltribe Collection, from *Peoples of the Golden Triangle*, Thames and Hudson, 1984.
153 Woman embroiderer, Heini Schneebeli.
Woman's outfit.
Embroidered saddlecloth.
Wooden ancestor figure used in Yao ritual.
Silver ornament.
Painting depicting Taoist pantheon, 1880.
154 Embroidered boy's jacket (bottom left).
Blue Hmong woman's burial clothes.
Lock-shaped silver pendant.
Embroidered collar pieces (five).
155 Silver spiral bracelets (three).
Akha woman's headdress.
Silver chain with pendants.
Silver neck rings (two).
Silver pipes.
Silver containers for tobacco or betel nuts.
156 Recently discovered Chiang Saen image.
Wat Phra That Chom Kitti, Chiang Saen (two).
Chiang Saen street scene.
157 Akha village, Doi Mae Salong.
Saa paper making at Mae Fah Luang Foundation,

© Charlotte Shalgosky.
Doi Tung Royal Villa Gardens, Chiang Rai, © Rachot Visalarnkul.
Opium poppy.
Opium smokers, from F.A. Neale, *Narrative of a Residence at the Capital of the Kingdom of Siam*, London, 1858.

Illustrators

Contents page:
Osman Asari, Cheong Yim-Mui, Soong Ching-Yee, Anuar Bin Abdul Rahim.

Nature :
9 : Osman Asari, Anuar Bin Abdul Rahim.
10 : Osman Asari, Anuar Bin Abdul Rahim.
11 : Cheong Yim-Mui, Soong Ching-Yee, Anuar Bin Abdul Rahim.
12 : Manfred Winkler, Anuar Bin Abdul Rahim.
13 : Seah Kam-Chuan, Anuar Bin Abdul Rahim.
14 : Jimmy Chan, Cheong Yim-Mui, Anuar Bin Abdul Rahim.
15 : Soong Ching-Yee, Anuar Bin Abdul Rahim.
16 : Soong Ching-Yee, Anuar Bin Abdul Rahim.

Arts and traditions:
26, 37 : Anuar Bin Abdul Rahim.
39 : Paul Yip.

Architecture :
Bruce Granquist
Kittisak Nualvilai

Itineraries :
180, 184, 203, 212 : Anuar Bin Abdul Rahim.
232 : Julian Davison.
233 : Julian Davison, Tan Tat Ghee.
235 : Tan Tat Ghee.

Maps:
Anuar Bin Abdul Rahim : 71, 87, 104, 108, 112, 114, 118, 121, 124, 133, 142, 145, 156.
Julian Davison : 145
Bruce Granquist : 7, 71, 76, 79, 87, 100, 124, 129, 131, 133, 148,

Labels : Paul Coulbois
Laurent Gourdon
Danièle Guitton

We have not been able to trace the heirs or publishers of certain documents. An account is being held open for them at our offices.

◆ A ◆

Akha tribe 152, 157
Albuquerque, Afonso de 59
Allegri, Carlo 92
Allied War Cemetery 97
Amphornsathan Throne Hall 92
Ananda Samakhom Throne Hall 92, 164
Ancient City 98
Anderson, H.N. 89
Ang Thong Province 126
animism 17
art, contemporary Thai 22, 84, 94, 135
Arunothai Somsakul 53, 73
Asiawan Tippaya Asna pavilion (Bang Pa-In Palace) 126
Assumption Cathedral 87, 89
Ayutthaya 19, 52, 69, 87, 124
– architecture 47
– Buddha images 81
– Period 30, 32–4, 36, 106
– temple buildings 47

◆ B ◆

bai sema 46
bai-sri 26
bamboo 9, 12
Bamrung Muang Road (Bangkok) 86
Ban Chiang 18, 117
Bangkok 63–5, 67, 71–97
– early Bangkok 57–8, 73
– history of 72–3
– markets 95
nightlife 65, 93, 161–2
– shopping 95, 162–3
– side trips 96
Bangkok bicentennial celebrations 29, 77, 92
Bang Pa-in Summer Palace 126
Bang Po Bay 104–5
Bang Saen 98
Bang Sai 126

Ban Ko Noi excavations 131
Ban Tawai 138, 140, 165
banteng 9
Baphuon style 120
basket weaving 140–1
baskets in traditional life 39
beaches,
– Ao Nang (Krabi) 115
– Bang Niang (Khao Lak) 111
– Bang Tao (Phuket) 108
– Big Buddha (Koh Samui) 104–5
– Bophut (Koh Samui) 104 5
– Chaweng (Koh Samui) 104–5, 170
– Hat Khlong Dao (Koh Lanta) 116
– Hat Khuat (Koh Pha-ngan) 106
– Hat Rin (Koh Pha-ngan) 104–6
– Hat Su San Hoi (Krabi) 115
– Jomtien 98
– Karon (Phuket) 108, 110
– Karon Noi (Phuket) 108
– Kata (Phuket) 108, 110
– Kata Noi (Phuket) 108, 110
– Kata Yai (Phuket) 68, 110
– Laem Phrom Thep (Phuket) 108, 110
– Lamai (Koh Samui) 104–5
– Long (Koh Phi Phi Don) 114
Maenam (Koh Samui) 104–5, 170
– Mai Khao (Phuket) 108, 110
– Nai Han (Phuket) 68, 108, 110
– Nai Yang (Phuket) 110
– Nopparat Thara (Krabi) 114–5
– Pan Sea (Phuket) 110
– Patong (Phuket) 108, 110
– Rawai (Phuket) 108, 110, 168
– Samila (Songkhla) 107
– Surin (Phuket) 108, 110, 167
Beauvoir, Marquis of 53, 75, 91
beetle battles 37
betel boxes 138
benjarong 163
Bhumibol Dam 135
bhumisparsa mudra 24
birds' nests, edible 15, 108, 114

bird-watching 107, 122
boat songs 29
Bock, Carl Alfred 35, 62, 90, 100, 128, 140, 142, 150
bodhi tree 24
Bodhisattva Avalokitesvara 24, 81
bodhisattvas 24
Boisselier, Jean 54, 141
Bor Sang 135, 138, 166
Boromphiman Mansion 75, 92
Bowring, Sir John 75
Brahmin temple 86
Brahmini kite 12
Buddha 24
Buddha images 26–7, 81, 106, 127, 129
Buddha's Footprint 127
Buddhaisawan Chapel 80, 82
– mural paintings of 82
Buddhism 17, 24
– in Thai life 25, 84
Buddhist art 25
Buddhist images 18
Buddhist Lent 38, 121, 146
Buddhist monks 25, 27, 32, 46, 70, 96, 103
Buddhist precepts 83
Buddhist temples 109
Buddhists 17, 109
buffalo fighting 104
bun bang fai 38
Buri Ram 118, 120
Burmese
– era 20
– invasion 20
– religious influences 51, 137, 144
– style temples 144, 149

◆ C ◆

Candle festival 38
Cape Phanwa 108
Cape Phra Nang 115
Casualties of War 108
Catholic churches 89
caves,

– Erawan 121
– Phrathat 97
– Phraya Nakhon 102
– Princess 115
– Chiang Dao 150
– limestone 115
– sea 112
– Sua 115
– Tham Keo 113
– Tham Lot (Krabi) 115
– Tham Lot (Pai) 147
– Tham Phi Hua To 115
– Tham Sadet 115
– Viking 114
– Wang Badang 97
– Yai Nam Nao 122
celadon ware 138, 165
Central Department Store 95, 162, 165, 169
Central Plains 87, 124–7
– houses 45, 94, 100, 126
– gate 45
– paneling 45
– root gable (ngao) 45
Central Thais 17
ceramics 131, 169
Chaiya 50, 81, 98, 103
Chaiyaphum 120, 122
chakhay 33
Chakrabongse House 87
Chakraphand Posayakrit 36
Chakri Dynasty 19, 72
Chakri Maha Prasat 75
– Audience Hall 75
Chalermchai Kositphiphat 151
Chalieng 131
Chang Klan Road (Chiang Mai) 135
Chantaboon 99
Chantaburi 99
Chao Inta 156
Chao Phraya Express 87
Chao Phraya River 56, 67, 72–3, 87–9
Chao Phraya River valley 17, 118
Chao Phraya Wichayen 127
Charoen Prathet Road

(Chiang Mai) 135
Chatuchak
– Park (Bangkok) 95
– Market, see market, weekend (Bangkok)
Chaumont, Chevalier de 19, 52, 61
chedi 46, 50
– bell-shaped 50
– Chula Pathon 96
– Golden (Wat Phra That Doi Suthep) 140
– Lanna 51, 143
– Phra Prathom 50, 96
– Sat Mahal Pasada (Wat Ku Kut) 141
– Srivijaya 50
– Sukhothai, Lotus Bud 50, 129
– Wat Chiang Man 51
– Wat Lai Hin 51
– Wat Phra Singh (Chiang Mai) 51
– Wat Pongsanuk Tai 51
Chetuphon Road (Bangkok) 78
Chiang Khong 121, 156–7
Chiang Mai 14, 20, 62, 133–40
Chiang Man Gate 133
Chiang Puak Gate (Chiang Mai) 133
Chiang Rai 14, 20, 134, 150–1, 156
Chiang Saen 20, 156
Chiang Saen Buddha image 141
Chiang Saen refugees 143
Chieng Sen 62–3
Chinatown (Bangkok) 73, 91
– temples of 91
Chinese 17, 108, 157
Chinese architectural styles 48
Chinese houses, old 108
Chinese Muslims 157

Chinese shophouses 45, 72
Chinese temples 109
Chini, Galileo 57–8, 92
Chitralada Palace 92
Choisy, l'Abbé de 52, 61
Choloklam Bay 104, 106
Chonburi 98
Chuan Leekpai, Prime Minister 22
chula kites 37
Chulalongkorn Day 38
Chumphon 103
Church of the Immaculate Conception 89
City of Angels 140, see also Bangkok
cliffs, limestone 114–5
Club Méditerranée (Phuket) 110
coconut plantations 105
Coffman, Sarah 100
communists 107, 157
Conrad, Joseph 56, 64
contemporary Thai design 22, 134, 139
coral reefs 16, 115–6
Coronation Day 38
costumes 30
– ceremonial 32
– northerners 54
– regal 31
– Siamese court 58
coups 21–2
Coward, Noël 89
Crawfurd, John 63
crocodiles 12, 98

◆ D ◆

Damnern Saduak 70, 96
"Death Railway" 97
décor
– interior 22, 134, 139
– Thai temple 139
Democracy Monument 71, 84, 87

Democratic Party 22
demography 17
Diamond Wall 126
Doi Chiang Dao 150
Doi Chomthong 151
Doi Inthanon 27, 140
Doi Kong Mu 149
Doi Mae Salong 156–7
Doi Suthep 135
Dongrek Mountains 135
durian 42
Dusit district 73, 92
Dusit Maha Prasat 74
Dusit Palace 92
Dusit Sawan Thanya Maha Prasat 127
Dvaravati
– architecture 50
– art 81
– Buddha images 82
– musical instruments 33
– Period 18, 30, 106, 127
– stuccoes 96

◆ E ◆

Earl, George Windsor 60, 63–4
East Asiatic Company 87, 89
egrets 13
Ekachai Barge 29, see also royal barges
Elephant Corral 125
elephant roundup 28, 117
elephants 10, 28, 122–3
– shows 125
elephant-training Camp 150
Emerald Buddha 70, 88, 151
Erawan Shrine 93

◆ F ◆

Fang 150
Ferro, Cesare 92
Ferroci, Corrado 83 4, 92
festivals 22, 38, 84, 139
films made on location in Thailand,
– The Beach 84
– The Bridge on the River Kwai 97
– The Killing Fields 102, 108–9
– The King and I 19
– The Kingdom of the Yellow Robe 90, 97, 146
– The Man with the Golden Gun 108, 113
Fine Arts Department 80, 119–20, 125
fishing boats 107
floating houses 45, 72, 132
flower arrangements 26

foreign embassies 89
Fua Haripitak 88

◆ G ◆

Garden of the Transplanted Tree 79
garuda 74
gems 95
Gervaise, Nicolas 61
Giant Swing (Bangkok) 71, 86–7
gibbons 9, 122
Golden Buddha 91
Golden Hansa 29
Golden Mount 85
Golden Triangle 62, 151, 156
Gollo, E.G. 92
Gorman, Chester 18
Great Crown of Victory 31
Great White Umbrella of State 74
Groslier, Bernard 119
gunboats 29

◆ H ◆

Haadyai 107
hairstyles 30
Hallett, Holt S. 62, 91, 134, 140
Hamilton, Captain 98
handicraft villages 140
Hang Dong 140
Haripunchai 20, 134, 141
Hat Nopparat 114
Hat Sompin 103
Hat Yao 114
Herbert, Thomas 59
Hildebrandt, Eduard 56
hill tribes 17, 146, 152
hill tribe treks 151
Himavat 77
Hlnayana Buddhism 24
Hinduism 118
Hin Ta and Hin Yai 104–5
Hmong tribe 17, 152
– textiles 154
Ho Amok 142–3
Holy Rosary Church 87, 89
Ho Minfong 65

Ho Phra Trai Pidok (Wat Rakhang) 88
ho trai 46
hornbills 9, 122
hot springs 147
hotels 22, 160–1, 165–70
howdahs 28
Hua Hin 102
Huay Kaeo Road (Chiang Mai) 135, 139, 165–6
"Hung Huntraa" 89
hun krabok 36
hun lek 36, 164
hun marionettes 36
Hunter, Robert 89

◆ I ◆

Indian influence 18
Indo-Chinese war 117, 121
Inner Palace 75
Isan 117–23
Islam 17
islands (Koh),
– Adang 116
– Chang 99
– Dam Hok 115
– Dam Khwan 115
– Fan 105
– Hai 116
– Hi 111
– Hong 112–3
– Keo 110
– Khien 113
– Kradan 116
– Lanka Chiu 103
– Lanta 116
– Larn 98
– Lawa Yai 111
– Libong 116
– Mae 106
– Mai Thong 111
– Mak 112–3
– Miang 111
– Mook 116
– Nakha Noi 108, 111
– Nakha Yai 111
– Nang 115
– Nang Yuan 104, 106
– Nom Sao 112

– Pannyi 112–3
– Pa Yam 103
– Pha-ngan 104–6
– Phing Kan 112–3
– Phi Phi Don 114
– Phi Phi Le 68, 114
– Poda 115
– Sak 98
– Samet 99
– Samui 103–5
– Surin 111
– Taen 104
– Talu 112
– Tao 106
– Tarutao 116
– Wua Ta Lap 106
– Yao Noi 112
Iyer, Pico 65

◆ J ◆

jad paan 26
James Bond Island 113
Jek Seng 54, 136
jewelry 30, 95
Jim Thompson Company 117, 163, 167, 169–70
Jim Thompson's House 94, 164
Jongkhum Lake 148–9
jongkrabane 30, 54

◆ K ◆

Kadwua 140
kaeng 41
Kaeng Phed Ped Yang (recipe) 41
kalae 45, 135
Kamthieng House 94, 164
Kanchanaburi 18, 97
–river resorts 97
Karens 17, 152
Katu Village (Phuket) 108
Kawila of Lampang 20, 143
Kelang Nakhon 142
Khamphaeng Laeng 101

Khamphaeng Phet 128
Khamu tribe 146
khanom krok 42
khantoke dinner 139
Khao Chang Krachok 102
Khao Laem Ya 99
Khao Luang 101
Khao Rang 109
Khao San Road 84
Khao Wang 100
Khmer
– art 120
– empire 18
– people 17
– temples 118–20, 127
khon 34–6, 43, 77
Khon Kaen 121
Khong Chiam 121
khong wong 33
Khrua In Khong 55, 84, 101
Khruba Srivijaya 140, 143, 145
Khun Chang and Khun Phan 66, 125
King Ramkhamhaeng, statue of 129
kings,
– Ananda 21
– Athitayaraj 141
– Bhumibol Adulyadej 21, 152
– Boromaraja I (1370–88) 125
– Boromaraja II 124
– Ekatat 19
– Intradit 19, 128
– Jayavarman II (AD 802–50) 24, 118–9
– Jayavarman VII (AD 1181–1218) 118
– Kham Fu 136
– Ku Na (1355–85) 137
– Li Thai (1347–74) 130
– Mengrai 20, 134, 141, 151
– Mongkut, see King Rama IV
– Narai (1656–88) 19, 61, 106, 124, 127
– Naresuan (1590–1605) 19, 20, 28, 125
– Ngam Muang 134
– of Lampang 20
– Pha Yu 136

– Rama I 19, 20, 29, 72, 76, 79
– Rama II 33, 63, 79, 86
– Rama III 78–9, 84, 89
– Rama IV (1851–68) 19, 28, 31, 79, 84, 100
– Rama V (Chulalongkorn) 19, 20–1, 31, 74–5, 84, 92
– Rama VI (1910–25) 21, 31, 92
– Rama VII 21, 102
– Rama IX, see Bhumibol Adulyadej
– Ramathibodi 19, 124
– Ramkhamhaeng (1279–98) 19, 33, 43, 106, 128, 134
– Suriyavarman I (AD 1002–50) 18, 118
– Suriyarvarman II (AD 1113–50) 118
– Taksin 19, 20, 124, 134
– Tilokaraja (1441–87) 51, 134
King's Birthday 38, 80
kite-fighting 37
Klai Klangwan 102
klawng yao (drum) 33
klong tad thapon (drum) 33
klongs 90, 126,
– Bangkok Noi 90
– Bangkok Yai, 90
– Banglamphu 71
– Damnern Saduak 96
– Lot 71
– Ong Ang 91
– Thonburi 90
– Toey 73
Kok River 151
Korat 117
Krabung 39
Krabi 18, 115
Kra Isthmus 23, 103
Krathong 26
Krua Khonpae 90
Krung Thep 72
ku, Wat Phra That Lampang Luang 49, 145
Kukrit Pramoj, Prime Minister 94
Ku Ya Sudha 143
Kwai Noi River 97
Kwai Yai River 97
Kwang River 141

◆ L ◆

lacquerware 138–9, 165
Laem Nang 115
Laem Ngob 99
Lahu Shis 17, 152
lakhon 35
lak muang 35, 71, 83, 109, 128, 164
Lampang 14, 18, 134, 142–5
Lampao 121
Lampao Dam 121
Lamphun 20, 129, 139, 141
lamyai 139, 141
Lanna chedis 51, 143
Lanna decoration 139
Lanna Kingdom 20, 62, 134
Lanna religious architecture 49
Lanna Thai 134
Lanna-style temples 98, 143, 145
Lao embroidery 30
Lao Yuan 17
Laos 20, 121
Laos, the 17
Lawas 17
Leonowens, Anna 63, 76, 85
Li Thi Miew 91
Ligor 18, 106
likay 35, 83
lingam 83
Lisu tribe 17, 152
Lodalam Bay (Koh Phi Phi Don) 114
Loei Province 122
Lohaprasad (Wat Rajanadda) 85
long-tail boat 90, 115, 150
look choop 42
Lopburi 18, 127
Loubère, Simon de la 56, 61
Lower Suriwong Road (Bangkok) 93
Loy Krathong festival 26, 38, 128, 137, 149, 128, 137, 139, 149
Luang Prabang 20
Luang Pibulsonggram 21
Luang Vichit Chetsada 90
Lulofs, M.H. 111
Lumpini Park

(Bangkok) 67, 93, 164
Lunar New Year 104

◆ M ◆

Mae Chaem 14
Mae Chan 156
Mae Hong Son 14, 18, 147–9
Mae Hong Son Loop 147
Mae Rim 150
Mae Sai 156–7
Mae Sai River 157
Mae Sariang 148
Mae Sa Valley 150
Mae Sa Valley Resort 150
Mae Surin rain forest 14
Maha Tera Sumana 137
Mahayana Buddhism 18, 24, 118–9
malai 26
Mallarmé, Stephane 57
Manfredi, Hercules 92
mangrove swamps 112–3
mangroves 9, 12, 115
Manora 35
Mara 24
Market, Banglamphu 84
market, floating
– Damnern Saduak 70, 96
– Samut Songkhram 96
Market, Pratunam (Bangkok) 95
Market, Thung Kwian 144
market, weekend (Bangkok) 95
Marre, de la 127
martial arts 37
massage, traditional Thai 22, 78
Maugham, Somerset 64, 89, 90, 127
May, Reginald Le 62–3, 156–7
Maya Bay 114
McEachern, C.A. 97
McKean, Dr James W. 141
McKean Institute 141
meditation 24–5
Mekong River 121, 156

Memorial Bridge (Bangkok) 71, 87–8
Mengrai Shrine 133, 136
Middle Palace (Grand Palace) 74
Mien (Yao) tribe 17, 152–3, 157
Mishima, Yukio 64
mondop 47, 76
Mons 17
Monument to Phuket's

Heroines 108
Morand, Paul 91
mor hom 30
Mouhot, Henri 99, 100–1
Mount Meru 125
Muang Boran 98
Muang Kung 140
mudmee 117
mudra 24 , 81
mudskippers 112
Mukdahan 121
Mun River 119, 121
museums,
– Banyen Folk Art 133
– Chao Sam Phraya 124
– Chiang Mai City Museum 135
– Chiang Mai University Art Museum 135
– Chiang Saen 156
– Coins and Royal Decorations 75
– JEATH Museum 97
– King Prajadiphok Museum 84
– Museum of the Department of Forensic Medicine 88
– National Museum (Ayutthaya) 124–5
– National Museum (Bangkok) 71, 80–2, 87
– National Museum (Chiang Mai) 135
– National Museum (Lamphun) 141
– National Museum (Nakhon Si Thammarat) 106
– private 94
– Ramkhamhaeng National Museum (Sukhothai) 129
– Royal Barge

Museum 90
– Songkhla Museum 107
Muslims 17, 107, 109

◆ N ◆

naga 131
nak 25
Nakhon Nayok Province 122
Nakhon Pathom 18, 66, 96
Nakhon Phanom 121
Nakhon Ratchasima Province 117–8, 120, 122
Nakhon Si Thammarat 18, 106
Nakorn Kasem (Bangkok) 91
Nan boat races 146
nang 36
nang talung 36, 107
nang yai 36
Nan River 132, 146
Nan Valley 146
Nathon Town 104–5
National Gallery 71, 84
national marine parks
– Ang Thong 106
– Tarutao 116
national parks
– Doi Inthanon 140, 147
– Doi Suthep-Doi Pui 140
– Erawan 97
– Huay Nam Dang 147
– Kaeng Tana 121–2
– Khao Phanom Bencha 115
– Khao Phra Thaeo 111
– Khao Sam Roi Yot 102
– Khao Sok 111
– Khao Yai 122–3
– Koh Similan 111
– Nam Nao 121–2
– Phang-nga 113
– Phu Kradung 122
– Phu Pan 121
– Saiyok 97
– Srina-kharin 97
National Theater 71, 83, 87
Nawarat Bridge (Chiang Mai) 134
Neale, Frederick A. 125
New Road (Bangkok) 93
nielloware 106
night bazaar (Chiang Mai) 133, 135, 138
Nirat Phra Prathom 66
Nongkhai 117, 121
Northern Thai design 134, 139

◆ O ◆

Ob Luang Gorge 147
Octagonal Throne 74
offerings 27

oil palms 115
Old Customs House 87, 89
Old Sukhumwit Road 98
opium 152, 156–7
orchid farms 150
orchids 11, 122
Overlap Stone (Koh Samui) 105

◆ P ◆

Pai River 147
Pak Klong Talaad 87–8
Pak Tai Thais 17
Pakthongchai 117
palaces
– Chantarakasem Palace 125
– Grand Palace, The 72, 74–7
– Marukhathayawan Palace 102
Palladia 76
Pallegoix, Bishop Jean-Baptiste 89
pannung 32
Pan Sea Bay 108, 167
Pasang 138
pasin 30–1
Pathet Laos 152
Patpong 73, 93
Pattalung 107
Pattani 60, 107

Pattaya 98
Payao 20
Perelman, S.J. 65
Petchabun 122
Phae Muang Phi 146
Phakoma 30, 138
Phang-nga Bay 68, 111–3
Phaulkon, Constantine 63, 127
Phaulkon's Residence 127
Phetchaburi 100–1
phi 27, 150
Phi Phi Islands 114–5
phi pob people 150
Phi Thong Luang 146
Phimai 118
Phiman Phetmathet Halls 100
phiphat 33
Phitsanulok 132
Phom Chao Indra 128
Phom Phet 128
Phra Apaimani 99

Phra Buddha Chakyamuni 86
Phra Buddha Chinaraj 92, 132
Phra Buddha Setang Khamanai 136
Phra Buddha Si Hing 80, 151
Phra Chan Thong Thip 146
Phra Chao Saen Pu 156
Phra Chao Tan Jai 141
Phra Chao Thongthip 141
Phra Keo Don Tao 144–5
Phra Mongkut Military Hospital 92
Phra Narai Rajanivet 127
Phra Petchara 127
Phra Phutthabat 127
Phra Pokklao Road (Chiang Mai) 136
Phra Ruang Highway 131
Phra That Chom Phet (Phetchaburi) 100
Phra Thinang Phet Phum Phairot (Phetchaburi) 100
Phra Thinang Santha Kam Sathan (Phetchaburi) 100
Phra Thinang Wechayan Wichien

Prasat (Phetchaburi) 100
Phra Trai Lok Chet (Wat Suthat) 86
Phrae 146
Phrom Thep 110
Phu Khao Thong 85

Phu Khieo Wildlife Sanctuary 122
Phu Wua Wildlife Sanctuary 121
Phuket 108–11
Phuping Palace 140
Phya San 20
Phya Thai Palace 92, 164
Pibul, Field Marshal 21
Pierre, Pia 55
pinai 33
Ping River 128, 135
Pinto, Fernão Mendez 59
Pires, Tomes 59
Piriya Krairiksh 120

Pittaya Boonag 151
pla duk 121
plowing ceremony 32, 38, 80
Poi Sang Long 149
pottery 138, 140
Prabu Chinaraj 86
Prachinburi Province 122
Prachuab Khiri Khan 102
Pramane Ground 80, see also Sanam Luang
prang 50
Prang, Hin Daeng (Prasat Hin Phimai) 119
Prang Ku 120
Prang, Meru Baromathat (Prasat Hin Phimai) 119
Prang, Wat Raja Burana 50
Prasat Ban Phluang 120
Prasat Hin Non Ku 120
Prasat Hin Phimai 119
Prasat Hin Sikhoraphum 120
Prasat Muang Tham 118, 120
Prasat Phanom Rung 118, 120
Prasat Phanom Wan 118
Prasat Phra Thep Bidom 76
Prasat Thamuen Thom 120
Pratu Chai (Prasat Hin Phimai) 119
Prem Tinsulanonda, General 22
Pridi Panomyong 21
prik 40
Prince Ananda Mahidol 21
Prince Chakrabongse 102
Prince Naris 92
Princess Mother 157
printed fabrics 30
pukpao kites 37
puppet theater 36, 164
Purchas, Rev. Samuel 60

◆ Q ◆

Queen Chamadevi 141–3
Queen Rambhai Barni 80
Queen Sirikit 92, 117, 126
Queen Sowabha Phongsri 75, 83, 92
Queen's Birthday 38
Queen's Gallery 84, 164

◆ R ◆

Rachini School 87

railways 19
rainforest 9, 10, 122
Rajadamnoen Road (Bangkok) 71, 73, 84, 92
Ramakien 34, 77
Rama II Memorial Park 96
Rama V Road 93
ranad (xylophone) 33
Ranong 103
Rasada Street (Phuket) 109
Ratchaphanikai Road (Chiang Mai) 136
Rattanakosin 72, 80–6
– architecture 48, 88
– Period 72
Rayong 99
Reclining Buddha (Wat Po) 79
Red House, see Tamnak Daeng
Relax Bay 110
restaurants 161–2, 165, 167–70
rice barges 126
rice baskets 39
rice farming 13, 126
rice paddies 147
Rigoli, Carlo 92
Rigotti, Annibale 57, 92
Rishi figures (Wat Po) 78
River Kwai 97
rock paintings 114, 117
rocket festival 38
Roi Et 117
Rojana Road (Ayutthaya) 125
royal barges 29, 90
Royal Household Bureau 75
royal houses 45
Royal Palace (Bangkok) 67, 71–2
Royal Pantheon 76
royal regalia 31, 74
rubber 108, 111

◆ S ◆

sabai 30
sai (fish trap) 39
Sakyamuni 24
sala 45–6
Sala Nang Riam 107
Sala Rim Nam 87

Salak Phra Wildlife Sanctuary 97
Sam Poh Kong 88
Sampet Prasat Throne Hall 47
Sampheng Lane (Bangkok) 91
San Khamphaeng 138, 140
San Tha Pha Daeng 129–30
Sanam Luang 32, 71, 80, 83
sangha 25
Santa Cruz Church 87, 89, 160
Santi Kiri 157
sanuk 37
Sao Chin Cha, see Giant Swing
Saraburi Province 122, 127
Saranrom Palace 83
Saraphi 141
Carosin Bridge (Phuket) 108
sarb (fish trap) 39
Sarit Thanarat, Field Marshall 21
Sathorn Bridge (Bangkok) 87
Sat Mahal Pasada (Wat Chamadevi) 141
Saulo, Georges 92
saw sam sai 33
Sawankhalok ceramics 131
School for Traditional Medicine (Wat Po) 78
School of Fine Arts 83
Sea Gypsies 110–1, 114, 116
– village 108
shadow puppets 36
Shan Buddhists 150
Shan ordination ceremony 139, 149
Shans 17, 148
Shearer, Alistair 77, 111
shell cemetery (Krabi) 115
shrimp farming 12
Si Racha 98
Si Satchanalai 128, 131
Siam, early accounts of 31
Siam Society 94
Siamese architecture 47
Siamese Kingdom 19
Siamese twins 89
Siddhartha 25
Sikhoraphum 118
silk industry 14
Silom Road (Bangkok) 73, 93
Silpa Bhirasri 83
Silpakorn University 80, 83
silverware 138
Singora 107
Sirirat Hospital

(Bangkok) 87–8, 164
Sisaket 118
Siwalai Gardens 75
SkyTrain 23
Smith, Dr Malcolm 75
Smith, H. Warrington 103, 113
snorkeling 110, 114–5, 115
Soi Cowboy 93
Songkhla 107
Songkran 38, 84, 137, 139
spa 22, 160–1, 163, 165–8, 170
special attire 32
spirit houses 27
spirits, belief in 27
spiritual abodes 27
squirrel fish 100
Srivijaya empire 18, 103, 106
Srivijayan architecture 50, 103
stuccoes 81–2
stupa 46, 82
Suan Dok Gate (Chiang Mai) 133
Suan Pakkard Palace 94, 164
Suan Prung Gate (Chiang Mai) 133, 136
Suchinda Kraprayoon, General 22
Sukhothai 19, 26, 60, 128–30
– ceramics of 82
– Hindu statues of 82
Sukhothai architecture 47
– chedi 50, 129
– mondop 47
– viharn 47
Sukhothai Buddha images 84, 129
– seated image 81
– standing image 106
– walking image 81
Sukhothai kings 130
Sukhumwit Road (Bangkok) 73
Sukhumwit Soi 23 93, 162
sunbirds 11
Sunthorn Phu (1786–1856) 66, 99
Suphanahongsa 29, 90
Surat Thani 103
Surin 117–8
Surin Province 118, 120
Suwannakhet 121

◆ T ◆

Tachard, Father Guy 29, 52, 61, 127
Tai Lue artists 146
Tai Yuan 17
takraw 37
talat kao 142
Tamagno, M. 92
Tamnak Daeng 45, 80
Tao Than village (Krabi) 115
Tapae Gate (Chiang Mai) 134
Tapae Road (Chiang Mai) 134, 136
tapir 10
tattoos 30
teak 122, 140
temples 46, 64, 139,
– Brahmin Temple (Bangkok) 86
– Burmese 144
– of Chiang Mai 136
– of Chiang Rai 151
– of Lampang 143–5
– of Lampang Luang 144–5
– of Sukhothai 129–30
– Khmer 118–20, 127
– Lanna 98, 142–3
– Temple of the Buddha's Footprint 127
textiles 138
Thai boxing 37
Thai classical music 33
Thai food 40–1, 110
Thai fruits and sweets 42
Thai houses,
– traditional 45, 126
Thai language 19, 43
Thai New Year 38, 104, 139, 137
Thai pleasures 37
Thai puppets 36
Thai religious monuments 50
Thai silk 95, 117
Thai village 44
Thai Yai 17
Thais, migration of 18
Thaksin Shinwatra, Prime Minister 22–3
Thale Noi 107
Thale Sap 107
Thammasat University 71, 80, 87
Thaniya Road (Bangkok) 93
Tha Rua 109
That Phanom 121
theater 34
– popular 35

Theater Festival, Bangkok 84
Thepanom Sukhothai glazed stoneware 82
Theravada Buddhism 18, 25
Theroux, Paul 93
Thewarat Mahesuan 74
thod kathin 27
Thompson, Jim 94–5
Thompson, John 31
Thonburi 20, 73, 87
– klongs of 90
Thong Sala (Koh Pha-ngan) 104, 106
Three Pagodas Pass 97
Tibetan Plateau 121
Tip Chang 145
Ton Sai Bay 114
Tong Yang (Koh Samui) 104
Tonsure ceremony 31, 75
Tourist Bureau, Bangkok 84, 160
Trat Province 99
trekking 151
Tribhumikatha 33, 130
tuk-tuk 93
turtles 16, 109, 111

◆ U ◆

Ubon Ratchathani 38, 117–8, 121
ubosot 46
Udon Thani 121
Udon Thani Province 18, 117
umbrella-making 138
underwater world 16
U Thong 18

◆ V ◆

vegetarian festival (Phuket) 109
Vehat Chamroon Palace 126
Vientiane 20, 121
viharn 46
– Daeng 47
– Khao Phra 118, 120
– Laikam (Wat Phra Singh, Chiang Mai) 49, 136
– Luang of Wat Mahathat (Nakhon Si Thammarat) 106
– Nam Tam 145
– Phra Chao Thong Tip 143
– Phra Mongkol Bopit 124–5
– Wat Chieng Khong 49
Vimarn Mek Palace 92
Vincent, Frank 4, 72, 101

◆ W ◆

Wang Lee House 87–8
Wang Long Bay 114
Warin Chamrap 121

"Superior services ... not as a duty, but from the heart" Centre Point Culture

9 properties in prime locations around Bangkok

Grande Centre Point Hotels & Residences
Ratchadamri • Sukhumvit–Terminal 21

Centre Point Hotels & Residences
Petchburi 15 • Sukhumvit 10 • Langsuan • Wireless Road